EMPLOYMENT LAW

EMPLOYMENT LAW

Third Edition

Ann E.M. Holmes,
BA, M. Phil, Pg.D (Occupational Health and Safety)
Principal Lecturer in Law, Staffordshire University

Richard W. Painter, LLB, MA
Professor of Law and Dean of the Law School,
Staffordshire University

Series Editor: C.J. Carr, MA, BCL

BLACKSTONE
PRESS LIMITED

First published in Great Britain 1988 by Blackstone Press Limited,
9–15 Aldine Street, London W12 8AW. Telephone 0181–740 1173

© Ann E. M. Holmes and Richard W. Painter 1988

First edition, 1988
Second edition, 1991
Third edition, 1995

ISBN: 1 85431 340 1

British Library Cataloguing in Publication Data
A CIP catalogue record for this book is available from the British Library

Typeset by Style Photosetting Ltd, Mayfield, East Sussex
Printed by Bell & Bain Ltd, Glasgow

CONTENTS

Preface   ix

List of abbreviations   x

Table of cases   xi

1 *How to avoid labouring employment law*   1

The nature of the subject — The importance of the European
perspective — The lecture in labour law — *Parlez-vous* employment law? The tutorial — 'Know your enemy': the assignment
— The subject's literature and how to handle it — No 'shrinking
violets', please! — Conclusion

2 *How to cope with assessment*   18

Introduction — Why do students fail or under-perform in
assessments? — How to get the best out of assessment —
Conclusion — Reading

3 *The nature and content of the contract of employment*   34

Employed or self-employed? — Constructing the contract of
employment — The examination — Reading

4 *Legal constraints on terms and conditions of employment 1* 66

Introduction — Equal pay — The relationship of UK law with European law — The Equal Pay Act 1970 — The examination — Conclusion — Reading

5 *Legal constraints on terms and conditions of employment 2: Sex and race discrimination* 91

Introduction — The relationship of UK law with European law — Overview — Substantive difficulties — The examination — Conclusion — Reading

6 *Termination of contract* 122

Introduction — Overview — The problem areas of termination — The examination — Dismissals at common law — Reading

7 *Unfair dismissal* 146

Introduction — Overview — The examination — Reading

8 *Redundancy payments* 174

Introduction — Qualification to claim — The concept of redundancy — Unfair redundancy dismissals — The examination — Conclusion — Reading

9 *Health and safety at work* 198

Introduction — Overview — Civil law — Criminal law — The examination — Conclusion — Reading

10 *The law of industrial conflict 1: the economic torts and trade dispute immunities* 218

Introduction — The importance of a historical perspective — Breaking the mould: the new policies of restriction — Finding your way through the legal maze — Stage one: civil liabilities for industrial action — Stage two: the immunities — Stage three: removal of the immunities — Civil remedies and enforcement — The examination — Reading

11   The law of industrial conflict 2: picketing   253

Introduction — Civil liabilities — Criminal liability — The
examination — Reading

Bibliography   273

Index   276

PREFACE

Three years may seem a relatively short period between editions of a book but, for the labour lawyer, it is a lifetime.

Since publication of the second edition, we have witnessed a consolidation of the complex statutory provisions governing collective labour relations with the passage of the Trade Union and Labour Relations (Consolidation) Act 1992. This rationalisation was extremely welcome to all students of employment law but it was only a temporary respite, for the Trade Union and Labour Relations Act 1993 has made a number of significant amendments to the consolidation statute.

The tension between UK and EC policy has been a feature of employment regulation since 1979. Most recently, this can be seen in the UK's 'opt-out' from the Maastricht Treaty's Social Chapter. Even so, UK government's opposition to the EC's social legislation has not been wholly successful. EC Directives required enactment, via TURERA, of a variety of improved or additional individual employment rights and ECJ case law has continued to shape UK judicial approaches in the area of discrimination, equal pay and transfer of undertakings.

As with the previous editions we have aimed not only to offer advice on study and revision strategies but also to update the reader in the light of some very recent developments. We have attempted to state the law as at 1 February 1995. In this endeavour, we have been greatly assisted by Stephen Hardys, (Research Scholar) and Alison Stubbs (Law Tutor Librarian) at Staffordshire University.

Ann Holmes and Richard Painter wish to thank their respective spouses, Stephen Migdal and Kate Painter for their contributions and support.

The book is again dedicated to our children: James (aged 8), Daniel (aged 6), James (aged 17) and Adam (aged 7).

Richard W. Painter
Ann Holmes
Stoke-on-Trent
February 1995

LIST OF ABBREVIATIONS

ACAS	Advisory, Conciliation and Arbitration Service
CA	Court of Appeal
CRE	Commission for Racial Equality
CROTUM	Commissioner for the Rights of Trade Union Members
EA	Employment Act
EAT	Employment Appeal Tribunal
ECJ	European Court of Justice
EOC	Equal Opportunities Commission
EPA	Equal Pay Act, Employment Protection Act
EPCA	Employment Protection (Consolidation) Act
GOQ	genuine occupational qualification
HASAWA	Health and Safety at Work etc. Act
HSC	Health and Safety Commission
HSE	Health and Safety Executive
ICFTD	in contemplation or furtherance of a trade dispute
ILO	International Labour Organisation
IT	industrial tribunal
NIRC	National Industrial Relations Court
RRA	Race Relations Act
SDA	Sex Discrimination Act
TUA	Trade Union Act
TULRA	Trade Union and Labour Relations Act
TULR(C)A	Trade Union and Labour Relations (Consolidation) Act
TURERA	Trade Union Reform and Employment Rights Act
UMA	union membership agreement

TABLE OF CASES

A. Simpson & Son (Motors) Ltd v Reid and Findlater [1983] IRLR 401   191
Abernethy v Mott, Hay & Anderson [1974] ICR 323   152
Adams v GKN Sankey Ltd [1990] IRLR 416   151
Addis v Gramophone Co. Ltd [1909] AC 488   141
Ainsworth v Glass Tubes & Components Ltd [1977] ICR 347   82
Albion Shipping Agency v Arnold [1982] ICR 22   83
Alexander v Home Office [1988] 1 WLR 968   113
Alexander v Standard Telephones & Cables Ltd (No. 2) [1991] IRLR 286   47
American Cyanamid Co. v Ethicon Ltd [1975] AC 396   244, 245
Anderson v Dalkeith Engineering Ltd [1985] ICR 66   197
Amalgamated Society of Railway Servants v Osborne [1910] AC 87   221
Arbeiterwohlfahrt der Stadt Berlin eV v Bötel [1992] IRLR 423   71
Arnold v Beecham Group Ltd [1982] ICR 744   77
Associated Newspapers Group Ltd v Wade [1979] ICR 664   222
Avon County Council v Howlett [1983] IRLR 171   53
Aziz v Trinity Street Taxis Ltd [1986] IRLR 435   110, 119

B.G. Gale Ltd v Gilbert [1978] IRLR 453   128
Bailey v BP Oil (Kent Refinery) Ltd [1980] IRLR 287   155, 156
Bain v Bowles [1991] IRLR 356   98
Balgobin v Tower Hamlets London Borough Council [1987] ICR 829   101
Banerjee v City & East London Area Health Authority [1979] IRLR 147   170
Barber v Guardian Royal Exchange Assurance Group [1991] 1 QB 344   70, 112
Barretts & Baird (Wholesale) Ltd v Institution of Professional Civil Servants
[1987] IRLR 3   222
Bass Leisure Ltd v Thomas [1994] IRLR 104, EAT   65, 185
Batchelor v British Railways Board [1987] IRLR 136   151
Beaverbrook Newspapers Ltd v Keys [1978] ICR 582   222
Benveniste v University of Southampton [1989] ICR 617   84
Bessenden Properties Ltd v Corness [1977] ICR 821   190
Bettany v Royal Doulton (UK) Ltd (1993) 219 HSIB 20   201
Bhudi v IMI Refiners Ltd [1994] ICR 307   72, 103
Bilka-Kaufhaus GmbH v Weber von Hartz [1987] ICR 110   72, 84, 89

Blackpool and the Fylde College v National Association of Teachers in Further
  and Higher Education [1994] ICR 648, CA — 242
Blaik v Post Office [1994] IRLR 280 — 70
Bliss v South East Thames Regional Health Authority [1985] IRLR 308 — 141
Bolton Metropolitan Borough Council v Malrod Insulations Ltd [1993] ICR 358 — 211
Bolton v Stone [1951] AC 85 — 206
Bowater Containers Ltd v McCormack [1980] IRLR 50 — 170
Bracebridge Engineering Ltd v Darby [1990] IRLR 3 — 100, 132
Bradford v Robinson Rentals Ltd [1967] 1 WLR 337 — 201
Breach v Epsylon Industries Ltd [1976] ICR 316 — 54
Briggs v North Eastern Education & Library Board [1990] IRLR 181 — 103
Brighton Borough Council v Richards (1993) EAT 431/92 — 98
British Aircraft Corporation Ltd v Austin [1978] IRLR 332 — 132
British Airports Authority v Ashton [1983] ICR 696 — 258
British Broadcasting Corporation v Beckett [1983] IRLR 43 — 133
British Broadcasting Corporation v Hearn [1977] ICR 685 — 235
British Coal Corporation v Smith [1994] ICR 810 — 82
British Home Stores Ltd v Burchell [1978] IRLR 379 — 162
British Labour Pump Co. Ltd v Byrne [1979] ICR 347; [1979] IRLR 94 — 142, 156, 157, 166, 171
British Leyland UK Ltd v Ashraf [1978] IRLR 330 — 127, 138
British Leyland UK Ltd v McQuilken [1978] IRLR 245 — 47
British Leyland UK Ltd v Swift [1981] IRLR 91 — 169
British Railways Board v Liptrot [1969] 1 AC 136 — 206
British Railways Board v NUR [1989] IRLR 349 — 242, 250
British Telecommunications plc v Ticehurst [1992] IRLR 219, CA — 53
Bromley v H & J Quick Ltd [1988] ICR 623 — 77
Brook v London Borough of Haringey [1992] IRLR 478 — 103
Broome v Director of Public Prosecutions [1974] AC 587 — 259, 270
Brown v Cearns & Brown Ltd (1985) 304 IRLIB 10 — 80, 88
Brown v Knowsley Borough Council [1986] IRLR 102 — 126, 139
Browning v Crumlin Valley Collieries Ltd [1926] 1 KB 522 — 50
Buchanan v Tilcon Ltd [1983] IRLR 417 — 191
Bullock v Alice Ottley School [1993] ICR 138 — 98, 112
Burdett-Coutts v Hertfordshire County Council [1984] IRLR 91 — 56, 63
Burns v Joseph Terry & Sons Ltd [1951] 1 KB 454 — 208
Burrett v West Birmingham Health Authority [1994] IRLR 7 — 118
Burton v British Railways Board [1982] QB 1080 — 112
Bux v Slough Metals Ltd [1973] 1 WLR 1358 — 201

Cadoux v Central Regional Council [1986] IRLR 131 — 46
Calder v Rowntree Mackintosh Confectionery Ltd [1993] ICR 811 — 84
Camellia Tanker Ltd SA v International Transport Workers' Federation [1976] ICR 274 — 230
Capper Pass Ltd v Lawton [1977] ICR 83 — 75
Carr v Alexander Russell Ltd [1976] IRLR 220 — 163
Carr v Mercantile Produce Co. Ltd [1949] 2 KB 601 — 206, 208
Chakki v United Yeast Co. Ltd [1982] ICR 140 — 136, 137
Chapman v Goonvean & Rostowrack China Clay Co. Ltd [1973] ICR 310 — 186
Chappell v Times Newspapers Ltd [1975] ICR 145 — 144
Charlton v Forrest Printing Co. Ltd [1978] IRLR 559 — 201
Chattopadhyay v Headmaster of Holloway School [1982] ICR 132 — 98
Chubb Fire Security Ltd v Harper [1983] IRLR 311 — 195
Churchill v A. Yeates & Sons Ltd [1983] ICR 380 — 150
Clarke v Eley (IMI) Kynoch Ltd [1982] IRLR 482; [1983] ICR 165 — 102, 105, 116, 117, 190
Clay Cross (Quarry Services) Ltd v Fletcher [1979] ICR 1 — 83
Close v Steel Co. of Wales Ltd [1962] AC 367 — 202, 206, 208
Clwyd County Council v Leverton [1985] IRLR 197 — 82, 87
Clymo v Wandsworth London Borough Council [1989] ICR 250 — 103

Coddington v International Harvester Co. of Great Britain Ltd (1969) 6 KIR 146   201
Collier v Sunday Referee Publishing Co. Ltd [1940] 2 KB 647   54
Commission of the European Communities v United Kingdom of Great Britain &
   Northern Ireland [1982] IRLR 333; [1984] IRLR 29   67, 72, 77, 92
Coulson v Felixstowe Dock Co. [1975] IRLR 11   166
Council of Civil Service Unions v Minister for the Civil Service [1985] ICR 14   149
Courtaulds Northern Textiles Ltd v Andrew [1979] IRLR 84   132, 140
Cowen v Haden Ltd [1983] ICR 1   185, 194
CRE v Amari Plastics Ltd [1982] IRLR 252   114
CRE v Dutton [1989] QB 783   97
Cresswell v Board of Inland Revenue [1984] ICR 508   56, 65
Crofter Hand-Woven Harris Tweed Co. v Veitch [1942] AC 435   231
Crompton v Truly Fair (International) Ltd [1975] ICR 359   176
Crouch v British Rail Engineering Ltd [1988] IRLR 404   201
Crown Suppliers (Property Services Agency) v Dawkins, [1993] ICR 517   97, 119

D. C. Thomson & Co. Ltd v Deakin [1952] Ch 646   229, 230
Daily Mirror Newspapers Ltd v Gardner [1968] 2 QB 762   230
Davidson v Handley Page Ltd [1945] 1 All ER 235   202
Davies v Francis Shaw & Co. (Manchester) Ltd (1987) 324 IRLIB 9   79
Davies v Presbyterian Church of Wales [1986] IRLR 194   37
De Souza v Automobile Association [1986] ICR 514   100, 106, 111
Deane v Ealing London Borough Council [1993] ICR 329   114
Dedman v British Building & Engineering Appliances Ltd [1974] ICR 53   149
Defrenne v Sabena [1976] ICR 547   68
Dekker v Stichting Vormingscentrum voor Jong Volwassenen (VJV-Centrum) Plus
   [1992] ICR 325   108
Delaney v Staples [1991] 2 QB 47, CA; [1992] 1 AC 687, HL   50
Devonald v Rosser & Sons [1906] 2 KB 728   50
Dibro Ltd v Hore [1990] ICR 370   77
Dietman v Brent London Borough Council [1987] ICR 737   144
Dimbleby & Sons Ltd v National Union of Journalists [1984] ICR 386   237, 245, 251
Dines v Initial Healthcare Services Ltd [1994] IRLR 336, CA   7
Dixon v British Broadcasting Corporation [1979] ICR 281; [1979] IRLR 114, CA   125; 138
Doughty v Turner Manufacturing Co. Ltd [1964] 1 QB 518   200
Dr Sophie Redmond Stichting v Bartol [1992] IRLR 366, ECJ   178
Drew v St Edmundsbury Borough Council [1980] ICR 513   227
Duffy v Yeomans and Partners Ltd [1994] IRLR 642, CA   157, 171
Dugdale v Kraft Foods Ltd [1977] ICR 48   76
Duke v GEC Reliance Ltd [1988] AC 618   94
Duport Steels Ltd v Sirs [1980] ICR 161   235, 245

Ealing London Borough Council v Race Relations Board [1972] AC 342   97
Earl v Slater & Wheeler (Airlyne) Ltd [1972] ICR 508   156
East Lindsey District Council v Daubney [1977] IRLR 181   166
East Sussex County Council v Walker (1972) 7 ITR 280   128
Eaton Ltd v Nuttall [1977] ICR 272   75, 77
Eaves v Morris Motors Ltd [1961] 2 QB 385   206, 207
Edwards v Bairstow [1956] AC 14   38
Edwards v National Coal Board [1949] 1 KB 704   211, 212
Egg Stores (Stamford Hill) Ltd v Leibovici [1977] ICR 260   165
Electrolux Ltd v Hutchinson [1977] ICR 252   75
Ellis v Brighton Co-operative Society [1976] IRLR 419   170, 195
Emerald Construction Co. Ltd v Lowthian [1966] 1 WLR 691   229
Enderby v Frenchay Health Authority [1994] ICR 112   72, 84, 88, 103
Etam plc v Rowan [1989] IRLR 150   113
Evans v Elemeta Holdings Ltd [1982] ICR 323   195

Express Newspapers Ltd v McShane [1979] ICR 210; [1980] AC 672; [1980] ICR 42
222, 235, 245, 249

F. C. Gardner Ltd v Beresford [1978] IRLR 63   140
F. C. Shephard & Co. Ltd v Jerrom [1986] IRLR 358   125, 136
Faccenda Chicken Ltd v Fowler [1987] Ch 117   57, 59
Falconer v ASLEF and NUR [1986] IRLR 331   230
Ferguson v John Dawson & Partners (Contractors) Ltd [1976] 1 WLR 1213   40
Ferodo Ltd v Barnes [1976] ICR 439   163
Fitzgerald v Hall, Russell & Co. Ltd [1970] AC 984   180
Flack v Kodak Ltd [1986] ICR 775   181
Ford v Warwickshire County Council [1983] 2 AC 71   181, 182
Foster v British Gas plc [1991] 2 AC 306; [1991] 1 QB 405   73, 94
Fulton v Strathclyde Regional Council (1986) 315 IRLIB 19   104
Futty v D. & D. Brekkes Ltd [1974] IRLR 130   128

Gallagher v Post Office [1970] 3 All ER 712   47
Gannon v J.C. Firth Ltd [1976] IRLR 415   139
Gascol Conversions Ltd v Mercer [1974] IRLR 155   43, 44, 47
Gateway Hotels Ltd v Stewart [1988] IRLR 287   180
Gibbons v Associated British Ports [1985] IRLR 376   46
Gilbert v I. Goldstone Ltd [1977] ICR 36   130
Gorictree Ltd v Jenkinson [1984] IRLR 391   180
Gorris v Scott (1874) LR 9 Ex 125   203
Greater Glasgow Health Board v Carey [1987] IRLR 494   103, 117
Greencroft Social Club & Institute v Mullen [1985] ICR 796   104
Greer v Sketchley Ltd [1979] IRLR 445   59
Grieg v Community Industry [1979] ICR 356   99, 116
Griffin v London Pension Fund Authority [1993] IRLR 248   74
Grimaldi v Fonds des Maladies Professionelles [1990] IRLR 400   101
Groener v Minister for Education [1990] 1 CMLR 401   94
Groves v Lord Wimborne [1898] 2 QB 402   202
Grundy (Teddington) Ltd v Plummer [1983] IRLR 98   191
Gunton v Richmond-upon-Thames London Borough Council [1981] Ch 448   144
Gwynedd County Council v Jones [1986] ICR 833   97

Habermann-Beltermann v Arbeiterwohlfahrt, Bezirksverband [1994] IRLR 364   108
Hadmor Productions Ltd v Hamilton [1983] 1 AC 191; [1981] IRLR 210   232, 236, 248, 249
Hall v Lorimer [1994] 1 WLR 209   40
Hampson v Department of Education and Science [1989] ICR 179, CA;
[1991] 1 AC 171, HL   107, 113, 117, 119
Handels- og Kontorfunktionaerernes Forbund i Danmark v Dansk Arbejdsgiverforening
[1989] IRLR 532; [1991] IRLR 31   71, 84, 108
Handley v H. Mono Ltd [1979] ICR 147   89
Hanley v Pease & Partners Ltd [1915] 1 KB 698   49
Hare v Murphy Brothers Ltd [1974] ICR 603   124, 136
Harman v Flexible Lamps Ltd [1980] IRLR 418   125
Harrington v Kent County Council [1980] IRLR 353   136, 137
Harris (Ipswich) Ltd v Harrison [1978] ICR 1256   163
Harris v Courage (Eastern) Ltd [1982] ICR 530   163
Harris v Select Timber Frame Ltd (1994) (IT Case No. 59214/93)   209
Hasley v Fair Employment Agency [1989] IRLR 107   82, 87
Hawkins v Ian Ross (Castings) Ltd [1970] 1 All ER 180   202
Hayes v Malleable Working Men's Club & Institute [1985] ICR 703   107
Hayward v Cammell Laird Shipbuilders Ltd [1988] AC 894   74, 78, 86
Heatons Transport (St Helens) Ltd v Transport & General Workers' Union [1973] AC 15   270
Hellyer Bros Ltd v Atkinson [1994] IRLR 88, CA   127

Herbert Clayton & Jack Waller Ltd v Oliver [1930] AC 209 — 54
Hill v C. A. Parsons & Co. Ltd [1972] Ch 305 — 144, 145
Hindle v Percival Boats Ltd [1969] 1 WLR 174 — 187, 188
Hivac Ltd v Park Royal Scientific Instruments Ltd [1946] Ch 169 — 57
HM Inspector of Factories v Austin Rover [1989] IRLR 405 — 211
Holland v London Society of Compositors (1924) 40 TLR 440 — 45
Hollister v National Farmers' Union [1979] ICR 542; [1979] IRLR 238 — 63, 170, 195
Home Office v Holmes [1985] 1 WLR 71 — 103, 106, 108, 111
Hornby v Close (1867) LR 2 QB 153 — 220
Hubbard v Pitt [1976] QB 142 — 256
Hudson v Ridge Manufacturing Co. Ltd [1957] 2 QB 348 — 201
Hugh-Jones v St John's College, Cambridge [1979] ICR 848 — 73
Hughes v Department of Health & Social Security [1985] AC 776 — 149
Hughes v London Borough of Southwark [1988] IRLR 55 — 145
Hurley v Mustoe [1981] ICR 490 — 109

Iceland Frozen Foods Ltd v Jones [1982] IRLR 439 — 155, 169
Igbo v Johnson Matthey Chemicals Ltd [1986] IRLR 215 — 127, 138
International Computers Ltd v Kennedy [1981] IRLR 28 — 188
International Sports Co. Ltd v Thomson [1980] IRLR 340 — 167
Irani v Southampton & South West Hampshire Health Authority [1985] ICR 590 — 145
Irwin v White, Tomkins & Courage Ltd [1964] 1 WLR 387 — 208
Isle of Wight Tourist Board v Coombes [1976] IRLR 413 — 55, 140

J. Lyons & Sons v Wilkins [1896] 1 Ch 811; [1899] 1 Ch 255 — 220, 256
J. T. Stratford & Son Ltd v Lindley [1965] AC 269 — 221, 229, 232
James v Eastleigh Borough Council [1990] 2 AC 751 — 98, 118
James v Hepworth & Grandage Ltd [1968] 1 QB 94 — 202
Jayes v IMI (Kynoch) Ltd [1985] ICR 155 — 203
Jean Sorelle Ltd v Rybak [1991] IRLR 153 — 150
Jenkins v Kingsgate (Clothing Productions) Ltd [1981] ICR 592 — 71, 72, 85, 89
John Summers & Sons Ltd v Frost [1955] AC 740 — 206, 207
Johnson & Bloy (Holdings) Ltd v Wolstenholme [1987] IRLR 499 — 57
Johnson v Nottinghamshire Combined Police Authority [1974] ICR 170 — 186, 193, 194
Johnson v Timber Tailors (Midlands) Ltd [1978] IRLR 146 — 101
Johnston v Chief Constable of the Royal Ulster Constabulary [1987] QB 129 — 94
Johnstone v Bloomsbury Health Authority [1991] IRLR 119 — 200
Jones v Associated Tunnelling Co. Ltd [1981] IRLR 477 — 185

Kent County Council v Gilham [1985] IRLR 18 — 63
Khanna v Ministry of Defence [1981] ICR 653 — 97
Kidd v DRG (UK) Ltd [1985] ICR 405 — 104, 108, 117, 190
King v Great Britain–China Centre [1992] ICR 516 — 99
Knowles v Liverpool City Council [1993] 1 WLR 1429 — 201

Lambeth London Borough Council v CRE [1990] ICR 768, CA — 113
Langley v Beecham Proprietaries (1985) COIT 1683/206 — 78, 82, 87
Langston v Amalgamated Union of Engineering Workers [1974] ICR 180 — 54
Lanton Leisure Ltd v White and Gibson [1987] IRLR 119 — 162
Larner v British Steel plc [1993] ICR 551 — 203
Laws v London Chronicle (Indicator Newspapers) Ltd [1959] 1 WLR 698 — 55
Lawson v Britfish Ltd [1987] ICR 726 — 82
Lee v Chung and Shun Shing Construction & Engineering Co. Ltd [1990] IRLR 236 — 38
Lesney Products & Co. Ltd v Nolan [1977] ICR 235 — 186, 193
Leverton v Clwyd County Council [1989] AC 706 — 74, 81, 82, 87
Lewis v Surrey County Council [1987] IRLR 509; [1988] AC 323 — 9, 183
Lister v Romford Ice & Cold Storage Co. Ltd [1957] AC 555 — 48

Litster v Forth Dry Dock & Engineering Co. Ltd [1990] 1 AC 546   179, 196
Littlewoods Organisation Ltd v Harris [1977] 1 WLR 1472   59
Lloyds Bank Ltd v Secretary of State for Employment [1979] ICR 258   182
Lochgelly Iron & Coal Co. Ltd v M'Mullan [1934] AC 1   202
London Transport Executive v Clarke [1981] IRLR 166; [1981] ICR 355   140, 144
Lonrho Ltd v Shell Petroleum Co. Ltd [1981] 2 All ER 456   202
Lonrho Ltd v Shell Petroleum Co. Ltd (No. 2) [1982] AC 173   231
Lonrho plc v Fayed [1992] 1 AC 448   231
Lumley v Gye (1853) 2 E & B 216   220, 228
Luxor (Eastbourne) Ltd v Cooper [1941] AC 108   48

Macarthys Ltd v Smith [1981] QB 180   68, 71, 82, 89
Macfisheries Ltd v Findlay [1985] ICR 160   194
Machine Tool Industry Research Association v Simpson [1988] IRLR 212   150
Maidment v Cooper & Co. (Birmingham) Ltd [1978] ICR 1094   75
Malloch v Aberdeen Corporation [1971] ICR 893   142
Mandla v Dowell Lee [1983] 2 AC 548   97, 119
Marina Shipping Ltd v Laughton [1982] QB 1127   227
Market Investigations Ltd v Minister of Social Security [1969] 2 QB 173   39
Marley v Forward Trust Group Ltd [1986] IRLR 369   46, 63
Marriott v Oxford & District Co-operative Society Ltd (No. 2) [1970] 1 QB 186   129, 140
Marshall v Gotham Co. Ltd [1954] AC 360   212
Marshall v Harland & Wolff Ltd [1972] ICR 101   124, 164
Marshall v Southampton & South West Hampshire Area Health Authority (Teaching)
    [1986] QB 401   73, 92, 94, 112, 117, 118
Marshall v Southampton and South West Hampshire Area Health Authority (Teaching)
    (No. 2) [1994] QB 126, ECJ   6, 113
Martin v Automobile Proprietary Ltd [1979] IRLR 64   195
Martin v MBS Fastenings (Glynwed) Distribution Ltd [1983] IRLR 198   128
Martin v Yeoman Aggregates Ltd [1983] IRLR 49   129
Massey v Crown Life Insurance Co. [1978] ICR 590   40
McAlwane v Boughton Estates Ltd [1973] ICR 470   127
McAuley v Auto Alloys Foundry (1994) (IT Case No. 62824/93)   100
McAuley v Eastern Health and Social Services Board [1991] IRLR 467   78
McCarthy v Coldair Ltd [1951] 2 TLR 1226   212
McKechnie v UBM Building Supplies (Southern) Ltd [1991] ICR 710   75
McLaren v Home Office [1990] IRLR 338   143
McLeod v Hellyer Brothers Ltd [1987] IRLR 232   37
McPherson v Rathgael Centre for Children and Young People [1991] IRLR 206   78
McWilliams v Sir William Arrol & Co. Ltd [1962] 1 WRL 295   201
Meade v Haringey London Borough Council [1979] ICR 494   221
Mears v Safecar Security Ltd [1983] QB 54   34, 43, 48, 49, 64
Mecca Leisure Group plc v Chatprachong [1993] ICR 688   100
Meek v Port of London Authority [1918] 1 Ch 415, affirmed [1918] 2 Ch 96   60
Meeks v National Union of Agricultural & Allied Workers [1976] IRLR 198   98, 104
Meer v London Borough of Tower Hamlets [1988] IRLR 399   102
Meikle v McPhail (Charleston Arms) [1983] IRLR 351   191
Melon v Hector Powe Ltd [1981] ICR 43   176, 196
Mercury Communications Ltd v Scott-Garner [1984] Ch 37   234
Merkur Island Shipping Corporation v Laughton [1983] 2 AC 570   227, 230
Mersey Dock & Harbour Co. v Verrinder [1982] IRLR 152   256
Merton London Borough Council v Gardiner [1981] QB 269   177
Messenger Newspapers Group Ltd v National Graphical Association (1982)
    [1984] ICR 345   246
Midland & Low Moor Iron & Steel Co. Ltd v Cross [1965] AC 343   207
Miles v Wakefield Metropolitan District Council [1987] IRLR 193   52
Millard v Serck Tubes Ltd [1969] 1 WLR 211   203

Ministry of Defence v Cannock [1994] ICR 918   114
Ministry of Defence v Jeremiah [1980] ICR 13   99, 106, 111
Mirror Group Newspapers Ltd v Gunning [1986] ICR 145   81, 87, 110
Mitchell v North British Rubber Co. Ltd 1945 JC 69   206
Monie v Coral Racing Ltd [1981] ICR 109   163
Moorcock (1889) 14 PD 64   48
Morgan v Civil Service Commission (1990) COIT 19177/89   96
Morgan v Fry [1968] 2 QB 710   227
Moroni v Firma Collo GmbH [1994] IRLR 130   70
Morris v Breaveglen Ltd [1993] IRLR 350   200
Morrish v Henlys (Folkestone) Ltd [1973] ICR 482   55
Morton Sundour Fabrics Ltd v Shaw (1967) 2 ITR 84   188
Moss v McLachlan [1985] IRLR 76   259
Mughal v Reuters Ltd [1993] IRLR 571   201
Murco Petroleum Ltd v Forge [1987] IRLR 50   140
Murphy v A. Birrell & Sons Ltd [1978] IRLR 458   182
Murphy v Bord Telecom Eireann [1988] ICR 445   80
Murray v Powertech (Scotland) Ltd [1992] IRLR 257   113

N. C. Walling & Co. Ltd v Richardson [1978] ICR 1049   190
Nagarajan v Agnew [1994] IRLR 61   110
Nagy v Weston [1965] 1 WLR 280   259
National Coal Board v Galley [1958] 1 WLR 16   45
National Coal Board v Sherwin [1978] ICR 700   76
Navy Army & Air Force Institutes v Varley [1977] ICR 11   81
Neath v Hugh Steeper Ltd [1994] IRLR 91   70
Nelson v BBC [1977] IRLR 148; [1977] ICR 649   65, 185
Nethermere (St Neots) Ltd v Taverna [1984] IRLR 240   36, 37
News Group Newspapers Ltd v Society of Graphical & Allied Trades 1982
    [1986] IRLR 337   257, 264, 267, 269
Nokes v Doncaster Amalgamated Collieries Ltd [1940] AC 1014   178
Norris v Southampton City Council [1982] IRLR 141   125
North Riding Garages Ltd v Butterwick [1967] 2 QB 56   56, 186
North West Thames Regional Health Authority v Noone [1988] ICR 813   98
Notcutt v Universal Equipment Co. (London) Ltd [1986] ICR 414; [1986] IRLR 218
    125, 137, 164
Nothman v Barnet London Borough Council [1979] ICR 111   149
NWL Ltd v Nelson [1979] ICR 867   234
NWL Ltd v Woods [1979] ICR 867   233, 245

O'Brien v Associated Fire Alarms Ltd [1968] 1 WLR 1916   185
O'Brien v Sim-Chem Ltd [1980] ICR 573   73, 77
O'Kelly v Trusthouse Forte plc [1983] IRLR 369   36, 37
O'Reilly v National Rail & Tramway Appliances Ltd [1966] 1 All ER 499   201
Ojutiku v Manpower Services Commission [1982] ICR 661   107
Opie v John Gubbins (Insurance Brokers) Ltd [1978] IRLR 540   183
Orman v Saville Sportswear Ltd [1960] 1 WLR 1055   49
Orphanos v Queen Mary College [1985] AC 761   103
Ottoman Bank v Chakarian [1930] AC 277   55
Outlook Supplies Ltd v Parry [1978] ICR 388   85

P Bork International A/S v Forgeningen af Arbejdsledere i Danmark [1989] IRLR 41   179
Paal Wilson & Co. A/S v Partenreederei Hannah Blumenthal [1983] 1 AC 854   124, 136
Palmanor Ltd v Cedron [1978] IRLR 303   132
Palmer v Southend-on-Sea Borough Council [1984] ICR 372   150
Parsons v East Surrey Health Authority [1986] ICR 837   112
Parvin v Morton Machine Co. Ltd [1952] AC 515   206

Peake v Automotive Products Ltd [1978] QB 433 — 99
Pearse v City of Bradford Metropolitan Council [1988] IRLR 379 — 104, 109, 116
Pederson v Camden London Borough Council [1981] ICR 674 — 131
Pel Ltd v Modgill [1980] IRLR 142 — 101
Perera v Civil Service Commission (No. 2) [1983] ICR 428 — 102, 105
Pickstone v Freemans plc (1993) (IT Case No. 28811/84) — 80
Pickstone v Freemans plc [1989] AC 66 — 68, 78, 80, 87, 88, 89
Piddington v Bates [1961] 1 WLR 162 — 258
Pink v White [1985] IRLR 1489 — 185
Polkey v A. E. Dayton Services Ltd [1988] AC 344 — 157, 158, 163, 166, 170, 192, 195
Porcelli v Strathclyde Regional Council [1986] ICR 564 — 99, 111
Porter v Bandridge Ltd [1978] ICR 943 — 162
Post Office v Union of Communication Workers [1990] IRLR 143 — 241
Powell v London Borough of Brent [1987] IRLR 466 — 145
Power Packing Casemakers Ltd v Faust [1983] QB 471 — 227
Price v Civil Service Commission [1978] ICR 27 — 102, 105, 109, 117

Quinn v Leathem [1901] AC 495 — 220, 231
Quinnen v Hovells [1984] ICR 525 — 81, 110

R v Associated Octel Co. Ltd [1994] IRLR 540 — 211
R v Birmingham City Council, ex parte EOC [1989] AC 1155 — 98, 118
R v Board of Trustees of the Science Museum [1993] 1 WLR 1171 — 211
R v British Broadcasting Corporation, ex parte Lavelle [1983] ICR 99 — 144
R v Bunn (1872) 12 Cox CC 316 — 220
R v CRE, ex parte Cottrell and Rothon [1980] 1 WLR 1580 — 114
R v Derbyshire County Council, ex parte Noble [1990] IRLR 332 — 143
R v East Berkshire Health Authority, ex parte Walsh [1985] QB 152 — 143, 145
R v Lord Chancellor's Department, ex parte Nangle [1991] IRLR 343 — 143
R v Secretary of State for Employment, ex parte EOC [1994] 2 WLR 409, HL — 6, 71, 180, 183
R v Swan Hunter Shipbuilders Ltd [1981] ICR 831 — 211
Rainey v Greater Glasgow Health Board [1987] AC 224 — 72, 83, 87, 88, 107, 117
Rao v Civil Aviation Authority [1994] ICR 495, CA — 171
Rask v ISS Kantineservice A/S [1993] IRLR 133, ECJ — 178
Raval v Department of Health and Social Security [1985] ICR 685 — 102, 106, 117
Rayware Ltd v TGWU [1989] IRLR 134 — 254
Ready Mixed Concrete (South East) Ltd v Minister of Pensions & National Insurance [1968] 2 QB 497 — 39
Red Bank Manufacturing Co. Ltd v Meadows [1992] ICR 204, EAT — 171
Reed Packaging Ltd v Boozer [1988] ICR 391 — 79
Reid v Rush & Tomkins Group plc [1989] IRLR 265 — 200
Ridge v Baldwin [1964] AC 40 — 141, 142
Rigby v Ferodo Ltd [1987] IRLR 516 — 56, 63
Riley v Tesco Stores Ltd [1980] ICR 323 — 150
Rinner-Kühn v FWW Spezial-Gebäudereinigung GmbH [1989] IRLR 493 — 70
RMC Roadstone Products Ltd v Jester [1994] ICR 456 — 211
Robb v Green [1895] 2 QB 315 — 57
Robert Cort & Sons Ltd v Charman [1981] ICR 816 — 151
Roberts v Birds Eye Walls Ltd [1994] ICR 338 — 70
Roberts v Cleveland Area Health Authority [1979] 1 WLR 754 — 111
Roberts v Tate & Lyle Industries Ltd [1986] ICR 371 — 73, 112
Robertson v British Gas Corporation [1983] IRLR 302 — 44, 45, 47, 62
Robinson v Carrickfergus Borough Council [1983] IRLR 122 — 191
Roger Bullivant Ltd v Ellis [1987] IRLR 491 — 57
Rolls-Royce Ltd v Walpole [1980] IRLR 343 — 167
Rolls-Royce plc v Doughty [1987] ICR 932 — 73, 94
Rookes v Barnard [1964] AC 1129 — 221, 231
Rummler v Dato-Druck GmbH [1987] ICR 774 — 77

S.W. Strange Ltd v Mann [1965] 1 WLR 629   126
Sagar v H. Ridehalgh & Son Ltd [1931] 1 Ch 310   60, 64
Sanders v Ernest A. Neal Ltd [1974] ICR 565   189
Saunders v Richmond-upon-Thames Borough Council [1978] ICR 75   110, 117
Saunders v Scottish National Camps Association Ltd [1980] IRLR 174   169
Savoia v Chiltern Herb Farms Ltd [1982] IRLR 166   133
Scott v Beam College Ltd (1985) 284 IRLIB 6   78
Secretary of State for Employment v Associated Society of Locomotive Engineers &
    Firemen (No. 2) [1972] 2 QB 455   59, 60, 277, 248
Secretary of State for Employment v Newbold [1981] IRLR 305   177
Secretary of State for Employment v Spence [1987] QB 179   178
Seide v Gillette Industries Ltd [1980] IRLR 427   96, 99
Sharifi v Strathclyde Regional Council [1992] IRLR 259   113
Sheffield Metropolitan Borough Council v Siberry [1989] ICR 208   79
Sheffield v Oxford Controls Co. Ltd [1979] IRLR 133   128
Shields v E. Coomes (Holdings) Ltd [1978] ICR 1159   76
Showboat Entertainment Centre Ltd v Owens [1984] ICR 65   98
Sime v Sutcliffe Catering Scotland Ltd [1990] IRLR 229   203
Simmons v Hoover Ltd [1977] ICR 61; [1977] QB 284   189, 227
Simon v Brimham Associates [1987] ICR 596   96
Singh v British Rail Engineering Ltd [1986] ICR 22   107, 119
Singh v Rowntree Mackintosh Ltd [1979] ICR 554; [1979] IRLR 199   106, 107, 117, 119
Sisley v Britannia Security Systems Ltd [1983] IRLR 404   113
Smith v Du Pont (UK) Ltd [1976] IRLR 107   57
Smith v Glasgow City District Council [1987] ICR 796   152
Smith v Stages & Darlington Insulation Co. Ltd [1989] IRLR 177   202, 203
Smith v Vange Scaffolding & Engineering Co. Ltd [1970] 1 WLR 733   201
Snowball v Gardner Merchant Ltd [1987] ICR 719   100, 111
Snoxell v Vauxhall Motors Ltd [1977] ICR 700   85
Sothern v Franks Charlesly & Co. [1981] IRLR 278   128
Sovereign House Security Service Ltd v Savage [1989] IRLR 115   129
Spencer v Paragon Wallpapers Ltd [1977] ICR 301   165, 166
Springboard Sunderland Trust v Robson [1992] ICR 554   77
Stapp v The Shaftesbury Society [1982] IRLR 326   151
Star Sea Transport Corporation of Monrovia v Slater [1978] IRLR 507   222
Steel v Union of Post Office Workers [1978] ICR 181   106
Stevenson v Teesside Bridge & Engineering Ltd [1971] 1 All ER 296   185
Sutcliffe v Hawker Siddeley Aviation Ltd [1973] ICR 560; [1973] IRLR 304 65, 129, 185
System Floors (UK) Ltd v Daniel [1982] ICR 54   43, 62

Taff Vale Railway Co. v Amalgamated Society of Railway Servants [1901] AC 426   220
Tanks and Drums Ltd v Transport and General Workers' Union [1992] ICR 1   241
Tanner v D.T Kean Ltd [1978] IRLR 110   128
Taylor v Kent County Council [1969] 2 QB 560   194
Taylor v Rover Co. Ltd [1966] 1 WLR 1491   201
Taylorplan Catering (Scotland) Ltd v McInally [1980] IRLR 53   166
Tejani v Superintendent Registrar for the District of Peterborough [1986] IRLR 502   97
Ten Oever v Stichting Bedrijfspensioenfonds voor het Glazenwassers- en
    Schoonmaakbedrijf [1993] IRLR 601   70
Tennants Textile Colours Ltd v Todd [1989] IRLR 3   79, 88
Thomas Marshall (Exports) Ltd v Guinle [1979] Ch 227   144
Thomas v National Coal Board [1987] ICR 757   76
Thomas v National Union of Mineworkers (South Wales Area) [1986] Ch 20
                                                     257, 260, 267, 268, 269, 271
Times Newspapers Ltd v O'Regan [1977] IRLR 101   162
Torquay Hotel Co. Ltd v Cousins [1969] 2 Ch 106   221, 230
Tottenham Green under Fives' Centre v Marshall (No. 2) [1991] IRLR 162   113

Tower Hamlets London Borough Council v Qayyum [1987] ICR 729   102
Turley v Allders Department Stores Ltd [1980] ICR 66   107
Turner v Australian Coal & Shale Employees' Federation (1984) 55 ALR 635   145
Turner v Goldsmith [1891] 1 QB 544   54
Turner v Sawdon & Co. [1901] 2 QB 653   54
Turvey v C. W. Cheyney & Son Ltd [1979] IRLR 105   131
Tynan v Balmer [1967] 1 QB 91   259

Uddin v Associated Portland Cement Manufacturers Ltd [1965] 2 QB 582   206
United Bank Ltd v Akhtar [1989] IRLR 507   65, 133
United Kingdom Atomic Energy Authority v Claydon [1974] ICR 128   185
University College of Swansea v Cornelius [1988] ICR 735   110
University of Liverpool v Humber [1985] IRLR 165   127
University of Manchester v Jones [1993] ICR 474   104, 109

Vaux & Associated Breweries Ltd v Ward (1969) 7 KIR 308   186

W. & J. Wass Ltd v Binns [1982] ICR 486   157
W. Devis & Sons Ltd v Atkins [1977] AC 931; [1976] ICR 196   146, 152, 157, 158
W. E. Cox Toner (International) Ltd v Crook [1981] IRLR 443   140
W. Weddell & Co. Ltd v Tepper [1980] ICR 286   163
Wadman v Carpenter Farrer Partnership [1993] IRLR 374   101
Waite v Government Communications Headquarters [1983] ICR 653   149
Walker v Northumberland County Council [1995] IRLR 36   201
Wall's Meat Co. Ltd v Khan [1978] IRLR 499   150, 162
Ward Lock & Co. Ltd v Operative Printers' Assistants' Society (1906) 22 TLR 327   256
Wearing v Pirelli Ltd [1977] ICR 90   203
Webb v EMO Air Cargo (UK) Ltd [1993] 1 WLR 49; [1994] QB 718   107, 119
Wells v F. Smales & Son (Fish Merchants) Ltd (1985) 281 IRLIB 11   79, 86
Wessex Dairies Ltd v Smith [1935] 2 KB 80   57
West Midlands Co-operative Society Ltd v Tipton [1986] AC 536   158, 163
West v Kneels Ltd [1986] IRLR 430   151
Western Excavating (ECC) Ltd v Sharp [1978] QB 761   130, 132, 140
Wheeler v Patel [1987] ICR 631; [1987] IRLR 211   180, 197
Whitbread & Co. plc v Thomas [1988] IRLR 43   163
White v Reflecting Roadstuds Ltd [1991] IRLR 331   133
Whitfield v H. & R. Johnson (Tiles) Ltd [1990] IRLR 525   202
Wickens v Champion Employment [1984] ICR 365   37
Wigan Borough Council v Davies [1979] IRLR 127   132
Wigley v British Vinegars Ltd [1964] AC 307   202, 205
Wileman v Minilec Engineering Ltd [1988] IRLR 144   100, 111
Williams v Compair Maxam Ltd [1982] ICR 156   190, 191, 192
Williams v Watsons Luxury Coaches Ltd [1990] ICR 536   125
Wilson v M. Racher [1974] IRLR 114; [1974] ICR 428   55, 141
Wilsons & Clyde Coal Co. Ltd v English [1938] AC 57   200
Wiltshire County Council v National Association of Teachers in Further & Higher
  Education [1980] IRLR 198   126, 138
Wiluszynski v Tower Hamlets London Borough Council [1989] ICR 493   52
Woodhouse v Peter Brotherhood Ltd [1972] ICR 186   176, 196
Woods v Durable Suites Ltd [1953] 1 WLR 857   201
Woods v WM Car Services (Peterborough) Ltd [1982] ICR 693   131, 133
Worringham v Lloyds Bank Ltd [1981] IRLR 178   71
Wright v Rugby B.C. (1985) 276 IRLIB 10   109, 117
Wylie v Dee & Co. (Menswear) Ltd [1978] IRLR 103   113

Young & Woods Ltd v West [1980] IRLR 201   40

Zarczynska v Levy [1979] 1 WLR 125   98

1 HOW TO AVOID LABOURING EMPLOYMENT LAW

THE NATURE OF THE SUBJECT

Students of labour law, or employment law as it is often called these days, should have no difficulty in maintaining their interest throughout their course. The subject has an immediate day-to-day relevance and is frequently the topic of media attention. The last decade or so has seen frequent newspaper comment on the impotency of the law in preventing picket-line violence, the morality of an employer's legal right to sack his striking workforce or the 'stupidity' of the law as evidenced by 'eccentric' industrial tribunal decisions in the realm of unfair dismissal, equal pay or discrimination claims. However inaccurate or otherwise these comments may be, the students of employment law will very rapidly gain the impression that they are studying a highly contentious area of law which since the 60s has rarely been absent from the agenda of public debate.

Yet it was only 35 years ago that one industrial relations commentator was able to observe accurately that: 'When British industrial relations are compared with those of the other democracies they stand out because they are so little regulated by law' (H. Phelps Brown, *The Growth of British Industrial Regulations,* quoted in Wedderburn, *The Worker and the Law,* 3rd ed, p. 1). This description of the State's traditional approach to the conduct of British industrial relations, known variously as legal abstentionism, voluntarism or *'collective laissez-faire',* was, by the 70s, in need of considerable modification.

The droplets of legal intervention discernible in the 60s assumed torrential proportions during the following decade. Today there are the 'statutory floor' employment rights provided by the Employment Protection (Consolidation) Act (EPCA) 1978; legislation on sex and race discrimination (Sex Discrimination Act 1975; Race Relations Act 1976; Equal Pay Act 1970) and a statutory regime regulating occupational safety (Health and Safety at Work etc. Act 1974). In addition, and more recently, collective labour relationships between employers and trade unions have become increasingly enmeshed within a legal framework via the changes brought about by the Employment Acts 1980, 1982, 1988 and 1990, the Trade Union Act 1984 and the Trade Union Reform and Employment Rights Act 1993. Legal abstentionism is no longer the major strand in the British State's industrial relations strategy and many contemporary labour law academics now talk in terms of the 'juridification' of the employment relationship, i.e., State intervention, via legislation, case law and administrative measures, which limits the autonomy of individuals and groups to determine their own affairs. (For an explanation and critique of the juridification thesis see J. Clark, 'The juridification of industrial relations: a review article' (1985) 14 ILJ 69.)

The dynamic and controversial nature of the subject, of course, also has its practical drawbacks. It is a fortunate student indeed who finishes an employment law course without having to take on board a new piece of legislation during the year of study. Since the early 70s governments have frequently resorted to legislation aimed at dismantling the structure of labour law erected by the previous administration in an attempt to move closer to their own conception of the role of law in promoting 'good industrial relations'. Even if the student manages to avoid a change in legislation, it can be guaranteed that what was at the start of the course the most up-to-date textbook will, in a variety of significant ways, be rendered inaccurate by the end as a result of developments in the case law.

Given the nature of employment law, you should not expect to spend the whole course examining legal rules in isolation. Most law lecturers would now accept that the law in general cannot be fully understood by students unless they gain insights from the social context in which it operates. In no subject is this more clearly illustrated than in employment law. For example, you will have a great difficulty in understanding the reasons for and significance behind the lengthening of the period of employment necessary in order to claim unfair dismissal unless you can relate it to the current government's economic policy of 'lifting the burdens' from business. Similarly, the impact of the increasingly restrictive provisions concerning 'blacking' and sympathy action which have been introduced over the last decade or so will be impossible to understand without an appreciation of what part 'secondary action' played in the industrial relations context of the 70s and early 80s. In short, as Roy Lewis has observed: 'An appreciation of industrial relations is essential for any lawyer who wishes to understand labour law as something more than a set of technicalities' ('Collective labour law', in G. S. Bain (ed.), *Industrial Relations In Britain*).

Many law lecturers often express the frustration that if they commence a lecture with a discussion of contextual issues, students' pens are put down and eyes glaze over, only to regain their shine when the lecturer begins to discuss the legal rules themselves. In our view, this is a dangerous attitude for any law students to adopt; for those studying employment law it could prove disastrous.

Finally, it is important to appreciate that in discussing employment law and industrial relations, there is no such thing as an objective position. All of us, whether we be lecturers, students, employers, trade unionists, politicians or even judges, have value systems or frames of reference. A particular frame of reference will determine how we view the behaviour of others and determine the steps we would take to change that behaviour. Whilst frames of reference have been widely used in industrial relations literature, employment lawyers are relatively new to the concepts. Nevertheless, there is an increasing tendency to employ the concepts in books and articles on employment law and a number of courses include discussion of frames of reference as a means of giving the subject a theoretical underpinning. It is impossible in a book such as this to provide a detailed explanation of this area, but it might be useful to describe briefly four possible frames of reference which we might possess.

Unitary

The work organisation is viewed as a harmonious whole. There is no conflict of interest between management and employees; they are all part of the same team striving together for the common good. When conflict occurs it is seen as the result of faulty communications or it is stirred up by agitators. Trade unions are seen as threats to the cohesion of the team and its captain, the employer. Those holding this frame of reference would advocate legal restrictions on trade unions whilst, at the same time, arguing for the removal of laws which limit the scope of managerial prerogative to operate according to the demands of the market. This approach is reflected in the current Conservative government's legal policy towards industrial relations.

Traditional pluralist

This perspective recognises that conflicts of interest are inevitable in industry but that conflicts can be resolved through the institutions of collective bargaining. Trade unions are viewed as a legitimate source of countervailing power and as equal partners in the dispute resolution process. Voluntary collective bargaining is seen as the best way of conducting industrial relations as opposed to legal intervention by the State. Strikes should be resolved through voluntary conciliation and compromise rather than through a framework of legal restriction. However, the State should provide a 'statutory floor' of basic employment law rights to protect workers who are not covered by collective bargaining. The policy of the Labour government of 1974–9 reflects this approach and it was also influential in the writings of many notable industrial relations academics during the 60s and 70s, e.g., Otto Kahn-Freund, Hugh Clegg and Lord McCarthy.

Radical pluralist
This frame of reference is critical of the traditional pluralist view that conflict can be tamed by the institutions of collective bargaining. The radical argues that collective bargaining, with the limited range of corporate decisions it covers, does not alter the massive disparity in power between employers and workers. However, by offering a limited involvement in decision-making, the traditional pluralist ideology attempts to distract workers from making more radical demands. In many ways the radical pluralist analysis resembles that of the *Marxist,* our fourth frame of reference, but it differs in what it prescribes as a solution. The radical pluralist would advocate evolutionary social change, involving a fundamental redistribution of income, wealth and power. The Marxist, on the other hand, would argue that until the capitalist mode of production is overturned by a revolution on the part of the proletariat, the inherent inequalities in society cannot be removed. The Marxist therefore dismisses any framework of legal rights granted to workers by the capitalist State as merely a means of disguising or masking their objective exploitation.

For a more detailed discussion of frames of reference see W. M. Rees, 'Frames of reference and the "public interest"', in Lord Wedderbum of Charlton and W. T. Murphy (eds), *Labour Law and the Community: Perspectives for the 1980s.*

THE IMPORTANCE OF THE EUROPEAN PERSPECTIVE

In associating the Conservative administrations of the 80s and 90s with the unitary perspective described in the previous section, we have highlighted their policies aimed at deregulating the individual employment relationship. These policies have increasingly come into conflict with the interventionist stance adopted by the Commission of the European Community.

Pressure from Europe brought about the introduction of the Transfer of Undertakings (Protection of Employment) Regulations 1981, the Equal Pay (Amendment) Regulations 1983 and the Sex Discrimination Act 1986. In addition, the European Commission's Charter of Fundamental Social

Rights proposed a number of measures aimed at improving the living and working conditions for EC workers including: the right to a 'decent wage'; the legal regulation of the withholding or seizure of wages; restrictions on working time; the right to annual paid leave and to a weekly rest period; and limitations on the use and terms of employment of fixed-term, part-time and casual workers.

The United Kingdom government strongly opposed the Charter, on the ground that it would lead to excessive regulation and would impede rather than foster the creation of jobs. Indeed, Mrs Thatcher described the Charter as 'inspired by the values of Karl Marx and the class struggle'. It was, therefore, unsurprising when at the meeting of the European Council in Strasbourg in December 1989 the UK was the only dissenting voice amongst 'the twelve' on the question of the adoption of the Charter.

However, since the coming into force of the Single European Act in July 1987, certain Community legislation can be adopted by qualified majority voting rather than requiring the agreement of all Member States. This includes measures which relate to the establishment or functioning of the internal market but, significantly, specifically excludes provisions 'relating to the rights and interests of employed persons' (art. 100A of the Treaty of Rome). On the other hand, provisions on 'improvements, especially in the working environment, as regards the health and safety of workers' are covered by qualified voting (art. 118A).

Under the qualified majority voting procedure, Council members' votes are weighted according to the size of their state's population. The UK, for example, has ten votes, whereas Luxembourg has only two. Currently with 15 Member States, a total of 87 votes can be cast, and 62 constitute the qualified majority.

Given the UK government's opposition to the Charter, it is unlikely to result in EU legislation unless its content can fit within the scope of the qualified voting majority procedure. Since the scope of that procedure is far from clear, it may require a ruling from the European Court of Justice to establish which provisions of the Charter can be implemented with only majority support and which cannot progress without unanimity. Indeed, on several occasions, the UK government has threatened to take such action.

At the Maastricht summit in December 1991, the UK strongly resisted the expansion of European legislative activity in the area of social policy. The Treaty on European Union which resulted from the negotiations was signed by all the then 12 member States at Maastricht on 7 February 1992. However, the accompanying protocol and agreement which extends the scope of the qualified voting procedure into new areas of social policy will cover only 11 States, the UK being in a minority of one (for a detailed discussion, see B. Bercusson, 'The dynamic of European labour law after Maastricht' (1994) 23 ILJ 1).

The basis of the protocol is that all member States apart from the UK 'wish to continue along the path laid down in the 1989 Social Charter'.

In the Council of Ministers, qualified majority and unanimous voting will take place as if the UK was not a member State. Controversially, both the UK representatives in the European Parliament and the Commissioners from the UK will be able to influence the adoption of legislation in the social field which would not be applicable in the UK.

The UK's situation is further complicated by the fact that the Commission will retain its powers to propose and press for Directives in the social field on the basis of arts. 100, 100A and 118A of the EC Treaty.

A good example of the problems caused by the conflict between UK and EC policy is provided by the Directive on the organisation of working time (No. 93/104) which was adopted on 23 November 1993. The UK government has called into question the legal basis for treating the Directive as a health and safety measure, arguing that the Directive's requirements for minimum daily rest periods, annual paid holidays, a 48-hour working week, and restrictions on night work are totally irrelevant to the proper control of health and safety at work. Consequently, the UK contends, the measure should have been adopted under art. 100, which requires unanimity. In March 1994, the UK government lodged a formal challenge to the legality of the Directive before the European Court of Justice.

It remains to be seen whether, in the years to come, the Commission will continue to rely, as far as possible, on the Treaty to have its proposals on social legislation adopted and implemented throughout the entire Union. If the Commission follows this approach, and as the adoption of measures under arts. 100A and 118A requires only qualified majority voting in the Council, the UK could still, in principle, be overruled and be required to comply with these Directives. In any case, it seems clear that if the Commission anticipates that a social measure which it intends to propose under the agreement of the other 11 States might be acceptable to the UK, it will invoke the Treaty, presumably art. 100, to allow the UK to participate.

It should be said that the Maastricht opt-out may have only a limited effect in reducing the influence of EC regulation. For example:

(a) EC Directives and the threat of infringement proceedings by the Commission forced the government to introduce a variety of amendments to domestic law via TURERA 1993. These changes included additional rights to pregnant women and enhanced rights of consultation to recognised trade unions in the context of impending redundancies or business transfers.

(b) ECJ case law has continued to shape UK judicial approaches in the area of discrimination (*Marshall v Southampton and South West Hampshire Area Health Authority (Teaching) (No. 2)* [1994] QB 126, ECJ), equal pay (*R v*

Secretary of State for Employment, ex parte EOC [1994] 2 WLR 409, HL) and the transfer of undertakings (*Dines* v *Initial Healthcare Services Ltd* [1994] IRLR 336, CA).

All students of law should have a clear grasp of the relationship between EC law and UK domestic law and this appreciation is particularly important for those studying employment law. Before embarking on your employment law course, it may be helpful to 'dig out' your notes on EC law which you made when you were studying constitutional or public law in order to refresh your memory. You will also find that we offer some further guidance in chapter 4.

THE LECTURE IN LABOUR LAW

Given what has already been said about the massive growth in the laws relating to employment, it is unrealistic and perhaps dangerous to expect that the lecturer will cover all the material to be found in the textbook. Assuming you receive two lectures a week and that the lecture series spans around 24 weeks, the lecturer will have something less than 48 hours to present the material. So how do you spot the 'wood from the trees'?

In order to help students gain an understanding of the structure of the course, most lecturers produce a lecture programme showing which topics are to be dealt with in depth and giving an indication of areas which are to receive less emphasis or are to be omitted altogether. If such a programme is not produced, why not ask for one to be prepared and distributed? One of the secrets of success in any course of study is that the students should know their course and that must include its structure.

The lecture will not only give you a clear indication of the structure and focus of the course, it will provide statements of legal principles, relevant case law and legislation, perspectives on legal policy and decision-making, and references which allow you to follow up the information and will suggest aspects of the topic which are worthy of deeper investigation. Just as it is standard practice for lecturers to issue students with a lecture programme, it is now widespread for them to issue lecture hand-outs listing the statutes, cases and other sources to be referred to in the lecture. From the lecturer's point of view, hand-outs repay the effort of preparation in the sense that they free the lecturer from the turgid and laborious process of dictating case references etc. or writing them on the board, thus saving valuable time and allowing the lecture to flow. From the students' perspective, hand-outs relieve some of the pressure of note-taking but, more importantly perhaps, give them a clear indication of major issues surrounding the topic.

Lectures have often been criticised as an essentially passive exercise for students which consequently create boredom and result in a less-than-effective learning medium. A number of lecturers have taken these criticisms on board and have sought by a variety of mechanisms to involve students more actively in the lecture. Students themselves can also take steps to ensure that they maintain concentration and do not find themselves ruminating, for example, on whether the lecturer actually chose the colour of the shirt he is wearing or whether it was a Christmas present from his mother-in-law.

First, do not behave like some passive and unquestioning empty vessel ready to be filled to the top with somebody else's ideas. Follow the lecturer's line of argument carefully, and continually ask yourself whether you agree with the decision in the particular case which the lecturer is discussing or the lecturer's own analysis of the policy implications flowing from a particular decision or statutory provision. If, during the course of the lecture, a point arises on which you require further clarification or amplification, note it down and resolve to raise it with the lecturer at a suitable juncture. Lecturers have different views on what stage in the lecture is best for receiving questions. Some are quite happy to field questions at any time; others will reserve five or ten minutes at the end for this purpose. The individual's personal predilection in this regard will be flagged in the opening lecture of the course. At whatever stage this facility is offered, resolve to use it. What might be a relatively minor point in need of clarification following the lecture can, if unresolved at this stage, assume staggering proportions of difficulty during the pre-examination revision period.

Secondly, concentration will be maintained during the lecture by the adoption of an efficient system of note-taking. Educationalists regard note-taking in lectures as having the dual benefit of keeping students active during the lecture and also providing the basis for the written material they will later use for the purpose of revision. Now employment law students in the second or third year of their degree studies might regard this advice as akin to the instruction of elderly female relatives in the art of egg-sucking, but our experience has been that, even by their third year, many undergraduates have still not mastered the art of note-taking and are still risking sprained wrists and pen melt-downs by attempting to produce a verbatim record of everything the lecturer says. Such students can gain little in the way of understanding of the lecture topic and if they do ask a question in the lecture it will have little to do with clarification or amplification but is likely to be a request to the lecturer to adopt a speed of delivery equivalent to a dictation machine.

Efficient note-takers will produce a set of notes which provide a coherent structure for the area under study, together with the main points and issues, and will avoid muddying the water with large amounts of irrelevant detail. Given the huge amount of case law which is generated in employment law, economical noting of cases is of particular importance. As an illustration, let us eavesdrop on the following extract of a lecture concerned with continuity of employment.

'Many workers found themselves excluded from employment law protections because of the general rule that to count towards a period of continuous employment the employee had to work, or normally be required to work, 16 hours or more. For those who could not meet this criterion, they would only cross this particular threshold of employment law rights after five years' continuous employment at eight hours or more per week — see EPCA 1978, schedule 13, paragraphs 3, 4 and 6.' Lecturer refers students to the lecture hand-out. 'It may be extremely difficult for part-timers and casual workers to fit themselves within the strictures of the continuity provisions. A brief reference to the case law in this area may illustrate the problems which have to be overcome.

It is submitted that an unduly strict view of schedule 13's already tight requirements was adopted by the House of Lords in *Lewis* v *Surrey County Council* [1987] IRLR 509. Over a period of some 14 years Mrs Lewis had been employed by the council as a teacher on a term-by-term basis at three different colleges maintained by the council. When her employment finally came to an end Mrs Lewis made an unfair dismissal and redundancy claim. Her ability to cross the hours threshold depended on whether she could aggregate the contracts with the three colleges in order to produce one overall contract sufficient to make her claim. The House of Lords, overturning the decision of the Court of Appeal, held that such an aggregation was not possible, even when the contracts were all with the same employer. In the view of Lord Hailsham, the whole structure of the Employment Protection (Consolidation) Act 1978, read with schedule 13, is built on the supposition that to create the qualifying period there must be a single relationship contained in a single contractual complex. There was no room, therefore, for importing into paragraph 4 of schedule 13 any such phrase as would give the meaning, "a contract *or contracts* of employment which normally, whether *singly or collectively,* involve employment for 16 hours".

It may be argued that this decision weakens still further the statutory protections accorded to part-time workers and casual workers. In the next lecture we shall examine the House of Lords decision in *R* v *Secretary of State for Employment, ex parte EOC* [1994] 2 WLR 409. In this case, the weakness of part-time workers within UK employment protection law and the UK government's obstruction of EC draft Directives aimed at ensuring equal protection under the law for such workers, prompted the EOC to make a spectacularly successful legal challenge.'

The lecture note on this might look something like this:

	Threshold to employment law rights:
	emplee must work, or normally be required to work, 16 hrs/wk +
	UNLESS emplee worked for 5 yrs at 8 hrs/wk + (ECPA 1978, sch. 13, paras 3, 4 & 6).
How many workers may be excluded? Is the number of such workers increasing?.	This causes problems for p/t & casual workers.
	See LEWIS v SURREY CC [1987] IRLR 509 HL, held that where emplee empld by same empler under series of concurrent contracts, hrs of work under all the contracts may not be aggregated for continuity calculation.
To what extent have the cts & tribs shown sympathy with the position of p/t & casual workers in their interpretation of the statute? Does the EOC case mark a change in judicial attitude?	'Contract' in para. 4 should not be read as plural. Decision weakens further position of p/t & casual workers.
	But see R v SS for Employment ex p EOC [1994] 2 WLR 409.

It will be seen that this student has been able to distil the information given down to a concise but accurate note. The *ratio decidendi* of the *Lewis* decision has been noted and there are no irrelevant details. Because the student has not spent the time slavishly attempting to record the lecturer's every word, the student has been able to question mentally what the lecturer has been saying and several questions have arisen which have been noted in the margin. If these questions are not addressed later in the lecture, the student will have two valuable issues to raise.

Note also that our hypothetical student in the example above has also developed a system of abbreviating common employment law terminology which also helps in providing time in order to follow the lecture. You should develop forms of abbreviation with which you are most comfortable but here is a list of some that are in common use: ACAS — Advisory, Conciliation and Arbitration Service; c of e — contract of employment; cb — collective bargain; CRE Commission For Racial Equality; emplee — employee; empler — employer; EAT — Employment Appeal Tribunal; EOC — Equal Opportunities Commission; icftd — in contemplation of or furtherance of a trade dispute; EPCA — Employment Protection (Consolidation) Act; HASAWA — Health and Safety at Work etc. Act; IT — industrial tribunal; TULR(C)A — Trade Union and Labour Relations (Consolidation) Act .

One final point to note about our exemplary student's approach is the manner in which the notes are structured. Remember that these notes will provide the basis of the materials you will use for revision. The need to be in a form which is capable of addition and refinement. It may be expensive and perhaps ecologically unsound but writing on every other line and on only one side of A4 sheets allows plenty of room for additions and revisions to the notes should there be any important developments in the case law — an extremely likely possibility in this subject! For the same reasons use a loose-leaf binder to store your lecture notes: this will allow you to keep all your notes on a given topic together — whether you obtained them from lectures or from your own reading.

PARLEZ-VOUS *EMPLOYMENT LAW? THE TUTORIAL*

There are students, and we all have known them, who are quite happy to subscribe to the 'empty vessel' learning model. In most lectures, their entirely passive attitude will not be exposed and they can cheerfully pursue their task of transcribing the lecturer's every word even down to the very last *bon mot*. The lecture notes themselves are not sufficient to develop the understanding necessary to pass the employment law course: as stated above, they merely provide the basis for the materials necessary for revision. The 'empty vessels' who are not prepared to study and think independently will find themselves badly exposed and embarrassed in the tutorial or seminar.

Successive surveys of employers have shown that, when appointing graduates, they are less concerned with the depth of knowledge of a particular discipline than with the inter-personal and research skills possessed by the graduate. Teachers in higher education have responded by introducing elements in our courses designed to help students develop confidence in oral communication. Indeed, these days some lecturers formally asses student performance in tutorials.

Properly used, these forums for small-group discussions are the most valuable learning medium you will encounter during your time spent in higher education. If you can clearly and confidently articulate ideas and exchange views on employment law then you are well on the way to developing the level of understanding necessary for success in the examination. Like all skills, however, this ability to confidently express your own views and to question those of others has to be worked for. Students who claim to have contributed well to tutorial discussion having done little or no preparation are either attempting to 'psych out' their fellow students or are fooling themselves.

Most tutors will distribute a tutorial worksheet some time in advance and this will contain an assignment, such as a hypothetical legal problem or a discussion question. More often than not, the assignments have appeared on past examination papers and therefore provide a valuable form of guidance as to what form examination questions on a given topic might take.

The tutorial worksheet will also frequently contain a list of recommended reading and it is this material which should absorb your attention in the period you spend preparing for the tutorial. The study skills which are required for tutorial preparation are essentially similar to those that need to be applied to the initial stages of preparing an essay assigned perhaps as assessed course work.

'KNOW YOUR ENEMY': THE ASSIGNMENT

Clearly familiarise yourself with what the assignment is asking you to do. This will provide the structure for your preparation. Assignments will sometimes ask students to be prepared to 'discuss', 'critically analyse', 'contrast', 'assess the impact or significance of' or, if the assignment takes the form of a hypothetical problem question, 'to advise'.

These key words or phrases give valuable pointers to how you will need to use the information you are about to gather: they set the boundaries between a relevant and an irrelevant response to the assignment. In our experience, one of the major reasons why students perform badly in tutorial written assignments and in examinations is because they fail to pick up on the guidance offered by these key words and phrases and thus do not answer the question as set. It may, therefore, be useful at this stage to offer a glossary of certain of the most common of these key words and phrases. Developing the habit of providing relevant responses to tutorial assignments from the outset could pay massive dividends when the examination is confronted.

'Discuss'. Perhaps the most commonly used of the key words, usually appearing after a quotation or pair of quotes. The word asks you to argue the case for and against the assertion made by the quotation and to reach a conclusion: a purely descriptive survey of the area will not do.

'Contrast'. This might appear where the student is asked to examine the approaches to the same employment law issue by two different courts, judges or academics. The word 'flags' the need on the part of the student to analyse and contrast the two approaches so as to clearly bring out their differences. Obviously, if you are to cope with this type of question adequately in either the tutorial or later in the examination, it is important that you are closely acquainted with the cases or articles on which the question is based: an answer framed in non-specific or general terms is not likely to be impressive. Let us assume, for example, that the assignment or examination question asked you 'To contrast the respective views of Elias and Collins on the extent to which the law of unfair dismissal has controlled managerial prerogative'. It would be suicidal to attempt to respond by offering your own views or even those of other writers, no matter how erudite, on the effects of the law of unfair dismissal without comparing the opinions of the writers named in the question.

'Critically analyse'. This phrase requires you to offer a detailed examination of perhaps a line of authority or statute but it also requires you to be able to view this matter with a critical or questioning perspective. Once again there is a need for you to display an awareness of academic opinion surrounding the area under scrutiny before proffering your own views of the matter.

'Assess the impact or significance of.' What is required here is a discussion of the content of a statute, judgment etc., followed by an informed opinion of the likely consequences and implications. The lecturer who uses this phrase in an assignment is often expecting a response which transcends 'black letter' legal analysis and which deals with the practical or socio-economic effects wrought by legal policy. For this sort of question, then, the student might require to be familiar with research and statistics drawn from outside the field of legal scholarship.

'Advise'. Along with 'discuss', this word is commonly used in association with hypothetical problem questions. Note carefully which of the characters in the problem you are asked to advise. In a trade dispute problem, the legal advice you offer to 'Capital plc' on its chances of obtaining an injunction to restrain industrial action by its work-force may be impeccable, but you will lose credibility in your tutorial group and marks in the exam if the question requires you to advise the 'Amalgamated Labour Union'.

It is rare, if not unknown, for a tutorial assignment, assessed essay or examination question to be set which merely requires the student to *describe* the law on a particular topic. Students who adopt the 'kitchen sink' approach — throwing everything in that they know about a topic in the hope that some of it is relevant — will end up boring their tutor and the rest of their tutorial group and failing their assessment!

Having clarified exactly what is required by the tutorial assignment, the next stage is how to handle the material on the tutorial work-sheet.

THE SUBJECT'S LITERATURE AND HOW TO HANDLE IT

The material you are advised to read may be sections of an employment law textbook or reader, an article or casenote in an academic or practitioners' journal or a law report.

The number of textbooks and readers on employment law has grown in line with the expansion of the area. Writing a textbook on employment law is very much like what they used to say about painting the Forth Bridge: as soon as the project is complete, it has to be begun again.

A list of significant works with full titles and other publication details is given in the bibliography at the end of this book.

Of the leading textbooks, Smith and Wood's *Industrial Law* perhaps offers the most comprehensive legal analysis, while a broader contextual approach is adopted in the books by Anderman (1993), Davies and Freedland (1993), Lewis (1986) and Wedderburn (1986). The long-awaited publication in 1986 of the third edition of Wedderburn's seminal work was welcomed by tutors and students alike. Earlier editions of this book were as influential in shaping the debate on industrial relations and the law as the work of the late Otto Kahn-Freund (see *Kahn-Freund's Labour and the Law*, 3rd ed. by P. Davies and M. Freedland). Once again, a new edition of the work by Wedderburn is long overdue.

A book which provides a clear and concise treatment of the area without sacrificing its critical perspective is *Textbook on Labour Law* by Bowers and Honeyball. This is a volume to which you might usefully refer if you are experiencing difficulties with the subject. Hopefully, the same can be said of *Employment Rights* by Painter and Puttick.

In addition to the texts which aim to offer a more or less comprehensive treatment of the subject, there are those which provide a close examination of one part of employment law (e.g., C. Bourn and J. Whitmore, *Race and Sex Discrimination*; G.S. Morris and T.J. Archer, *Trade Unions, Employers and the Law*; J. McMullen, *Business Transfers and Employment Rights*) whilst encyclopaedic detail is provided by works produced under the respective general editorships of Harvey and of Hepple and O'Higgins.

For over a decade, the subject lacked an up-to-date cases and materials book. This problem has now been remedied with the recent publication of collections by Pitt and by Painter, Holmes and Migdal.

Employment Law has two main series of law reports: the *Industrial Cases Reports* (ICR) and the *Industrial Relations Law Reports* (IRLR). Two features of the IRLR which are worth commending to new students of the subject are its attractively set out headnotes, together with its monthly editorial which identifies major points arising from the cases reported in each month's issue.

You may also be referred to or wish to consult one or other of the principal up-dating periodicals: *IDS Brief and Industrial Relations Review and Report*. Both journals are published twice a month and carry commentaries on recent case law together with briefings or guidance notes on particular topics. A more considered approach to developments in employment law is provided by the *Industrial Law Journal*. Published quarterly, the journal carries substantial articles on particular issues in employment law together with detailed case commentaries. It is highly likely that you will be referred to this journal on a regular basis and you should resolve to follow up these references. Familiarity with contemporary academic commentary will deepen understanding and will pay dividends in the examination. Given the pace of development of the subject as evidenced by the breadth of the literature, the tutorial reading lists you receive may look extremely daunting and you may begin to wonder if the employment law tutor is aware that you are studying three or four subjects in addition to employment law!

Whilst there is no doubt that preparation for tutorials will occupy a considerable proportion of study time, many students spend more time than they have to on this task as a result of inefficient reading and note-taking techniques. Symptoms of this problem manifest themselves in the following ways:

(a) Students who need a removal van to transport their employment law notes: the proliferation of A4 caused by the fact that they have started to take notes on the first reading of the material without first surveying it in order to get an idea of the main points. The notes, which are the product of hours of labour, are virtually useless for tutorial or revision use: they are far too lengthy.

(b) Students who spend all their grant on photocopier charges: these students somehow believe that if they possess a copy of the report, article etc. then understanding will be achieved by a process akin to osmosis. Contribution in tutorial and performance in examination are again likely to be disappointing because they have not distilled the material down to the main points, expressed in their own words — both key elements in the process of understanding and learning.

Large amounts of time, trees and 10p pieces will be saved if what is called the 'SQ3R' strategy is adopted. The abbreviation stands for the five steps which should be taken in studying any piece of text, be it book, article or law report:

Survey the text as a whole to derive an overview of its contents. If you are studying a chapter of a book or an article, for instance, reading the first and last paragraphs should allow you to survey what is to come or what has been said. If you are dealing with a law report, then scanning the headnote will provide you with a feel for the issues involved before the court.

Question. You should never begin a detailed reading of any piece of text without having in mind a series of questions that you wish to have answered. In this way the reading process becomes a much more positive activity and avoids the 'empty-vessel' model of study referred to above. If a tutorial assignment is being prepared then you should begin by asking yourself to what extent the main ideas of the article, report or chapter support or controvert the stance you were proposing to adopt. In reviewing your lecture notes you may find that the lecturer has expressed a view on the matters dealt with in the text: resolve to compare this with the ideas, contained in the text itself.

Read. Having accomplished the first two steps, you should now actively read the text in order to seek answers to these questions. *Do not attempt to make notes at this stage* — it will distract your reading and will slow you down.

Recall the main ideas of the text and, if possible using your own words, note down what you consider to be the key points.

Review by briefly repeating the previous four steps and checking that your notes provide answers to all the questions you posed.

NO 'SHRINKING VIOLETS', PLEASE!

The steps outlined above should ensure that you can now face the tutorial with confidence, looking forward to deepening your understanding of the topic even further through discussions with your tutor and your fellow students. Do not ruin all this good work by 'clamming up' in tutorial. Prepare a written answer to the assignment in note form as an *aide-mémoire* — you may have done your library research a week previously. Always be prepared to offer your views. If your views are correct you will help the rest of the group. If, despite your excellent preparation, you still have problems, others in the group will help you to resolve them.

Remember that the tutorial is your most valuable learning resource and you should aim to get the most out of it. If, for some reason, your tutorial group is not working as well as it should, then ask your tutor to set aside some time at the end of the tutorial to allow the group to analyse the reasons for this. Such a suggestion should not be resented by the tutor. Indeed, the tutor may well welcome the fact that the proposal to review performance has come from the student group as opposed to the tutor's own initiative.

CONCLUSION

This chapter has sought to give an indication of the nature of the body of information which is encompassed by employment law and has sought to offer some advice and guidance on the study skills which will help you to move efficiently through the lecture and tutorial programme and the assigned literature. It is our view that the adoption of the study techniques advocated in this chapter throughout the currency of the course will provide a level of understanding which will mean that your assessments can be faced with confidence. Chapter 2 will offer some advice on how you can reinforce this good work as you prepare your assessments.

Subsequent chapters will attempt to highlight the issues within the employment law syllabus which frequently put in an appearance on examination papers in the subject. Using sample examination questions, we will suggest appropriate strategies for handling those key issues. In accomplishing this task we have necessarily had to be selective and do not pretend to offer a comprehensive coverage of the substantive law. Remember that the aim of the books in the 'SWOT' series is to offer guidance in assessment and revision technique, not to produce standard textbooks.

2 HOW TO COPE WITH ASSESSMENT

INTRODUCTION

The change to modularity and semesterisation of many courses has encouraged consideration, and in some cases implementation, of alternative assessment methods. In many instances this has resulted in a move away from the traditional three-hour examination. Whilst assessment in some form is unavoidable, some relief can be found from the fact that the three-hour examination is, or should be, a thing of the past. Indeed some courses may have abandoned examinations as the sole method of assessment in favour of continuous assessment of course work. Those of you who feel that you are not good at exams may be able to rely on your assignment work, but hopefully even where you have examinations these will not be the nerve-racking experience of the past. Whatever form of assessment is utilised on your course, progression between years or levels and final classification will depend on how well you cope with the range of assessment tasks. Whilst there is no magic formula to guarantee that success, the starting-point must be that you the student must take responsibility for the learning input which is necessary not only to pass, but to achieve the highest marks possible. There is a lot at stake and there are no short cuts to developing the requisite skills for succeeding in assessment.

If you are on a course which has modularised and semesterised, you may find that you are assessed at the end of each semester. This has the advantage that your assessment comes in 'bite-sized' chunks. Even if your course has not modularised, you may find a more enlightened approach has been taken and that the three-hour closed-book examination has been replaced.

WHY DO STUDENTS FAIL OR UNDER-PERFORM IN ASSESSMENTS?

Failure to perform well in assessment can arise for a variety of reasons and may vary with the nature and type of assessment. It is accepted, for example, that some students are better at assignment work than examinations. However, it is unlikely that you can select the method of assessment at which you perform best, so the first thing to do is to sit down and evaluate your own performance under the type of assessment to which you will be subjected.

The general reasons for poor performance in any assessment are:

(a)   Lack of preparation; for example, allowing insufficient revision time before an examination or failing to manage time effectively in researching and writing assignments.

(b)   Insufficient comprehension of the area or topic or failure to comprehend what is required in the assessment. If you fall into this category you must take great care when reading examination papers or planning assignment work as this kind of error usually results in very low marks being awarded. Such misunderstandings can mean the difference between a pass or fail or a good degree classification as opposed to a poor one.

If you fall into either of the above categories you must attempt to remedy the situation as soon as possible. For students in the first category there is a lot of hard work to be done and even then there is no guarantee of success; it may, however, still be possible to scrape through by the skin of your teeth. A warning: students in this category tend to receive little sympathy from their lecturers.

If you fall into the second category you will have to set aside longer periods for preparation, particularly at revision time, in order to ensure comprehension of the subject area being assessed. If you leave revision or, in the case of assignments, writing until the last possible moment and then discover that there are numerous areas of the subject or topic which you do not understand, you may find that, in seeking clarification your lecturer's patience is stretched, especially if these problems could have been sorted out at the time the topic was studied.

Obviously poor performance may be due to other reasons such as illness or personal problems and there is little one can do to avoid the unforeseen. However, if you are beset by such problems, check the assessment regulations to ensure that you follow the correct procedure for ensuring that information such as medical notes are brought to the attention of the external examiners or in the case of assignment work to obtain an extension to any deadlines which may have been set.

HOW TO GET THE BEST OUT OF ASSESSMENT

It is unlikely that many of you will have to sit a three-hour closed-book examination, so what are the alternatives? The range of assessment options are wide and varied. For example, you may find yourself sitting open-book or seen examinations, writing extended essays of 4,000 words or take part in an oral assessment. If we consider the main types, some clues to improving performance can be given.

Assignment Work

Assignments may either replace examinations altogether or form a percentage of the assessment in a particular subject. The advantage of assignment work is that your performance is not being judged over the space of two or three hours in an examination hall. The disadvantage is that the assessor may have higher expectations, given that there has probably been ample time set aside for preparation and research. Assignments may take a number of forms, e.g., problem, essay titles or writing a report. Leaving aside content, poor performance in assignment work can arise from the following:

(a) failure to meet deadlines,
(b) exceeding word limits,
(c) failure to submit the correct number of assignments.

These points are so fundamental that many of you must wonder why we bother to mention them, but in our experience of continuous assessment, each year an unacceptable number of students fail to comply with one or even all of the above and are deemed to have failed.

It is imperative that you familiarise yourself with the assessment regulations for individual subjects as word limits may vary and you may be penalised for exceeding the stipulated word length. Find out what penalty is imposed for missing deadlines: it may be a maximum mark of 40 per cent or, if you are so late that the return date for the course work has passed, you may find that 0 is automatically recorded. Evaluate why you fail to meet deadlines; it is likely to be connected with poor time-management skills. These need to be addressed because time-management is a skill which you need to develop in any profession, but particularly if you see your future in the law. To help you evaluate this skill, keep a diary over a few weeks to assess how much time you are spending on academic work. It is important that you are honest with yourself. If you choose to play rugby or football on Wednesday afternoons, there is little point in ignoring this fact in your diary and pretending that you have this time for academic work — likewise if you are addicted to watching *Neighbours*! The main factor is to strike a balance between academic work and leisure time — no one wants you to give up your social life but keep it in perspective. Once the diary is complete and you can evaluate it, sit down and prioritise the work and other commitments and slot them into your plan of work for each week — remember work must come first if you want to obtain the best grades.

If you know that you do not fall into the above category, what else can be done to improve performance?

Consider the assessment criteria. There will be general assessment criteria applicable to all subjects and specific assessment criteria relating to the assignment title. Regarding the former, marks will usually be given for structure, accuracy of argument, depth, originality (i.e., creative thought and evidence of research), style (i.e., fluency, succinctness), presentation (i.e., legibility, layout, word-processing, length), sources (i.e., accurate acknowledgement of and correct citation of references), grammar and spelling. As you can see the list is fairly extensive and compliance with the general criteria to the best of your ability will improve your marks.

Whether you will lose marks for failing to type or word-process an assignment will depend on the rules. For example, at Staffordshire University when 50 per cent of assessment was based on course work, students were required to submit at least one piece per subject either typed or word-processed. Support was provided in the form of word-processing workshops and ready access to a computer suite — teaching and learning facilities should match academic expectations. Furthermore word-processing improves your presentation skills and allows you to amend drafts easily.

A good lecturer will provide specific assessment criteria relating to a particular assignment title. Such criteria should make quite clear what will earn marks and this should help you to submit a good piece of work.

For example, in a problem question, marks will be awarded for:

(a) correct explanation of the law;
(b) correct and succinct application of the law;
(c) use of case law;
(d) evidence of further research.

Essay titles always seem to pose a greater problem for the student in that, in many cases, the student does not instantly recognise what the lecturer wants from the title. Again specific criteria will help. However, it is unlikely that the lecturer wants a regurgitation of lecture notes or the main text which is a common fault in legal essay work. You must appreciate that the 'answer' is unlikely to be found in your notes or a textbook and that what is required is research on your part supported by discussion, critique, and evaluation. There are two essentials to be considered before answering an essay title:

(a)   what is the essay about?
(b)   what approach is required?

This requires some thought on your part by reference to the specific assessment criteria. Before researching and writing you should make a plan. This is true for problem work but is absolutely essential for essay work. A plan will help you to focus on what is required and determine the limits of the work so that you do not become bogged down in irrelevant areas of research and writing.

Pay some attention to the 'instruction' words found at the beginning or end of the essay title. For example, 'evaluate' requires some judgment to be made; it may be preceded by the word 'critically', which does not require you to give a polemic of your own stance but will require some objective thought and reference to articles and other works.

At this stage many students fall into the trap of photocopying lots of articles but then not reading them — articles are not transferred to the brain by osmosis! An essay should be used as a vehicle for showing your standard of comprehension and depth of legal research within the confines of the title and any word limits.

Plagiarism is a great problem in essay work. You must familiarise yourself with the rules that your institution has on dealing with plagiarism. They are likely to be strict because plagiarism is equated with cheating in examinations.

Do you know what plagiarism is? It is generally accepted that copying from texts or articles without attributing source, or copying from another student's work, or allowing your work to be copied all amount to plagiarism. Even if you reference sources correctly, beware. A piece of work which is made up predominantly of quotes from texts and articles probably does not address the essay title and will not therefore be awarded a good mark. It illustrates an inability to transfer your research into your own words.

Assignment work may be followed by formal or informal feedback sessions. Take advantage of them. You may also be given the opportunity to improve on your marks by submitting an additional piece of work. Learn from your mistakes.

If assignment work is your only form of assessment, take advantage of that fact by planning your work carefully so that you are confident that you have submitted the best piece of work possible.

Portfolio Assessment

In some subjects or modules you may be asked to produce a portfolio as the means of assessment. Instead of one lengthy piece of work, this normally involves five or six shorter pieces to be produced throughout the semester and handed in together at the agreed date. Usually a portfolio will be used for the student to illustrate prowess in a variety of exercises. In employment law it may be reporting on a visit to an industrial tribunal, research work on stereotyping, writing a report on a disciplinary matter etc. Apart from the demands of the assessment criteria, it is essential that particular attention be paid to time-management skills so as to avoid the danger of rushing the work and spending too little time on the last two exercises in the portfolio. Presentation skills come to the fore and word-processing is therefore essential.

Oral Assessment

You may be given the opportunity to replace written assessment by some form of oral assessment or, indeed, it may form a compulsory feature of assessment on your employment module. If you have the choice, as students at Staffordshire do, then our advice is do not opt for it unless you are confident that your presentation skills will meet the demands of the assessment. Look at the assessment criteria and find out how the marks are divided, e.g., for content, research, response to questions, use of extrinsic aids.

Some guidance and training should be given on how to make a presentation and it pays to practise. The use of a video at this stage is essential. If you plan to use the OHP or flip charts you need to consider carefully how they will be incorporated into your presentation. Remember you will probably have been given a limited time in which you will have to focus on a particular topic and there is little point in using these aids if they detract from rather than enhance your presentation.

The other point which will probably determine whether you select oral presentation as a method of assessment is whether you are allowed to select your own topic. If, for example, all oral presentations have to be made on the Transfer of Undertakings Regulations and this is a topic you cannot abide then opt out if you can. At Staffordshire students are allowed to select a topic from the field of discrimination law with the approval of the lecturer. Many students think they can turn up and talk about 'equal pay'. This would be a pointless exercise as in the 30 minutes set aside for this assessment, that topic would prove too cumbersome — hence the need to obtain approval. The topic selected must have a specific focus, so that depth and rigour of knowledge can be illustrated through the presentation itself and the response to questions.

You may be videoed or perform in front of two members of staff. This takes confidence, not only in your ability to give the presentation but also in your own knowledge about the topic selected. Again time-management and research skills are required.

Assessment of Tutorial Performance

On some courses you may find that your tutorials are assessed, i.e., your contribution to the tutorial. Such assessment may form part of your overall assessment. If this is the case you should familiarise yourself with the assessment criteria and the percentage of marks available. It is usual for marks to be allocated for understanding of the subject-matter, use of authorities, application of legal principles to hypothetical cases, analysis and critical evaluation, and constructive contribution to the tutorial. The effect of assessed tutorials, apart from an instant improvement in attendance and preparation, is to encourage independent thought, confidence in research and making contributions. We have all sat through tutorials where students, for whatever reason, are inhibited from speaking or entering into discussions. This form of assessment focuses the student's mind on active rather than passive learning. Failure to attend will normally result in nought being recorded! To perform well in this type of assessment, your study skills will come to the fore. You must ensure that you are well prepared which will involve time-management, research, reading and oral skills. The disadvantage of this method of assessment is that tutorials in other subjects which do not adopt this approach tend to suffer as students put all their efforts into the assessed subject.

Examinations

It is unlikely that on any course you will be able to avoid examinations completely. However, you should be prepared for examinations not to be, necessarily, the onerous burden of the past. As we have seen, they may take a variety of forms, e.g., open book, seen, closed book or be limited in length to anywhere between one and three hours. Whichever form of examination is imposed, the key to success is preparation.

Revision

Every student has to do some revision, do not be persuaded otherwise by your fellow students who want to go to the pub for a swift half. It is true that some people have a more retentive memory than others and therefore probably do not have to spend quite so much time revising — the fortunate few! Once you accept that revision is unavoidable you can set out to reduce its tiresomeness as far as possible. You will usually be given two to three weeks before the examination as a revision period. Use those weeks wisely. There are a number of pointers which you should try to follow:

(a) Make a revision plan. This should not be too complicated but should ensure that an equal time is spent on each topic.

(b) Avoid having to revise new material when you are tired.

(c) Avoid revising late at night. Get a good night's sleep, especially before the examination.

(d) Do not rely on last-minute revision of new material. The evening or morning before an examination should be used only to read through and check your understanding of the material which you have already revised.

(e) Ensure that your plan allows an equal amount of time for each subject. Do not be tempted to spend time on a weaker subject at the expense of one at which *you* feel you are good.

(f) Incorporate rest periods into your plan, e.g., 15 minutes in front of the television with a cup of coffee. You may need to be strong willed to get yourself going again especially if you have become bored, but you must.

The method of revision tends to be personal. By this stage most students will have successfully completed examinations and will have found what suits them best. For example, you may need total silence in which case if you share a house with four noisy art students who do not have examinations it may be wise to return home for a few weeks where you may have understanding parents who will feed you and look after you through this period; or, you may need the radio on full blast, if so think of the other students and buy a set of headphones.

You must find the best method of revision for yourself, by trial and error. In employment law you will probably be faced with a vast quantity of material which you cannot learn 'parrot fashion', so do not be tempted. Employment law can be broken down into areas for revision purposes. You should therefore collect all the material, that is, lecture notes, tutorial sheets, hand-outs, articles etc. together into their topic areas. In this way you can ascertain whether there are some materials which you may no longer need. You can then précis the material into a form which you find easy to recall. However, do not fall into the trap of oversimplifying the material as you may end up with only a superficial knowledge of the topic.

Here is an example of a revision summary for the topic, equal pay:

'Like work' (s. 1(2) EPA 70).
Meaning s. 1(4): includes broadly similar nature.
Capper Pass Ltd v *Lawton* (1977).
Electrolux Ltd v *Hutchinson* (1977).
Eaton Ltd v *Nuttall* (1977).

Maidment v *Cooper & Co. (Birmingham) Ltd* (1978).
E. Coomes (Holdings) Ltd v *Shields* (1978).
National Coal Board v *Sherwin* (1978).
Thomas v *National Coal Board* (1987).
Need to refer to the meaning of 'pay' and 'employed': s. 1(6).
Hayward v *Cammell Laird Shipbuilders Ltd* (1988).
Leverton v *Clwyd County Council* (1989).
British Coal Corporation v *Smith* (1994).
[Any relevant articles.]

If you do this in good time you will be able to discuss any problems you have with the lecturing staff and keep up to date, which is imperative in employment law, but you must not go fishing. There is nothing more irritating for an examiner than attempts to discover the examination questions; especially when made under the cloak of lack of understanding. Examination questions are set months in advance (at least six months) and, for security reasons, examiners usually do not keep copies of the papers they have set and so are unlikely to remember their exact contents. It is even more difficult where there are two or more examiners. If you really want to try question spotting then look at past papers (where they are set by the same examiners) to give you some idea of the likely topics. We do not recommend that you drop any topic from your revision programme in the belief that it will not be examined, as you may find that you are unable to answer the required number of questions which will damage your chances of success. In a subject like employment law, as you will see, there is a chance that topics may be mixed up in a problem. You should appreciate the dangers if you attempt to compartmentalise the topics you have covered. However, it does no harm to spend a few minutes jotting down the topics actually covered by the lecturer and the permutations into which they *might* fall. For example:

Employment law
(a)   Formation of the contract of employment.
(b)   Relationship of the parties.
(c)   Wages.
(d)   Discrimination.
(e)   Equal pay.
(f)   Health and safety at work.
(g)   Termination of the contract.
(h)   Trade union membership.
(i)   Industrial conflict.

Your own employment law course may be different to this and you may wish to expand upon what is included under the topic headings. However, you can see from this that potentially topics (a) and (b) or (a) and (d) or (e) may be combined in a problem; or topics (g) and (f) or (g) and (d). Therefore, although one topic may be treated in isolation in the examination, perhaps in an essay question, the possibility that questions will involve combinations of topics means that it is perilous to ignore any topic altogether.

Before the examination
As the revision period draws to a close, check once more the date, time and room of the examination for the subject concerned. A fatal mistake which is made each year by a few students is turning up to the wrong examination. Usually they get the date or time wrong. This is such a fundamental mistake that you cannot really expect the examiner to have much sympathy. It pays to check where the examination room is, if it is in a part of the building which you do not usually frequent. You do not want to end up rushing up and down corridors and stairs searching for the room five minutes before the examination is due to commence.

Read the examination regulations. These are generally given to all students or are available in the departmental office. They will inform you of your rights and should things not go according to plan you may need to make use of them. For example, you may find that if you are late for the examination then the regulations will prevent you sitting it.

Make sure you allow plenty of time in which to get to the examination. If you are late and are not in breach of the examination regulations you may be allowed some extra time but it is doubtful whether you will be allowed the full time. Furthermore you will be sitting the examination under a disadvantage as no doubt you will be in quite a panic. If you are travelling by car to the examination check such basic things as petrol, battery and tyres including the spare; if by train or bus, catch an earlier one than you would normally. If you are going to be delayed try to telephone the department and they will inform the examination room.

Finally make sure you have got all that you need for the examination: a number of pens in working order, an eraser or correcting fluid, ruler, ink, sweets, a watch, blotting-paper — and lucky mascot if you must! Remember no bags will be allowed inside the examination room and certainly no paper will be allowed on your desk except the question paper, answer book, statutes (if permitted) and, if it is an open-book examination, your notes.

Inside the examination room
Let us presume you have made it to the examination without mishap. Once you have settled yourself in your seat the time approaches for the start of the examination. You may or may not be given 10 minutes' reading time

before the actual examination commences. On being told to turn over the paper by the invigilator do not panic. Read through the whole paper carefully at least twice before putting pen to paper. Do not be put off by your fellow candidates who appear to be writing reams in the first few minutes.

On your first read-through of the paper, concentrate on giving yourself some idea of the topics covered. Try not to make your final selection of questions to be answered at this stage. Then, in the second reading, which you can do more slowly, as you select the questions which you wish to attempt, make a rough plan of anything, e.g., statutes, sections, rules, cases, academic arguments, which strike you as relevant to that question. This plan is for your benefit so it does not have to look like a work of art. It should be in note form and should not take long. It may pay you to do it in the answer book because you may wish to refer the examiner to it if you run out of time. When you have completed the answer you can then put a pencil line through the plan. Use your plan when you actually start answering the question to ensure that your answer is structured and does not jump about from rule to rule in an incomprehensible or illogical way. Although this plan is rough, make sure you at least understand it, especially if you abbreviate case names, for example, 'AA' may not necessarily mean 'Automobile Association'! A warning: do not spend too much time on the plan. There is no need to make full plans at this stage. You can add to your plan before you commence answering the individual question.

Whilst you are reading the question paper make sure you understand the rubric and stick to it. You may have to answer two from four or four out of nine questions; there may even be a compulsory question. You *must* attempt the required number; to fail to do so is literally throwing away marks. Even if you answer one out of two questions reasonably well you have limited your chances of success. Examiners rarely have sympathy with candidates who make this fundamental mistake. Also do not hedge your bets by answering more questions than is necessary. You are wasting your time as the examiner will only mark the first answers in the book up to the required number. The examiner will not select your best answers.

It follows therefore that the allocation of time is very important. You must allow time to read through the paper carefully even if you are given additional reading time. Also it is advisable to allow 10 minutes at the end of the examination to read through the answers, underline case names and statutes and ensure that you have completed the front of the answer book correctly. You must adhere to the time limits which you set for each question. If you exceed them you will have difficulty in completing the paper. This will affect your chances of passing the examination. Rather than exceed your time limits, leave a side free after an incomplete answer and return to it if you have time. The evidence is that you would gain few marks if you continued to answer the question, as most marks are gained in the first 20 minutes of writing the answer.

Style and content
Style is to some extent a personal thing. Certainly what suits one examiner will not necessarily suit another. You are therefore advised to speak to your examiners if you are unsure of the style which they find acceptable. There are, however, a few basic rules which you can adopt:

(a) Ensure that your writing is legible. There is nothing more frustrating to an examiner than to have to plough through pages of indecipherable writing when there are another hundred scripts to mark; you may not gain the marks you deserve.

(b) Ensure that your spelling is correct, especially of legal words. Let us give you an example from personal experience: one student answered a problem on defamation, spelling it as deformation all the way through the answer, even though he had been referred to the textbook, a tutorial sheet and a hand-out on the subject; this student failed that question.

(c) Ensure that your answer is grammatically correct. You must write in complete sentences. As a general rule it is unlikely that an examiner will mark an answer which is completely in note form. There is, however, one exception: should you run out of time you may attempt to complete your answer by writing in note form. This may enable you to gain a few marks which you would not otherwise have done.

(d) Do not write across the whole page: leave the margins for the examiner's use.

(e) Start each answer on a new page.

(f) Underline case names, statutes and articles.

(g) Get to the point. Try not to ramble or repeat yourself because the examiner will lose interest and you will not be doing yourself justice.

(h) Do not write out the question in your answer book. This is a complete waste of your time and totally unnecessary.

(i) Do not add your own words to the question to enable you to answer the question you wanted rather than the one the examiner set.

(j) Try to remember case names. If you cannot, then a sentence identifying the facts will suffice. As a general rule no marks will be gained for regurgitating the facts of the case. What is important is the decision and your application of it. We shall consider the correct time to recite the facts later.

Now let us turn to the content of your answer book. Remember that you start with no marks so there is everything to be gained and nothing to lose.

The examiner can usually tell very quickly whether you have understood the problem or essay subject and will not be deceived by a display of learning which is actually irrelevant. If you have run out of things to write which are pertinent to the question, there is no point in writing about some closely related topic. If you have no idea how to apply the law to the problem, do not instead write 'all you know' about the area. We would like to stress that this is one of the worst crimes a student can commit and will certainly result in failure. No examination question will require you to 'write all you know' about a given topic. If you feel yourself falling into this trap stop immediately and reassess the question and answer, and if you are still in doubt about what is required then abandon the answer and attempt another question. Remember you only gain marks for relevant points.

Probably the most important question for the student is which is better to answer, problems or essays? On an employment law paper there will probably be both, and you may have to attempt both. Glanville Williams in *Learning the Law* suggests that the better student should concentrate on answering problems because essays take longer to answer and the evidence shows that examiners are meaner with marks. Whilst this may be true, you should answer the questions which you feel competent to do. To some extent if you are confident about your ability to apply the law, for example, in a problem on discrimination then this question should be selected. If you have read widely on the law surrounding industrial conflict then an essay on this topic would be a wise choice. As we see it, the main problem with essays is that it is much easier for students to fall into the trap of writing 'all they know' about the area because there is less guidance in the question. It could be argued therefore that the weaker student should stick to problem questions. Whether you favour problems or essays, our advice is: answer the questions which you feel will bring you the best marks first.

Answering a problem
To some extent the guidance given for the writing of assignments applies equally to examinations, but even more so as you are under pressure in the examination room.

You should have identified the issues in your rough plan and be prepared to write your answer in a logical form. It is best to tackle a problem as if you are writing for someone who has no knowledge of this area of law. There are therefore a few points which you can follow:

(a) State the law as it relates to the problem. In employment law this may involve reference to sections of statutes, so make sure you know the section number and the gist of the wording.

(b) Use cases in applying the law and in giving reasons for your application to the problem. Always remember that a bald statement of the law is insufficient, nor does the examiner want to see a regurgitation of all the law on this topic without any application. Be careful because this is a common fault.

(c) Make sure your answer is in line with the requirements of the problem. Usually the examiner will either want you to 'discuss' the problem or 'advise' a particular party. You will inevitably have to raise the same issues but there may be a particular slant to your answer if you are required to advise one party as opposed to a general discussion which will require you to look at all the parties.

(d) Do not worry if the facts of the problem appear to be incomplete and there is therefore insufficient evidence for you to reach a conclusion. The examiner is probably not looking for an exact answer. What you have to do is recognise and discuss all of the issues raised in the problem. Do not be afraid to say that from the facts there is insufficient evidence to conclude on liability if you are confident that you have raised all the necessary points.

(e) There may be an opportunity to introduce academic argument or social or economic policy into a problem on employment law, especially where the area of law is not settled, but do not get bogged down, just refer to the argument and the cases involved. Political, social and economic policy is an integral part of employment law and although there is more scope for discussing it in an essay, do not overlook an opportunity to raise it in a problem. For example, it may be relevant to the attitude of the tribunal in an unfair dismissal case.

(f) Remember to use remedies and defences. These tend to be forgotten, yet you should be able to gain a few marks by referring to any relevant remedies and defences. Do not get carried away unless an extensive discussion is specifically required in the question.

Writing an essay
To write a good essay in an examination is to some extent a more difficult task than answering a problem because you need time to structure your thoughts, or you might end up writing a garbled mess. The main problem you are faced with is deciding what is required from the essay question. If you misinterpret the question or even fail to understand the title you will be throwing away marks as you write, not just about the wrong area (which is an unlikely mistake) but probably about the wrong *aspect* of the topic. If you are in any doubt about the essay question do not attempt it.

When tackling an essay question you will probably be faced with the words 'critically examine', or 'assess' or 'discuss'. In employment law as in any other area of law it is unwise to answer such a question unless you know more than the bare bones of the topic. You will need to draw on all the additional material such as articles, EOC publications, and statistics which you have been referred to over the academic year. There are a number of points which you may find helpful:

(a)   Do not be afraid to be critical as long as you are constructive. You must be able to support your criticisms by reference to statistics, academic works etc. Remember there can be a very find dividing line between dogmatism and criticism.

(b)   Make use of academic debate. If, for example, you are faced with an essay such as, 'Critically assess the current position of the work for equal value provision in the Equal Pay Act 1970', then you need to refer in detail to the key legal cases and the contentious points raised by those cases as well as academic argument in this field. You would then have to refer to learned articles such as C. McCrudden, 'The effectiveness of European equality law' (1993) 13 Oxford J Legal Stud 320, or B. Hepple and E.M. Szyszczak (eds.), *Discrimination: the Limits of the Law* (London: Mansell, 1992), or C. Kilpatrick, 'Deciding when jobs of equal value can be paid unequally: an examination of s. 1(3) of the Equal Pay Act 1970' (1994) 23 ILJ 311.

(c)   If the question is in the form of a quotation attributed to a particular author you should use this as a guide to the approach you should adopt in writing the essay. Obviously if you have never read the work or at least considered it then you probably will not know what is required.

(d)   This is stating the obvious, but make sure you use cases to support your arguments. There is a tendency for students when writing essays to forget the use of authorities.

General points
The following points are applicable to both essays and problems in examinations. Ask the examiner whether you can use abbreviations for common words, e.g., 'c. of e.' for contract of employment. The examiner may accept abbreviations of case names after you have written them out once, e.g., *Hayward* v *Cammell Laird Shipbuilders Ltd* becomes *H* v *CL*, but please check.

The facts of cases should be set out only where it is necessary for you to assess the impact of a series of cases and/or where it is necessary for you to distinguish cases. Other than that, no marks are gained for regurgitation of the facts. When using a case as an authority it may be important to refer to the level at which the decision was reached bearing in mind the doctrine of precedent. There is little point in using an EAT decision as support for your argument when it has been superseded by a CA decision.

CONCLUSION

We hope the guidance contained in this chapter is of some value to you. We suggest you adopt a pragmatic approach to assessment: you cannot avoid it so you may as well make the best of it. It is important for your future career to gain the best mark possible and you are the only person who has the control over this. Do not be put off by fellow students calling you a swot, you will have the last laugh.

READING

Clinch, P., *Using a Law Library* (London: Blackstone, 1992).

Fairbairn, G., and Winch, C., *Reading, Writing and Reasoning* (Buckingham: Society for Research into Higher Education and Open University Press, 1991).

Holborn, G., *Butterworths Legal Research Guide* (London: Butterworths, 1993).

Maughan, C., and Webb, J., *Lawyering Skills and the Legal Process* (London: Butterworths, 1995).

Northedge, A., *The Good Study Guide* (Milton Keynes: Open University, 1990).

Williams, G., *Learning the Law*, 11th ed. (London: Stevens, 1982).

3 THE NATURE AND CONTENT OF THE CONTRACT OF EMPLOYMENT

As we stated in chapter 1, the individual employment relationship has been altered quite radically by the legislation of the 70s which created the statutory floor of employment rights and a specialised system of industrial tribunals through which disputes over these rights are adjudicated. Does this mean that the law of contract no longer provides the foundation of employment law? Is possession of the *status* of 'employee' the all-important issue given that it is that status and not contract which attracts the rights bestowed by statute? To accept this view would be going too far for two reasons:

(a) There are still many situations for which statute has not provided and it is up to the law of contract to fill the gap and supply the answers to questions such as whether there is a right to receive wages when absent through sickness (see *Mears v Safecar Security Ltd* [1983] QB 54).

(b) Even when it comes to adjudicating statutory rights, the courts and tribunals will often look to the guidance of contractual theories in reaching a decision, e.g., in the context of unfair dismissal, whether an employee's repudiation of the contract requires acceptance by the employer in the form of a dismissal or whether the repudiation automatically brings the contract to an end.

In view of this, the common law rules of contract remain of crucial importance to the student of employment law and are worthy of careful study.

EMPLOYED OR SELF-EMPLOYED?

Nowhere is the residual importance of the common law better illustrated than when it comes to identifying whether a worker possesses 'employee'status. This is a confused area and wherever confusion reigns, expect to find the examiner seeking to pose an examination question which will test the student's powers of legal analysis to the full! A question drawn from this topic area may be either in the form of an essay or a problem (the latter usually raising the status issue as part of a wider problem concerned with unfair dismissal and/or redundancy payments). We shall look at a problem question later in this section but first of all let us examine a recent essay question on the definition of employee status.

Why is it necessary to distinguish between contracts of employment and those of self-employment? Do you consider the tests used by the courts and tribunals to be satisfactory?

Analysis

The question itself obligingly provides a structure for the answer. We are first asked to identify the factors which make the distinction important. The question then asks us to evaluate the quality of judicial decision-making in this area.

The distinction between contracts of and contracts for service is crucial for workers for a number of reasons. Only employees qualify for:

(a)   Social security payments such as unemployment benefit, statutory sick pay etc.
(b)   Employment protection rights such as unfair dismissal, redundancy payments, minimum notice on termination etc.
(c)   Certain health and safety provisions, including the Factories Act.
(d)   The benefit of the employer's duty of care at common law.

But perhaps the primary importance of the distinction concerns taxation. 'Employees' are taxed under Schedule E of the Income and Corporation Taxes Act 1970, while the self-employed enjoy more favourable treatment, being taxed under Schedule D with its more generous allowances. It is therefore tempting for workers to have themselves classified as self-employed and the advantages to the employer are obvious from what has just been stated. Of course the benefits to the employee tend to be of a short-term nature. As Smith and Wood maintain:

. . . the independent contractor may be in a better monetary position while working, but at a grave disadvantage if he falls off a ladder or is sacked (*Industrial Law*, p. 9).

Given the fundamental importance of the distinction, it is unfortunate that the formulation of the test of employee status has come from the courts and tribunals rather than from statute. The only guidance on the question in the legislation is so completely circular as to be absolutely useless (see EPCA 1978, s. 153).

The case law on this subject is confusing and contradictory. Historically, the leading approach was to apply the test of 'control', i.e., could the employer control how, when and where the worker was to work. If he could then that worker was his employee. However, as nowadays many employees possess skills not held by their employer, control as the sole determinant of status has been rejected. Along the way the test of 'integration' was floated, i.e., whether the worker was fully integrated into the employing organisation, but the test was never widely adopted. The modern approach has been to abandon the search for a single test and adopt a multifactorial test weighing up all the factors for and against the existence of a contract of employment to determine whether the worker was 'in business on his own account'. Factors which are influential include the method of payment (payment on a commission basis indicative of self-employment); whether tax and national insurance are deducted; the degree of control exercised over the worker; the provision of tools and equipment and who bears the risk of loss and chance of profit.

Recent case law involving the question of the status of 'peripheral workers' has seen an emphasis placed on the concept of mutuality of obligation as a possible factor in the equation. The concept was explained by Kerr LJ in *Nethermere (St Neots) Ltd* v *Taverna* [1984] IRLR 240 as follows:

> The inescapable requirement concerning the alleged employees however . . . is that they must be subject to an *obligation* to accept and perform some minimum, or at least reasonable, amount of work for the alleged employer.

The implications of this test for workers with irregular working patterns are highly disadvantageous — at least if it is applied in a strict sense. The dangers are highlighted in *O'Kelly* v *Trusthouse Forte plc* [1983] IRLR 369 in which the Court of Appeal was not prepared to find that 'regular' casual waiters were employees, even though they had a well-established and regular working relationship with Trusthouse Forte. It was held to be quite 'unreal' to maintain that the long-standing arrangement, which involved a reliance by the employer on its regular casuals and of the regulars receiving priority in the allocation of work, lacked the essential 'mutuality of obligation' to classify them as employees. Mutuality was lacking because technically they could refuse work when it was offered even though, in practice, they did not do so because refusal would result in removal from the regular casual list.

This sort of narrow reasoning is also to be found in the judgment of the EAT in *Wickens v Champion Employment* [1984] ICR 365 where 'temps' engaged by a private employment agency were not accorded employment status because of the lack of binding obligation on the part of the agency to make bookings for work and the absence of any obligation by the worker to accept them.

A more realistic approach is to be found in the majority judgments of the court in *Nethermere (St Neots) Ltd v Taverna*. Here, homeworkers making clothing on a piecework basis were accorded employee status on the basis that the regular giving and taking of work over a period of time evidenced the necessary mutuality of obligation. This was so even though the workers were under no obligation to undertake a particular quantity of work and in certain weeks did no work at all. As Stephenson LJ put it:

> I cannot see why well-founded expectations of continuing homework should not be hardened or refined into enforceable contracts by regular giving and taking of work over periods of a year or more, and why outworkers should not thereby become employees under contracts of service.

In its establishment of the concept of the global or umbrella contract, covering weeks where no work was available, the *Nethermere* decision offered a means of pushing peripheral workers through the 'gateway' to employment protection. However, more recently the Court of Appeal has shown a marked reluctance to apply the concept, again taking a narrow view on the 'mutuality' question (see *McLeod v Hellyer Brothers Ltd* [1987] IRLR 232).

The confusions which abound in this area are multiplied because of the view that the question of employment status is one of mixed fact and law rather than a pure question of law (see *O'Kelly v Trusthouse Forte plc*). As a result, the powers of the EAT and Court of Appeal to interfere with decisions of industrial tribunals on status are much reduced and the chances of inconsistency thereby heightened. Those who regretted the adoption of this view welcomed the House of Lords decision in *Davies v Presbyterian Church of Wales* [1986] IRLR 194 where it appeared that Lord Templeman unequivocally held that whether the claimant was an employee was a pure question of law. That case, in which *O'Kelly* was not referred to, turned entirely upon the construction of a document, whereas *O'Kelly* had to be decided partly on the interpretation of various written documents and partly on inferences to be drawn from the parties' conduct. This difference was seized upon by the Court of Appeal in *McLeod v Hellyer Brothers Ltd* in order to distinguish *Davies* and to continue to apply the *O'Kelly* approach, that an appellate court is entitled to interfere with the decision of an industrial tribunal on whether the applicant was employed under a contract of employment only if the tribunal had misdirected itself in law or its decision was one which no tribunal properly instructed could have reached (see also *Edwards* v *Bairstow* [1956] AC 14). In *Lee* v *Chung and Shun Shing Construction & Engineering Co. Ltd* [1990] IRLR 236, the Privy Council implicitly approved of the distinction adopted in *McLeod* and approved the fundamental test for employee status as: 'Is the person who has engaged himself to perform these services performing them in business on his own account?'.

An answer along these lines will satisfy the question: you have explained the importance of the employment status question and have illustrated the unsatisfactory nature of the tests as formulated and applied by the courts. Although the question does not explicitly solicit your views on how matters might be improved, a brief discussion of any proposals on reform will give your answer added weight and make a neat conclusion.

Your discussion of the case law has shown that the courts have experienced great difficulty in classifying so-called 'atypical' workers, those whose work is temporary, part-time or casual. Given that they at present make up an estimated one-third of the labour force and their numbers are increasing, you may wish to argue that employment protection legislation should be extended to cover this increasingly inaptly named group of 'atypical' workers.

Commentators such as Hepple 15 ILJ 169 and P. Leighton, 'Marginal workers', in R. Lewis (ed.), *Labour Law in Britain*, ch. 18, have argued for a radical change of approach by our legislators, maintaining that any reform in this area is likely to be frustrated is statutory rights continue to rest on the nebulous concept of the 'contract of service'.

Hepple has proposed that the 'contract of service' should be replaced by a broad definition of the 'employment relationship' between the worker and the undertaking by which the worker is employed. The relationship would continue to be based on voluntary agreement between the worker and the undertaking to work in return for pay but 'it would be a contract of a new kind, one that encompassed both the intermittent exchange of work for remuneration, and the single continuous contract'.

Hepple accepts that this legislative protection should exclude genuinely independent workers, those 'in business on their own account', but argues that there can be no watertight legal definition of who is 'independent'. He proposes a statutory presumption that the worker is covered by the legislation, with the burden of proof on the employer should it be alleged that the worker is independent.

A Problem on Employment Status

Eric, a student at Bogwell College, has taken a summer job selling ice-cream. The arrangement is that he hires the van from Frosto Ltd, buys the ice-cream from that company and is allocated the 'park and library patch'. The prices are fixed by Frosto. Eric is paid a 'fee' of £30 per week, plus the mark-up on the ice-cream he sells. He is told 'No cards, mate' when he joins, but is given a copy of 'The Frosto Code' which prescribes uniforms, standards of hygiene and cash procedures. His earnings average £130 a week.

Advise Eric on his employment status.

Analysis

We have seen that the modern approach has been to adopt a multifactorial approach in answering the fundamental question of whether the worker could be said to be 'in business on his own account' (see *Ready Mixed Concrete (South East) Ltd v Minister of Pensions & National Insurance* [1968] 2 QB 497; *Market Investigations Ltd v Minister of Social Security* [1969] 2 QB 173).

The *Market Investigations* decision offers the basis of a check-list for employment status and, given the infrequency with which guidance is offered in this area, the following extract from Cooke J's judgment (at pp. 184–5) is useful:

> No exhaustive list has been compiled and perhaps no exhaustive list can be compiled of the considerations which are relevant in determining [the] question, nor can strict rules be laid down as to the relative weight which the various considerations should carry in particular cases. The most that can be said is that control will no doubt always have to be considered, although it can no longer be regarded as the sole determining factor; and that factors which may be of importance are such matters as whether the man performing the services provides his own equipment, whether he hires his own helpers, what degree of financial risk he takes, what degree of responsibility for investment and management he has, and whether and how far he has an opportunity of profiting from sound management in the performance of his task.

We can now consider each of the factors identified by Cooke J in an attempt to clarify Eric's position:

(a) Control. There are elements in Eric's 'arrangement' with Frosto which evidence a relatively high degree of control which might help categorise the relationship as a contract of employment — the fact that Frosto fixes the prices, allocates the sales territory and lays down standards to be adhered to in relation to uniform, hygiene and cash-handling.

(b) Equipment. It appears that Eric does not supply his own equipment but on the other hand the arrangements concerned with the hire of the van and purchase of the ice-cream do not fit easily into the usual employer-employee relationship.

(c) Financial risk and chance of profit. Eric begins to look less like an employee and more like an entrepreneur given that the major part of his earnings depends on how much ice-cream he sells (there are factual similarities here with the *Ready Mixed Concrete* case). The facts do not tell us whether Eric can delegate his tasks to another or whether he is free to determine the hours he works. If such was the case we might be able to more confidently declare Eric's status as self-employed.

(d) Self-description. To what extent will the courts be influenced by the purported declaration that the relationship is one of self-employment — 'No cards, mate'? After a period of uncertainty, where it was not clear whether the courts would allow the stated intentions of the parties to determine the matter of status (see *Ferguson* v *John Dawson & Partners (Contractors) Ltd* [1976] 1 WLR 1213 and compare with *Massey* v *Crown Life Insurance Co.* [1978] ICR 590), it now appears that the subjective intention of the parties will not override what in other respects has the attributes of a contract of employment (see *Young & Woods Ltd* v *West* [1980] IRLR 201).

(e) The Court of Appeal has recently warned against a mechanistic application of Cooke J's checklist (see *Hall* v *Lorimer* [1994] 1 WLR 209). While the checklist should not be regarded as laying down an all-purpose definition, it does offer valuable guidance in many cases.

Having gone through this exercise you may still be uncertain about Eric's status. Do not worry about this. As long as you have correctly stated the law then the precise weight you give to the various factors in reaching your conclusion is largely a matter for you. In other words, it is as difficult for the examiner to challenge your conclusion on status as it is for the EAT to challenge that of an industrial tribunal!

CONSTRUCTING THE CONTRACT OF EMPLOYMENT

In theory the employment contract is subject to the contractual rules regarding offer, acceptance, intention to create legal relations etc. However, there has long been an awareness that the 'normal rules' do not fit easily (see R. Rideout in *Current Legal Problems* (1966), pp. 111–17). At the time the contract is made often very little is said and perhaps even less is written down. Moreover, classical contract's idea of parties of equal strength bargaining at arm's length has never reflected the reality of how the vast majority of contracts of employment are entered into. Such a view totally ignores the superior bargaining power of the employer.

Given the informal manner in which one of the more important legal relationships can be entered into, the terms and conditions of the contract of employment may derive from a variety of documents and sources. The courts have supplemented the express terms of the bargain by a process of implication and, latterly, statute has enacted provisions which operate by becoming incorporated in the individual contract of employment (see, for example, the equality clause under the equal pay legislation).

In this section of the chapter we shall consider the various sources of the contract of employment using the following structure:

(a) Express terms.
(b) The products of collective bargaining.
(c) Implied terms.
(d) Work rules.
(e) Custom and practice.
(f) Statute.

Express Terms

Only in exceptional cases must the contract be in writing, e.g., Merchant Shipping Act 1970, contracts of apprenticeship. However, since 1963 most employees have possessed the right to receive a written statement of some of the most important terms within a certain period of entering employment (see now part I of EPCA 1978). Prior to the passage of TURERA 1993, the statement had to be provided within 13 weeks of entering employment. An employee had to work for 16 hours or more a week in order to qualify or have been continuously employed for five years under a contract of employment requiring eight hours' work or more per week. The adoption of the EC Directive on proof of an employment relationship (91/533) requires that essential aspects of the contract or employment relationship should be given to all employees, except where the member State is able to justify excluding those working less than eight hours a week, or those who have been employed for less than a month, or those whose work is of a casual and/or specific nature. The necessary information must be provided within two months of the beginning of the employment. In terms of the type of information which is required, in many areas UK law already went further than the Directive. But there were certain aspects where our law was lacking. TURERA 1993 is designed to comply with the Directive and substitutes new ss. 1 to 6 of EPCA.

Under the TURERA 1993 amendments, employers have now to give the following additional information to that already required: the place of work; where the employee is required (or permitted) to work in various places, an indication of that fact and the address of the employer; any collective agreement which directly affects the terms and conditions of employment of the individual employee (including the identity of the parties by whom such collective agreements were made); where the employment is not intended to be permanent, the period of the expected duration of the contract; where the employee is to work outside the UK for a period of one month, certain additional information.

An employer will have to give this written statement no later than two calendar months after the beginning of employment. In addition, all employees will be entitled to this statement as of right, unless their contract involves less than eight hours' work a week.

Under the previous law, instead of giving a written statement of particulars in statutory form to each employee, the statement could merely refer the employee to some other document which the employee had reasonable opportunities of reading in the course of employment or which is made reasonably accessible to the employee. Secondly, whilst any changes in terms had to be communicated to the employee within one month of the alteration, the employer could indicate that any further changes in the document to which the employee is referred will be made in that document within the permissible period.

TURERA 1993 tightens up the law in a number of important respects. It is no longer sufficient to refer employees to another document (e.g., a collective agreement) for details of hours of work, pay or holiday entitlement. These must be given in the statement of terms itself. However, it is still permissible to refer the employee to another reasonably accessible document for sickness and pension provisions, and to the law or a collective agreement for details regarding notice rights. It is also still possible to cross-refer in relation to disciplinary rules and procedures. All the other required particulars now have to be included in a single document. Previously, it was not necessary for a written statement to be given if an employer gave a written contract or made a copy reasonably accessible and the written contract might be scattered across a number of documents.

The limitations mean that cross-referral to a staff handbook will no longer comply with the law. As a result, employers will have to redraft much of their employment documentation. It could also result in much greater formality and detail in employment agreements.

If there is a change to any of the terms of which particulars must be provided or referred to in the document, the employer now has to notify employees individually in writing. This must be given at the earliest opportunity, and, in any event, no later than one month after the change. Where the change results from the employee being required to work outside the UK for a period of more than one month, the change must be notified no later than the time the employee leaves the UK, if that is earlier. The statement of change may refer the employee to other reasonably accessible documents, or the law or a collective agreement as appropriate, *but only in respect of changes to sickness, pension, notice and disciplinary provisions.*

By virtue of EPCA 1978, s. 11, an employee can complain to an industrial tribunal if provided with no statement at all or an incomplete statement or a complete but inaccurate statement. The tribunal is empowered to determine what particulars ought to have been provided, or to amend inaccurate particulars (see *Mears* v *Safecar Security Ltd* [1983] QB 54, CA).

Given the weakness of the remedy it is not surprising that research has shown that many employers do not keep their employees informed in writing of their principal terms of employment (see P. Leighton and S. Dumville, 'From statement to contract (1977) 6 ILJ 133). Any new employee who successfully complained to an industrial tribunal about not receiving the statutory statement may well achieve a Pyrrhic victory. The employer's response may well be to dismiss an 'employment protection rip-off artist' who will have insufficient continuity to claim unfair dismissal. Fortunately, by virtue of an amendment introduced by TURERA 1993, it is now automatically unfair to dismiss an employee for asserting a statutory right, including failure to supply written particulars (see EPCA 1978, s. 60A).

The statement is not a contract itself

This point is a difficult one for many students to grasp when it is brought to their attention for the first time and as such it often features as an issue in employment law examination questions. The point will crop up in one of the problems we shall consider later in this chapter.

Following *Gascol Conversions Ltd* v *Mercer* [1974] IRLR 155, it was thought that s. 1 statements had been accorded virtually equivalent weight to a written contract, i.e., were affected by the parol evidence rule. In that case, the employee actually signed the written statement. Lord Denning MR stated that, by reason of the parol evidence rule, the statutory statement being reduced to writing was 'the sole evidence of the contract and its terms'. As a result, the statement's reference to the number of hours of work per week could not be contradicted. In *Gascol Conversions Ltd* v *Mercer*, however, the written statement was actually described as the 'new contract of employment', so it was not simply a case of the employee signing a receipt to say that the document had been received by him. If the latter was the case, it would not be so easy to construe the document as a written contract.

This was the view taken by the EAT in *System Floors (UK) Ltd* v *Daniel* [1982] ICR 54. In this case the employee had been given and had signed a statutory statement which stated that he started employment one week earlier than the actual commencement of his employment. On his dismissal, the correct starting date was the crucial issue in determining whether he had sufficient service to claim unfair dismissal. The employee sought to rely on *Gascol Conversions Ltd* v *Mercer* to argue that the starting date contained in the signed statement could not be contradicted. This was rejected by the

EAT which distinguished *Gascol Conversions Ltd* v *Mercer* on the basis that it involved a signed contract of employment, whereas in the instant case Daniel were merely signing to acknowledge he had received the statement.

In the course of his judgment, Browne-Wilkinson J provided this widely cited analysis of the effect of the written statement:

> It provides very strong prima facie evidence of what were the terms of the contract between the parties, but does not constitute a written contract between the parties. Nor are the statements of the terms finally conclusive: at most, they place a heavy burden on the employer to show that the actual terms of contract are different from those which he had set out in the statutory statement.

This approach was later approved by the Court of Appeal in *Robertson* v *British Gas Corporation* [1983] IRLR 302, a useful case because, as we shall see, it also provides guidance on the incorporation of terms from collective agreements.

The Products of Collective Bargaining

The collective agreement performs two functions. First, it regulates the relationship between the union and the employer or employers' association. Unlike other countries, collective agreements in Britain are presumed not to be legally binding (see TULR(C)A 1992, s. 179). Secondly, it has a normative function providing a set of substantive rules, relating to wages, hours, holidays etc., which regulate the individual contract of employment. In order for the terms of the collective agreement to be incorporated, there must be some sort of 'bridge' between the collective bargain and the individual contract. Conceptual problems abound in this area which can be crafted into problem questions or which you might be asked to discuss through the medium of a quotation along the following lines:

> 'Despite its major importance for a large number of employees, the precise legal effect of collective bargain in the contracts of employment of employees affected by it is a matter of some difficulty.'
> Discuss.

Analysis

There are three possible ways in which the 'bridge to incorporation' might be constructed:

(a) Incorporation by agency.

(b) Express incorporation.
(c) Incorporation by conduct.

Agency
One superficially attractive method is that individual contracts are affected by the collective bargaining process because the union acts as agent for its members. Whilst this concept eliminates any difficulty as to the mechanics of incorporation, the courts and tribunals have tended to be very wary of the idea of the union as agent. The problem is that the agency concept would restrict the union to acting only on behalf of union members. Also there would be a serious difficulty if a union member as principal purported to withdraw his authority from the union to act as his agent — hence the courts' suspicion (see *Holland* v *London Society of Compositors* (1924) 40 TLR 440).

Express incorporation
This is the most frequent mechanism of incorporation and is achieved by express reference in the actual contract or in the written statement of terms (see *National Coal Board* v *Galley* [1958] 1 WLR 16).

Within this area it is possible to identify several difficulties.

First, what is the effect on the terms of an individual contract when an incorporated collective agreement is terminated? A valuable case to retain in your armoury here is *Robertson* v *British Gas Corporation* [1983] IRLR 302, not only will it provide you with guidance on this point but, as we have seen, you can also use it as an authority on the legal status of EPCA 1978, part I, statements. For these reasons the case is worth examining in some detail.

In 1970, the offer letter to men appointed as meter readers/collectors stated that 'Incentive bonus scheme conditions will apply to meter reading and collecting work'. At this time there was in existence a collective agreement made between the employers and the union which regulated the amounts payable under the bonus scheme. In 1977 the men received a s. 1 statement which stated:

The provisions of the agreement of the National Joint Council for Gas Staffs relating to remuneration will apply to you. Any payment which may, from time to time, become due in respect of incentive bonuses will be calculated in accordance with the rules of the scheme in force at the time.

In 1981, the employer gave the union notice that it was terminating the bonus aspect of the agreement at the end of the year. Robertson and another successfully sued British Gas in the county court for the loss of what amounted to a third of their wages.

Before the Court of Appeal the employer argued that the men's contracts were to be found in the 1977 s. 1 statement which, on its understanding was to be interpreted as meaning that if there was no bonus scheme in force then no bonus was payable.

The Court of Appeal disagreed with the employer's interpretation of the 1977 statement but were of the view that, even if it were correct, the s. 1 statement could not be used as an interpretation of the 1970 letter which was the contract itself. Kerr LJ explained that it was open to the employer to withdraw from the collective agreement, since it was not legally enforceable. But the terms of the agreement had been incorporated into individual employees' contracts and only if those terms were varied by agreement could the individual contract be varied. In this case, however, there had been no agreed variation; the employer had unilaterally withdrawn from the agreement, leaving the individual contracts unaffected. See also *Gibbons* v *Associated British Ports* [1985] IRLR 376; cf. *Cadoux* v *Central Regional Council* [1986] IRLR 131.

A second and related area of confusion has arisen over the import of the legal status of the source of the contractual term. Just because the collective agreement is not contractually binding does not mean that those of its terms which are incorporated in the individual contract will also fail to possess a legally binding quality. This is well illustrated by the decision of the Court of Appeal in *Marley* v *Forward Trust Group Ltd* [1986] IRLR 369.

Marley's contract of employment with Forward Trust Group Ltd expressly incorporated the terms of a collective agreement which had been negotiated with the trade union, ASTMS, and was subject to modifications to that agreement. There had always been a 'mobility clause' in his contract of employment which obliged him to work in any department of the company to which he might be posted.

Early in 1983, the union negotiated an amendment to the collective agreement which introduced certain provisions as to redundancy. These provided that, in the event of redundancy, employees who were offered significant changes to the terms of their employment such as location would have the right to a six-month trial period. If at the end of this trial period, they rejected the job their right to an agreed scheme of redundancy payments would be preserved.

At the end of 1983, the employer, faced with redundancies, closed the Bristol office where Marley was employed and he was transferred to London. Marley, having tried the job, was unhappy and decided to leave and claim under the redundancy agreement. The company resisted his claim because in its view he had been transferred under the mobility clause and not under the redundancy agreement. Further, the redundancy clause did not have the force of law because the collective agreement was expressed to be 'binding in honour only'. Astonishingly, this argument was accepted by both the industrial tribunal and EAT despite the fact that the collective agreement had been expressly incorporated into the individual contract.

Fortunately, this heresy was rejected by the Court of Appeal. Lawton LJ, applying the *Robertson* decision, held that the terms of an enforceable collective agreement once incorporated into an individual contract assumed a legally binding character.

A third problem concerning express incorporation involves the question as to whether certain terms of a collective agreement are appropriate for inclusion in the individual contract of employment. This is very much a grey area compounded by the fact that the courts have never developed a test for what makes a particular clause 'appropriate'. The most that can be said is that much will depend on whether the particular clause is seen as relating to collective rather than individual relationships, such as union recognition (*Gallagher* v *Post Office* [1970] 3 All ER 712) or redundancy planning (*British Leyland UK Ltd* v *McQuilken* [1978] IRLR 245; *Alexander* v *Standard Telephones & Cables Ltd (No. 2)* [1991] IRLR 286).

A final issue concerns the inclusion of 'no-strike' clauses and their relationship to the individual contract of employment. It may be argued that such 'peace clauses' create collective rather than individual obligations and therefore are inappropriate for incorporation (see the discussion of this point by Wedderburn, *The Worker and the Law* at p. 340). However, the legislature has proceeded on the basis that no-strike clauses are able to cross the bridge and has laid down certain restrictions relating to incorporation (see TULR(C)A 1992, s. 180).

Incorporation by conduct
This is sometimes called implied incorporation or, in the words of Kahn-Freund, 'crystallised custom'. An important point to note is that terms implied from collective agreements on the basis of conduct or custom cannot oust an express term covering the same subject-matter (see *Gascol Conversions Ltd* v *Mercer* [1974] IRLR 155).

Implied Terms

Although an increasing role has been played by statutory obligations which cannot be contracted out of by the employer, the common law implied terms of employment are still of considerable importance.

The judges of the common law laid down two tests, or probably one combined test, to determine whether a term should be implied into the contract. These tests, with which you will be familiar from your days as a contract student, allow the court to imply a term:

of which it can be predicated that 'it goes without saying', some term not expressed but necessary to give to the transaction such business efficacy as the parties must have intended (per Lord Wright in *Luxor (Eastbourne) Ltd v Cooper* [1941] AC 108 at p. 137).

This subjective basis for implication always had an air of unreality about it given, as Kahn-Freund has observed, 'It is . . . sheer Utopia to postulate a common interest in the substance of labour relations' (*Labour and the Law*, 3rd ed., p. 28). Also, as we shall see, the courts have long been willing to hold that at common law there are certain terms which will be implied to most if not all employments not on the basis of the intention of the parties but because they were a 'necessary condition of the relation of master and man' (per Viscount Simonds in *Lister v Romford Ice & Cold Storage Co. Ltd* [1957] AC 555 at p. 576). Finally, in recent years there has been a distinct shift away from a subjective test as the basis for incorporation towards an objective test which questions whether it is 'necessary' to imply a term.

This is well illustrated in the reasoning of the Court of Appeal in *Mears v Safecar Security Ltd* [1983] QB 54, an important case concerning whether or not there is an implied right to sick pay where the written contract is silent on the matter. Stephenson LJ expressed the view that in supplying missing terms, industrial tribunals were not tied to the requirements of the subjective test for commercial contracts as in cases such as *The Moorcock* (1889) 14 PD 64, but can and should consider all the facts and circumstances of the relationship between the employer and the employee concerned, including the way in which they had worked the particular contract of employment since it was made. So where, as in *Mears v Safecar Security Ltd* the contract was silent on sick pay, the court could look to past practice of not paying sick pay to the work-force as the best indication that no right to sick pay should be implied.

Common law implied terms
It is now possible to list the most important implied terms of the contract of employment. As with other areas of labour law, laying down an overall structure will aid understanding and help revision:

(a)   Duties of employer:

    (i)   To pay wages.
    (ii)   To provide work(?).
    (iii) To exercise care.
    (iv) To cooperate.

(b)   Duties of employee:

(i)   To obey reasonable orders.
(ii)   To exercise reasonable care and competence.
(iii) To maintain fidelity, which may be broken down into the following subheadings:

(1)   honesty,
(2)   not to compete,
(3)   not to misuse confidential information,
(4)   not to impede the employer's business,
(5)   the duty to account.

A number of these obligations will be discussed in other chapters of this book. For instance, the duty to obey reasonable orders has an obvious relevance to the chapters concerned with unfair dismissal and redundancy, whilst discussion on the duty of reasonable care will be found in the chapter on health and safety at work. Our intention here is to focus on a number of legal issues which, because of their complexity and/or the fact that they have recently been the subject of discussion by the courts, may provide examination material.

Obligation to pay wages   A number of key legal issues have arisen in relation to this fundamental obligation:

(a)   What is the effect of sickness absence on wages? In most cases, questions of pay during sickness will be governed expressly by the contract of employment. If there is no express term, and no collective agreement which can be incorporated, the question arises whether a term can be implied. Until relatively recently, it was thought that there was a presumption at common law that the employer's obligation to pay continues unless and until a term to the contrary could be shown (see *Orman* v *Saville Sportswear Ltd* [1960] 1 WLR 1055).
Following the decision of the Court of Appeal in *Mears* v *Safecar Security Ltd* [1983] QB 54 it is now misleading to talk in terms of a presumption that wages will be payable. In each case the court must decide, in the light of all the circumstances, the nature of the implied term governing sick pay. So the basis of the obligation is now implication rather than presumption.
(b)   Does the common law recognise the right of the employer to lay off without pay? At common law a lay-off will be regarded as a suspension without pay and therefore a repudiation of contract (see *Hanley* v *Pease & Partners Ltd* [1915] 1 KB 698).
However, there may be exceptions to this rule:

(i)   Where the lay-off is for reasons wholly beyond the control of the employer (see *Browning* v *Crumlin Valley Collieries Ltd* [1926] 1 KB 522 — employer not in breach when the lay-off was in order to allow the mine to be returned to a safe condition; compare with *Devonald* v *Rosser & Sons* [1906] 2 KB 728 where a lay-off was held to breach the contract where it was because of lack of profitable orders).

(ii)   An express term or custom may permit lay-off without pay.

From the Second World War there have developed many collectively bargained provisions for guaranteed minimum weekly wages in the event of lay-off or short-time working, though these payments are generally subject to suspension in the event of industrial action. In the absence of collectively agreed arrangements, statute has implied a restricted right to guarantee payments in every contract of employment (see EPCA 1978, ss. 12 to 18).

(c)   Deductions from wages and the Wages Act 1986. Part I of the Wages Act 1986 came into force at the beginning of 1987. It replaced the protection, formerly provided by the Truck Acts, from arbitrary deductions from wages. Section 1 of the 1986 Act allows deductions to be made only if they are authorised or required by a written term of the contract of employment or of some other agreement, or by a term (whether oral or written) whose existence has been explained in writing.

'Wages' is defined in s. 7 as any sum payable to the worker by the employer in connection with the employment, including 'any fee, bonus, commission, holiday pay or other emolument referable to his employment, whether payable under the contract or otherwise'.

Section 8(3) states that

Where the total amount of any wages paid on any occasion by an employer to any worker . . . is less than the total amount of wages that are *properly* payable by him to the worker . . . then, except in so far as the deficiency is attributable to an error computation, the amount of the deficiency shall be treated . . . as a deduction.

In *Delaney* v *Staples* [1991] 2 QB 47, CA; [1992] 1 AC 687, HL, the Court of Appeal and House of Lords settled two principal points of controversy over Part I of the Wages Act, namely whether it applies in the case of; (i) non-payment of a sum which the employee says was due under the contract; and (ii) failure to pay wages in lieu of notice. The EAT case law had been contradictory on both these points:

(i)   Can the Act apply to a simple non-payment? One division of the EAT consistently held that the Act only applied to a 'deduction', not a failure to pay altogether (which therefore remained a matter for the county court). However, the Court of Appeal approved the view of other EAT decisions, that the statutory definition of a deduction in s. 8(3) has to be applied literally, thus ignoring any common law distinction between non-payment and deduction.

> The Act is, indeed, concerned with unauthorised deductions. But s. 8(3) makes it plain that, leaving aside errors of computation, any shortfall in payment of the amount of wages properly payable is to be treated as a deductions. That being so, a dispute on whatever ground as to the amount of wages properly payable cannot have the effect of taking the case outside s. 8(3) (per Nicholls LJ).

It followed, therefore, that the employee in the case could bring IT proceedings to recover £55.50 unpaid commission and holiday pay outstanding on her dismissal, as an unauthorised deduction. That point was not the subject of further appeal.

(ii) Can the Act apply to non-payment of wages in lieu of notice? The employee had been dismissed without notice; she was given a cheque for £82, stated to be in lieu of notice, but this was later stopped. She sought to recover this also as an unauthorised deduction. This time, however, she was unsuccessful. The House of Lords held that where an employee is dismissed without notice due under the contract, a claim for 'pay in lieu of notice' is in effect a claim for damages for wrongful dismissal and that sums payable by way of damages for wrongful dismissal do not fall within s. 7(1)(a).

Confusions concerning the scope of the IT's jurisdiction under part I of the Wages Act 1986 should be much less frequent now that the government has finally issued an Order under EPCA 1978, s. 131 (see the Industrial Tribunals Extension of Jurisdiction (England and Wales) Order 1994). The Order provides that an employee may bring a claim before an industrial tribunal for breach of his or her contract of employment, or for a sum due under the contract, if the claim arises or is outstanding on the termination of the employment. The employer is also able to make such a claim against an employee, but only where the employee has already claimed under the Order. The maximum award that an industrial tribunal can make in respect of a contract claim, or a number of claims relating to the same contract is £25,000. Certain types of claim are excluded from the tribunal's jurisdiction. Broadly, these relate to claims about the provision of living accommodation, intellectual property (for example, copyright), obligations of confidence on the employee and covenants in restraint of trade.

(d) Deductions from wages of those taking industrial action. Section 1(5)(e) of the Wages Act exempts such deductions from the requirements of the Act. The subsection does not provide any positive authority to the employer to make deductions from salary. Whether such a right exists remains a question governed by the common law: hence the importance of *Miles* v *Wakefield Metropolitan District Council* [1987] IRLR 193.

The central question in this case was: if an employee, entitled to a weekly wage for a defined number of hours, refuses to work the whole or part of a week, is the employer entitled, without terminating the contract and without relying on damages for breach of contract, to withhold the whole or a proportion of a week's pay?

The House of Lords upheld the principle of 'no work, no pay' as the basis for the mutual obligations between employer and employee. This principle was described by Lord Templeman as follows:

> In a contract of employment wages and work go together . . . In an action by a worker to recover his pay he must allege and be ready to prove that he is ready and willing to work.

Therefore, in Miles' case the employer was entitled to withhold wages for the Saturday mornings on which the superintendent registrar of births, marriages and deaths had refused to carry out marriage ceremonies as part of his normal contractual duties in furtherance of industrial action.

This is an important case but the House of Lords did not definitely answer the question of what would be the situation where the employee goes slow or works to rule in breach of contract and the employer accepts the reduced work as partial performance of the contract. Lords Templeman and Brightman expressed the opinion that in such a situation the employee will not be entitled to his full contractual earnings but will be entitled to be paid on a 'quantum meruit' basis, i.e., an amount equal to the value of the reduced services performed. Lord Bridge expressed doubts about this view whilst the remaining Law Lords declined to express an opinion.

The principle of 'no work, no pay' was again applied by the Court of Appeal in *Wiluszynski* v *Tower Hamlets London Borough Council* [1989] ICR 493 where it was emphasised that where the employer has made it clear that it will not accept partial performance, then partial performance will mean no pay. Having told the employee in advance that incomplete performance will not be accepted, an employer is entitled not to accept or pay for that part of the work which the employee continues to do.

An interesting feature of this case was the rather narrow view taken as to what constitutes 'acceptance' by the court. On the facts, the employee was informed that he should not attend work if he was not prepared to carry out his full duties and that if he carried out work it would be regarded as unauthorised and undertaken in a voluntary capacity. However, throughout the month-long dispute, Mr W (an estate officer in the housing department) continued to report for work and carried out his duties normally and conscientiously — except for a limited form of industrial action which involved refusing to deal with enquiries from councillors about their constituents' housing problems. Estate officers normally received only a handful of such queries per week. Indeed, once the dispute was over, Mr W dealt with all the outstanding councillor enquiries in less than three hours. Nevertheless, the council saw the answering of councillor queries as a significant part of officers' duties and refused to pay Mr W and the other officers any salary for the whole month of the dispute. The Court of Appeal upheld the employer's right to take that course of action.

Lord Justice Nicholls stated:

> . . . a person is not treated by the law as having chosen to accept that which is forced down his throat despite his objections. The rationale underlying the principle of waiver is that a person cannot have it both ways; he cannot blow hot and cold; he cannot have his cake and eat it; he cannot eat his cake and have it; he cannot approbate and reprobate. But this does not mean that the employer of a large workforce is required physically to eject a defaulting employee from his office, or prevent him from going round the estate of houses for which he is responsible, on penalty that if he, the employer, does not do so he must pay the employee for the work which the employee insists on carrying out contrary to the employer's known wishes.

(See also *British Telecommunications plc* v *Ticehurt* [1992] IRLR 219, CA.)

(e) Overpayment of wages. Whether an employer can recover sums overpaid will depend on whether the overpayment has been made under mistake of law, where the overpayment is generally irrecoverable, or under mistake of fact, which allows the employer a prima facie right of recovery. In *Avon County Council* v *Howlett* [1983] IRLR 171, however, the Court of Appeal held that, even where the payment was made under mistake of fact, the employer may be estopped from claiming restitution. The estoppel argument could succeed if:

(i)   the overpayment was accompanied by an express or implicit representation of fact which led the employee to believe that he was entitled to treat the money as his own;

(ii)   the employee, without notice of the employer's claim, had changed his position; and

(iii) the overpayment had not been primarily caused by the fault of the employee.

An obligation to provide work   We have said that the reciprocal obligation on the employer in return for the employee's availability to perform contractual duties is the obligation to pay wages. It is *not* the obligation to provide work. This means that, in general, the employer will not be in breach of contract by failing to supply work as long as he continues to pay wages.

The general principle is encapsulated in the famous statement of Asquith J in *Collier* v *Sunday Referee Publishing Co. Ltd* [1940] 2 KB 647 at p. 650: 'Provided I pay my cook her wages regularly she cannot complain if I choose to take any or all of my meals out' (see also *Turner* v *Sawdon & Co.* [1901] 2 QB 653).

This principle is the reason why an employer will not be in contractual breach for giving wages in lieu of notice. The courts, however, have identified certain exceptions to the general rule and, indeed, more recent applications of the exception threaten the very rule itself:

(a)   A duty exists to offer work where remuneration depends wholly or perhaps partially on piecework or commission payments. This might apply, therefore, in the case of a commercial traveller as in *Turner* v *Goldsmith* [1891] 1 QB 544.

(b)   In special cases it may be understood that part of the consideration is the opportunity to gain publicity, as in the case of an actor (*Herbert Clayton & Jack Waller Ltd* v *Oliver* [1930] AC 209).

(c)   Where the employee is engaged on skilled work and his skills may only be maintained by being allocated work. In *Breach* v *Epsylon Industries Ltd* [1976] ICR 316, the EAT considered that a chief engineer who was being paid but for whom no work could be provided might have been constructively dismissed and redundant. In the course of the judgment, the view was expressed that the general principle was somewhat out of date and that, in the modem context, consideration of the facts would more often than not lead to the conclusion that an obligation to provide work existed.

This view is very much in line with Lord Denning's attempt to sweep the rule away in *Langston* v *Amalgamated Union of Engineering Workers* [1974] ICR 180. In this case, the Master of the Rolls, having considered the dictum of Asquith J in *Collier* stated:

That was said 33 years ago. Things have altered much since then. We have repeatedly said in this court that a man has a right to work, which the courts will protect . . . I would not wish to express any decided view, but simply state the argument which could be put forward for Mr Langston. In these days an employer, when employing a skilled man, is bound to provide him with work. By which I mean that the man should be given the opportunity of doing his work when it is available and when he is ready and willing to do it.

When the *Langston* case came up for full consideration by the National Industrial Relations Court [1974] ICR 510, Sir John Donaldson was not so expansive in approaching the right to work and preferred to fit the case within exception (a) above. The NIRC concluded that the plaintiff's contract contained the right to be paid at premium rates for overtime and thus, by implication, the right to be in a position to earn such rates by being available when it was offered. Therefore, by suspending him on basic pay, the employers were in breach of contract. (For a penetrating analysis of the problems associated with implying a general right to work into a contract of employment you should read Hepple 10 ILJ 65.)

Duty to cooperate   We shall see in the chapter on termination of contract that, in the context of unfair dismissal, the courts have been prepared to hold that contracts of employment generally are subject to an implied term that the employer must not destroy or seriously damage the relationship of trust and confidence between employer and employee. Therefore, a managing director who accused his personal secretary of being 'an intolerable bitch on a Monday morning' was found to have repudiated the contract (see *Isle of Wight Tourist Board* v *Coombes* [1976] IRLR 413).

The duty of cooperation is not merely one way and, as we shall see, is placed equally on the employee.

Obedience to reasonable orders   Refusal to obey a reasonable order within the scope of the contract of employment is a breach of contract, although, as in all other classes of breach, the breach may not be so fundamental a rejection of the contract as to justify rescission in the form of dismissal. Indeed, with the changing social attitudes, many of the earlier decisions upholding the employer's right to dismiss summarily for one act of disobedience would not be decided in the same way today (for evidence of this more 'enlightened' attitude see *Laws* v *London Chronicle (Indicator Newspapers) Ltd* [1959] 1 WLR 698 and *Wilson* v *Racher* [1974] ICR 428).

Of course, an order which is unreasonable (such as ordering an employee into immediate danger: *Ottoman Bank* v *Chakarian* [1930] AC 277) or which is illegal (*Morrish* v *Henlys (Folkestone) Ltd* [1973] ICR 482) may properly be disobeyed.

In the modern context, dismissal for disobedience will be tested under the statutory regime of unfair dismissal where the fairness of the sacking will not necessarily be determined by the fact that the employee was in breach of contract. We shall give greater attention to these matters in our chapter on unfair dismissal.

One final but crucially important issue in this area concrns the extent to which an obligation to adapt to new techniques or other new working conditions can be read into the contract of employment.

This question arose in *Cresswell* v *Board of Inland Revenue* [1984] ICR 508 where the civil service unions objected to the computerisation of certain clerical tasks, previously performed manually. In the course of legal proceedings arising out of the industrial action which followed, it became necessary to know whether the employer had acted within its contractual rights in directing staff to adapt their jobs to the use of computers. It was held that this change was legitimate — even in the absence of any specific term in the contract allowing for the transition to computers — and that the employer was acting within the limits of its lawful authority in insisting upon the change. The refusal of the workers to comply with this lawful command meant that they had forfeited their right to be paid.

In coming to this decision, Walton J felt that:

> . . . there can really be no doubt as to the fact that an employee is expected to adapt himself to new methods and techniques introduced in the course of his employment . . . Of course, in a proper case the employer must provide any necessary training or retraining.

On the facts, Walton J was of the view that the function of the job had not changed; it was 'recognisably the same job but done in a different way'. This judicial emphasis on job function, as opposed to the manner of doing the job will also be seen when we look at the test for redundancy (see *North Riding Garages Ltd* v *Butterwick* [1967] 2 QB 56) and its adoption strengthens managerial prerogative to institute change. For a critical analysis on this aspect of the *Cresswell* decision you should read the commentary by R. Fentman 14 ILJ 51.

Whilst this decision would be welcomed by employers planning to introduce computerisation, it cannot be seen as offering a legal *carte blanche* to those who seek to bring about more fundamental changes. Walton J recognised that in certain situations it would still be legitimate to argue that a particular change required the acquisition of such 'esoteric skills' that it amounted to a redefinition of the job itself.

In order to introduce such fundamental changes without being in breach of contract, the employer would have to establish one of two things:

(a) a term authorising fundamental variation; or
(b) the agreement of the employee to the making of such a change.

If the employer unilaterally insists on a change, the employee has the choice of resignation (and claiming unfair dismissal) or working on under protest and claiming damages. Two important cases which illustrate this point are *Burdett-Coutts* v *Hertfordshire County Council* [1984] IRLR 91 and *Rigby* v *Ferodo Ltd* [1987] IRLR 516.

Duty of fidelity: competition whilst in employment The courts are very reluctant to accept that what workers do in their own spare time should be any concern of the employer. However, sometimes they are bound to do so. An employer's interests would clearly be harmed by an employee's spare-time work if this involved direct competition with the employer's business (see *Hivac Ltd v Park Royal Scientific Instruments Ltd* [1946] Ch 169 where an injunction was granted to restrain workers engaged on the highly specialised work of manufacturing electronic components for hearing aids from working for a competitor).

Working in competition or disclosing confidential information may provide a fair reason for dismissal (see *Smith v Du Pont (UK) Ltd* [1976] IRLR 107).

Duty of fidelity: competition by ex-employees As a general rule, an ex-employee is free to go into competition with his former employer. This is subject to two exceptions.

The first is that an employee may not do anything while still employed which is in breach of the duty of fidelity, e.g., a milkman canvassing customers on the last day of his employment before he set up business on his *own* (*Wessex Dairies Ltd v Smith* [1935] 2 KB 80), copying out a list of his employer's customers before he left to set up in competition (*Robb v Green* [1895] 2 QB 315; *Roger Bullivant Ltd v Ellis* [1987] IRLR 491; *Johnson & Bloy (Holdings) Ltd v Wolstenholme* [1987] IRLR 499).

However, an ex-employee is entitled to make use of knowledge and skill acquired whilst in his employer's business and in this sense the implied duty of confidentiality is narrower than the duty of fidelity in the case of an existing employee.

This point is illustrated by the leading case of *Faccenda Chicken Ltd v Fowler* [1987] Ch 117 (one case name you're unlikely to forget!). Fowler had ben employed as a sales manager of Faccenda Chicken Ltd's chicken marketing business until he resigned, along with eight other employees, in order to establish a rival operation selling fresh chickens from refrigerated vehicles. Neither Fowler nor any of the other former employees were subject to any express agreement restricting activities after leaving Faccenda's employ. Faccenda claimed that Fowler and his colleagues had broken their contracts by using confidential sales information, relating to the requirements of the customers and the prices they paid, to the detriment of the company.

The Court of Appeal laid down the following guidelines in order to determine whether any particular item of information falls within the implied term so as to prevent its use or disclosure by an employee after his employment has ceased:

(a)   The nature of the employment. Employment in a capacity where confidential information' is habitually handied may impose a high obligation because the employee should be expected to appreciate its sensitive nature.

(b)   The nature of the information itself. Information will only be protected if it can properly be classed as a 'trade secret' or as material which in all the circumstances if of such a highly confidential nature as to require the same protection as a trade secret, e.g., secret processes of manufacture such as chemical formulae designs or special methods of construction.

(c)   Whether the employer impressed on the employee the confidentiality of the information.

(d)   Whether the relevant information can be easily isolated from other information which the employee is free to use or disclose. The fact that the allegedly 'confidential' information is part of a package and the remainder of the package is not confidential is likely to throw light on whether the information in question is really a trade secret.

Applying those principles, the Court of Appeal held that Fowler and his colleagues were not in breach of an implied term of their contracts for the following reasons:

(a)   The sales information contained some material which was not confidential if looked at in isolation, e.g., van routes.

(b)   The information about prices was not clearly divisible from the rest of the sales information.

(c)   Neither the sales information in general, nor the information about prices in particular, though of some value to a competitor, could reasonably be regarded as plainly secret or sensitive (though Neill LJ thought that certain types of price information would fall into this category, e.g., the price to be charged for a new model of car or the price put forward in a tender document).

(d)   The sales information, including the information about prices, was necessarily acquired by Fowler and his colleagues in order that they could do their work. Each salesperson could quickly commit the whole of the sales information relating to his or her own area to memory.

(e)   The sales information was generally known among the van drivers and others at quite a junior level within the company: this was not a case where the information was restricted to senior staff.

(f)   There was no evidence that Faccenda had ever expressly given instructions that information about prices was to be treated as confidential.

This is an important decision and, indeed, Professor R. W. Rideout has stated 'that there is no question but that this decision rewrites the duty of confidentiality contained in the law of employment' (15 ILJ 183, at p. 187).

The second exception to an ex-employee's freedom to go into competition with his former employer may be a restraint of trade clause in the contract of employment. Given the weakness of the implied term of confidentiality once employment has ended, many employers would be well advised to protect themselves against the divulgence of trade secrets or loss of customers by the insertion of such clauses in the contract of employment. You should note, however, that in *Faccenda Chicken Ltd v Fowler* the Court of Appeal expressly disagreed with the statement of Goulding J, at first instance, that confidential information which became part of the employee's skill and knowledge could be protected by an express restraint clause. Therefore, only trade secrets (as defined in *Faccenda Chicken Ltd v Fowler*) or customer connections may be protected by such a clause. Furthermore, the restrictive covenant must be shown to go no further, in terms of the time and area of restraint, than is reasonable for the protection of the employer's proprietary interests and must be generally in the public interest.

We do not intend to say much more on the question of restraint of trade clauses because many employment law courses do not dwell on the issue given that it has probably been comprehensively covered in a first-year contract course. Two relatively recent Court of Appeal decisions are worth reading, however, in order to refresh your memory of the area: *Littlewoods Organisation Ltd v Harris* [1977] 1 WLR 1472 and *Greer v Sketchley Ltd* [1979] IRLR 445.

Impeding the employer's business   Part of the duty of fidelity comprises the duty of cooperation. The leading authority on the employee's side of the cooperation 'coin' is *Secretary of State for Employment v Associated Society of Locomotive Engineers & Firemen (No. 2)* [1972] 2 QB 455.

In this case, the Court of Appeal had to determine whether the respondent union's 'work to rule' was in breach of contract. In disputing this, the union claimed that it was merely following the employer's rule book. In finding a breach of contract, Lord Denning MR thought that 'a worker must not wilfully obstruct the employer' in his business so as 'to produce chaos'. Roskill LJ implied a term that workers, although they could withdraw their goodwill, could not seek to obey the working rules in 'a wholly unreasonable way which has the effect of disrupting the system'. Indeed, Buckley LJ went even further, laying stress on a more positive implied obligation of faithful service:

> . . . within the terms of the contract the employee must serve the employer faithfully with a view to promoting those commercial interests for which he is employed.

Which frame of reference is evidenced by such a statement?

Work Rules

Many employers, particularly large ones, lay down work rules or company rules on matters such as safety, discipline, sickness etc. and it is possible for these to become incorporated in the contract. This may come about if the employee agrees to be bound by them before or at the time of entering employment.

As a result of *Secretary of State for Employment* v *ASLEF (No. 2)* [1972] 2 QB 455, however, it is clear that not all work rules will have a contractual effect. Remember that in that case the union had argued that by sticking to the working rules its members could not be found to be in breach of their contracts. On his way to finding a breach of the implied term of cooperation, Lord Denning MR stated:

> Each man signs a form saying that he will abide by the rules, but these rules are in no way terms of the contract of employment. They are only instructions to a man as to how he is to do his work.

Notice the wide scope that this finding gives to managerial prerogative. If a work rule is found to be non-contractual, it can be changed unilaterally by the employer and if the employee refuses to operate the changed rule he or she is refusing a lawful order and at common law might be lawfully dismissed.

Note further, however, that these contractual approaches are now heavily overlaid by statute and, as we shall see, breaches of work rules (whether contractual or not) do not prevent an industrial tribunal from looking at the overall merits of the case in the context of an unfair dismissal claim.

Whilst the *ASLEF* decision is important, it is probable that those parts of the work rule book or company handbook which covers matters of which written notice must be given by statute will provide strong prima facie evidence of the true contractual terms.

Custom and Practice

Writers on industrial relations and labour history have attached importance to custom and practice as a form of worker regulation: though, in the more formalised context of modem industrial relations, they are now less significant. If a custom is to carry a legal effect it must be 'reasonable, certain and notorious'. There is some confusion as to whether there is an additional requirement that the individual worker must be aware of the practice. This was not required in the leading case of *Sagar* v *H. Ridehalgh & Son Ltd* [1931] 1 Ch 310; cf. *Meek* v *Port of London Authority* [1918] 1 Ch 415, affirmed [1918] 2 Ch 96.

Statute

The growth of statutory intervention over the last decade or so has seen the use, on occasion, of the statutory implied term in the contract of employment, e.g., the rights to equal pay, guarantee payment and minimum notice. In addition, in the next chapter we shall see that statute will sometimes operate to void certain contractual terms (EPCA 1978, s. 142).

THE EXAMINATION

As we stated in the introduction to this chapter, the common law rules of contract still very much provide the foundations for the study of employment law. The issues discussed in this chapter may seem somewhat unrelated in the early stages of your course. You should not worry unduly about this because, as the course progresses, you will find yourself drawing again and again on the legal principles we have discussed in this part of the book. You may have experienced a similar confusion when you commenced your study of criminal law with a study of general principles of criminal liability eventually finding that everything falls into place as you started to study substantive offences. Just as you could not hope to pass a criminal law paper without a good knowledge of the general principles of criminal liability, in employment law you must ensure that you have a sound grasp of the nature and content of the contract of employment. The next section will provide you with an opportunity to test your level of understanding of a number of the legal issues.

Question 1

Henry has worked for Capital plc for the past 10 years. When he joined Capital he was sent a letter stating, *inter alia*:

> Your terms of work are determined by the collective agreements, as set out in the rule book available in the Chief Personnel Officer's Department.

Henry's pay has been made up from his basic wage of, currently, £186 per week and productivity bonuses averaging another £25 per week. A few weeks ago, and as part of an efficiency drive, employees were informed that work was to be regraded and bonus payments discontinued. Henry's wages would now be £205 per week. He objects to this and seeks your advice.

At the same time, Capital wrote to all employees informing them that 'the informal holiday for the Bursley Annual Christmas Fair is to be ended. All employees to report to work as usual'.

The fair had been attended by Capital workers since 1962. Advise the workers as to their contractual position.

Analysis

This two-part problem is concerned with the legal mechanisms for the incorporation of terms of the contract of employment.

Henry's problem

(a) The letter. You should first determine the legal status of this document. Is this the contractual document or is it a statutory statement? Remember that if it is the latter, it has been held that it is not the contract itself and can be controverted by external evidence (see *System Floors (UK) Ltd* v *Daniel* [1982] ICR 54 and *Robertson* v *British Gas Corporation* [1983] IRLR 302). You should also note that the cross-reference to the rule book available in the chief personnel officer's department would no longer comply with the more stringent requirements of part I of the EPCA 1978, as amended. However, those requirements only apply to employees who are employed on or after 30 November 1993. Employees who were employed before that date may request the more detailed particulars to be supplied to them within two months of their request. But, in the absence of such a request, the employer is under no obligation to supply the more detailed statement. Employees who were in employment before 30 November 1993 are also entitled to be individually notified in writing of any change in the particulars which now need to be provided, whether or not they have requested a new-style statement.

(b) Are the terms of the collective agreement incorporated into the individual contract? This appears to have been achieved here by express incorporation so that the terms of the collective agreement regulate the basic wages and the system of bonus payments.

(c) Has the employer unilaterally terminated the collective agreement? This is not absolutely clear from the wording of the problem and so it will pay dividends if you argue in the alternative. If the union has agreed to vary the terms of the collective agreement, there is very little that Henry can do given that he has agreed to allow his terms and conditions to be regulated by collective bargaining. The agency concept of incorporation has gained little favour with judges in this country and therefore Henry will be bound by any agreed variation whether or not he is a union member and whether or not he resigned membership before the variation was finalised.

If the employer has, on the other hand, sought unilaterally to change the collective agreement there is a breach of the contract of employment (*Robertson* v *British Gas Corporation*). Whilst the employer can generally lawfully withdraw from a collective agreement (TULR(C)A 1992, s. 179) once a term deemed appropriate for incorporation has crossed the 'bridge' into the individual contract, it assumes a legally binding quality and can only be varied by consent (see *Marley* v *Forward Trust Group Ltd* [1986] IRLR 369).

If the latter is the case two possibilities open up for Henry. The first option is to resign and to lodge a claim for 'constructive' and unfair dismissal. We shall not spend too much time discussing this issue at this stage given that we shall be examining the law of unfair dismissal later in the book. However, it is worth noting that constructive dismissal requires a fairly prompt resignation in response to a repudiation of contract on the part of the employer. Even where a constructive dismissal takes place, the industrial tribunal must still go on to consider the overall fairness of the employer's actions. On this last point, there is authority, as we shall see, which upholds the fairness of such dismissals, despite contractual breach by the employer, on the grounds that it was for a 'sound, good business reason' (*Hollister* v *National Farmers' Union* [1979] ICR 542 per Lord Denning MR at p. 551). Indeed it may be argued that Capital's efficiency drive might be seen in this light. On the other hand, the employer's unilateral withdrawal from an incorporated collective agreement has provided the ground for a finding of unfair dismissal in at least one case (see *Kent County Council* v *Gilham* [1985] IRLR 18).

Given the uncertainties surrounding the outcome of the unfair dismissal claim, it may be preferable to advise Henry to seek a contractual remedy in the county court or High Court. In order for Henry to succeed it is important that his conduct in remaining at work should not be taken as an affirmation of the contract. In *Burdett-Coutts* v *Hertfordshire County Council* [1984] IRLR 91 a solicitor's letter to the employer sufficiently negatived the affirmation argument.

Provided this obstacle can be overcome it would appear that Henry will be able to recover the arrears of pay which are due to him under the contract. The case of *Rigby* v *Ferodo Ltd* [1987] IRLR 516 holds that damages should not be limited to the period after which, by the terms of the contract of employment, the plaintiff employee could have been lawfully dismissed.

The annual holiday

(a) The first task here would be to check whether the contract or written statement of terms refers to this particular holiday entitlement. Assuming that there is no express reference to the December holiday, the question then becomes whether a term can he implied on the basis of custom and practice. It may well be that a practice which has been regularly followed for something like a quarter of a century is sufficiently 'reasonable, certain and notorious' to assume a legally binding quality. In *Sagar v H. Ridehalgh & Son Ltd* [1931] 1 Ch 310 a practice of making deductions for bad work which had prevailed for some 30 years was held to be incorporated in a weaver's contract of service.

(b)   If a statutory statement has been issued, as opposed to a copy of the whole contract, any aggrieved Capital employee may apply to an industrial tribunal for determination of the accuracy of those particulars (see *Mears v Safecar Security Ltd* [1983] QB 54).

(c)   Should management make deductions from the pay of those who take the holiday then an action for recovery of the lost wages may be mounted in an industrial tribunal, alleging a breach of the Wages Act 1986.

Question 2

The Yuppy Bank (a merchant bank) has its headquarters in London and employs 2,500 people. During the past 10 years, the bank has suffered a decline due to the recession and difficulties in the international money market. In April 1994 the board of directors presented a paper, which was made available to all staff, entitled 'Strategy for Survival'. It proposed that the bank move its premises to the south-east London suburbs, which would be cheaper. It also proposed that more sophisticated business machines be installed, involving about 50 staff developing new skills. The bank issues a contract of employment to all employees when they join. Clause 6 states: 'Your place of work is 23 Bodkin St, London EC1. Management reserve the right to move you to any work place within the UK'.

Sarah, an accounts clerk, who has worked for Yuppy at Bodkin St since 1988, objects to the proposals, especially as she is one of those who will be expected to learn new skills involving the use of computerised databases. In her contract of employment, she is referred to as a 'clerical officer, grade 3'. She has been exclusively engaged in bookkeeping since she joined the organisation.

Advise Yuppy as to its legal position regarding Sarah.

The Relocation Issue

The question of law involved here is whether management have contractual authority to issue the order to relocate. This issue will often arise in the context of a redundancy payments claim where one of the tests of redundancy is whether the requirements for an employee to carry out work of a particular kind 'in the place where the employee was so employed' have ceased or diminished or are expected to do so. 'Place' has been interpreted to mean where an employee could be obliged to work under the terms of the contract of employment, not merely where the employee had in fact been working prior to the order to move (see *Sutcliffe* v *Hawker Siddeley Aviation Ltd* [1973] IRLR 304 and contrast with *Bass Leisure Ltd* v *Thomas* [1994] IRLR 104, EAT, discussed at page 185).

The question then becomes one of construing the terms of Sarah's contract of employment. Clause 6 contains a clear express term and the courts are generally opposed to allowing such terms to be varied by the implication of a term based on past practice (see *Nelson* v *BBC* [1977] IRLR 148). An arbitrary and unreasonable exercise of a mobility clause power may amount to a constructive and unfair dismissal (see *United Bank Ltd* v *Akhtar* [1989] IRLR 507, discussed at page 133) but there is little or no evidence to suggest that Yuppy Bank has broken the implied trust of confidence in Sarah's case. It would appear, therefore, that Sarah will be in breach of the obligation to obey reasonable orders if she refuses to transfer.

The Requirement to Develop New Skills

Once again this is a matter of construing Sarah's contract. If the initiative proposed by Yuppy is seen as merely updating the job of 'clerical officer, grade 3' as opposed to bringing about a change in job function then it may well be that there is no breach of contract on the part of management. This view may be supported on the basis that there is an implied term in the contract of employment that the employee will adapt to new methods and techniques introduced in the course of employment (see *Cresswell* v *Board of Inland Revenue* [1984] ICR 508).

READING

Anderman, S.D., *Labour Law: Management Decisions and Workers' Rights*, 2nd ed. (London: Butterworths, 1993), ch. 1–5.

Napier, B., 'The contract of employment', in R. Lewis (ed.), *Labour Law in Britain* (Oxford: Blackwell, 1986).

Painter, R.W., and Puttick, K.A., *Employment Rights* (London: Pluto Press, 1993), ch. 4–9.

Smith, I.T., and Wood, J.C., Industrial Law, 5th ed. (London: Butterworths, 1993), ch. 3.

Wedderburn, Lord, *The Worker and the Law*, 3rd ed. (Harmondsworth: Penguin, 1986), pp. 172–87, 318–43.

4 LEGAL CONSTRAINTS ON TERMS AND CONDITIONS OF EMPLOYMENT 1

INTRODUCTION

In this chapter we shall be looking at the difficulties arising out of the substantive law on equal pay and in the following chapter we shall be considering sex and race discrimination. However, we should remind you that the topic 'legal constraints on terms and conditions of employment' is wider than the remit of this and the following chapter. For example, it also covers maternity rights (EPCA 1978, ss. 33 to 47 as amended by TURERA 1993), time off for public duties (EPCA 1978, ss. 29 and 30), time off for trade union duties (officials) and activities (members) (TULR(C)A 1992, ss. 168, 169, 244 and 152 respectively). It is possible, because of the limited time available, that these topics are not covered in your employment law course. You should therefore seek the guidance of your lecturers regarding the detail in which you should study the areas referred to above. Do not presume that because they are not within the scope of this book that they will not appear on your examination paper.

EQUAL PAY

One thing the student quickly learns when studying labour law is that the Equal Pay Act (EPA) 1970, as amended, is one of the shortest statutes yet in many ways is one of the most contentious. The volume of case law can seem quite daunting and certainly at the present time is a veritable minefield. The Equal Pay Act 1970 has only been in force a relatively short time (remember it did not come into effect until 1975 in order to give industry time to make the necessary provisions) yet it has already been questioned by the Court of Justice of the European Communities (ECJ) with significant results — see *Commission of the European Communities* v *United Kingdom of Great Britain & Northern Ireland* [1982] IRLR 333, leading to the Equal Pay (Amendment) Regulations 1983 (SI 1983 No. 1794).

The concept of equal pay for men and women has been in existence for many years — see the ILO Convention No. 100 of 1951. In comparison with many other European countries it has taken the UK a long time to legislate for what is in effect a basic right. As women in the work-force have increased — in the 1970s over 40% of the work-force was female — so the issue of equal pay has come to the forefront as a major employment problem. The 'New Earnings Survey' (HMSO, 1994) reveals that the differential between women's pay and men's pay is closing albeit slowly. For example, the statistics show that in respect of manual work women's gross hourly earnings are 72.5% of men's and for non-manual work women's earnings are 67.9%. The question you should be asking is: Why are women paid less than men? Why should there be this differential? The evidence is that the answer is historical and social. Rubenstein in *Equal Pay for Work of Equal Value* states that 'women are paid less than men because of the attributes they bring to the job, because of the jobs they are in and because they are women'. Therefore it can only be after complete re-education that equal treatment for women in employment can come about. It is the status of women which needs to be improved. However, you should not overlook the position of the male employee. He too is protected by EPA 1970; but the fact is that the majority of claims have been made by women. The 1970 Act did not have a far-reaching effect as it was confined to 'like work' and 'work rated equivalent' and has been given a conservative interpretation by the courts which have been quick to consider the economic implications of increasing a woman's pay. Indeed, in real terms the 'like work' provisions have made little difference to women's pay because few women are in the same type of employment as men. As a general rule, men and women follow traditional job patterns i.e., women's work and men's work'. For a more detailed discussion see R. Townshend-Smith, *Sex Discrimination in Employment* (London: Sweet & Maxwell, 1989), ch. 1–2. It was hoped that the 1983 amendment to the Equal Pay Act 1970 would remedy the pay variation. Initially the outlook was bleak due to some rather restrictive interpretations by the lower courts. However, in recent years the House of Lords in particular has been at the forefront of interpreting the EPA 1970 in the light of art. 119 and Directive 75/117. This has ensured that the principle of equal pay for work of equal value and the concept of 'pay' are to be as flexible as possible.

Before you even consider answering a question on equal pay in an examination, you should not only be confident that you have a thorough knowledge of the current state of play regarding the case law but also that you have a good working knowledge of the sections of the statute. The flow chart in figure 4.1 shown opposite should help you.

Even if you are supplied with the relevant sections of the Act, you are wasting time by constantly thumbing through them — it should only be used as an *aide-mémoire*.

THE RELATIONSHIP OF UK LAW WITH EUROPEAN LAW

No answer to an equal pay question will be complete without some reference to the Treaty of Rome and European Directives. You must, therefore, ensure that you understand the practical effect of European law within the UK by reference to current judicial thinking. However, we shall not be considering the wording of the Treaty and Directives but merely the problems and issues arising from their interpretation by the courts.

Let us now consider art. 119 of the Treaty of Rome. As you will be aware this imposes a requirement of equal pay for equal work. (We shall be considering the word 'pay' in detail later.) As every law student knows the Treaty of Rome is directly applicable in the United Kingdom by virtue of the European Communities Act 1972. The effect of this is twofold:

(a)   The United Kingdom should amend its existing law accordingly (to some extent this has been done by the Equal Pay Act 1970 as amended).

(b)   It is directly enforceable by our domestic courts as emphasised in *Defrenne* v *Sabena* [1976] ICR 547 and *Macarthys Ltd* v *Smith* [1981] QB 180. In theory the domestic court will consider its domestic law first and then have regard to the European Court's decisions under art. 119.

In practice, therefore, applicants may have two strings to their bow. This was illustrated in *Pickstone* v *Freemans plc* [1989] AC 66 where both the domestic and European arrows were fired by the applicant at her employer. The Court of Appeal in choosing to apply art. 119 and Directive 75/117 as opposed to the EPA 1970, found in favour of the applicant. On appeal by the employer, the House of Lords went one step further in finding for the applicant on the basis that the EPA 1970 must be interpreted subject to art. 119. They concluded that the existing interpretation of s. 1(2)(c) was inconsistent with art. 119 as it permitted an equal value claim to be defeated where there was a man employed on 'like work'. The right to equal pay for work of equal value is not dependent on there being no man who is employed on the same work as the woman. To avoid this construction the court stated that 'there must be implied in s. 1(2)(c) after the word

Figure 4.1   Equal Pay Act 1970

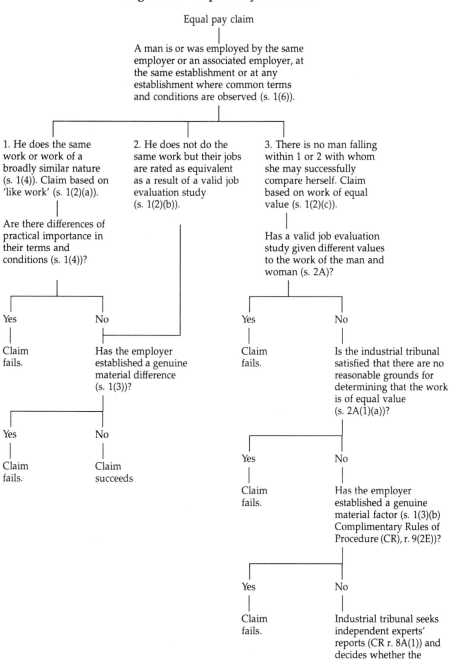

"applies", the words as between the woman and the man with whom she claims equality"'. *Blaik* v *Post Office* [1994] IRLR 280 makes it quite clear that if there is a sufficient remedy given by domestic law, it is unnecessary and impermissible to explore the same complaint under the equivalent provisions in a Directive. It is only if there is a disparity between the two that it becomes necessary to consider whether the provisions in European law are directly enforceable by the complainant.

The potency of European regulation can also be seen from the case of *Barber* v *Guardian Royal Exchange Assurance Group* [1991] 1 QB 344 where the ECJ held that benefits paid under a contracted-out occupational pension scheme amounted to 'pay' under art. 119. Existing employees are therefore entitled to equal benefits from such schemes, e.g., where such a scheme provides for a woman to take a pension at 60, a male employee will have the right to insist on the same option, on the same terms. The *Barber* decision in effect overrides UK law which previously allowed discrimination in respect of pension entitlements and benefits. The ECJ also held that redundancy benefits, whether contractual, statutory or voluntary in nature constitute 'pay' within art. 119. As a result these too must be offered to men and women on the same terms. The statutory redundancy scheme already complies with this ruling. The case of *Ten Oever* v *Stichting Bedrijfspensioenfonds voor het Glazenwassers- en Schoonmaakbedrijf* [1993] IRLR 601 confirms that the impact of the decision in *Barber* is confined to periods of employment subsequent to 17 May 1990 when it was decided, except where legal proceedings have already been initiated before that date. This has since been reaffirmed in *Neath* v *Hugh Steeper Ltd* [1994] IRLR 91. In *Moroni* v *Firma Collo GmbH* [1994] IRLR 130 the ECJ said that *Barber* was not confined to contracted-out occupational pension schemes and extended its application to supplementary pension schemes.

See also *Roberts* v *Birds Eye Walls Ltd* [1994] ICR 338 in which the ECJ held that it was not contrary to art. 119 to reduce the amount of a bridging pension to take into account the amount of State pension which the employee will receive, even though the result is that a female ex-employee (aged between 60 and 65) receives a smaller bridging pension than is paid to her male counterpart. Any other decision would result in some women gaining a twofold benefit by paying reduced contributions and receiving a bridging pension which compensates for the corresponding reduction in State pension.

Cases from other member States heard by the ECJ also have an impact on UK law and how the EPA 1970 and SDA 1975 should be interpreted. In *Rinner-Kühn* v *FWW Spezial-Gebäudereinigung GmbH* [1989] IRLR 493 the ECJ held that sick pay amounted to 'pay' within art. 119. As a result German national law was found to discriminate against part-time workers, the majority of which were female, in that the qualifying period (i.e. number of hours worked) to obtain such benefits discriminated against women. See also *Arbeiterwohlfahrt der Stadt Berlin eV* v *Bötel* [1992] IRLR 423 in which paid leave or overtime pay for participation in training courses given by the employer in accordance with statutory provisions amounted to 'pay' within art. 119.

The House of Lords has finally ruled in *R* v *Secretary of State for Employment, ex parte EOC* [1994] 2 WLR 409 that the qualifying number of hours worked per week for unfair dismissal and redundancy compensation is incompatible with art. 119 and Directives 75/117 and 76/207, it being recognised that the great majority of employees who work for more than 16 hours per week are men and the great majority who work for less than 16 hours per week are women, resulting in discrimination against women. As to whether the threshold could be objectively justified, it was concluded that there was no real evidence to support the view put forward by the Secretary of State that the thresholds resulted in greater availability of statutory part-time work than would be the case without them. Interestingly whether unfair dismissal compensation is to be regarded as 'pay' has yet to be decided by the ECJ.

Note that the case of *Handels- og Kontorfunktionærernes Forbund i Danmark* v *Dansk Arbejdsgiverforening* [1989] IRLR 532 has an impact on the 'genuine material difference/factor' defence. The ECJ ruled that where pay grading structures are not transparent, i.e., where it is not clear to the employee why they have been put on a particular point on the pay scale, the onus is on the employer to show that such a practice is not discriminatory. In addition, employers should assess the criteria used for paying increments or grading to ascertain whether they have an adverse impact on women and, if so, whether they are justifiable. In effect an employer can pay more for quality but not for flexibility or adaptability, e.g., male employees being able to work unsociable hours.

As you can see there are clear advantages to the applicant in having recourse to art. 119 and the ECJ. A wider interpretation of the law may be available, as in *Macarthys Ltd* v *Smith* where comparison with a male predecessor was allowed under art. 119. This form of comparison was not available under EPA 1970. The advantage of recourse to art. 119 can also be seen in *Worringham* v *Lloyds Bank Ltd* [1981] IRLR 178 where a pension scheme was found to be in breach of the article although there was no breach of EPA 1970.

However, you should appreciate that the ECJ in its earlier decisions has not always addressed the issue to the benefit of female employees. In *Jenkins* v *Kingsgate (Clothing Productions) Ltd* [1981] ICR 592 albeit recognising that the majority of part-time workers were women, the ECJ decided that a difference in pay between full-time and part-time employees did not automatically contravene art. 119 'unless it is in reality merely an indirect way of reducing the pay of part-time workers'. The case was referred back to the EAT who interpreted this as providing a genuine material difference/ factor defence where part-time workers are employed, thereby allowing a lower rate of pay to part-time workers if it was reasonably necessary to achieve an objective unrelated to sex. This decision certainly allows a different rate of pay between full-time and part-time workers on economic grounds which in the current economic and political climate allows employers to maintain low pay in industries which are traditionally low paid and in which the majority of employees are female, e.g., clothing industry.

You should also consider the case of *Bilka-Kaufhaus GmbH* v *Weber von Hartz* [1987] ICR 110 which provides a defence under art. 119 whereby an employer is permitted to show that his pay policy is objectively justified on economic grounds. Section 1(3) of the EPA 1970 has been interpreted accordingly in *Rainey* v *Greater Glasgow Health Board* [1987] AC 224.

Jenkins and *Bilka-Kaufhaus* should also be noted for introducing the concept of indirect discrimination into the EPA 1970 and art. 119 in that where entitlement to pay or related benefits depends on satisfying a condition which men can more easily comply with than women, art. 119 and the EPA 1970 may be contravened. The concept has been considered in *Enderby* v *Frenchay Health Authority* [1994] ICR 112 in which the ECJ concluded that where indirect discrimination in respect of pay is alleged, art. 119 does not require proof of the existence of a requirement or condition as the SDA 1975 does. However, a requirement or condition must still be established under the SDA 1975 for indirect discrimination (*Bhudi* v *IMI Refiners Ltd* [1994] ICR 307).

Finally let us consider the relationship of the Directives to our domestic law. Directive 75/117, the 'equal pay Directive', has led to one of the most far-reaching decisions of the ECJ in *Commission of the European Communities* v *United Kingdom of Great Britain & Northern Ireland* [1982] IRLR 333 — a case with which you should be familiar. In this case the Commission alleged that the UK equal pay legislation did not comply with the requirements of European Community law, in particular Directive 75/117. It was held that the UK had not adopted 'the necessary measures' and there was 'at present no means whereby a worker who considers that his post is of equal value to another may pursue his claims if the employer refuses to introduce a job classification system' (under EPA 1970, s. 1(5)). This decision resulted in the Equal Pay (Amendment) Regulations 1983 (SI 1983 No. 1794) which introduced the 'equal pay for work of equal value' concept into UK law. So, as you can see, any deficiencies in UK legislation can be dealt with by the Commission — although it may be a slow process given that the Directive originated in 1975. The quickest way of challenging UK law, as we have seen, is to enforce art. 119 directly in the domestic courts, but can this be done with Directives?

Generally the point of a Directive is to lay down the law to be achieved by the Member State and to leave to the State the form and method of implementation. Directives as such are not intended to be directly enforceable. Directive 75/117 clarifies art. 119 and to this end is 'enforceable'. However, should an individual wish to rely on this Directive, they would be unlikely to succeed. Indeed in *O'Brien* v *Sim-Chem Ltd* [1980] ICR 573 it was considered by the Court of Appeal that Directive 75/117 was not directly enforceable. Further, in *Hugh-Jones* v *St John's College, Cambridge* [1979] ICR 848 it was decided that Directive 76/207, the 'equal treatment Directive', could only be used to prevent enforcement by a member State of laws conflicting with the Directive and could not be used by individuals in proceedings against another person within the member State.

You should make sure you are aware of the current state of play, which is that the ECJ has ruled that a Directive may be relied upon by an individual before a national court where the Directive is 'sufficiently precise and unconditional'. The action can, however, only be brought against a government authority acting as an employer, see *Marshall* v *Southampton & South West Hampshire Area Health Authority (Teaching)* [1986] QB 401. You should note that even the Court of Appeal was unsure of the enforceability of the Directive and asked for a preliminary ruling and it may well be that only the ECJ is capable of deciding whether a Directive is 'sufficiently precise and unconditional'. As you can see there is a limitation on the direct enforcement of Directives which to some extent has been upheld in *Foster* v *British Gas plc* [1991] 1 QB 405. In this case the House of Lords referred the question of the enforceability of Directives in our national courts to the ECJ. It ruled that Directives can only be enforced against the State or organs or emanations of the State. However, a wide interpretation was given to these terms which include

a body, whatever its legal form, which has been made responsible for providing a public service under the control of the State and has for that purpose special powers beyond those which result from the normal rules applicable in relations between private individuals.

British Gas, prior to being de-nationalised was found to be within that wording. This has been confirmed in *Foster* v *British Gas plc* [1991] 2 AC 306.

It is unlikely that a Directive will ever be held to be directly enforceable against a private employer as it is hardly the fault of the employer that the member State has failed to bring its domestic law into line with the Directive — see *Roberts* v *Tate & Lyle Industries Ltd* [1986] ICR 371; *Rolls-Royce plc* v *Doughty* [1987] ICR 932.

THE EQUAL PAY ACT 1970

We can now consider the problem areas within the UK substantive law. It is necessary to stress yet again that you must have a thorough knowledge of EPA 1970, s. 1 — the requirement of equal treatment for men and women in the same employment.

Pay

First we must briefly look at the scope of the Act and the meaning of the word 'pay' as far as the courts are concerned. It is clear from the wording of the Act that the equality clause applies in respect of any term in a woman's contract of employment which is less favourable than that of her male comparator. However, the majority of the equal pay claims are confined to pay. This is quite natural as pay is probably the biggest issue for most employees. It was initially thought that the word 'pay' was not to be restricted to the rate of pay but regard should be had to the whole of the remuneration package. Following the House of Lords decision in *Hayward* v *Cammell Laird Shipbuilders Ltd* [1988] AC 894 this is clearly not the case. The effect of the decision is that each of the terms of the contract should be considered separately and individually. The applicant is entitled to equality in respect of each clause. However, it is pertinent to consider the reservations of the lower courts. Both the EAT and the Court of Appeal expressed concern that considering rate of pay as an isolated term without regard to other benefits received under the contract of employment would result, in mutual enhancement and leap frogging, leading to a spiral of equal value claims as the male employees claimed the same contract benefits. This fear is unfounded as in reality whilst there may be an initial impact there cannot be the spiral of claims anticipated by the Court of Appeal. For example, a woman may earn £2.00 per hour; her male comparator earns £2.60 per hour. In addition she receives luncheon vouchers. If her equal value claim is upheld, he may then claim luncheon vouchers, and whilst he may well succeed that is the end of the claims spiral. Obviously there is an economic impact arising from this decision. However, we are left to consider the question of how far should the economic issue be relevant in equal pay claims? Furthermore, would such a claim be defeated by EPA 1970, s. 1(3). (See the Lord Chancellor in *Hayward, obiter* at p. 904 and *Leverton* v *Clwyd County Council* [1989] AC 706.) Most of the remaining contentious issues on the meaning of 'pay' relate to the dividing line between statutory social security benefits which do not fall within art. 119 and occupational 'benefits' which usually do (see *Griffin* v *London Pension Fund Authority* [1993] IRLR 248). Both redundancy payments and *ex gratia* payments have been held to fall within the definition of 'pay' (*McKechnie* v *UBM Building Supplies (Southern) Ltd* [1991] ICR 710).

Finally, remember to refer to art. 119 and the ECJ decisions on what is included in the word 'pay' which we considered earlier.

Like Work

The main issue which you have to consider is: What amounts to 'like work' as far as the courts are concerned? Well we know from EPA 1970, s. 1(4), that it includes the same work or work of a broadly similar nature. Obviously if the woman is employed on the same work as the man there is no problem. In deciding whether work is of a 'broadly similar nature' the EAT in *Capper Pass Ltd* v *Lawton* [1977] ICR 83 issued clear guidelines in laying down what is known as the 'broad-brush approach'. There are as follows:

(a)   The skill and knowledge required for the job should be considered, but a minute examination of the work involved is not necessary.

(b)   The differences between the two jobs (if any) should not be of any practical importance. The *de minimis* rule is to be taken into account.

The case law has resulted in an interesting interpretation of s. 1(4). The frequency with which different duties may occur is relevant. In *Electrolux Ltd v Hutchinson* [1977] ICR 252 the male employees were paid a higher piece-work rate for doing work of a 'broadly similar nature' to female employees; however, the men could be asked to do more demanding work, to work nights and to do non-production work. Did these extra duties justify a higher rate of pay? It was concluded by the EAT that they did not. The question to be asked is: How frequently are the men asked to do this extra work? The answer must be 'to a significant extent' if the employer is to justify the difference in pay.

The nature of the job is relevant. Does it require additional skills or training, or perhaps more importantly, does it impose an added responsibility? In *Eaton Ltd* v *Nuttall* [1977] ICR 272, where the male production schedulers handled more valuable items, it was decided that male and female staff were not doing work of a broadly similar nature because of the additional responsibility — 'failures by the applicant in the discharge of her duties would lead to less grave consequences than would failures by the men with whose work she had sought to compare her own'. So such things as handling money or having to secure the premises may justify the difference in pay. However, the court cannot disregard some aspect of what the man does just because he is paid extra for doing it. For example, in *Maidment* v *Cooper & Co. (Birmingham) Ltd* [1978] ICR 1094 a female packer sought equality of pay with a male packer even though both of them had other duties which took up 10% of their time and for which the male packer was paid extra. The EAT declared that it was not permissible to compare part only of the duties undertaken by a claimant with part only of the duties of the person she sought comparison with. It may well be this extra duty which prevents him from being on like work.

The case law also reveals that what happens in practice rather than in theory must be considered. So logically we must look at the reality as in *Shields* v *E. Coomes (Holdings) Ltd* [1978] ICR 1159 where it was alleged that the higher rate of pay for male counter hands could be justified on the grounds that one of their duties was to prevent trouble. However, the evidence revealed that there had never been any trouble and that even if there were the men employed had no particular skills to deal with it.

Finally it had been thought that the time at which a person worked was to be disregarded, i.e., the payment of a higher basic rate of pay to men on the night shift and a lower rate to women on the day shift could not be justified — as in *Dugdale* v *Kraft Foods Ltd* [1977] ICR 48 and *National Coal Board* v *Sherwin* [1978] ICR 700. However, you should be aware of *Thomas* v *National Coal Board* [1987] ICR 757 where the facts were the same as in *Sherwin* yet the EAT held that female canteen assistants employed during the day were *not* engaged in like work to a male employed alone and at night. The effect of this decision is to make the time at which work is done relevant to the consideration of 'like work' if it results in additional responsibility, for example, working alone as this may be a 'difference of practical importance'.

Work Rated as Equivalent

This area of comparison poses fewer problems for students because it has seldom been an issue in the courts, and it is significant that job evaluation studies are not in general popular with trade unions. However, you should not presume that there are no problematic areas. Section 1(2)(b) of EPA 1970 is to be regarded as an alternative area of comparison to s. 1(2)(a), i.e., it can only be pleaded where there is in existence a valid job evaluation study within s. 1(5). Certainly where this is the case, an action should be brought under the heading of work rated equivalent as opposed to 'like work' or 'work of equal value'. The main criticism of the UK law was that the employee had no right to insist upon the introduction of a job classification scheme without the consent of the employer and therefore if the employer refused the door was immediately closed on any equal value claim. Even after recent amendments to the Act the position under s. 1(5) remains the same.

The question which you must consider is what amounts to a *valid* job evaluation scheme? It is now clear that a valid job evaluation scheme should be analytical and non-discriminatory. Following *Eaton Ltd v Nuttall* [1977] ICR 272 (at p. 277) a valid scheme ought to consider all matters connected with the nature of the work, including effort, skills and responsibilities, and when this has been done the employee should slot automatically into position on a particular grade within that study. If the employer still has to make a subjective judgment before this can be done then the study is *not* valid. In *Bromley v H & J Quick Ltd* [1988] ICR 623 it was decided that a valid job evaluation scheme has to be analytical, i.e., it requires a study to be made of the demands on the worker under various headings. You should also note that Directive 75/117 applies as regards job evaluation studies which discriminate on grounds of sex (see art. 1 as applied in *Rummler v Dato-Druck GmbH* [1987] ICR 774). As far as the courts are concerned, where a job evaluation scheme has been used as the basis for a grading structure, two jobs which end up in the same pay grade are to be viewed as having been rated as equivalent (*Springboard Sunderland Trust v Robson* [1992] ICR 554).

There is no need for you to become an expert on what should or should not be contained in a job evaluation scheme, but it is in your interests as far as the examination is concerned to be aware of the principal job evaluation methods, as laid down by ACAS (Guide No. 1). Fortunately these are listed with brief descriptions in the appendix to the report of *Eaton Ltd v Nuttall* [1977] ICR 272 at p. 278.

You may have to consider is whether a valid job evaluation study has to be implemented by the employer. The case law creates an anomaly. In *O'Brien v Sim-Chem Ltd* [1980] ICR 573 the House of Lords concluded that if such a study came within s. 1(5) then it must be implemented, i.e., if necessary the equality clause should operate. But in *Arnold v Beecham Group Ltd* [1982] ICR 744 it was concluded that there could be no implementation of a job evaluation study until the parties who agreed to it have accepted its validity. It would appear that even if the tribunal accepts the study there is nothing to compel the employer to do so. Can this really be the law? If so why should any employer implement a scheme which is going to cost him money? Of course the answer must be that either party must have proper grounds for challenging the scheme's validity; just because it is not in one party's favour is not a sufficient reason. If a case on this were to reach the ECJ it would most probably conclude in the light of *Commission of the European Communities v United Kingdom of Great Britain & Northern Ireland* [1982] IRLR 333 that a valid job evaluation study must be implemented. An employer may use a job evaluation scheme to defend an equal pay claim even though it was not in existence at the time proceedings were commenced, so long as it complies with s. 1(5) and relates to facts and circumstances existing at the time when the proceedings began (*Dibro Ltd v Hore* [1990] ICR 370). However, where a job evaluation study has been undertaken which relates to workers in another undertaking, that study cannot prevent an equal value claim from proceeding, even if the work and pay structures are the same (*McAuley* v *Eastern Health and Social Services Board* [1991] IRLR 467).

Work of Equal Value

Section 1(2)(c) of EPA 1970 provides a different avenue for the applicant from those considered above and is the UK attempt to comply with Directive 75/117. As a result there has been an initial rush of cases, and since the decision in *Hayward* v *Cammell Laird Shipbuilders Ltd* [1988] AC 894, a steady flow has been maintained. Many of the larger trade unions have mounted test cases, e.g., NUPE, COHSE, TGWU and USDAW, which have resulted in settlements.

The first problem arises out of the relationship between paras (a), (b) and (c) of s. 1(2). It was thought from *Scott* v *Beam College Ltd* (1985) 284 IRLIB 6, that under domestic law an equal value claim can only be considered where there is no substance for a claim under 'like work' or 'work rated equivalent'. In effect this approach prevented the applicant from 'hedging her bets' but it also put a stop to a genuine equal value claim as long as there was a token man doing the same job as the woman. However, the decision in *Pickstone* v *Freemans plc* [1989] AC 66, allows her claim to proceed on the basis of 'equal worth', notwithstanding that a man doing the same job is being paid the same rate as she is. In deciding this, the House of Lords has upheld the view that the EPA 1970 must be construed so that it does not conflict with European law. There must, therefore, be implied into s. 1(2)(c) after the word applies', the words 'as between the woman and the man with whom she claims equality'. You should note, however, that this decision still requires the applicant to consider whether 'like work' is more appropriate than an equal value claim (see *McPherson* v *Rathgael Centre for Children and Young People* [1991] IRLR 206). It ensures, more importantly, that the employer cannot avoid the requirements of the Act by employing a token man on 'like work'.

You should ensure that you understand the importance of the role of the tribunal in equal value cases. Under the Industrial Tribunals (Constitution and Rules of Procedure) Regulations 1993, sch. 2, the tribunal must:

(a)   Decide whether there are reasonable grounds for determining that the work is of equal value. This is based on the evidence of the parties (see *Langley* v *Beecham Proprietaries* (1985) COIT 1683/206). At this stage in deciding whether there is a prima facie case, the industrial tribunal is duty bound to consider any genuine material difference/factor defence (s. 1(3)) raised by the employer. If the industrial tribunal is satisfied that the defence is proved, then it must not refer the matter to the independent expert, the time and expense involved being of the essence (see *Reed Packaging Ltd* v *Boozer* [1988] ICR 391; *Sheffield Metropolitan Borough Council* v *Siberry* [1989] ICR 208). The IT rules of procedure were changed in 1994 so that if an s. 1(3) defence is considered before reference to the independent expert, then it cannot be reconsidered at a later stage, other than in exceptional circumstances. This allays one of the criticisms made by the EOC, as the employer is no longer permitted two attempts at raising the defence. Also to speed up the procedure the independent expert must now notify the IT of the date by which he or she intends to report and must give further notification if there is likely to be a delay and explain why there is such a delay. The IT now has the power to revoke the expert's instructions and appoint a new expert.

(b) If satisfied that there are reasonable grounds, require an independent expert to prepare a report. The government intends to remove the 'reasonable grounds' stage. It has been suggested that this is because the present form of the equal value procedure is so complex that it infringes the spirit of European law.

Proceedings are adjourned whilst this is being done. It is significant that the tribunal need not accept the independent expert's report: see *Tennants Textile Colours Ltd* v *Todd* [1989] IRLR 3, where it was made clear that although the report carried considerable weight the onus was still on the applicant to show that she was employed on work of equal value. Furthermore, a tribunal may reach a conclusion contrary to that of an independent expert without concluding that the report is inherently wrong. However, where there is a total rejection of the report as in *Davies* v *Francis Shaw & Co. (Manchester) Ltd* (1987) 324 IRLIB 9, it may require a new expert to make a further report. In *Davies's* case the report was rejected on the grounds that it did not comply with the regulations. In *Wells* v *F. Smales & Son (Fish Merchants) Ltd* (1985) 281 IRLIB 11, where the tribunal overruled part of the independent expert's report when it concluded that all 14 fish packers were doing work of equal value to that of a male labourer as opposed to only 9 out of 14 as assessed by the expert. The tribunal did not reject the report wholesale and for the most part agreed with its findings. There was therefore no need to request a further report by a new expert.

This leads us to the contentious area of what amounts to work of equal value?

The problem with which you are faced concerns the approach adopted by the courts. We have to consider two industrial tribunal decisions. The first being the *Wells* case itself where the independent expert identified 13 separate jobs carried out by the applicants and considered each of these

jobs under four main headings: skill and experience; responsibility; working conditions and effort. Marks were then awarded and the final score
given as a percentage. Not all of the women scored the same; the range of
marks being within 79% to 95% of the comparator's score. The independent
expert concluded that only 9 of the 14 women were doing work of equal
value to the male comparator. However, the tribunal adopted a 'broad-
brush' approach in concluding that all of the women were employed on
work of equal value in that the differences between the five remaining
women and the male comparator were not relevant as the demands made
of them were equal to those of the male comparator.

Clearly the tribunal, in adopting this approach, was not looking for
anywhere near 100% equivalence in value between the job of the applicant
and the comparator; indeed 79% was acceptable. However, the broad-brush
approach was rejected in *Brown v Cearns & Brown Ltd* (1985) 304 IRLIB 10,
where the expert's report concluded that the applicant's work was 95% of
her comparator's. The tribunal declined to hold that their work was of
equal value as 'it was not of precisely equal value'. The industrial tribunal
criticised the broad-brush approach on the basis that it stemmed from
s. 1(4) of the Equal Pay Act 1970, i.e., work of a broadly similar nature, and
there were no equivalent words in the equal value provisions, nor in the
relevant EEC article.

Presumably the tribunal was looking for 100% equivalence between the
job of the applicant and the comparator. Realistically this is going to be an
extreme rarity and we can only question the feasibility of this approach if
this provision is ever to be successfully pleaded. Whilst it is not a binding
decision it highlights the attitude of the tribunals in this type of case and
clearly there is a need for a higher court to give some guidance in this area.
The broad-brush approach has since been adopted in *Pickstone v Freemans
plc* (1993) 28811/84 where the IT, disagreeing with the independent expert's
report, rules that female warehouse operatives were employed on work of
equal value with male checker warehouse operatives, even though the
women only scored 19 on the evaluation compared to the male comparator's score of 22. The IT recognised that it was difficult for a system of
evaluation to attain 100% precision.

Finally in *Murphy v Bord Telecom Eireann* [1988] ICR 445, it was confirmed
that 'equal' includes 'higher'. Accordingly, a woman employed on work of
a higher value than her male comparator is not barred from bringing an
equal value claim.

The Comparator

In considering with whom the applicant should be compared you are faced
with a number of problems. The first arises out of s. 1(6) of EPA 1970. The

applicant must be employed by the same employer or an associated employer of her comparator. Let us consider the word 'employed'. Usually this means 'employed under a contract of service'. Section 1(6)(a) gives a different meaning, to include a contract personally to execute work or labour, i.e., a contract for services (see chapter 3 for a more detailed discussion of these words). However, this does not necessarily mean that every independent contractor is covered by the Act. The position is illustrated by the following cases. In *Quinnen* v *Hovells* [1984] ICR 525 it was said (*obiter*) that 'those who engage, even cursorily, the talents, skill or labour of the self-employed are wise to ensure that the terms are equal as between men and women and do not discriminate between them'. A stricter approach has been adopted by the Court of Appeal in *Mirror Group Newspapers Ltd* v *Gunning* [1986] ICR 145 (a sex discrimination case) where it was held that the question to be asked is: Is the sole or dominant purpose of the contract the execution of work or labour by the contracting party? If the answer is no then clearly the applicant is not employed. The performance of a task which is a minor obligation of the contract considered as a whole does not mean that the contracting party is employed.

Secondly, s. 1(6) poses the problem of 'same employment'. There does not appear to be any difficulty as long as the applicant is employed at the same establishment as her comparator — see *Navy Army & Air Force Institutes* v *Varley* [1977] ICR 11. However, if she is employed by the same or an associated employer but at a different establishment, then she has no claim unless common terms and conditions of employment are observed at both establishments either generally or for the relevant class of employee. You must appreciate the interpretation given by the courts to the words 'common terms and conditions of service'. In *Leverton* v *Clwyd County Council* [1989] AC 706 the applicant, a nursery nurse, chose as her comparators clerical officers employed by the county council but employed at different establishments. The applicant worked shorter hours and had longer holidays. It was held by the Court of Appeal that she was not employed in the same employment as, although the comparators were employed under the standard conditions of service relevant to all of the county council employees, any individual contractual obligations had to be considered — in this case the shorter hours of work and the longer holidays. These were felt to be so radically different from those of her comparators that she could not be said to be employed on common terms and conditions. The House of Lords, however, overturned this decision. It concluded that although there was a difference in the hours worked and the holidays received, she was still employed on common terms and conditions. The correct construction of s. 1(6) called for a comparison between the terms and conditions of employment observed at the establishment at which the woman is employed and the establishment at which the men are employed, applicable either generally (as in this case), or to a particular class or classes of employees to which both the woman and the men belong. Note that the comparison is not between the two employees but between their terms and conditions. If these are found to be 'common' then the claim may proceed. In effect the issue is whether the applicant would have been employed under the same contract had she been doing the same job at her comparator's establishment. The Court of Appeal considered s. 1(6) again in *British Coal Corporation* v *Smith* [1994] ICR 810 and held that the words 'common terms and conditions' meant the same terms and conditions rather than terms and conditions which are broadly similar or to the same overall effect. If only one of the terms is the same, s. 1(6) is not satisfied. Furthermore the comparator selected by the applicant must be representative of the group or an s. 1(3) defence may apply. It is therefore imperative in claiming an s. 1(6) comparator that if any men were employed at the female's establishment, they should be employed on the same terms and conditions as men at the male comparator's establishment.

Remember the common terms and conditions requirement only applies where the applicant and her comparator are employed at different establishments, not the same establishment (see *Lawson* v *Britfish Ltd* [1987] ICR 726).

You may need to consider the meaning of the words 'associated employer'. In *Hasley* v *Fair Employment Agency* [1989] IRLR 107, the Northern Ireland Court of Appeal held that two employers are to be treated as associated if one employer is a company of which the other employer (not necessarily a company) has control. In this particular case neither the Fair Employment Agency nor the EOC (NI) were companies within the meaning of the Act; they were statutory bodies.

Once you have dealt with the problem of 'same employment', you are faced with the selection of the comparator. Here most of the issues have been resolved:

(a) Multiple comparators are permitted — see *Langley* v *Beecham Proprietaries* (1985) COIT 1683/206, applying Interpretation Act 1978, s. 6.

(b) Where an applicant cannot name her comparators she is not barred from bringing a claim as long as she has a prima facie case. She can rely on discovery to obtain the relevant names (*Clwyd County Council* v *Leverton* [1985] IRLR 197) but be aware of the dangers of spreading the net too widely (*Leverton* v *Clwyd County Council* [1989] AC 706).

(c) The applicant may select the comparator of her choice (*Ainsworth* v *Glass Tubes & Components Ltd* [1977] ICR 347).

(d) The applicant may be compared with her predecessor (*Macarthys Ltd* v *Smith* [1981] QB 180).

(e) The applicant cannot be compared with a hypothetical male or female.

Genuine Material Differences

An employer has a 'defence' under EPA 1970 by virtue of s. 1(3). You should understand that it is quite acceptable for this defence to be considered as a preliminary issue by the Tribunal (Industrial Tribunals (Rules of Procedure) Regulations 1985 (SI 1985 No. 16), reg. 7A(1)). However, the Regulations have been amended so that if a s. 1(3) defence is raised at the preliminary hearing it cannot be considered after the independent expert has reported (Industrial Tribunals (Constitution and Rules of Procedure) Regulations 1993 (SI 1993 No. 2687) Sched 2). The plan to abolish the 'no reasonable grounds' provision (EPA 1970, s. 2A(1)) should also be noted.

This defence requires the employer to show on a balance of probabilities that the variation in pay is 'genuinely due to a material factor other than sex'. In the case of like work or work rated as equivalent, this material factor 'must be a material difference between the [applicant's case] and [her comparator's]', whilst in the case of equal value, 'it may be such a difference'. Following the decision of the House of Lords in *Rainey v Greater Glasgow Health Board* [1987] AC 224, it would now appear that, despite this difference in wording, the ambit of the defence is probably the same in all equal pay cases.

The major issue relating to the scope of the defence is whether the material factor justifying the difference in pay can encompass 'market forces'. Given that men have traditionally been able to demand higher rewards in the labour market, the acceptance of 'market force' arguments has serious implications for the degree of protection offered by the equal pay legislation.

In *Albion Shipping Agency* v *Arnold* [1982] ICR 22 the market forces defence was allowed. This permitted the employer to pay a female office manager less than her male predecessor on the grounds that the employer's volume of business had been reduced which had led to a decrease in his profits. The EAT concluded that 'economic factors affecting the employers' business' might justify the payment of different wages to a man and a woman successively employed. *Arnold's* case can be distinguished from the decision in *Clay Cross (Quarry Services) Ltd* v *Fletcher* [1979] ICR 1 on the basis that the male and female in the former were not employed *simultaneously*. This case has particular significance in the current economic climate.

The decision in *Fletcher* has now been overruled by *Rainey* v *Greater Glasgow Health Board* [1987] AC 224. In *Fletcher's* case, the Court of Appeal decided that a difference in pay could only be justified after comparing the personal factors of the respective male and female, e.g., length of service, skill, qualifications and productivity, and no consideration should be given to extrinsic factors, such as market forces. However, in *Rainey*, new recruits to the prosthetic service from the private sector were offered their existing rate of pay whereas people recruited straight into or from within the National Health Service were paid on existing scales which were lower. The applicant had been recruited directly into the Health Service and was therefore on a lower point on the pay scale than her comparator. This was justified on the grounds that it was necessary to attract well-qualified prosthetists; and that the different method of entry was a material difference other than sex. In rejecting the decision in *Fletcher*, the House of Lords held that both personal and extrinsic factors were relevant and that all the circumstances of the case must be considered. It decided that the reason given was an objectively justified ground for offering the male prosthetist a higher rate of pay, and that there were sound administrative reasons for doing so. So, it appears that both market forces and administrative grounds are available as, a defence to any claim under s. 1. Indeed the ECJ, in applying art. 119 in *Bilka-Kaufhaus GmbH v Weber von Hartz* [1987] ICR 110, concluded that a variation in pay may be justified on economic grounds. However, note the decision in *Benveniste v University of Southampton* [1989] ICR 617, where a female lecturer employed on the same work as her comparators was initially appointed on a lower point in the pay structure because of economic restrictions. It was held that whilst such financial constraints might justify paying a new appointee less than another employee on like work, when the constraints no longer applied parity must be restored. *Enderby v Frenchay Health Authority* [1994] ICR 112 confirms that the burden of proof moves to the employer to show that the pay differential is not discriminatory and is based on objectively justified factor. The fact that the difference in pay arises from a collective agreement is not necessarily a sufficient objective justification for the difference in pay. However, 'market forces' may constitute an objectively justified economic ground for the difference in pay. It is time for the IT to determine what proportion of the difference in pay is attributable to market forces. If this can be done then that part of the differential is objectively justified and any award should reflect this proportionality.

You will need to refer to the decision in *Handels- og Kontorfunktionærernes Forbund i Danmark v Dansk Arbejdsgiverforening* [1989] IRLR 532, where the issue of transparent, non-discriminatory pay grading systems was considered. If the only defence for such schemes is the of differentials between classes or types of worker, and this has an adverse impact on female employees, such schemes would be in breach of art. 119 and the EPA 1970 although the employer may have a defence using *Bilka-Kaufhaus* or *Rainey*. See *Calder v Rowntree Mackintosh Confectionery Ltd* [1993] ICR 811.

There are two other issues which you may have to consider as a genuine material factor. The first is part-time work, which is traditionally done by females and in the past has attracted a lower rate of pay. In the most recent ecision of note, the EAT held that a difference in pay between male full-time employees and female part-time employees can only be justified if the employer can show that the difference is 'reasonably necessary in order to achieve an economic or other objective' — in this case the reduction of absenteeism and the greater use of plant and equipment (*Jenkins* v *Kingsgate (Clothing Productions) Ltd* [1981] ICR 592). Does it follow that if cheap part-time labour is employed to enable the employer to be competitive in home and foreign markets, the difference in pay between full and part-time employees, male and female respectively, would be reasonably necessary?

The second issue is 'red-circled' agreements, which allow the employer to protect an employee's or group of employees' salary even though he or they may have been moved to a lower grade of work. As far as you are concerned the first question is: Is the red-circling discriminatory or is it evidence of past discriminatory practices? If it is then there is no defence (*Snoxell* v *Vauxhall Motors Ltd* [1977] ICR 700). Secondly, how long has the red-circled agreement been in existence? Such agreements are not intended to be indefinite (*Outlook Supplies Ltd* v *Parry* [1978] ICR 388). They should clearly only survive as long as the last person in the group.

THE EXAMINATION

As far as the examination is concerned the topic of equal pay may not necessarily be examined on its own. It could be mixed in with problems on sex discrimination or dismissal and you must ensure that you have recognised all of the issues when answering a problem in order to gain optimum marks. We stress yet again the importance of making a rough plan before you commence writing in order to structure your thoughts and your written answer. Furthermore you should maintain a strict time-limit for each question, allowing yourself 5–10 minutes at the end of the examination to read through what you have written.

Illustrative Problem

Maggie and Kath have been employed as packers by Clean Chem Co. Ltd for three years. All full-time packers are female and they are paid £1.75 per hour for a 36-hour week. They have free meals at lunch-time in the works canteen; a productivity bonus is paid weekly if the number of items packed exceeds the weekly target figure; and on Fridays they finish at 4 p.m. whereas the rest of the work-force finishes at 5.15 p.m. Jean is employed to do the same work as Maggie and Kath but on a part-time basis. She works on the twilight shift 6–10 p.m. She is paid £1.25 per hour and does not receive any other concessions. All packers are given protective overalls which are laundered free of charge.

Maggie discovers that fork-lift truck drivers employed by Any-Way Handlers Ltd, a subsidiary of Clean Chem situated in the next town, are paid £2.50 per hour. However, they are obliged to work a 40-hour week and work overtime when necessary, but they do not receive any other concessions. Maggie feels that her job is worth as much to the company and that she and the other packers should therefore be paid the same rate as the fork-lift truck drivers. Two months before this issue is decided by the tribunal, Kath decides to leave for a better paid job. Jean discovers that some years previously only men were employed as packers on the twilight shift at the rate of £1.30 per hour plus productivity bonus.

Clean Chem have responded to Maggie's claim by arguing that there is no intention to discriminate in respect of pay as the difference between the packers' pay and the fork-lift truck drivers' pay arises from a collective agreement.

Discuss.

Analysis

First you must consider carefully what is required. In this particular problem you are required to discuss the position of all the parties concerned, not merely to advise one particular party. You must therefore ensure that all of the issues are covered in respect of all of the applicants and the defendant.

Maggie and others v Clean Chem Co. Ltd

The point should be made that Maggie, with the support of her trade union, if there is one, will probably bring a representative action on behalf of the full-time packers. This is usually the case where people are employed on exactly the same terms and conditions. However, if there are differing terms and conditions then the other packers may be joined in the same action but the individual merits of each claim will be considered separately by the tribunal as in *Wells v F. Smales & Son (Fish Merchants) Ltd* (1985) 281 IRLIB 11. The case will automatically be referred to ACAS for conciliation and settlement. In the event of this failing and the case being referred to the industrial tribunal, the tribunal must decide whether there are reasonable grounds on which the case should proceed. In so doing it will consider any s. 1(3) defence.

Although Maggie receives a number of benefits as part of her remuneration package, she is entitled to proceed with her equality claim in respect of individual terms, in this particular case rate of pay (*Hayward v Cammell Laird Shipbuilders Ltd* [1988] AC 894).

Before considering whether the 'equality clause' will operate, the first question must be: 'Is Maggie employed within the meaning of EPA 1970,

s. 1(6)(a)?' She cannot proceed unless she is employed by Clean Chem. This does not pose a problem here because s. 1(6)(a) includes in its meaning contract of service and contract for services as in *Mirror Group Newspapers Ltd* v *Gunning* [1986] ICR 145 and Maggie is more likely to be employed under a contract of service although we do not have all of the facts to prove this. Secondly, are she and her male comparator employed on 'like work', 'work rated equivalent' or 'work of equal value'? Under the EPA it is necessary to decide which ground is the most appropriate for her claim. You may wish to point out that if a 'like work' claim is available and likely to succeed she should proceed on that ground. However, she is not barred from pursuing an equal value claim just because there is a token man employed on like work (*Pickstone* v *Freemans plc* [1989] AC 66). To proceed on the ground of s. 1(2)(a) she must come within s. 1(4), i.e., her work and her comparator's are the same or of a broadly similar nature. From the facts there are no men employed as full-time packers, and fork-lift drivers cannot be said to be employed on work of a broadly similar nature, no matter how wide the interpretation given by the tribunal. She does not come within s. 1(2)(b) as there does not appear to be in existence a valid job evaluation scheme within s. 1(5), and she cannot demand that one is carried out. Her claim, therefore, must proceed on the basis that she is employed on work of equal value to that of a man in the same employment (s. 1(2)(c)).

Before deciding whether her work is of equal value, we have to look at her comparator. As long as she can name them she can have multiple comparators (*Langley* v *Beecham Proprietaries* (1985) COIT 1683/206). In order to name her comparators she can apply for discovery, which will not prevent her case from proceeding (*Clwyd County Council* v *Leverton* [1985] IRLR 197). Her comparator must, however, be employed in the 'same employment' within s. 1(6)(b). We know that the fork-lift truck driver is not employed by the same employer nor at the same establishment, but is he employed by an associated employer at an establishment where common terms and conditions of employment are observed? Clearly the employers are associated within s. 1(6)(c): *Hasley* v *Fair Employment Agency* [1989] IRLR 107. However, it is impossible to deduce from the facts whether common terms and conditions are observed. You should conclude that Maggie cannot proceed under s. 1(2)(c) if there are no common terms and conditions, e.g., a collective agreement, within the meaning laid down in *Leverton* v *Clwyd County Council* [1989] AC 706, but you should continue on the basis that there may be in existence such an agreement.

Once Maggie has established that she has a prima facie case, her employer may argue that the case should not proceed because there is a genuine material difference or factor between her and her comparator. Applying *Rainey* v *Greater Glasgow Health Board* [1987] AC 224 Clean Chem can put before the tribunal not only personal factors, such as skills, productivity, hours worked, length of service and place of work, but also extrinsic factors such as market forces and administrative reasons — all acceptable as long as they are 'genuine' and can be 'objectively justified'. In this case the longer hours of work, the productivity bonus, the free meals and overalls are all relevant. It is likely, therefore, that there are genuine material factors which will prevent Maggie's case from proceeding. However, if the tribunal does not accept Clean Chem's defence and concludes that there are reasonable grounds for determining that the work is of equal value, it will then appoint an independent expert to prepare a report. Reference should also be made to *Enderby* v *Frenchay Health Authority* [1994] ICR 112, in which it was held that where one group of workers who are almost exclusively women is paid less than another group made up predominantly of men for doing work of equal value, there is a prima facie case of discrimination under art. 119. Furthermore whilst 'market forces' may be a defence, reliance on a collective agreement may not suffice.

The independent expert will make a study of Maggie's work and her comparator's under various headings, e.g., effort, skill, responsibilities etc., which usually results in a percentage conclusion. The tribunal is not obliged to accept the independent expert's conclusion (*Tennants Textile Colours Ltd* v *Todd* [1989] IRLR 3). Indeed it is a matter for debate whether the tribunal will find in favour of Maggie depending upon whether it adopts the broader approach in *Wells* v *F. Smales & Son (Fish Merchants) Ltd* and *Pickstone* v *Freemans plc* or the narrower approach in *Brown* v *Cearns & Brown Ltd*. If Clean Chem have already pleaded the s. 1(3) defence, they will not be able to rely on it again at this stage. Following the decision in *Rainey* v *Greater Glasgow Health Board* the tribunal can consider both personal and extrinsic factors. This would allow the market forces defence to prevail as well as economic factors. On the basis of those decisions it is doubtful, therefore in considering all the terms and conditions of Maggie's contract with that of her comparator that Maggie will succeed under EPA 1970 or art. 119.

Kath v *Clean Chem Co. Ltd*
As long as Kath is employed on the same or similar terms and conditions to Maggie she may be joined to the action. The only issue relates to the qualifying period. Kath must ensure that the action against Clean Chem is brought within six months of her leaving its employment (s. 2(4)).

Jean v *Clean Chem Co. Ltd*
The first issue is: Can Jean be represented in Maggie's action? The answer is no because she is not employed on the same or similar terms or conditions and therefore she would need to bring her own representative action on behalf of the part-time workers.

Secondly, Who is her comparator? Unfortunately for her she cannot be compared with the full-time female packers. She could, however, be compared with a male predecessor as in *Macarthys Ltd* v *Smith* [1981] QB 180. This would enable her to bring a claim on the basis of 'like work' under s. 1(2)(a) and, as long as her work was of the same or a broadly similar nature within s. 1(4), she might well succeed. If she has the basis for a successful like work claim, then she should proceed on that ground. If not, she may make an equal value claim, selecting as her comparator, for example, the fork-lift truck drivers at Any-Way Handlers (see *Pickstone* v *Freemans plc*). Whoever she selects, under s. 1(2)(c) she would have to face the same issues as Maggie regarding s. 1(6). Her main problem in selecting a full-time male as her comparator relates to a genuine material factor. Clean Chem could plead that the variation in pay between full-time and part-time employees was necessary on economic grounds, e.g., 'to obtain maximum utilisation of his plant' as pleaded in *Jenkins* v *Kingsgate (Clothing Productions) Ltd* [1981] ICR 592). Furthermore, in the earlier case of *Handley* v *H. Mono Ltd* [1979] ICR 147 the EAT concluded that a difference in pay between full-time male and part-time female employees was justified as they contributed less to the running of the plant. Any s. 1(3) defence would have to be objectively justified by the employer. Following *Bilka-Kaufhaus* the employer would need to show that the difference in pay met 'a real need on the part of the undertaking and that this was appropriate with a view to achieving the objective and necessary to that end'.

In conclusion Maggie and Kath do not have a clear-cut case and perhaps should take some time to find a more suitable comparator, subject to the six-month time-limit for Kath. Jean may have to settle for a 'like work' claim unless she can find a comparator employed on a part-time basis for her claim of equal value.

Essay Questions

You may be faced with an essay question in the examination, although a problem is more likely. Essays in this field tend to require a critical examination of the working of the statute; they should not be attempted unless you are confident that you have a thorough understanding of the wider issues surrounding this area and have read more than the standard text. Most essays will require you to refer to the social, economic and political issues which affect labour law, and in particular equal pay. Reference to current statistics would be invaluable. The reading list at the end of the chapter provides you with further guidance on this.

CONCLUSION

You should at the very least find this area interesting and this should compensate for the complexity of the case law. In perspective it is probably less than in other areas of labour law. To understand the subject fully you should ensure that you read widely and do not adopt a purely legalistic approach. Equal pay is certainly a 'banker' at least for half a question in the examination and it is therefore worth spending the extra time on its 'little subtleties'.

READING

Bourn, C., and Whitmore, J., *Race and Sex Discrimination*, 2nd ed. (London: Sweet & Maxwell, 1993).

EOC, *Equal Pay for Men and Women: Strengthening the Acts* (Manchester: EOC, 1990).

Kilpatrick, C., 'Deciding when jobs of equal value can be paid unequally: an examination of s. 1(3) of the Equal Pay Act 1970' (1994) 23 ILJ 311.

Leonard, A.M., *Judging Inequality* (London: Cobden Trust, 1987).

McColgan, A., *Pay Equity: Just Wages for Women* (Institute of Employment Rights, 1994).

Meehan, E.M., *Women's Rights at Work* (Basingstoke: Macmillan, 1985).

Morris, J., *No More Peanuts* (NCCL).

Palmer, C., *Discrimination at Work*, 2nd ed. (London: Legal Action Group, 1992).

Szyszczak, E., 'Pay inequalities and equal value claims' (1985) 48 MLR 139.

Townshend-Smith, R., *Sex Discrimination in Employment* (London: Sweet & Maxwell, 1989).

West Midlands Low Pay Unit, *Undervalued and Underpaid* (1991).

5 LEGAL CONSTRAINTS ON TERMS AND CONDITIONS OF EMPLOYMENT 2: SEX AND RACE DISCRIMINATION

INTRODUCTION

We shall be considering sex and race discrimination together and merely taking note of any differences where it is relevant to do so. As far as you are concerned the provisions of the Sex Discrimination Act (SDA) 1975 and the Race Relations Act (RRA) 1976 are virtually the same and certainly the decisions made by the courts in respect of these statutes are for the most part interchangeable. It is up to you to make yourself knowledgeable of the wording of the relevant sections of the respective statutes as it is not the object of this book to do this. However, we have included some guidance by way of an overview which you will see a little later in the chapter. Both statutes cover not only discrimination in employment but also discrimination in education, provision of services etc., but we shall only be considering the substantive difficulties arising out of discrimination in employment.

Even though both statutes have been in force for over a decade this area of law is still beset by problems, and there is considerable doubt about their effectiveness in eliminating discrimination. The law has attempted to change overt behaviour but it unfortunately cannot change people's attitudes and that poses the real problem.

As long ago as 1958, the International Labour Organisation (Convention No. 111) wanted countries ratifying the convention to take measures against discrimination on the grounds of race, colour, sex, religion, political opinion or national and social extraction in employment. As you will appreciate it was some years on before the UK implemented legislation in this field and it has yet to ratify the convention. Although the UK may have gone some way towards the elimination of discrimination, there are still loopholes. For example, discrimination on religious or political grounds is not included in the statutes, so it is still possible to be anti-Semetic without fear of infringing the law. Northern Ireland is the exception as the Fair Employment (Northern Ireland) Act 1989 makes it an offence to discriminate on grounds of religion and political opinion. It is interesting that the legislature does not feel that the rest of the UK suffers from this type of discrimination.

Other statutes have attempted to prevent discrimination in employment in respect of disabled people and people with criminal records — see the Disabled Persons (Employment) Acts 1944 and 1958 (although there are proposals to repeal and replace this legislation) and the Rehabilitation of Offenders Act 1974 respectively which provide limited protection. Furthermore, in the USA concern has been expressed about discrimination on the grounds of bodily and facial appearance as there is evidence that the most physically unattractive members of society suffer severe discrimination, especially in employment — see 'Facial discrimination: extending handicap law to employment discrimination on the basis of physical appearance' 100 Harv L Rev 2035. Should this be under consideration in the UK? Another area of discrimination which has yet to be considered seriously in the UK, although there has been some research, is ageism. Does this type of discrimination require specific legislation? How do we prioritise those areas of discrimination which do not have adequate protection? (See *Age: No Barrier*, METRA, 1991.)

The UK sex discrimination law has been criticised by the ECJ in *Commission of the European Communities* v *United Kingdom of Great Britain & Northern Ireland* [1984] IRLR 29. SDA 1975 was not in line with art. 4(b) of Directive 76/207 in that it did not cover such things as internal work rules, nor rules governing the independent occupations and professions; nor did it apply to private households or undertakings where five or fewer were employed. Also (*Marshall* v *Southampton & South West Hampshire Area Health Authority (Teaching)* [1986] QB 401), as far, as public sector employment is concerned, the difference in retirement age of men and women contravened Directive 76/207. As a result of these two decisions we now have the Sex Discrimination Act 1986.

The Sex Discrimination Act 1986 not only made the necessary changes to the existing statute to comply with the ECJ rulings, i.e., extending application of the Act to undertakings with five or fewer employees, removing the complete exemption for private households and extending the coverage to collective agreements, works rules, professional associations etc., but went much further, possibly out of fear of being called into question yet again by the European Commission. Section 7 of the 1986 Act removed (by repealing the relevant section or statute) the protection afforded to women by the Factories Act 1961 and related statutes in respect of shift work, overtime and maximum working hours. These provisions were intended to prevent the abuse of women at work. Any exemptions from these provisions in the past would be granted by the Health and Safety Executive subject to investigation of the necessity for the limitation on working hours to be lifted. This protection has now been removed and the only source of protection remains with the Health and Safety at Work etc. Act 1974 which imposes a lesser standard. Are we therefore at the stage denounced by the Low Pay Unit where:

> the absence . . . of effective overall regulation of exploitative shift-work patterns and long hours for both men and women may be at the expense of a general deterioration of conditions for the most vulnerable ('Equality government style: women's hours of work', *Low Pay Review*, Spring 1985, p. 33).

Section 7 has now been repealed and replaced by the Employment Act 1989.

Before we consider the substantive difficulties we must consider why there is a need for statutes to prevent sex and race discrimination. Both women and ethnic minorities are seen as candidates for low-paid mundane jobs. These are the types of job where there is a lack of opportunity for the persons concerned to get out of the stereotyped role in which society has put them.

As is illustrated in *Stereotypes and Selection* by M. Curran, stereotyping coupled with the perception by employers of jobs as having male or female characteristics leads to discrimination. This discrimination is not always against the female applicant, e.g., sales assistant is seen as a female job. However, this research has shown that 'female jobs' generally offer lower rates of pay, inferior pension provisions and lesser prospects of promotion than 'male jobs'. Statutes alone are not necessarily going to improve the prospects of women/men or ethnic minorities. A change of attitude is necessary, starting at recruitment level. Both the EOC and the CRE lay down guidelines for employers regarding selection and recruitment in their codes of practice. A positive step towards the elimination of discrimination would be a review by employers of their current procedures and practices in the light of these guidelines.

THE RELATIONSHIP OF UK LAW WITH EUROPEAN LAW

This was dealt with in chapter 4 and as we saw there the effect of the EC Treaty and Directives is the same. You would be wise therefore to reconsider the relevant part of that chapter. However, you should ensure that you know Directive 76/207 which is particularly relevant to sex discrimination. This is the equal treatment Directive; it has been adopted by the UK. The application of this Directive in the UK has been debated in *Johnston v Chief Constable of the Royal Ulster Constabulary* [1987] QB 129 in which it was confirmed by the ECJ that Directive 76/207 is unconditional and sufficiently precise for it to be relied upon by an individual against a member State in a national court. You should, however, be aware that the decision in *Duke v GEC Reliance Ltd* [1988] AC 618 has upheld the finding in *Marshall v Southampton & South West Hampshire Area Health Authority (Teaching)* [1986] QB 401 that an individual cannot enforce the Directive against a private employer, only against the State or 'an organ or emanation of the State'. The meaning of these words was clarified in *Foster v British Gas plc* [1991] 1 QB 405, ECJ, where it was held that they included a body, whatever its legal form, which has been made responsible for providing a public service under the control of the State and has for that purpose special powers beyond those which result from the normal rules applicable in relations between private individuals. The House of Lords has confirmed that British Gas falls within this definition (*Foster v British Gas plc* [1991] 2 AC 306). See also *Rolls-Royce plc v Doughty* [1992] ICR 538.

You ought also to be aware of another area of European law which may be of increasing importance. Article 48 outlaws discrimination based on nationality between workers of Member States. Regulation 1612/68 makes it unlawful for an employer to treat nationals differently by reason of their nationality. The application of these provisions can be seen in the case of *Groener v Minister for Education* [1990] 1 CMLR 401. Groener, a Dutch woman, applied for a post as lecturer in Dublin. A linguistic requirement was imposed in that the appointee had to have a certificate of proficiency in the Irish language or had passed a special oral examination in Irish. Groener was the best candidate but did not satisfy the language requirement. She alleged that the language requirement was discriminatory and contravened the article and the regulation. The case was referred to the ECJ which held that whilst a linguistic requirement is the only form of indirect discrimination permitted under the regulation, it can only be justified where the nature of the post demands it. The court felt that this was satisfied in this particular case but emphasised that such a requirement 'had to be in proportion to the aim it pursued and its discriminatory effect kept to the minimum necessary to achieve that aim'.

In effect, whilst it might be justifiable to impose a language requirement for a lecturer, would this be the case for anyone dealing with the public or offering a service? It certainly would not be justifiable for employment as, for example, a cleaner.

OVERVIEW

Before we consider the substantive difficulties, it may assist you to have an overview of this area because it can seem confusing when you have to consider two statutes.

Discrimination in Employment

Discrimination is unlawful if based on:

(a) Race, colour, nationality, ethnic origins or national origins (RRA 1976, ss. 1 and 3).
(b) Sex (SDA 1975, ss. 1 and 2).
(c) Marital status (SDA 1975, ss. 1 and 3).

What is Discrimination?

(a) Direct discrimination (SDA 1975, s. 1(1)(a); RRA 1976, s. 1(1)(a)), i.e., treated less favourably because of sex or race. Includes segregation (RRA 1976, s. 1(2)).
(b) Indirect discrimination (SDA 1975, s. 1(1)(b); RRA 1976, s. 1(1)(b)), i.e., requirement applies to all employees but the proportion of a particular sex or race who can comply with it is considerably smaller than the proportion outside that race or sex; and
the employer cannot justify the requirement; and
it is to the employee's detriment.
(c) Victimisation (SDA 1975, s. 4; RRA 1976, s. 2), i.e., treated less favourably because the employee:

(i) brought proceedings,
(ii) gave evidence,
(iii) helped the CRE or EOC,
(iv) made allegations of discrimination.

(d) By employers against applicants and employees (SDA 1975, s. 6; RRA 1976, s. 4):

(i) Prior to employment:
(1) determining who should be employed,
(2) terms on which employed,
(3) refusing or deliberately omitting to offer employment.

(ii) During employment:
   (1) access to promotion, transfer, training or other benefits and facilities,
   (2) dismissal or subjecting to any other detriment.

SUBSTANTIVE DIFFICULTIES

We can now turn to the substantive difficulties arising from the law on sex and race discrimination. SDA 1975 protects both men and women of any age from discrimination. Married persons have specific protection in the employment field (s. 3). RRA 1976 prevents discrimination on racial grounds and protects members of a racial group. Before we look at the types of discrimination we must consider the following terms which have posed problems.

Racial Grounds and Racial Group (RRA 1976, s. 3 (1))

These terms are used in relation to direct and indirect discrimination; and the same words are used in respect of the definition of each term. The difficulty with which you are faced, and indeed for the courts, is in determining the scope of the words used.

In *Seide* v *Gillette Industries Ltd* [1980] IRLR 427 one of the issues was whether being a Jew meant that a person was a member of a particular religious faith in which case such discrimination would not be covered by the Act, or whether it meant that a person was of a race or particular ethnic origin. Confusingly it was held that the word 'Jew' could mean any of these and the court has to look at why the person is being discriminated against. The EAT was not prepared to distinguish, by definition, between race and ethnic origin in this case. It may not therefore be necessary to meet one precise part of the definition in the initial stages.

You should also consider *Simon* v *Brimham Associates* [1987] ICR 596 where Simon was asked his religion at a job interview on the grounds that anyone of the Jewish faith might be excluded from selection as the job involved working for Arabs. Simon, who was Jewish, refused to answer the question and withdrew his application. It was held that although words or acts of discouragement on racial grounds can amount to discrimination, this was not the case here as the purpose behind the question was not discriminatory. Furthermore *Simon's* case was made more difficult because he alleged individual discrimination, i.e., direct discrimination, rather than discrimination against a member of an identified class or group. In other words he stood a better chance of success if he had adopted the approach in *Seide's* case. See also *Morgan* v *Civil Service Commission* (1990) COIT 19177/89.

In *Mandla* v *Dowell Lee* [1983] 2 AC 548, which was concerned with discrimination against a young Sikh boy who was not allowed into school unless he removed his turban and cut his hair, the issue was whether being a Sikh came within the definition of a racial group. It was held that within the definition given in s. 3, the word 'ethnic' is wider than 'race'. The reasoning of Lord Fraser of Tullybelton contains the definitive test for establishing 'ethnic origin'. 'Ethnic origin' means to be regarded as a distinct and separate community by reason of various characteristics including culture, language, history, descent, literature and religion and any racial characteristics. Therefore a Sikh was a member of a racial group. However, language alone is insufficient to define racial group (*Gwynedd County Council* v *Jones* [1986] ICR 833). The test in *Mandla* has had a significant impact. In *CRE* v *Dutton* [1989] QB 783, the Court of Appeal concluded that 'gipsies' as opposed to 'travellers' were an ethnic group as they came within the definition in s. 3 and satisfied the test in *Mandla's* case. Gipsies were a wandering race of Hindu origin; they had a long-shared history, common geographical origin, their own customs, language, folk tales and music. Yet in *Crown Suppliers (Property Services Agency)* v *Dawkins*, [1993] ICR 517, the Court of Appeal decided that Rastafarians were a religious sect rather than an ethnic group as they did not satisfy all of the guidelines laid down in *Mandla*. In particular, as the Rastafarian movement only commenced in 1930, it did not have a long shared history. Nor could Rastafarians claim group descent. Finally, it was felt by the court, that there were no apparent customs and practices and that there was insufficient evidence to distinguish them from the rest of the Afro-Caribbean community. You may like to consider whether Rastafarians would ever fulfil all of the elements of the test in *Mandla*.

The meaning of 'nationality' is wider than 'national origins'. The latter means race rather than citizenship or residence (*Ealing London Borough Council* v *Race Relations Board* [1972] AC 342 applied in *Tejani* v *Superintendent Registrar for the District of Peterborough* [1986] IRLR 502) whereas 'nationality' includes citizenship. In reality this only becomes an issue where a person born in another country takes out British citizenship and there may then be a dispute about his true nationality.

Types of Discrimination

Both SDA 1975 and RRA 1976 prohibit particular types of discrimination from the overt to the unintentional and we shall be considering the problems arising from each type.

Burden of proof
Although this is on the complainant and appears to be onerous, as a result of the decision in *Khanna* v *Ministry of Defence* [1981] ICR 653, if a prima

facie case of discrimination is indicated from the facts the onus is on the employer to give an acceptable explanation, and if one is not forthcoming, then an inference of discrimination can be made by the tribunal. See *North West Thames Regional Health Authority* v *Noone* [1988] ICR 813 and *Chattopadhyay* v *Headmaster of Holloway School* [1982] ICR 132, for example, failure to monitor an equal opportunities policy may result in the IT inferring that discrimination has taken place (*Brighton Borough Council* v *Richards* (1993) EAT 431/92). In attempting to establish discrimination, the statutory comparison imposed by SDA 1975, s. 5, and RRA 1976, s. 3, must not be overlooked, i.e., 'like must be compared with like', (*Bain* v *Bowles* [1991] IRLR 356; *Bullock* v *Alice Ottley School* [1993] ICR 138). You may need to consider the various academic arguments put forward for altering the burden of proof in discrimination cases.

Direct discrimination SDA 1975, s. 1(1)(a); RRA 1976, s. 1(1)(a)
The concept of direct discrimination is aimed at preventing overt and covert discrimination of the individual. When considering direct discrimination you have to establish two things:

(a)   A woman or a member of a racial group has been treated less favourably than a man or other person.
(b)   The reason for the treatment is based on her sex or racial grounds.

The main difficulty is reconciling the decisions of the courts with what appear to be straightforward sections of the respective statutes.

Notice the slightly different wording in the two statutes. Under RRA, discrimination is based on 'racial grounds', whereas under SDA, discrimination against a woman has to be 'on the grounds of *her* sex' (our italics). The wider phrase under RRA brings transferred discrimination within its remit. This means that discrimination may take place where a person is treated less favourably because of another person's race. For example, in *Showboat Entertainment Centre Ltd* v *Owens* [1984] ICR 65, Owens, who was white, was dismissed from his job as a manager of an amusement centre for failure to obey an order to exclude black people. Unlawful discrimination was held to have taken place (see also *Zarczynska* v *Levy* [1979] 1 WLR 125).

It is important for you to appreciate that unlike EPA 1970 comparison can be made with the hypothetical man. There is no need for the complainant to find a man or other person who has been treated more favourably (although of course this would help the complainant's case) (see *Meeks* v *National Union of Agricultural & Allied Workers* [1976] IRLR 198).

Following the decision in *R* v *Birmingham City Council, ex parte EOC* [1989] AC 1155, HL, and *James* v *Eastleigh Borough Council* [1990] 2 AC 751,

HL, there is a simple test for establishing direct discrimination. You need to ask the following questions:

(a) Was there an act of discrimination?

(b) *But for* the applicant's sex or race would they have been treated differently, i.e., 'less favourably'?

If both questions are answered in the affirmative, direct discrimination is established. The cases referred to above confirm that the intention or motive of the discriminator is irrelevant, e.g., in *James's* case the reason for the act of discrimination — the provision of free swimming for women over 60 years and men over 65 years — was to help the needy, i.e., those on a pension. Whilst this may be a worthwhile cause it is not a defence to an act of direct discrimination. It is, however, interesting to note that the Court of Appeal in this case felt that the reason for the discrimination was relevant to proof of discrimination. Imagine the repercussions had such a decision been allowed to stand. The fact that discrimination can be inferred has eased the problems of proving direct discrimination: see *King* v *Great Britain–China Centre* [1992] ICR 516, which provides guidance on proving direct discrimination.

Motive is irrelevant (*Grieg* v *Community Industry* [1979] ICR 356 and *Seide* v *Gillette Industries Ltd* [1980] IRLR 427). An unintentional or good intentioned act is therefore unlawful. However, irrespective of motive, a 'trivial' or insignificant act (at least in the eyes of the court) may not be unlawful. In *Ministry of Defence* v *Jeremiah* [1980] ICR 13 Lord Denning MR felt that there should be scope for the *de minimis* rule to apply so that a minor act which had little adverse effect would not be unlawful. In this way Lord Denning could defend his decision in *Peake* v *Automotive Products Ltd* [1978] QB 433.

Sexual and racial harassment

As you are aware, there are no specific provisions in the respective legislation dealing with sexual and racial harassment. Harassment falls to be considered under the remit of the direct discrimination provisions. This is in itself unsatisfactory as it is necessary to contrive to bring such acts within the wording of the sections. In recent years there has been a rapid growth in the number of harassment claims being made and the time has probably come for there to be separate provisions (see EOC, *Equal Treatment for Men and Women — Strengthening the Acts*). It is important for you to appreciate what amounts to harassment, as according to a number of considered decisions, a wide range of conduct can be caught by the Acts.

Following *Porcelli* v *Strathclyde Regional Council* [1986] ICR 564, it is clear that harassment is concerned with the treatment of the individual in a particular way because of their race or sex. Sexual harassment, therefore, does not have to involve sexual connotations such as touching or suggestive remarks but can be intimidating conduct. It is only necessary to show that the treatment of the applicant occurred in a particular way because of their sex or race. In this particular case, deliberately placing heavy laboratory equipment on the top shelf in the store room so that the female laboratory assistant had problems handling it, was an important factor in establishing harassment on the part of her male colleagues.

The case of *Bracebridge Engineering Ltd* v *Darby* [1990] IRLR 3, confirms that a single act of a serious nature will support a claim of discrimination. You should, therefore, appreciate that there does not have to be a course of conduct. The complainant does not have to show that she has tolerated such conduct over a period of time. *Bracebridge* suggests that the nature of the conduct is relevant. However, one could argue that no one should have to be subjected to any act of harassment no matter how insignificant it may appear to members of the tribunal.

Racial insults can amount to harassment but only where it can be shown that they were directed towards the complainant or were it was reasonably likely to have an effect on his or her feelings so that a detriment has been suffered (*De Souza* v *Automobile Association* [1986] ICR 514). See also *McAuley* v *Auto Alloys Foundry* (1994) IT Case No. 62824/93 in which the IT upheld a complaint by an Irishman who was subjected to racial insults which resulted in his dismissal following his complaints to his employer. The employer dismissed him for having an 'attitude problem'. See also *Mecca Leisure Group plc* v *Chatprachong* [1993] ICR 688.

Once the complainant has established that harassment has taken place, she must show that she has suffered a detriment within s. 6 of the SDA 1975 and s. 4 of the RRA 1976. We would argue that if harassment has been established this is in itself detrimental treatment of the person concerned. However, the EAT has ruled in *Snowball* v *Gardner Merchant Ltd* [1987] ICR 719, that evidence of the complainant's attitude to sexual (or racial) matters is admissible in establishing whether the harassment is to his or her detriment. In *Wileman* v *Minilec Engineering Ltd* [1988] IRLR 144, EAT, whilst, albeit *obiter*, deciding that the act of harassment amounts to 'subjecting to any other detriment', the tribunal went on to award £50 compensation based on the fact that the complainant wore scanty and provocative clothes to work.

Both the SDA 1975 and the RRA 1976, ss. 41 and 32 respectively, provide that the employer is vicariously liable for discriminatory acts including harassment on the part of their employees. The discriminator may or may not be in a superior position to the complainant (see *Bracebridge* which involved discrimination by a supervisor and *Porcelli* which involved employees in the same post).

You should note that an employer may avoid liability where he can show that he has investigated claims of harassment even though he has subsequently not taken any action because of the lack of evidence (*Balgobin* v *Tower Hamlets London Borough Council* [1987] ICR 829). Where an employer has a code of practice or policy on harassment he must be seen to put it into practice.

There have been developments relating to sexual harassment following the adoption by the European Council of Labour and Social Ministers of the resolution relating to sexual harassment (resolution No. 6015/90) which arose out of a report by Michael Rubenstein on the dignity of women and men at work. This led to a Commission recommendation and the publication of a code of practice on sexual harassment. Whilst the recommendation and the code of practice are not binding, in *Grimaldi* v *Fonds des Maladies Professionelles* [1990] IRLR 400 the ECJ ruled that national courts must take such non-binding measures into account in clarifying the interpretation of other provisions of European and national law; see also *Wadman* v *Carpenter Farrer Partnership* [1993] IRLR 374. Also note the effect of TURERA 1993 in restricting publicity in sexual harassment cases.

Finally the fact that the respondent employs other black people or men, for example, does not prevent an act being discriminatory; moreover, a single discriminatory act will suffice. In *Johnson* v *Timber Tailors (Midlands) Ltd* [1978] IRLR 146 a Jamaican was successful in his action under RRA 1976 even though there was only one act of discrimination against him, and a West Indian and Asians were employed by the defendant.

Segregation (RRA 1976, s. 1(2))

Segregation is a form of direct discrimination. You should appreciate that just because all the workers employed in a certain department or to do a certain job are of a particular racial group does not mean that there has been unlawful segregation on racial grounds. To be unlawful there has to be evidence that the segregation has arisen because of some policy on the part of the employer or person concerned. Following *Pel Ltd* v *Modgill* [1980] IRLR 142, there appears to be no onus on the employer to adopt a positive policy to prevent 'natural segregation' of races occurring.

Indirect discrimination

Indirect discrimination is aimed at conduct or practice which on its face appears to be neutral or innocuous rather than discriminatory but has an adverse or disparate impact on a particular sex or race. Unfortunately the wording of the legislation limits its scope. It also raises a number of legal issues as far as the student is concerned. Certainly the wording of s. 1(1)(b) of SDA 1975 and RRA 1976 has been open to a number of interpretations. It is important for you, when applying this section, not to lose sight of the fact that there are three elements which have to be established on the part of the applicant: requirement or condition, proportion and compliance and detriment.

Requirement or condition   As far as the tribunal is concerned there is a series of questions of fact which need to be answered before the act of indirect discrimination can be said to be unlawful. In race cases, following *Tower Hamlets London Borough Council* v *Qayyum* [1987] ICR 729, the tribunal should:

(a)   Identify the applicant's colour, race, nationality or ethnic group.
(b)   Ascertain whether there is a racial group similar to his.
(c)   See whether there has been a requirement or condition imposed generally irrespective of race.
(d)   Decide whether the proportion of the racial group to which he belongs and to which the requirement or condition applies is considerably smaller than the relevant comparable proportion of the indigenous group.

(Obviously only questions (c) and (d) are relevant to sex discrimination.) See also *Raval* v *Department of Health and Social Security* [1985] ICR 685.

The initial burden of proof is on the complainant or applicant to establish that there is a requirement or condition. This can be a precisely defined requirement, as in *Price* v *Civil Service Commission* [1978] ICR 27, or it can be a number of 'vague factors' as long as it *must* be complied with. In *Clarke* v *Eley (IMI) Kynoch Ltd* [1982] IRLR 482 it was held that the words 'requirement' and 'condition' should not be given a narrow construction and should include 'anything which fairly falls within the ordinary meaning of either word' (p. 485). This is a significant hurdle for the applicant. In *Meer* v *London Borough of Tower Hamlets* [1988] IRLR 399 one of the criteria used in selecting applicants for the post of head of the legal department was experience within Tower Hamlets. Meer, who was of Indian origin, had local government experience but had not worked for Tower Hamlets. He was not short-listed for the post. He complained that this experience amounted to a requirement or condition. The Court of Appeal held that the criterion relating to Tower Hamlets experience was not a 'must' even though all four people on the short list had such experience. It was therefore outside the Act, as a requirement or condition was something which must be complied with (see *Perera* v *Civil Service Commission (No. 2)* [1983] ICR 428 where it was held that a requirement or condition had to be an absolute bar to selection).

You may wish to note that M. Rubenstein in McCrudden (ed.), *Women, Employment and European Equality Law* (Eclipse, 1987), has suggested that any requirement or condition which operates as an absolute bar could be challenged using, Directive 76/207. In *Bhudi v IMI Refiners Ltd* [1994] ICR 307 it was concluded that there is no obligation on a UK court to construe s. 1(1)(b) in such a way as to disregard the express provision relating to proof of a 'requirement or condition'; thereby confining the decision in *Enderby v Frenchay Health Authority* [1994] ICR 112 to the interpretation and application of art. 119.

Whilst establishing a requirement or condition has proved to be a contentious area for students, this has also been the case for women who wish to work half or part-time. You need to be aware of the current state of play. It was thought that a requirement to work full-time amounted to a requirement or condition (*Home Office v Holmes* [1985] 1 WLR 71). However, in *Clymo v Wandsworth London Borough Council* [1989] ICR 250, it was held that full-time work may be, required because of the nature of the job; in which case it would not be a requirement or condition. The court distinguished between the requirement for a senior librarian to work full-time and a cleaner. In respect of the former, it would be the nature of the job and outside the SDA 1975, whereas, in respect of the latter, it would amount to a requirement or condition. It is hoped that the position has been clarified by *Briggs v North Eastern Education & Library Board* [1990] IRLR 181 in which it was held that even where it is the nature of the job which requires full-time attendance, this can still amount to a requirement or condition which is being applied to the complainant. Finally, even where the applicant is permitted to work on a half or part-time contract, she cannot necessarily select which days or hours she works. See *Greater Glasgow Health Board v Carey* [1987] IRLR 494, where the applicant was allowed to return to work on a half-time contract. She wanted to work five half days and her employer wanted her to work $2\frac{1}{2}$ full days. This requirement was found to be justified as leading to a more efficient and customer responsive health visitor service. Mere rejection for a post on an amalgam of factors does not amount to the application of a requirement or condition but is merely a failure to defeat competitors (*Brook v London Borough of Haringey* [1992] IRLR 478).

A contentious issue for the student is whether in applying the requirement or condition the employer must intend to discriminate. Certainly if we have regard to SDA 1975, s. 66(3), or RRA 1976, s. 57(3), no compensation is to be awarded for indirect discrimination where it is unintentional even though it is unlawful. There is therefore little point in bringing an action for unintentional indirect discrimination if the purpose of your action is compensation as can be seen from *Orphanos v Queen Mary College* [1985] AC 761.

Proportion or compliance Once you have overcome the first hurdle of establishing a requirement or condition you must show that the proportion of the applicant's race or sex who can comply with the requirement or condition is considerably smaller than the proportion of another race or sex. You must appreciate that the selection of the correct pool for comparison is of critical importance to the applicant's case. Should the applicant select the incorrect pool as far as the tribunal is concerned her case will fail; any statistical evidence must relate to the correct pool (see *Pearse* v *City of Bradford Metropolitan Council* [1988] IRLR 379). A contentious issue is the question with whom should the protected group be compared? In *Meeks* v *National Union of Agricultural & Allied Workers* [1976] IRLR 198, a race case, it was suggested that the group for comparison could be the whole country if appropriate. This is most certainly too wide to satisfy the tribunal in sex discrimination cases. In *Pearse* the EAT decided that the correct pool for comparison was those qualified for the post, as opposed to those eligible for the post: the former being a smaller pool than the pool selected by the applicant and about which she had no statistics. In *University of Manchester* v *Jones* [1993] ICR 474, the Court of Appeal held that the appropriate pool for comparison is all those with the required qualifications for the post not including the requirement complained of. The pool cannot be manipulated to fit the applicant's own situation. Remember the 'like with like' comparison is also relevant.

However, statistical evidence alone may not be sufficient because the applicant must show that a 'considerably smaller proportion' cannot comply with the requirement or condition. If statistical evidence is to be used successfully it must be specific; e.g., if the requirement or condition affects part-time workers and you want to show that the majority of part-time workers are female, your statistical evidence must show this (*Kidd* v *DRG (UK) Ltd* [1985] ICR 405). 'Proportion' is a question of fact in each case. A case which you might find helpful is *Greencroft Social Club & Institute* v *Mullen* [1985] ICR 796. In this case it was argued that where no women could comply with the requirement of membership this did not amount to a smaller proportion. Fortunately this argument was rejected by the EAT. 'Nil' can therefore be regarded as a proportion. In *Fulton* v *Strathclyde Regional Council* (1986) 315 IRLIB 19, the employer imposed a requirement of full-time employment for certain social work posts. The statistics showed that at least 90% of the women and all of the men employed as basic-grade social workers could comply with this condition. It was held that 90% was not a considerably smaller proportion than 100%. We would argue that the area of comparison selected by the tribunal was incorrect in this case. Instead of comparing all female social workers employed by the council with all of the men, only the part-time female workers should have been compared with the men.

Statistical evidence is of growing importance in establishing the disparate impact of the requirement or condition. The search for statistics places an unduly heavy burden on the applicant, who may have difficulty obtaining such information even if it is available. In *Perera* v *Civil Service Commission (No. 2)* [1983] ICR 428, EAT, it was accepted that the applicant need not produce elaborate statistical evidence. Whether this is still the case must be questionable.

The disparate impact of the requirement or condition is to be shown as a percentage. C. Palmer, Discrimination at Work, 2nd ed. (London: Legal Action Group, 1992), suggest the following template:

(a)   take the number of women in the pool;
(b)   take the number of women in the pool who can meet the requirement or condition;
(c)   divide (b) by (a) to give the proportion of women in the pool who can satisfy the requirement or condition.

The same calculation should now be done for the men and a comparison made.

As you will by now appreciate proving disparate or adverse impact can be a problem. In America a four-fifths rule operates whereby if the minority group is less than four-fifths of the majority group who can comply with the requirement or condition, disparate impact is proved. Would it help the applicant if a similar rule was adopted in the UK?

You must consider the proportion of women or men or the racial group *who can* comply with it. This does not include looking at past opportunities to comply. The relevant date is the date the discriminatory conduct operated so as to create the alleged detriment (*Clarke* v *Eley (IMI) Kynoch Ltd* [1982] IRLR 482). The words 'can comply' have been held to mean 'can comply in practice' (*Price* v *Civil Service Commission* [1978] ICR 27). It is not acceptable to argue theoretically that, for example, women or Sikhs are eligible when in reality they are not.

Detriment   You are then faced with the problem of 'detriment'. The applicant must show that the requirement or condition is to his or her detriment. This word arises in a different context in SDA 1975, s. 6(2)(b), and RRA 1976, s. 4(2)(c). There has been little legal discussion of the words in s. 1(1)(b) but some discussion of the words 'any other detriment' in ss. 6 and 4. The two issues are:

(a)   Should the word 'detriment' be given the same meaning in s. 1 as in ss. 6 and 4?
(b)   What is the meaning of 'detriment' in s. 1? This question stands irrespective of the first question.

Let us consider whether the word detriment means the same throughout both statutes. Some books, such as Smith and Wood, *Industrial Law*, and *Rideout's Principles of Labour Law* do not consider 'detriment' as a problem under s. 1(1)(b) and certainly do not clarify whether it should have the same meaning as in ss. 6 and 4. Bowers and Honeyball, *Textbook on Labour Law* only considers the meaning given to the words in ss. 6 and 4. However, Wedderbum suggests in *The Worker and the Law* that the word 'detriment' has the same meaning in each of the respective sections although to illustrate this he uses cases which have considered the interpretation of 'detriment' in respect of ss. 6 and 4, e.g., *Ministry of Defence v Jeremiah* [1980] ICR 13 and *De Souza v Automobile Association* [1986] ICR 514, i.e., there is a need to show 'injury'. We would suggest that to give 'detriment' the same meaning in s. 1 as in ss. 6 and 4 is to consider the word out of context.

We would argue that in s. 1 'detriment' is merely limiting the applicant to a person who has actually been affected by the requirement or condition and prevents any other body from bringing an action on their behalf, e.g., a trade union, i.e., it provides locus standi. Furthermore we would submit that the decision in *Home Office v Holmes* [1985] 1 WLR 71 is the correct approach to the meaning of 'detriment' in s. 1(1)(b) in that if the complainant cannot comply with the requirement or condition it follows that it must be to his or her detriment. 'Detriment' can therefore be equated with mere incapacity to comply. However, there is at least one decision which runs counter to this approach (see *Raval v Department of Health and Social Security* [1985] ICR 685).

Justification   The onus now moves to the respondent to show that the requirement or condition is justifiable irrespective of the sex or race of the person to whom it is applied. The difficulty faced by the student is in respect of the criteria laid down by the courts in assessing justification. Whether a requirement or condition is justified is a question of fact in each case. In *Steel v Union of Post Office Workers* [1978] ICR 181 Phillips J stated that the tribunal, in considering justification, 'had to weigh up the needs of the enterprise against the discriminatory effect of the requirement or condition'. He went on to say that the tribunal must be satisfied that the requirement or condition is necessary not merely convenient. Furthermore it should look to the future when considering the effect if allowed to continue; and it should consider whether there is a non-discriminatory method of obtaining the same objective. We would suggest that this was the soundest criterion for establishing justification. However, as you must appreciate, this criterion has gradually been eroded in subsequent cases.

In *Singh v Rowntree Mackintosh Ltd* [1979] ICR 554 it was held that a requirement, to be justified, must be more than convenient but not absolutely essential. Commercial necessity, if reasonable, can be grounds for justifying a requirement or condition. This was certainly an erosion of the interpretation given in *Steel's* case. However, subsequent cases have gone even further. In *Ojutiku* v *Manpower Services Commission* [1982] ICR 661 the test of necessity in *Steel's* case was totally rejected. The Court of Appeal gave the following interpretation of the word 'justifiable':

> . . . if a person produces reasons for doing something, which would be acceptable to right-thinking people, as sound and tolerable reasons for so doing, then he has justified his conduct.

It was accepted by the court that this applied a lower standard than the word 'necessary'. However, the decision in *Ojutiku* is no longer to be regarded as good law. It has been overtaken by the decision in *Rainey* v *Greater Glasgow Health Board* [1987] AC 224 and *Hampson* v *Department of Education and Science* [1989] ICR 179. In *Hampson* the Court of Appeal concluded that the test of 'justifiability' should be consistent with the test used to justify a genuine material difference/factor in EPA 1970, s. 1(3), i.e., 'justifiable' requires an objective balance between the discriminatory effect of the condition and the reasonable needs of the party who applies the condition. Note that in the past such things as safety (*Singh* v *British Rail Engineering Ltd* [1986] ICR 22) and hygiene (*Singh* v *Rowntree Mackintosh Ltd* [1979] ICR 554) have justified an act of discrimination.

Pregnancy   Pregnancy has posed a particular problem for the courts as far as sex discrimination is concerned. To treat a woman differently because she was pregnant was thought, following *Turley* v *Allders Department Stores Ltd* [1980] ICR 66, not to amount to sex discrimination because there was no male equivalent for comparison. The EAT suggested that a pregnant woman could not be compared with an ordinary male. This approach was modified in *Hayes* v *Malleable Working Men's Club & Institute* [1985] ICR 703 and approved in *Webb* v *EMO Air Cargo (UK) Ltd* [1993] 1 WLR 49 where it was held that the treatment of the pregnant woman can be compared with the sick man', e.g., a man who is about to have time off work due to illness. However, the decision of the ECJ in *Webb* v *EMO Air Cargo (UK) Ltd* [1994] QB 718 has finally brought UK law in line with European law, by declaring that not only is it contrary to Directive 76/207 to dismiss a woman on grounds of pregnancy, but also that there is no question of comparing the situation of a woman who finds herself incapable by reason of pregnancy of performing the task for which she was recruited with that of a man similarly incapable for medical or other reasons. The ECJ did distinguish between pregnant women employed for an indefinite period, who are afforded protection, and those on limited-term contracts, e.g., to cover maternity leave.

You need to consider European law in this field as it has not taken the restrictive route pursued by the national courts and has proved to be the ultimate influence on UK law. In *Dekker* v *Stichting Vormingscentrum voor Jong Volwassenen (VJV-Centrum) Plus* [1992] ICR 325, the ECJ held that unfavourable treatment on grounds of pregnancy amounted to direct discrimination on grounds of sex because pregnancy is a condition unique to women so that where it can be shown that unfavourable treatment is on the grounds of pregnancy, that treatment is, by definition, on grounds of sex. The importance of this decision is that there is no need for the pregnant woman to compare herself with the hypothetical man, sick or healthy. However, the case of *Handels- og Kontorfunktionærernes Forbund i Danmark* v *Dansk Arbejdsgiverforening* [1991] IRLR 31, reintroduces the comparison with the sick man albeit in limited circumstances. The ECJ upheld the view that a pregnant woman is entitled to protection from discrimination not only during her pregnancy but also during any maternity leave to which she is entitled under national law. However, should the woman fall ill after the end of her maternity leave with a pregnancy related illness, her treatment by the employer should be compared with his treatment of the hypothetical sick man. Accordingly, if a woman worker is dismissed because of a pregnancy related illness but a sick man would have been treated in the same way, there is no breach of Directive 76/207. Whilst this case extends the protection to the pregnant female so that her maternity leave is also a protected period, once she returns to work we have to return to that false comparison with the sick man. Finally in *Habermann-Beltermann* v *Arbeiterwohlfahrt, Bezirksverband* [1994] IRLR 364, the ECJ blocked a potential loophole in the legislation by holding that an employer could not use a provision in German national law preventing night work during pregnancy as a reason for avoiding a contract in which work was to be performed at night as to do so would deprive the Directive of its effectiveness.

Furthermore you should note the impact of the pregnant workers Directive (92/95) which has already resulted in changes to statutory maternity leave and pay; in addition it has removed the qualifying period of two years for claims of unfair dismissal on grounds of pregnancy or maternity (TURERA 1993 amends EPCA 1978, s. 60).

Part-time workers   The cases suggest that there is a tendency by employers to regard part-time employees in a different light to full-time employees, e.g., part-time staff may well be selected for redundancy before full-time staff. This in turn may amount to discrimination where it can be shown that the majority of part-time staff are female. We know from the case law that it cannot be assumed as far as the courts are concerned that the majority of part-time employees are female because of their domestic roles (*Kidd* v *DRG (UK) Ltd* [1985] ICR 405) although it can be argued that the decision in *Home*

Office v *Holmes* [1985] 1 WLR 71 is to be preferred. However, the main problem when considering the position of part-time staff lies in establishing the fields of comparison. Some assistance may be found in *Wright* v *Rugby B.C.* (1985) 276 IRLIB 10 where a woman who returned from maternity leave was originally allowed to work different hours from her previous contract. This arrangement was then discontinued by her employer. It was decided that the pool of comparison should be women of child-bearing age and men of the same age seeking, or in, full-time employment. This being the case it was found that the proportion of women who could comply with the requirement to work fixed hours prescribed by the employer was considerably smaller than the proportion of men who could comply with it, 'having regard to the background of the custom in our society that women are usually those who have the greater responsibility for the care of extremely young children'.

This case recognises that the selection of the 'pool' for comparison is of importance and can obviously make a difference to the outcome of the case. In *Price* v *Civil Service Commission* [1978] ICR 27 it was stressed that it may be proper to consider as the pool available for this purpose something less than the total female and male population, for example, a particular age group.

When you are faced with this problem, you would be wise to think carefully about the pool of comparison as it can affect the complainant's chances of success (see *Pearse* v *City of Bradford Metropolitan Council* [1988] IRLR 379; *University of Manchester* v *Jones* [1993] ICR 474). You should also be aware that even if the correct pool is selected a successful outcome is not guaranteed.

Married persons Married persons are given specific protection from discrimination in the employment field (SDA 1975, s. 3). It is therefore unlawful to refuse to consider a person for a job because he or she is married. In *Hurley* v *Mustoe* [1981] ICR 490 a requirement that employees must not have young children was found to discriminate on grounds of marital status as more married women than unmarried have young children. The problem highlighted by this section is that there is no specific protection for single people in the employment field. It is therefore lawful for an employer to refuse to employ a person just because he or she is single. Section 3 does not comply with Directive 76/207, art. 2; there is therefore plenty of scope for SDA 1975 to be challenged yet again in the ECJ.

Victimisation (SDA 1975, s. 4; RRA 1976, s. 2)
You should find few problems with this area of discrimination. The alleged victimisation must be due to an act by the complainant which falls within

s. 2 or s. 4 respectively. However, we must stress that it is clearly not victimisation if the employer can show that he would have treated any one of his employees in the same way as he treated the complainant for doing what he did. This is illustrated in *Aziz v Trinity Street Taxis Ltd* [1986] IRLR 435 where Mr Aziz, who suspected he was being treated unfairly on the grounds of his race, taped conversations of fellow members of Trinity Street Taxis Ltd with the intention of using them in proceedings against the company. The tape recordings were not used in evidence but their existence was discovered during the proceedings and as a result Aziz was expelled from membership of the company. The EAT held that Aziz must prove that one of the activities laid down in s. 2 was the real and substantial cause for the expulsion if a claim for victimisation was to succeed. This was found not to be the case as the real reason for the expulsion was the making of the tapes which would have resulted in the expulsion of any member who had done the same as Aziz. See also *University College of Swansea v Cornelius* [1988] ICR 735. A complaint of victimisation must relate to the actions of the employer during the employee's employment, not action taken after the employee has ceased to be employed (*Nagarajan v Agnew* [1994] IRLR 61).

Employment   You must make sure that you make the link between s. 1 *et seq.* and SDA 1975, s. 6, and RRA 1976, s. 4, remembering that s. 1 *et seq.* lay down the types of discrimination whilst ss. 6 and 4 specifically cover acts of discrimination in the employment field. The latter is intended to cover every stage of employment from recruitment to dismissal.

Let us first consider any problems arising from the words 'employed' and 'employment'. 'Employed' has the same meaning as in EPA 1970 and you should refer to our earlier discussion of this — see *Quinnen v Hovells* [1984] ICR 525 and *Mirror Group Newspapers Ltd v Gunning* [1986] ICR 145 in the chapter on equal pay.

Whether an employer is in breach of SDA 1975, s. 6, or RRA 1976, s. 4, is a question of fact in each case. The sections themselves have rarely given rise to any substantive difficulties. All that you need do is ensure that you are aware of the types of factual situation found to be within the Acts. For example, you should note that the EAT has held that it is not unlawful in itself to ask questions of a female applicant which would not be asked of a male applicant, although it can show a discriminatory frame of mind (*Saunders v Richmond-upon-Thames Borough Council* [1978] ICR 75); such questions are not in themselves discriminatory and it is justifiable to ask such questions where it is proper to do so.

The only difficulty in relation to discrimination in the employment field is in respect of the meaning and interpretation of the words 'any other detriment'. We debated earlier whether detriment in SDA 1975, s. 6, and RRA 1976, s. 4, should have the same meaning as in s. 1. We know that the type of detriment suffered in ss. 6 and 4 can be the same as that suffered in s. 1 (*Home Office* v *Holmes* [1985] 1 WLR 71). Furthermore the courts have attempted to give an interpretation of 'detriment' as used in these sections. In *Ministry of Defence* v *Jeremiah* [1980] ICR 13 Brandon LJ (at p. 26) suggested that 'detriment' in RRA 1976, s. 6(2)(b), meant nothing more than 'putting under a disadvantage'. If this is the case, the question to be asked is: Does the difference in treatment put the women under a disadvantage by comparison with the men? This is certainly a wide interpretation of the Act and gives flexibility to the sections.

To some extent this flexibility has been maintained by the decisions in *Porcelli* v *Strathclyde Regional Council* [1986] ICR 564 and *De Souza* v *Automobile Association* [1986] ICR 514 where it was held that sexual and racial harassment can amount to 'any other detriment' within ss. 6 and 4. The wider *ratio* of these cases is that 'detriment' amounts to any conduct which would result in the reasonable worker taking the view that he had been disadvantaged in the circumstances in which he or she had to work. The Court of Appeal in *De Souza* v *Automobile Association* said:

. . . if . . . the discrimination was such that the putative reasonable employee could justifiably complain about his or her working conditions or environment, then whether or not these were so bad as to be able to amount to constructive dismissal, or even if the employee was prepared to work on and put up with the harassment, this too could contravene the subsections.

Obviously this can only be a question of fact in each case. The aftermath of the discriminatory act must be carefully considered to see if the employee has been disadvantaged. As we have seen, this interpretation has been accepted in *Snowball* v *Gardner Merchant Ltd* [1987] ICR 719 where it was held by the EAT that evidence about the employee's attitude to sexual matters is relevant to the issue of detriment in sexual harassment cases. The implication in this case is that if the employee is not embarrassed about discussing sexual matters, she is unlikely to succeed in a claim for sexual harassment because it is not to her detriment (see *Wileman* v *Minilec Engineering Ltd* [1988] IRLR 144). This is certainly an area where you should be on the look out for further developments.

Exceptions There are specific exceptions laid down in the legislation although SDA 1975, s. 6, has been amended so that most of the contentious issues have been removed. SDA 1975, s. 6(4), caused most problems by having a blanket exclusion of provisions in respect of death and retirement. The retirement exemption had been challenged unsuccessfully in *Roberts* v *Cleveland Area Health Authority* [1979] 1 WLR 754. The Court of Appeal at that time gave a very wide interpretation to the word 'retirement'. However, the ECJ in *Marshall* v *Southampton & South West Hampshire Area Health Authority (Teaching)* [1986] QB 401 held that a general policy concerning dismissal of a woman solely because she has attained the qualifying age for a State pension, this age being different under national legislation for men and women, constitutes discrimination on grounds of sex contrary to Directive 76/207. Furthermore, SDA 1975, s. 6(4), was found to conflict with the Directive. *Marshall's* case was subsequently applied in *Parsons* v *East Surrey Health Authority* [1986] ICR 837. As a result of the ECJ decision s. 6(4) was amended so that exclusions relating to retirement are restricted, but see *Bullock* v *Alice Ottley School* [1993] ICR 138 which permits an employer to have a variety of retiring ages for different jobs, provided that there is no direct or indirect discrimination based on gender. Although, in theory, monetary benefits or similar benefits obtainable on retirement, are excluded from the legislative provisions where they are linked to the State social security scheme, the Social Security Act 1989 which implements Directive 86/378 (the equal treatment for men and women in occupational social security schemes Directive) provides that any discriminatory scheme still in existence after 1 January 1993 will be overridden. The EPA 1970 and SDA 1975 will be amended with the result that it will become unlawful to discriminate on grounds of sex or marital status in respect of access to benefits, facilities and services under an occupational pension scheme. As you will by now be aware, the Social Security Act has been overtaken by events, e.g., the decision of the ECJ in *Barber* v *Guardian Royal Exchange Assurance Group* [1991] 1 QB 344. There must also be some doubt about the decision in *Burton* v *British Railways Board* [1982] QB 1080, although this case succeeded because the discrimination arose out of the State pensionable ages and therefore fell within the permitted acts excluded by the social security Directive 79/7. However, in *Roberts* v *Tate & Lyle Industries Ltd* [1986] ICR 371, the ECJ stressed the difference between retirement and pensionable ages, the exclusion only applying to State pensionable age. The effect of the amendment to the SDA 1975 is far-reaching, resulting in changes to the law on equal pay, unfair dismissal, redundancy etc. You may wish to refer to (1987) 337 IRLIB for a comprehensive discussion of these changes.

You also need to consider the effect of the Employment Act 1989 on the SDA 1975 as it removes the restrictions on the types of work which women can do. For example, women are no longer prohibited from working underground in mines or cleaning factory machinery; restricted on the number of hours worked, shifts etc.; also restrictions from applying to specific industries such as potteries and bakeries are removed. You should, however, be aware of s. 55 of the SDA 1975, which still provides a limited exception from the Act on grounds of health and safety.

Finally, for an interpretation of the words 'in pursuance of any instrument' in s. 41 of the RRA 1976 (excluded acts done under a statutory authority), see *Hampson* v *Department of Education and Science* [1991] 1 AC 171, HL, where it was decided that these words are confined to acts done in the necessary performance of an express obligation contained in the instrument and do not include acts done in the exercise of a power or discretion conferred by the instrument. It was reasoned that any other interpretation would have provided a wide loophole in this provision.

Genuine occupational qualification (SDA 1975, s. 7; RRA 1976, s. 5)   There are plenty of ways for an employer to escape the rigours of the statutes. On the one hand, he can attempt to justify any act of indirect discrimination or, on the other, he can show that sex or race is a genuine occupational qualification (GOQ). (Note that there are fewer GOQs in RRA 1976, s. 5.) The emphasis here is on the word 'genuine' and on the whole these sections have not been beset by substantive difficulties. You should ensure that you know the full range of GOQs and are *au fait* with such cases as *Wylie* v *Dee & Co. (Menswear) Ltd* [1978] IRLR 103; *Sisley* v *Britannia Security Systems Ltd* [1983] IRLR 404; and *Etam plc* v *Rowan* [1989] IRLR 150.

One contentious point has arisen regarding the meaning of 'personal service'. In *Lambeth London Borough Council* v *CRE* [1990] ICR 768, CA, it was held that the word 'personal' required direct contact between the provider of that service and the client if the GOQ was to apply. The provision would not therefore protect a post where there is no face to face contact. However, the 'personal service' does not have to be the main service provided by the post to fall within the GOQ provisions (see *Tottenham Green under Fives' Centre* v *Marshall (No. 2)* [1991] IRLR 162) as long as it is a required attribute of the post holder and not a sham or so trivial it should be disregarded.

Compensation
It is clear from the case of *Marshall* v *Southampton and South West Hampshire Health Authority (Teaching) (No. 2)* [1994] QB 126 that interest is payable on compensation awards for discrimination and that any award should not be subject to an upper limit set by national law. The reasoning behind this being that financial compensation must be adequate and that it must enable loss and damage actually sustained as a result of the discrimination to be made good. Note the Sex Discrimination and Equal Pay (Remedies) Regulations 1993 and the Race Relations (Remedies) Act 1994. All awards for compensation should also include a sum for injury to feelings (*Murray* v *Powertech (Scotland) Ltd* [1992] IRLR 257; *Sharifi* v *Strathclyde Regional Council* [1992] IRLR 259). Following *Alexander* v *Home Office* [1988] 1 WLR 968, compensation can include injury to feelings, humiliation and insult as

well as pecuniary loss. The decision in *Deane* v *Ealing London Borough Council* [1993] ICR 329 has thrown doubt on the availability of exemplary damages in discrimination cases, although it could be argued that the decision in the *Ministry of Defence* v *Cannock* [1994] ICR 918 provides a counter-argument as the EAT held that the correct measure of damages in a complaint brought directly under the EC Directive is tortious rather than contractual as discrimination is a statutory tort. Therefore the applicant must be put in the position he or she would have been in but for the unlawful conduct of the defendant.

Other Unlawful Acts

These are to be found in SDA 1975, ss. 37 to 42, and RRA 1976, ss. 28 to 33. They cover such things as discriminatory advertisements, instructions to discriminate etc. As yet they have not proved to be problematic for the student (or the courts). However, you should make sure you know and understand these provisions and the machinery for enforcing them.

The Role of the EOC and the CRE

The only substantive difficulty has arisen when the powers of the CRE and EOC have been called into question (see *CRE* v *Amari Plastics Ltd* [1982] IRLR 252; *R* v *CRE, ex parte Cottrell and Rothon* [1980] 1 WLR 1580) and this is really a matter of public law. You should, however, be aware of the importance of the role of the EOC and CRE, including their remit and powers. As mentioned earlier, the EOC has begun judicial review proceedings to challenge the validity of the limits on the employment protection rights of part-time workers. You should also be cognisant of their respective codes of practice.

Relationship of SDA 1975 and EPA 1970

This sometimes poses problems for students. The SDA 1975 and EPA 1970 are to be regarded as a single code promoting equal treatment. However, the basic rule is that there is no overlap between the two statutes. If the applicant is in any doubt regarding the statute under which his or her claim should fall the decision can be left to the tribunal. As a general rule, pay and related matters arising out of the contract of employment are covered by EPA 1970. A word of warning, as the word 'pay' receives a wider interpretation obviously more and more benefits will be regarded as 'related matters'. Different treatment in relation to any other matter, whether it arises before the existence of a contract of employment or out of the contract of employment, will be governed by SDA 1975. Figure 5.1 may assist you.

Figure 5.1

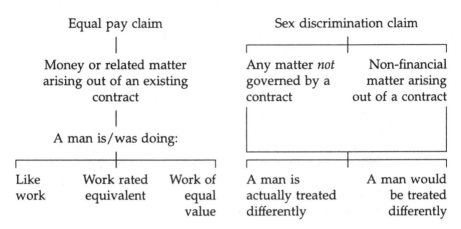

THE EXAMINATION

We stressed earlier when we considered equal pay that sex discrimination could easily be mixed in with a problem on equal pay or dismissal. You may even find that sex, race and dismissal are all to be found in one problem. Don't panic. Read through the question carefully and make a plan outlining all the issues. Remember this plan is for *your* benefit and should be used to ensure that your thoughts are structured into an order relevant to the problem or essay. Remember to stick to a strict time-limit!

Illustrative Problem

Westbury Health Authority has advertised for a supervisor to take charge of its domestic staff (i.e., cleaners). Mavis, aged 36 years, is employed as a part-time cleaner by the health authority. She used to work full-time for the authority but five years previously she took maternity leave and decided to work part time because of family commitments. She applies for the job as supervisor.

There are three other applicants for the job.

Peter, who has been employed as a cleaner for two years by the health authority; Edith, aged 58 years, who is an experienced cleaner, and Frank also aged 58 years who has only had experience of kitchen work.

Edith is told by personnel that she is not eligible for interview because she is too close to the State retirement age. Frank is interviewed but does not get the job because of his lack of experience.

Mavis attends a preliminary interview. She is asked questions about how she will cope working full time with a family to look after. She is subsequently informed by personnel that part-time staff are not eligible for the post. She later discovers that Peter, who is promoted to supervisor, did not have to attend a preliminary interview and when he was interviewed was not asked questions about his home life.

Brian, a white Rastafarian, was dismissed from his job as a mortuary attendant two months ago. The reason for his dismissal, according to personnel, is that he cannot wear a protective surgical cap when attending post-mortems because of his dreadlocks and will not have them cut off. He has received numerous warnings, some of which he has taped in case of such an eventuality; personnel's discovery of the tapes coincided with his dismissal although they claim the tapes have no bearing on their decision.

Ruth has been employed as a radiographer in the X-ray department for 12 months. Within two months of informing personnel that she is pregnant, she is dismissed.

Advise Westbury Health Authority.

Analysis

The first point you should note is that you have to consider the problem from the point of view of the health authority, i.e. how can it avoid liability. However, in considering this you must consider whether there is, as a matter of fact and law, a case against the authority. Remember, before the authority sets about justifying its actions the burden is on the complainant to establish discrimination. We shall still have to consider the position of each complainant and the health authority in turn.

Mavis v Westbury Health Authority

The first issue for consideration is: Has there been an act of discrimination by the health authority within SDA 1975, ss. 1 and 6? You must ask the question: Has Mavis been treated less favourably than a man by reason of her sex (s. 1(1)(a)) or is there a requirement or condition etc. within s. 1(1)(b)? On the evidence Mavis's strongest case probably rests on establishing indirect discrimination. You must then consider the three things which the complainant must establish. The requirement or condition poses little problem, i.e., the post is only open to full-time staff. Reference should be made to the dictum in *Clarke* v *Eley (IMI) Kynoch Ltd* [1982] IRLR 482. The health authority could argue that in applying the requirement it did not intend to discriminate. However, motive is irrelevant (*Grieg* v *Community Industry* [1979] ICR 356). She will then need to produce evidence that the proportion of women who can comply with the requirement or condition is considerably smaller than the proportion of men. This is a question of fact. You should stress the importance in selecting the correct pool for comparison (*Pearse* v *City of Bradford Metropolitan Council* [1988]

IRLR 379). She will probably need statistical evidence which shows that the majority of part-time workers are female. The point should be made that following *Kidd* v *DRG (UK) Ltd* [1985] ICR 405 the statistical evidence must specifically relate to the claims made. At this point the health authority could attempt to discredit such evidence by producing its own statistics, although, following *Wright* v *Rugby BC* (1985) 276 IRLIB 10 it may have some difficulty in disproving that traditionally women work part-time because of family commitmaning of 'can comply' (*Price* v *Civil Service Commission* [1978] ICR 27). The health authority could argue that in the past she had been able to comply with the requirement. You must point out that it is on weak ground because past opportunities to comply are not relevant (*Clarke* v *Eley (IMI) Kynoch Ltd*).

Mavis must then show that it is to her detriment that she cannot comply with the requirement. Now you are faced with the argument about the meaning of 'detriment'. You may argue that because the condition effectively bars her from being considered for promotion this must be to her detriment. The health authority could argue at this point that, applying *Raval* v *Department of Health and Social Security* [1985] ICR 685, it is not to her detriment because she could have easily met the requirement by becoming a full-time cleaner (bearing in mind that the supervisor's job is full-time so she must now be in a position to do this). If Mavis succeeds in establishing unlawful discrimination it is open to the health authority to justify it (s. 1(1)(b)(iii)). The heath authority could claim that the requirement is necessary on grounds of efficiency, i.e., full-time staff are tried and tested and the authority knows that they are able to cope with the demands of a full-time job (*Greater Glasgow Health Board* v *Carey* [1987] IRLR 484). You must refer to the criteria for judging 'justifiable' (*Singh* v *Rowntree Mackintosh Ltd* [1979] IRLR 199; *Rainey* v *Greater Glasgow Health Board* [1987] AC 224; *Hampson* v *Department of Education and Science* [1989] ICR 179, CA).

Finally you should refer to art. 119 and the possibility of Mavis using European Community law, including the Directive, which she can do following *Marshall* v *Southampton & South West Hampshire Area Health Authority (Teaching)* [1986] QB 401.

If Mavis succeeds in establishing indirect discrimination she will then have to refer to s. 6(2). She may raise *Saunders* v *Richmond-upon-Thames Borough Council* [1978] ICR 75 regarding the question she was asked about her family life. However, the health authority can argue that it was a proper question to ask in the circumstances. She may stand a better chance of establishing discrimination in respect of the preliminary interview to which Peter was not subjected.

If Mavis succeeds (and you should not be concerned that your answer is inconclusive as long as you have considered all of the issues) it is open to the health authority to establish one of the exceptions within ss. 6 or 7;

however, none of these apply to this particular case. You should refer to SDA 1975, s. 65 (remedies available to the complainant) and make the point that compensation would not be awarded for unintentional indirect discrimination. Also you would be awarded marks for mentioning assistance by the EOC (s. 75).

Edith v Westbury Health Authority

The burden is on Edith as complainant to establish discrimination. The first issue is, what type of discrimination is it? She may have grounds for claiming that her treatment by the health authority amounts to direct discrimination (s. 1(1)(a)) in that she has been treated less favourably than a man on grounds of her sex. She certainly has the evidence to do this as Frank, who is the same age, is treated more favourably. You need to refer to the test for establishing direct discrimination (R v Birmingham City Council, ex parte EOC [1989] AC 1155), i.e., has there been an act of discrimination and, but for the complainant's sex, would she have been treated differently. The discrimination must be gender based (see James v Eastleigh Borough Council [1990] 2 AC 751).

She then has to bring her claim within s. 6, and she will be able to do so under s. 6(2) (refusal of access to opportunities for promotion). You must then consider whether the health authority can avoid liability. It may argue that retirement is excluded from the Act (s. 6). However, in the light of s. 6(4) as amended it is unlikely to succeed because retirement is not an acceptable reason for refusing access to opportunities for promotion. Again you should refer to the compensation which may be payable by the health authority. Reference should be made to cases such as Marshall v Southampton & South West Hampshire Area Health Authority (Teaching) and Directive 76/207.

Brian v Westbury Health Authority

Once more the first issue which you have to consider concerns the type of discrimination committed by the health authority. Is it direct discrimination, i.e., less favourable treatment on grounds of race (RRA 1976, s. 1(1)(a)), in which case the requirement that Brian wears a surgical cap would amount to personal treatment, or indirect discrimination — does the application of the requirement or condition apply to everyone in the mortuary? Brian may have considered direct discrimination if he could show the implementation of a 'dress code' which applied only to one sex. However, a 'dress code' which applies equally to both sexes as in this case does not amount to direct discrimination even though it may result in different dress for the respective sexes (Burrett v West Birmingham Health Authority [1994] IRLR 7). However the evidence suggests an act of indirect discrimination (RRA 1976, s. 1(1)(b)). You must therefore show that (a) there is a requirement or condition — in this case the wearing of the surgical cap in the post-mortem room; (b) that Brian belongs to a 'racial group'. You must refer to the meaning in s. 3(1). This poses a problem as it could be argued by the health authority that Rastafarianism is a religion and therefore is outside the scope of the Act. You must refer to the test in *Mandla v Dowell Lee* [1983] 2 AC 548, and the decision in *Crown Suppliers (Property Services Agency) v Dawkins* [1993] ICR 517.

Whilst the latter case supports the view that Rastafarianism is a religion, should Brian succeed in establishing that he is a member of a racial group, he must then show proportion and compliance (s. 1(1)(b)(i)). You are then faced with similar problems to those discussed earlier, i.e., the pool of comparison, use of statistical evidence and the meaning of the words 'can comply'. The pool of comparison is particularly significant as the health authority will be able to show that the requirement applies equally to other racial groups such as Sikhs who would also have great difficulty complying with the requirement. However, if the statistical evidence shows that the majority of men not of that racial group can comply with it then Brian will only have to show 'detriment'. Again you must refer to the issues raised earlier in respect of 'detriment'.

If Brian surmounts these hurdles the health authority can attempt to justify the requirement (s. 1(1)(b)(ii)). You are now faced with the test in *Hampson v Department of Education and Science* [1991] 1 AC 171. On the evidence, if the health authority pleaded safety and hygiene as its reason for justifying the requirement it would probably succeed as these are recognised grounds subject to the test in *Hampson*. You should refer to *Singh v British Rail Engineering Ltd* [1986] ICR 22 and *Singh v Rowntree Mackintosh Ltd* [1979] ICR 554. Reference would have to be made to s. 4 as the alleged discrimination is in respect of his dismissal (s. 4(2)(c)).

Should Brian fail under s. 1(1)(b), you must consider whether, from the facts, there is any other type of discrimination, e.g., is there victimisation? You would have to show that the health authority dismissed Brian because either he alleged that it had discriminated against him and the act of discrimination would have contravened the Act or that the health authority knows or suspects that Brian has or intends to make these allegations. This in itself may be difficult to establish. Even if Brian can show that he was dismissed for taping the warnings, if the health authority can show that any employee would have ben treated in the same way, its conduct will not amount to victimisation (*Aziz v Trinity Street Taxis Ltd* [1986] IRLR 435).

Finally you must point out that if Brian wants to bring his action before an industrial tribunal then, by virtue of s. 68, he has only one more month in which to do this.

Ruth v Westbury Health Authority

Webb v Emo Air Cargo (UK) Ltd [1994] QB 718 has removed the need for comparison with the sick man or his equivalent. She must still show, however, that her unfavourable treatment arises out of her pregnancy. Furthermore as a result of TURERA 1993, amending EPCA 1978, s. 60, it is now automatically unfair to dismiss a woman on grounds of pregnancy or for a reason connected with pregnancy. As the qualifying period has also been removed, Ruth may pursue a claim using s. 60. In addition reference should be made to the pregnant workers Directive 92/85. The effect of the Directive is to require the employer to alter the employee's working conditions to avoid an identified risk and where it is not reasonable to do this, the employer should suspend the employee from work on full pay. These provisions can now be found in the Management of Health and Safety at Work (Amendment) Regulations 1994 (SI 1994 No. 2865).

Essay Questions

You could be faced with an essay that is legalistic in approach, e.g., 'How far have the recent amendments to SDA 1975 brought UK law in line with European Community law?'

Such an essay should not be attempted unless you are confident that you know the requirements and effect of the article and Directive and can refer in detail to the cases where UK law has been called into question in the ECJ. You should also know what the specific amendments to the current statutes are.

Another type of essay question which may be set is one which requires you to look at the effectiveness of SDA 1975 or RRA 1976 in eliminating discrimination. This not only requires you to have a thorough knowledge of the statute but you must be able to deal with the wider sociological and economic aspects of discrimination, such as stereotyping. You should therefore not attempt such an essay unless you have done a lot of reading in the research areas concerning discrimination. The reading list at the end of the chapter provides some guidance.

CONCLUSION

The task of looking at both sex and race discrimination may seem daunting to you. However, if you treat them as virtually the same statute with interchangeable cases you have only to consider one topic i.e., discrimination. As with equal pay, apart from understanding the law and in particular the substantive difficulties, it is important that you read widely so that not only do you understand the wider aspects of this area of law but do not fall into the trap of adopting a purely legalistic approach which could limit the questions which you could answer satisfactorily.

READING

Age Concern, *Age, the Unrecognised Discrimination* (1991).

Bamforth, N., 'The changing concept of sex discrimination' (1993) 56 MLR 872.

Byre, A., *Indirect Discrimination* (Manchester: EOC, 1987).

CRE, Annual Reports.

CRE, Code of Practice.

CRE, *Second Review of the Race Relations Act* (1992).

Curran, M., *Stereotypes and Selection* (Manchester: EOC, 1986).

Ellis, E., *European Sex Equality Law* (Oxford: Clarendon Press, 1991).

EOC, Annual Reports.

EOC, Code of Practice.

EOC, *Equal Treatment for Men and Women: Strengthening the Acts* (Manchester: EOC, 1988).

EOC, *Fair and Efficient Selection* (Manchester: EOC, 1993).

Hepple, B., and Szyszczak, E.M. (eds.), *Discrimination: the Limits of the Law* (London: Mansell, 1992).

Lacey, N., 'Legislation against sex discrimination: questions from a feminist perspective' (1987) 14 J Law and Soc 411.

McCrudden, C. (ed.), *Women, Employment and European Equality Law* (Eclipse Publications, 1987).

McCrudden, C., *Racial Justice at Work* (PSI, 1991).

McCrudden, C., 'The effectiveness of European equality law' (1993) 13 Oxford J Legal Stud 320.

McLean, S., and Burrows, N. (eds.), *The Legal Relevance of Gender* (Basingstoke: Macmillan, 1988).

Midgal, S., and Holmes, A., 'Harassment at work: guidelines for employers' (1991) 12 Bus Law Rev 112.

Morris, A.E., and Nott. S.M., *Working Women and the Law* (London: Routledge, 1991).

6 *TERMINATION OF CONTRACT*

INTRODUCTION

The ending of the employment relationship is the most obvious and frequent source of litigation between employer and employee. The common law action of wrongful dismissal and the statutory rights to claim unfair dismissal and redundancy payments all depend on a dismissal taking place. If the employer can successfully advance the argument that the relationship terminated in a manner which did not involve dismissal then he can stop the employee's action in its tracks. In view of the mechanics of termination's practical importance it is not surprising that it frequently appears in employment law examination problems.

OVERVIEW

At the outset let us attempt to establish an accurate overview of the various modes of termination. Setting out the topic in such a way provides an excellent means of structuring your study. As you work through the topic, the skeletal structure may be expanded to include the leading cases together with references to any texts or articles you have consulted in the course of your studies. If a new case on the topic is decided during the course of the year it can be inserted into your topic overview at the appropriate place. It may often be the case that this overview may be provided by the lecture hand-out. Whether this is the case or you develop your own, always try to keep the overview as concise as possible because it will provide an excellent means of testing your grasp of the topic in the final stages of revision. An overview of termination might look something like this in its early stages.

(a) Termination not involving dismissal at common law:

(i) Death or dissolution of the employer.
(ii) Frustration.
(iii) Expiry of fixed-term contracts.
(iv) Mutual agreement.

(b) Termination involving dismissal at common law:

(i) Dismissal by notice.
(ii) Dismissal for fundamental breach.
(iii) Wrongful dismissal.

(c) Terminations deemed to be dismissals by statute:

(i) An act of the employer or an event affecting the employer (including death) which has the effect of terminating the contract automatically at common law (EPCA 1978, s. 93).

(ii) Termination of the contract with or without notice by the employer (ss. 55(2)(a) and 83(2)(b)).

(iii) The lapse of a fixed-term contract without renewal (EPCA 1978, ss. 55(2)(b) and 83(2)(b)).

(iv) Where the employee terminates the contract, with or without notice, in circumstances such that the employee is entitled to terminate it without notice by reason of the employer's conduct: 'constructive dismissal' (EPCA 1978, ss. 55(2)(c) and 83(2)(c)).

Notice also that in three instances statute deems a dismissal to have taken place in circumstances where common law would not have recognised a dismissal. This represents a limited acceptance by the legislature that too wide an application of common law doctrines could leave employees extremely vulnerable. A conflict still exists as to the extent to which other common law modes of termination, such as frustration and mutual agreement, should be accepted by courts and tribunals given the fact that acceptance will prevent a review of the merits of the decision to dismiss.

In our discussion of the problem areas of termination we shall first of all examine some of the important legal issues involved in determining the precise borderline between dismissal and non-dismissal — this will cover the matters set out under (a) and (c) of our skeletal structure. We shall then offer you some further points on how to revise this section of the course and work through a sample problem question. The remainder of this chapter will concern section (b) of our structure and the common law action for wrongful dismissal which, after years in the shadows, has the potential for renewed prominence in employment law. The pertinent matters in this area will be discussed through the medium of an essay question.

THE PROBLEM AREAS OF TERMINATION

Termination not involving Dismissal at Common Law

Frustration
In order for the doctrine of frustration to apply, there are two essential factors which must be present. First, there must be some outside or extraneous change of situation, not foreseen or provided for by the parties at the time of contracting, which either makes it impossible for the contract to be performed at all, or at least renders its performance something radically different from what the parties contemplated when they entered into it. Secondly, the relevant outside event or extraneous change of situation must have occurred without the fault of either contracting party (see the speech of Lord Brandon of Oakbrook in *Paal Wilson & Co.* v *A/S Partenreederei Hannah Blumenthal* [1983] 1 AC 854 at p. 909).

Over the years, a number of cases have dealt with frustration of the contract of employment mainly in the context of two particular events: long-term absence through sickness or through imprisonment. A finding of frustration in these instances will mean no dismissal has taken place and thus a loss of unfair dismissal or redundancy payment rights. EPCA 1978, s. 93, cannot operate to produce a dismissal simply because illness or imprisonment are not events befalling the *employer*.

In the early 70s the courts evidenced a willingness to accept arguments based on frustration in appropriate cases. In *Marshall* v *Harland & Wolff Ltd* [1972] ICR 101, the National Industrial Relations Court (NIRC) applied the concept in a case involving long-term absence through sickness, laying down a number of factors which should be weighed by a tribunal in deciding whether a contract was frustrated. These included the length of time the employee has been employed, whether the employee held a 'key position', the length of time which the employee was likely to be away from work and the importance of getting someone to do the job meanwhile. These guidelines were subsequently used by Lord Denning MR in the Court of Appeal when he held that the doctrine was applicable to the case of a foreman of 25 years' service who had been sentenced to 12 months' imprisonment for an assault committed away from work (*Hare* v *Murphy Brothers Ltd* [1974] ICR 603).

Subsequently, doubts were cast on the applicability of the doctrine of frustration to the majority of contracts of employment by two decisions of the EAT. In *Harman* v *Flexible Lamps Ltd* [1980] IRLR 418, illness was held not to be a frustrating event. Bristow J was of the view that frustration only had a relevance to long-term contracts of employment which could not be determined by notice and did not apply to short-term periodic contracts which could be ended on relatively short notice. At the heart of the judgment is an awareness that a wide acceptance of the frustration doctrine could undermine the aims of the employment protection legislation. Such policy considerations were no doubt also prominent in the minds of the members of the EAT in *Norris* v *Southampton City Council* [1982] IRLR 141 when they held that, as a matter of law, a contract of employment is not frustrated by imprisonment. Reaching this conclusion involved the tribunal holding that the basis for the decision of the majority in *Hare* was not frustration and that the judgment of Lord Denning MR was in effect a dissenting judgment.

Recently, however, we have witnessed a return to the orthodoxy of the early 70s in the form of two Court of Appeal decisions. In *Notcutt* v *Universal Equipment Co. (London) Ltd* [1986] IRLR 218 a medical prognosis had been given that a worker of 27 years' service, who was two years from retirement age, was unlikely to work again because of a coronary. In the course of finding that illness had frustrated the contract, Dillon LJ concluded that he could see no reason why such a periodic contract of employment should not in appropriate circumstances be held to have been terminated without notice by frustration according to the accepted and long-established doctrine of frustration in the law of contract. The views expressed by Bristow J in *Harman* were seen by Dillon LJ as no more than a warning that the court must look carefully at any submission that the contract has been frustrated if it is put forward to avoid the provisions of EPCA 1978 (see also *Williams* v *Watsons Luxury Coaches Ltd* [1990] ICR 536 where the EAT warned against too easy an application of the doctrine).

Finally, there is the Court of Appeal's decision in *F.C. Shepherd & Co. Ltd* v *Jerrom* [1986] IRLR 358. This will play a key role in our answer to part of the sample problem to be examined later in this chapter because it unambiguously establishes that the imposition of a custodial sentence on an employee is capable in law of frustrating a contract of employment and, in doing so, clarifies a major confusion which had existed since the *Hare* decision; namely, whether imprisonment constitutes 'self-induced frustration'.

Fixed-term contract or 'task' contract?
A fixed-term contract is one which is to expire on a date which can be defined with reasonable precision. It does not cease to be a fixed-term contract even if it contains a clause allowing for termination by notice during its currency (*Dixon* v *British Broadcasting Corporation* [1979] IRLR 114, CA).

In *Wiltshire County Council* v *National Association of Teachers in Further &*
Higher Education [1980] IRLR 198, the Court of Appeal distinguished
between a fixed-term contract and a contract for the completion of a
particular task, at the end of which there is no dismissal. Such a contract is
discharged by performance, as would be the case on completion of a
fixed-term contract, were it not for EPCA 1978, ss. 55(2)(b) and 83(2)(b),
which create a statutory dismissal when such an engagement is not
renewed under the same contract. (It is, of course, possible to insert a
waiver of redundancy and unfair dismissal rights in fixed-term contracts of
two years or more.) As ss. 55(2)(b) and 83(2)(b) do not apply to contracts
which lack a definite completion date, a contract to perform a particular
task cannot give rise to a dismissal.

In *Brown* v *Knowsley Borough Council* [1986] IRLR 102 the distinction
between a fixed-term contract and a contract to perform a particular task
was extended to cover contracts terminable on the happening or non-
happening of a future event. In that case a contract expressed to last 'only
so long as sufficient funds are provided by the MSC or by other firms or
sponsors' was held to have automatically determined when MSC funds
ceased to be available. The distinction that is being made here is controversial and the principle enunciated is potentially of very wide application,
especially in universities, polytechnics and other research organisations
which are substantially dependent on short-term outside funding.

Indeed, the implications of a strict application of the EAT's reasoning in
this case could lead to some quite extraordinary results. Could it be argued
that contracts expressed to last for 'only so long as the company makes a
profit' are not terminable by dismissal? Or that contracts expressed to
expire when 'work is no longer available' would mean that redundancy
claims would be excluded? Alternatively if confronted in future with such
clauses would the courts hold that they were void as an attempt to exclude
or limit a right bestowed by EPCA 1978? Such matters are not resolved and
because the law on this issue is in an uncertain state it is ripe as an
ingredient in an examination problem.

Termination by mutual agreement
As with other contracts, a contract of employment may be terminated by
mutual consent of the parties (*S.W. Strange Ltd* v *Mann* [1965] 1 WLR 629).
If the courts were to too readily accept that the contractual relationship had
ended in this way then once again access to employment protection would
be severely threatened. As a result statute has intervened by providing that
where an employee under notice gives the employer notice that he or she
wishes to leave before the expiry of the employer's notice, the employee is
deemed still to have been dismissed for unfair dismissal and redundancy
purposes and not to have been party to an early termination by mutual

consent (EPCA 1978, ss. 55(3) and 83(2)). In general, the courts and tribunals have been reluctant to accept the argument that an employee has in reality agreed to give up his or her job and forego the possibility of an unfair dismissal or redundancy claim (see the judgment of Sir John Donaldson P in *McAlwane v Boughton Estates Ltd* [1973] ICR 470 at p. 473) and *Hellyer Bros Ltd v Atkinson* [1994] IRLR 88, CA).

These same policy considerations are present in the Court of Appeal decision in *Igbo v Johnson Matthey Chemicals Ltd* [1986] IRLR 215 where the court had to consider the effect of an agreement by which an employee agrees that if the employee does not return to work from a period of absence by a specified time then the contract of employment will come to an end. In overruling the earlier decision in *British Leyland UK Ltd v Ashraf* [1978] IRLR 330, the Court of Appeal held that these 'automatic termination' agreements are void under EPCA 1978, s. 140. This section makes void any provision in an agreement which purports to 'exclude or limit' any provision of EPCA 1978. We shall have an opportunity of applying the reasoning of the court when we consider the examination problem on termination later in the chapter.

The use of s. 140 in this way has generally been welcomed by employment law commentators for the reasons summarised by Upex (1987) 16 ILJ at p. 65:

First the obvious consequences of this decision is that industrial tribunals dealing with such cases will now be able to examine the merits of each case in which an employer's claims rely on agreement such as that which Mrs Igbo signed. Second, employers will not in future be able to rely on such agreements without more ado. To avoid the risk of losing a case in the tribunal, they will have to investigate each case and consider the employee's reason for failing to meet the deadline for return. In a case where the employee has a good reason for failing to return, one would have thought it unlikely that the tribunal would find the dismissal fair. Bearing in mind the prevalence of the practice amongst employees who have families in foreign countries of asking for extended periods of unpaid leave, this decision will make an important contribution to their protection.

This is not to say that an argument that the relationship has terminated by mutual consent can never succeed. In *Igbo*, the court seemed to think that if the employee is genuinely willing to leave then s. 140 would not invalidate the agreement. Thus, where a termination is agreed to by an employee, for example, in return for financial compensation or under an early retirement scheme. This was the case in *University of Liverpool v Humber* [1985] IRLR 165.

Terminations deemed to be dismissals by statute
We have seen that statute has extended the concept of dismissal beyond termination by the employer with or without notice to cover the non-renewal of a fixed-term contract and cases of 'constructive dismissal'. We have already examined some of the definitional problems surrounding the fixed-term contract and it is now appropriate to pinpoint some of the issues which have absorbed the attention of the courts and tribunals in relation to direct and constructive dismissal.

Direct dismissal (EPCA 1978, s. 55(2)(a))
This is the clearest and most obvious form of dismissal and consequently the concept has not generated the same amount of case law as the other statutory modes of dismissal. That is not to say that the examiner is robbed of all ammunition with which to load into a question.

'Resign or be sacked'   A resignation under threat of dismissal may constitute a dismissal (see *East Sussex County Council* v *Walker* (1972) 7 ITR 280 and *Sheffield* v *Oxford Controls Co. Ltd* [1979] IRLR 133). However, in order to succeed in this argument the employee must establish a certain and immediate threat (*Martin* v *MBS Fastenings (Glynwed) Distribution Ltd* [1983] IRLR 198).

*'**** off!'*   Many a boring employment law lecture has been livened up by a discussion of the colourful cases which determine whether the words used by the employer were words of dismissal or merely words of exasperation or exhortation (see, for example, *Futty* v *D. & D. Brekkes Ltd* [1974] IRLR 130 and *Tanner* v *D.T Kean Ltd* [1978] IRLR 110). Because of their appeal to students examiners may be tempted to include a similar sort of issue in a problem question on the basis that if the students cannot remember this series of cases they will remember nothing! Do not let the amusing facts blind your grasp of the legal principles they represent which might be broadly stated as follows:

(a)   If, taking into account the context in which they were uttered, the words unambiguously amount to a dismissal (or resignation) then this should be the finding of the tribunal (*Sothern* v *Franks Charlesly & Co.* [1981] IRLR 278).

(b)   Where, however, the words employed are ambiguous, because they have been uttered in the heat of the moment, the effect of the statement is determined by an objective test, i.e., whether any 'reasonable' employer or employee might have understood the words to be tantamount to a dismissal or resignation (*B.G. Gale Ltd* v *Gilbert* [1978] IRLR 453).

(c)   A dismissal or resignation given in the heat of the moment may be withdrawn. However, the change of mind must not be so late that it is impossible to recover the words' effect (*Martin* v *Yeoman Aggregates Ltd* [1983] IRLR 49).

Those principles have more recently been considered by the Court of Appeal in *Sovereign House Security Service Ltd* v *Savage* [1989] IRLR 115. The court confirmed that an industrial tribunal is entitled to look beneath what was said unambiguously and find that in the context or circumstances (such as a decision taken in the heat of the moment or the case of an immature employee) there was no real termination despite appearances.

Constructive dismissal (EPCA 1978, s. 55(2)(c))
The conceptual problems surrounding this form of dismissal have generated a plethora of case law over the years and, for the examiner, this makes the temptation to include a constructive dismissal point on any examination paper hard to resist.

By virtue of the concept of constructive dismissal, the law treats some resignations as dismissals and therefore extends statutory dismissal rights to employees who feel constrained to resign by virtue of their employer's conduct.

We have stated that the concept is a creation of statute and an extension of the modes of dismissal recognised at common law. It is submitted that this is a correct statement of the law despite the Court of Appeal's purported extension of direct dismissal to encompass an employee's resignation in reaction to his employer's breach of contract in *Marriott* v *Oxford & District Cooperative Society Ltd (No. 2)* [1970] 1 QB 186. Indeed, Lord Denning subsequently admitted that he and the rest of the court had 'stretched' the law in order to do justice in that particular case. The temptation to do this was understandable given the flawed definition of constructive dismissal when it first made an appearance as s. 3(1)(a) of the Redundancy Payments Act 1965. This paragraph was designed to cover cases such as a resignation in the face of a reduction in pay but it was flawed in that it required the employee to leave without giving notice. The reasonable employee who gave notice was therefore excluded from its ambit.

This was essentially the trap that Mr Marriott fell into when he responded to a reduction in pay by giving notice to his employer. Nevertheless, the court held that by insisting on the reduction in pay, the employers had automatically terminated the contract themselves and had directly dismissed Mr Marriott. Constructive dismissal was not expressly included when the right to claim unfair dismissal was first introduced by the Industrial Relations Act 1971 and so this stretching of the law was continued by later cases (see *Sutcliffe* v *Hawker Siddeley Aviation Ltd* [1973] ICR 560). The necessity to adopt what is now the largely discredited theory of automatic termination was only removed when TULRA 1974 expressly included a more widely defined concept of constructive dismissal in 1974. Under the current definition, which applies to both unfair and redundancy dismissals, it does not matter whether the employee left with or without notice provided the employee was entitled to leave by reason of the employer's conduct.

No sooner had this controversy been resolved than problems began to spring up relating to the criteria which should be used in order to determine whether a constructive dismissal had taken place. Specifically, a number of decisions suggested that constructive dismissal was not confined, as had previously been assumed, to fundamental breaches of contract, but applied to any case where the employer's behaviour was held to be unreasonable. In other words unfair constructive dismissal hearings were reduced to a single criterion (see *Gilbert* v *I. Goldstone Ltd* [1977] ICR 36).

Following a period of confusion, the Court of Appeal in *Western Excavating (ECC) Ltd* v *Sharp* [1978] QB 761 clarified matters, rejecting the reasonableness test, and holding that a contractual approach was the right one. This is the leading case in the area of constructive dismissal and therefore it is important that you read the case and any commentaries on it to which you may be referred. Given the importance of this case, it is also worthwhile to try to remember a key extract from the judgments and be able to attribute it. Lord Denning MR conveniently, and reasonably concisely, sets out the key elements of constructive dismissal. The passage is perhaps too long to learn verbatim but you should be able to paraphrase it:

> If the employer is guilty of conduct which is a significant breach going to the root of the contract of employment, or which shows that the employer no longer intends to be bound by one or more of the essential terms of the contract then the employee is entitled to treat himself as discharged from any further performance. If he does so, then he terminates the contract by reason of the employer's conduct. He is constructively dismissed. The employee is entitled in those circumstances to leave at the instant without giving any notice at all or, alternatively, he may give notice and say he is leaving at the end of the notice. But the conduct must in either case be sufficiently serious to entitle him to leave at once. Moreover, he must make up his mind soon after the conduct of which he complains: for, if he continues for any length of time without leaving, he will lose his right to treat himself as discharged. He will be regarded as having elected to affirm the contract.

Being able to paraphrase this definition and attribute it to Lord Denning will provide an answer to a question concerned with constructive dismissal with some authority but it will also provide a checklist which should be helpful in working through such a problem.

If we break down Lord Denning's statement we will be able to distil the key elements of the concept:

(a) Has the employer broken a term of the contract or evidenced a clear intention not to be bound?

(b) If yes, is the term which has or will be broken an essential or fundamental term of the contract?

(c) If yes, has the employee resigned with or without notice in response to the breach within a reasonable time? (We are cheating a little here because you will notice that Lord Denning does not mention a reasonable period being available to the employee in which to decide whether to resign but this has been emphasised in other cases — see, for example, *Turvey* v *C. W. Cheyney & Son Ltd* [1979] IRLR 105.)

Of course, setting things out in this way does clarify the questions to be asked but it is of no help in supplying the answers. After all, what constitutes a repudiation of a fundamental term and how long is a reasonable time? The difficulty in knowing where the employer or employee stand on these and other issues has been compounded by a development which has been referred to in other chapters of this book. This is the recent tendency of the Court of Appeal to hold that many of the issues in unfair dismissal, most notably for the purposes of this discussion the question whether there has been a repudiation, are issues of fact alone or mixed fact and law and therefore the findings of industrial tribunals are only reviewable following perverse decisions (*Pederson* v *Camden London Borough Council* [1981] ICR 674; *Woods* v *WM Car Services (Peterborough) Ltd* [1982] ICR 693). Whilst this uncertainty poses major problems for clients and their advisers it should not strike fear into the heart of the student of employment law. Most examiners try to set questions on issues where the law is unclear and so you should not worry if you cannot arrive at a definite conclusion having reviewed the relevant law. Indeed, you can gain credit by making a virtue out of a necessity by pointing out the 'grey' areas.

In the midst of this uncertainty, however, it is possible to produce a categorisation of acts or omissions which the courts and tribunals have held to repudiate the contract. Anderman, *The Law of Unfair Dismissal*, 2nd ed., p. 67, observes that repudiatory conduct by an employer has traditionally included two well-established types of conduct:

(a) In the first place an employer may unilaterally break an essential positive obligation owed by him to his employee under the contract, whether the obligation was expressed or implied. For example, an employer may withdraw an existing contractual right such as free transport, or fail to meet a contractual obligation such as the payment of wages. The essence of this type of repudiation is that the employer has failed to perform a positive contractual obligation and the employee is presented with a *fait accompli*.

(b) Secondly, an employer may insist that the employee agree to a change in existing working arrangements or terms and conditions of employment, or insist that the employee perform an act which he is not contractually obliged to do. In either case the employer is in effect renouncing the contract and his unjustified insistence on the change or act could constitute a repudiation of the contract.

This is a useful way of explaining the traditional categories and saves you trying to learn a long list of case names which merely illustrate the same points as the more concise statement set out above. Always be on the look out to cut down on the number of case names you are going to attempt to remember in the examination.

Following the adoption of the contractual test by the Court of Appeal in *Western Excavating (ECC) Ltd v Sharp*, a number of commentators argued that it would impose a great restriction on the ambit of constructive dismissal claims relative to the more generous reasonableness test. This fear has not been borne out because the EAT has been prepared to hold that contracts of employment generally are subject to an implied term that the employer must not destroy or seriously damage the relationship of trust and confidence between employer and employee (see *Courtaulds Northern Textiles Ltd v Andrew* [1979] IRLR 84). As a result the distinction between the *Western Excavating (ECC) Ltd v Sharp* approach and the discredited 'reasonableness' test looks slim indeed as is illustrated by looking at just some of the situations where the implied obligation has been held to be broken:

(a) Failing to respond to an employee's complaint about the lack of adequate safety equipment (*British Aircraft Corporation Ltd v Austin* [1978] IRLR 332).

(b) Undermining the authority of senior staff over subordinates (*Courtaulds Northern Textiles Ltd v Andrew*).

(c) Failing to protect an employee from harassment from fellow employees (*Wigan Borough Council v Davies* [1979] IRLR 127).

(d) Failing to properly investigate allegations of sexual harassment or treating the complaint with sufficient seriousness (*Bracebridge Engineering Ltd v Darby* [1990] IRLR 3).

(e) Foul language by employer (*Palmanor Ltd v Cedron* [1978] IRLR 303).

(f) Imposing a disciplinary penalty grossly out of proportion to the offence (*British Broadcasting Corporation* v *Beckett* [1983] IRLR 43).

(g) A series of minor incidents of harassment over a period of time which cumulatively amount to repudiation: the so-called 'last straw' doctrine (*Woods* v *WM Car Services (Peterborough) Ltd* [1982] ICR 693).

The potency of the implied obligation of trust and confidence can be seen in the case of *United Bank Ltd* v *Akhtar* [1989] IRLR 507 which suggests that the employers should ensure that they operate a wide mobility clause in a reasonable manner. Should they fail to do so, it may constitute a breach of contract and entitle the employee to claim constructive dismissal.

Mr Akhtar was a junior ranking and low paid worker who had been employed by the bank since 1978 in Leeds. A clause in his contract provided:

> The Bank may from time to time require an employee to be transferred temporarily or permanently to any place of business which the Bank may have in the UK for which a location or other allowance may be payable at the discretion of the Bank.

The EAT held that the employee was entitled to treat himself as constructively dismissed by reason of the employer's conduct in requiring him to transfer his place of employment from Leeds to Birmingham at short notice (six days) and with no financial assistance, even if this could be held to be within the terms of the express mobility clause in the employee's contract of employment. This is because the general implied contractual duty set out in *Woods* v *WM Car Services (Peterborough)* [1982] ICR 693 that employers will not, without reasonable or proper cause, conduct themselves in a manner calculated or likely to destroy the relationship of trust and confidence between employer and employee, is an overriding obligation independent of and in addition to the literal terms of the contract (cf. *White* v *Reflecting Roadstuds Ltd* [1991] IRLR 331).

Fairness and constructive dismissal
In answering a problem on constructive dismissal which asks you to determine the fairness of the dismissal it is important to remember that a constructive dismissal is not necessarily unfair. Therefore, having determined whether the elements of such a dismissal are present, you must then proceed to consider the fairness question under EPCA 1978, s. 57(3). In many cases this will not alter your conclusion but you may come across cases where, although the employee was entitled to resign, the employer's action which prompted the resignation was fair and reasonable in the circumstances (see *Savoia* v *Chiltern Herb Farms Ltd* [1982] IRLR 166).

THE EXAMINATION

Reference has already been made to the incremental nature of employment law and the topic of termination is an excellent example of this. You may often be confronted by issues in this area as preliminary obstacles in a problem concerned with unfair dismissal or redundancy payments. Moreover, the unfair dismissal applicant featured in any scenario may also have an alternative wrongful dismissal claim at common law. An essay question may ask you to compare and contrast the common law and statutory dismissal remedies. Thus it need hardly be said that selective revision is particularly dangerous in this area. To study unfair dismissal or redundancy payments without a sound grasp of the modes of termination of the contract of employment is like a production of *Hamlet* without the Prince.

Sample Examination Questions

In this section we shall analyse two past examination questions. The first question is a five-part problem which requires the candidate to determine whether in law a dismissal has taken place or whether the contractual relationship has come to an end by some other mechanism. The second question requires an essay discussing the reason for the renewed prominence of the common law action for wrongful dismissal. Our aim here is not primarily to offer you a model answer but to use the sample questions as a medium through which to emphasise the key issues which should be discussed and, on occasion, to promote a deeper understanding of those issues.

Question One

Sackem is the senior personnel officer of Capital plc. He has recently dealt with the following personnel problems in the manner described below:

(a) Some two months ago, Fred, a works foreman of some 10 years' service, was sentenced to 12 months' imprisonment for an assault committed outside work. Fred lodged a successful appeal against conviction and, on his release from prison, Fred asked Sackem when he might resume work. Sackem informed him that his job had been filled and there were no vacancies.

(b) Just over a month ago, Sackem granted Tish a period of four weeks' leave in order that she might visit her parents in Zimbabwe. Before her departure she signed a declaration which stated: 'I understand and agree that my employment will cease should I not return to work by the due date'. As a result of a baggage handlers' dispute, Tish's return flight was delayed and she reported for work two days late. Sackem refused to allow Tish to return to work.

(c)   Three years ago Capital plc was awarded a research grant by the government in order to investigate ways of improving the safety of one of the products it manufactures. At that time, Capital employed Boffin as research officer on the project.

There is a clause in Boffin's contract of employment which states that his contract of employment will continue 'until such time that government funding for the project is withdrawn'. Early last week the government informed Capital that it was ceasing forthwith to finance the project. The following day Sackem told Boffin that his employment was terminated with immediate effect.

(d)   Trevor, a production worker, was discovered by a supervisor to be sleeping during his night shift. As a result of his failure to tend his machine, it overheated and suffered a major breakdown. Sackem calls Trevor to his office and tells him that 'By your act of gross negligence you have sacked yourself. Please leave the premises immediately.'

(e)   Mrs Steel has been employed as Sackem's personal secretary. Four weeks ago, Sackem informed her that she would not be receiving an annual salary increase because her work was not satisfactory. Until then, she had received a pay increase every year. Mrs Steel was the only employee not to be given a pay rise. When Mrs Steel complained that she had never previously received any indication that Sackem was unhappy with her work, Sackem replied: 'Well I've always thought you were a lazy bitch'. This interchange was witnessed by Kate, Mrs Steel's assistant. Mrs Steel informed Sackem that she would be seeing her solicitor. Following this incident she continued to attend work until yesterday when she handed in her notice.

Examine each of these incidents and advise Sackem whether in legal terms dismissal has taken place.

This is a useful question for the purposes of this chapter because you will see that it is solely concerned with the mechanics of termination. Therefore we will not be forced to address any matters concerning the fairness of a dismissal. The examiner has evidently decided that there is quite sufficient required of the examination candidate without asking for a discussion of the overall fairness of the decision to dismiss. This is important because it means that you will get absolutely no credit for dealing with unfairness in your answer. It cannot be stressed too frequently that it is absolutely crucial to provide the answer to the question which the examiner has posed and not the answer to the question you wished had been asked!

Analysis

We have seen that with the advent of the statutory rights to claim unfair dismissal and redundancy payments it became tempting for employers to seek to avoid the application of the legislation by arguing that the contract of employment came to an end without dismissal. The five scenarios in this question require an analysis of how willing the courts and tribunals have been to accept such arguments and to allow Sackem to avoid having his personnel practices subjected to their scrutiny.

Obviously, in producing an answer to this five-part question you must ensure that your response is economical, relevant and accurate. Earlier in this chapter it has been suggested that there is often a clash between the application of common law doctrines of termination and policy considerations. Indeed that issue might itself provide the source of an examination question. Interesting though that issue is, however, it is not directly relevant to our problem question. Remember that you are asked to advise Sackem on the legal implications of his actions and, as a client with five troublesome personnel problems, he would not be interested in a discourse on, for example, the history of the relationship between frustration and employment contracts!

Fred

A structure to an answer to this part of the question might look something like this:

(a)   Identify the area of law concerned.

(b)   State the significance of a finding of frustration.

(c)   Define the doctrine of frustration. Lord Brandon of Oakbrook's speech in *Paal Wilson & Co. A/S* v *Partenreederei Hannah Blumenthal* [1983] 1 AC 854 provides an authoritative statement of the doctrine coming as it does from a Law Lord. Paraphrase his two-part definition and attribute it. Applying this definition will now provide a structure to the rest of your answer.

(d)   Determine whether what happened was capable in law of frustrating the contract. First, was there an event which was not foreseen or provided for by the parties at the time of contracting?. The sentence of imprisonment would seem to fit this category on the basis of Lord Denning MR's judgment in *Hare* v *Murphy Brothers Ltd* [1974] ICR 603, the EAT decisions in *Harrington* v *Kent County Council* [1980] IRLR 353 and *Chakki* v *United Yeast Co. Ltd* [1982] ICR 140 and, most importantly, *F. C. Shephard & Co. Ltd* v *Jerrom* [1986] IRLR 358 before the Court of Appeal.

Secondly, did the outside event occur without the fault of either party? This was a vitally important aspect of the *Jerrom* case with the apprentice seeking to rely on his own fault in order to prevent his former employer using frustration arguments and to establish his right to claim unfair dismissal. As we know, this slick argument was rejected by the Court of Appeal though all three judges differed slightly in their reasoning. Given that, together with *Notcutt v Universal Equipment Co. (London) Ltd* [1986] IRLR 218, *Jerrom* provides one of the most recent and authoritative statements on the applicability of frustration to employment contracts, the report of the case is well worth studying. If, having done so, you can give a brief indication of how the judges' reasoning differed this will make your answer that much more impressive. For example, Lawton LJ drew a distinction between Jerrom's criminal acts, which by themselves did not affect the performance of the contract, and the sentence passed by the judge. It was the latter which made it impossible to carry out the contract (this is the sort of reasoning which Lord Denning MR had used in *Hare*). Mustill LJ thought that it was an 'affront to common sense' for Jerrom to claim to improve his position by asserting that he had repudiated the contract. It was a fundamental rule that no man should be allowed to take advantage of his own wrong-doing. Balcombe LJ was of the view that in any event there was no repudiation of the contract by Jerrom. There would have been none if he had received a suspended sentence or probation: the custodial sentence passed by the judge was an external event capable of frustrating the contract.

(e) On the facts of the problem, was the event such as to render the performance of the contract radically different from what the parties had contemplated when they entered into it?

This issue is to be decided by the tribunal to which is entrusted the task of deciding issues of fact. Matters which need to be balanced are Fred's fairly lengthy service on the one hand as against his 'key' position as foreman and his potential absence of 12 months on the other.

(f) One final complicating factor arises from the fact that Fred has been sentenced to a fairly substantial period of imprisonment but has served only a small part of it. Remarks by Lord Denning in *Hare* lend support for the view that a prison sentence of substantial length could frustrate a contract of employment on the date of sentencing. This was followed in *Harrington v Kent County Council* where a teacher served only eight weeks of a 12-month sentence. Despite the fact that the employer knew of the employee's intention to appeal, the EAT held the contract to be frustrated.

This approach is contradicted by the later EAT decision in *Chakki v United Yeast Co. Ltd* where it held that the imposition of a sentence was not an automatically frustrating event. In that case, Chakki was sentenced to 11 months' imprisonment at the start of his 14-day annual holiday. He was released on bail pending an ultimately successful appeal after spending only one night in prison. When he reported for work he found that the employer had replaced him and refused to have him back. The EAT remitted the case to the industrial tribunal to decide if, at the time the employer took its decision to replace, a reasonable employer would have concluded that Chakki would be absent from work for such a long time that a permanent replacement was necessary. This of course was an unusual case where it was soon apparent to the employer that there was a good chance of a successful appeal. Thus the law here is somewhat unclear. The *Jerrom* judgments do not directly address this question though they seem to assume that frustration occurs on the date of sentence.

Tish

The chances of Sackem being able to argue that Tish has agreed to a mutual termination of the contract of employment should she fail to return from her period of extended leave are slim indeed following the Court of Appeal judgment in *Igbo* v *Johnson Matthey Chemicals Ltd* [1986] IRLR 215. The sort of declaration she signed is now rendered void by virtue of EPCA 1978, s. 140, and *British Leyland UK Ltd* v *Ashraf* [1978] IRLR 330 is no longer good law.

Try not to leave the answer at that and attempt to equate the process of reasoning used by the Court of Appeal to the facts of Tish's case. State the content of s. 140 which renders void any agreement 'in so far as it purports . . . to . . . limit the operation of any provision of this Act'. The declaration which Tish signed had a vital limiting effect on the operation of her right to claim unfair dismissal under ss. 54 and 55 of the Act.

Tish's unconditional right to the benefit of those sections was made a conditional right by the declaration, i.e., in order to retain the protection of the section she had to return to work by the due date. The agreement's effect was therefore to limit her right under EPCA 1978 and void.

Boffin

Is Boffin employed under a fixed-term contract, a periodic contract or a contract discharged by the happening of a specified event? Only in the first two instances will a dismissal have taken place so as to pave the way for an unfair dismissal or redundancy payment claim.

A fixed-term contract? We need a definition and the one provided by Lord Denning MR in *Dixon* v *British Broadcasting Corporation* [1979] ICR 281 at p. 285 is sufficiently concise to remember verbatim:

> . . . a 'fixed-term' contract is sufficiently satisfied if the contract is for a specific stated period, even though it is determinable by notice within that period.

It would seem that the clause in Boffin's contract will fall outside the definition following *Wiltshire County Council* v *National Association of*

Teachers in Further & Higher Education [1980] IRLR 198 and *Brown v Knowsley Borough Council* [1986] IRLR 102. In the EAT in the *Wiltshire case*, Phillips J said that he could see no reason why contracts which are terminable on the happening of an uncertain future event such as the duration of a government or the life of the sovereign could not constitute contracts for a fixed term. However, when the case came before the Court of Appeal, Lord Denning MR was strongly critical of his reasoning (see also the views of Kilner Brown J in *Ryan v Shipboard Maintenance Ltd* [1980] ICR 88 at p. 93). The Denning approach has now, of course, been applied in the Brown case where, unfortunately, given the importance of the distinction being made, leave to appeal to the Court of Appeal was refused.

Your reading round this area may have supplied you with two additional arguments with which to maintain that Boffin has been dismissed. The first is summarised by *IDS Brief* 317 (January 1986), p. 3, in a comment on the *Brown* decision:

> The definition of ordinary dismissal in EPCA 1978 talks only of 'the contract under which [the employee] is employed by the employer' being terminated. No one has ever seriously argued that the happening of purely extrinsic events (i.e., those quite unrelated to the actual job of work in question) can prevent termination other than by dismissal.

This is argument for classifying Boffin's termination as a direct dismissal under EPCA 1978, s. 55(2)(a) or s. 83(2)(a).

Secondly, you might argue that the contractual provision has the effect of excluding Boffin's rights under EPCA 1978 and is thus void under s. 140.

Trevor

This part of the question takes us into an area which we have not yet discussed but one which will feature in the final part of the chapter, namely, whether a repudiation of the contract of employment requires acceptance in the form of dismissal from the employer. From your study of the law of contract you may remember the judicial aphorism that an unaccepted repudiation is like 'a thing writ in water'. The question is whether contracts of employment form an exception to this general rule of contract.

In a number of cases in the 70s the EAT was prepared to accept that certain repudiatory actions by employees automatically terminated the contract without the need for the employer to accept the repudiation by dismissal. A good example of what was known as 'self-dismissal' or 'constructive resignation' is *Gannon v J.C. Firth Ltd* [1976] IRLR 415 where employees 'downed tools' and walked out of the factory leaving machinery in a dangerous state and were held to have dismissed themselves by their actions.

The widespread adoption of the concept of 'constructive resignation' would have opened up a huge gap in the framework of employment protection. Trevor's act of negligence could be seen as a breach of contract of sufficient gravity that he could be considered to have resigned by his own act.

Fortunately, it is now clear that Sackem cannot deploy this sort of argument because of the Court of Appeal's decision in *London Transport Executive* v *Clarke* [1981] IRLR 166. In this case, a majority of the Court of Appeal held that a contract of employment could not be 'automatically' terminated by a repudiation by an employee but required an acceptance of the repudiation by the employer.

Mrs Steel
This part of the question requires us to determine whether the treatment which Mrs Steel has received entitled her to resign and claim constructive dismissal. In order to succeed she must be able to show that Sackem is in fundamental breach of contract and not merely behaving unreasonably (it would be useful here to employ the paraphrase of Lord Denning's definition of the scope of constructive dismissal in *Western Excavating (ECC) Ltd* v *Sharp* [1978] QB 761 which we discussed earlier in the chapter).

Does the failure to award Mrs Steel a pay rise amount to a repudiation? Assuming that there was no express contractual term, is it possible to imply a term that the employee be given a yearly increase? The latter question was answered in the negative by the EAT in *Murco Petroleum Ltd* v *Forge* [1987] IRLR 50. However, Sir Ralph Kilner Brown did venture the opinion that if an employer in failing to award an employee a pay increase had acted arbitrarily or capriciously this would breach the implied duty of mutual trust and confidence (see also *F. C. Gardner Ltd* v *Beresford* [1978] IRLR 63). Even if his treatment of Mrs Steel on the matter of salary was not a repudiation, the words he used to her in front of a subordinate almost certainly was (see *Isle of Wight Tourist Board* v *Coombes* [1976] IRLR 413 and *Courtaulds Northern Textiles Ltd* v *Andrew* [1979] IRLR 84).

By her delay in tendering her resignation has she affirmed the contract? Probably not. She told Sackem that she would be consulting her solicitor and this clearly gave the indication that she did not accept the situation. Provided that the employee makes clear his or her objection to the employer's actions, the employee will not be taken to have affirmed the contract by continuing to work and draw pay for a limited period of time (see *Marriott* v *Oxford & District Co-operative Society Ltd (No. 2)* [1970] 1 QB 186 and *W. E. Cox Toner (International) Ltd* v *Crook* [1981] IRLR 443).

DISMISSALS AT COMMON LAW

At common law a contract of employment could be terminated by giving notice of a length which has been expressly agreed. In the absence of an expressed notice period, the law will imply a period of 'reasonable notice' whose length will depend on the circumstances of the employment. Moreover, the common law allowed an employer to dismiss an employee with no notice at all if the latter's conduct amounted to a repudiation of the contract of employment.

Until the introduction of the statutory right to claim unfair dismissal in 1971, the employer was left with an extremely wide managerial prerogative in the area of discipline given the largely obsolete and unjust legal principles which made up the action of wrongful dismissal. The major weaknesses in the action for wrongful dismissal may be summarised as follows:

(a) The low level of damages awarded to successful litigants, generally only compensating for the appropriate notice period (see *Addis* v *Gramophone Co. Ltd* [1909] AC 488 and *Bliss* v *South East Thames Regional Health Authority* [1985] IRLR 308).

(b) The inability of the dismissed employee to regain his or her job because of the general rule against ordering specific performance of contracts of employment.

(c) The archaic nature of some of the principles of summary dismissal reflecting 'almost an attitude of Tsar-serf' (per Edmund Davies LJ in *Wilson* v *M. Racher* [1974] IRLR 114).

(d) The lack of procedural protections for most employees, with only so-called 'office-holders' entitled to natural justice and the remedies of public law (see, *Ridge* v *Baldwin* [1964] AC 40).

With the advent of unfair dismissal, the action for wrongful dismissal was perceived as largely irrelevant in practical terms and this was reflected in the number of times we as examiners included it in the examination papers we drafted. Occasionally, we would set an essay question asking students to contrast wrongful and unfair dismissal or we would include a wrongful dismissal point in a problem. However, a number of recent developments have caused us to reassess the situation and it may well be that wrongful dismissal cannot be consigned to employment law's lumber room. The reasons for this reassessment should become clear as we work through the following question which is taken from a recent examination paper:

What developments have caused employees to look for alternative remedies to unfair dismissal in order to safeguard their rights to a fair disciplinary procedure?

Obviously in order to answer this question you will need to be able to explain why employees have felt it necessary in the first place to look for alternative remedies to the statutory remedy. We shall discuss some of the perceived shortcomings of the latter in the following chapter but they may be briefly summarised here as follows:

(a)   The generally low success rate of applicants in industrial tribunals.
(b)   The few cases in which the reinstatement remedy is awarded.
(c)   The low level of compensation.
(d)   The devaluation of the importance of procedural fairness in unfair dismissal cases as a result of the test laid down in *British Labour Pump Co. Ltd* v *Byrne* [1979] IRLR 94 (now no longer good law as we shall see).

As a result of these flaws in the framework of statutory protection, there has been a renewed interest in common law and public law remedies by employees who are seeking to prevent a dismissal taking place in breach of natural justice or because the power of dismissal has been exceeded.

This is a complex area which is still very much in a state of flux and it is important that you have a clear structure in mind for the presentation of the developments. The discussion of the area can be divided between (a) the public law remedies of judicial review and (b) the private law remedies of injunctions and declarations.

Public Law Remedies

The holder of a public office has always received special protection over and above that of an employee so that the officer has the right to the protection of natural justice before dismissal. A good example of this is *Ridge* v *Baldwin* [1964] AC 40.

However, there is immense difficulty in distinguishing a 'protected office' from 'mere employment'. In *Malloch* v *Aberdeen Corporation* [1971] ICR 893 Lord Wilberforce was moved to comment that:

A comparative list in which persons have been entitled to a hearing, or to observation of rules of natural justice looks illogical and even bizarre.

In *Malloch* v *Aberdeen Corporation* a Scottish teacher whose employment was regulated by statute was held to be an office-holder and thereby entitled to a hearing. Lord Wilberforce offered a wide definition of the concept and stated that natural justice would only be excluded in those 'pure master and servant cases' where there was 'no element of public employment or service, no support by statute, nothing in the nature of an office or status which is capable of protection'.

This statement opened up the possibility that many public sector workers possessed the status of office-holder and could challenge their employer's disciplinary actions by way of application for judicial review under RSC Ord. 53.

This potential alternative to unfair dismissal for large numbers of workers was severely restricted by the Court of Appeal in *R v East Berkshire Health Authority, ex parte Walsh* [1985] QB 152. In this case the judge at first instance accepted the proposition that the employee, a hospital senior nursing officer was entitled to judicial review of the health authority's decision to dismiss him on the grounds that it was *ultra vires* and in breach of natural justice. This view was firmly rejected by the Court of Appeal, holding that the relationship between the parties was one of pure master and servant and therefore a matter of private and not public law. According to Sir John Donaldson MR, the remedies of public law were only available to those individuals who were employed by a public authority under terms which were underpinned' by statute in one of two ways:

(a) By statute placing restrictions upon the authority's power to dismiss.

(b) By statute requiring the authority to contract with employees on specified terms.

It was not enough, as Hodgson J had held at first instance, for the employee to show that he was employed in a senior position by a public authority for public purposes, and that the public had an interest in seeing that public servants were treated lawfully and fairly (see also *R v Derbyshire County Council, ex parte Noble* [1990] IRLR 332; *McLaren v Home Office* [1990] IRLR 338; *R v Lord Chancellor's Department, ex parte Nangle* [1991] IRLR 343).

Thus our survey of developments in the public law field offers little in the way of alternative or additional protection to the vast majority of employees. Indeed it is the very existence of the right to claim unfair dismissal which is one of the reasons why the courts have taken the view that most workers do not require the additional protection of public law. What of the recent developments in the private law sphere?

Private Law Remedies

We have seen that the courts were traditionally reluctant to force an employer to take an employee back. As regards employees this rule is now enshrined in TULR(C)A 1992, s. 236, which provides that 'No court shall . . . [issue an order compelling] an employee to do any work or attend at any place for the doing of any work'.

The reasons which have been given by the courts in the past to justify their reluctance to grant the remedy have been based on two propositions.

First, it was wrong to order the parties to remain in the employment relationship where trust and confidence had broken down. Such an order would require constant supervision and, as such, could not be effectively policed by the courts. As Geoffrey Lane LJ put it in *Chappell* v *Times Newspapers Ltd* [1975] ICR 145, to order specific performance 'if one party has no faith in the honesty or integrity of the other . . . is a plain recipe for disaster'. In *Hill* v *C. A. Parsons & Co. Ltd* [1972] Ch 305 the Court of Appeal *did* issue an injunction to restrain an employer from treating an employee as dismissed in order to extend the duration of the contract, and so render Hill eligible for the benefit of unfair dismissal protection under the soon to come into force Industrial Relations Act 1971. But this was an unusual case because there was continuing trust and confidence between the parties as it was the trade union exerting pressure on the employers to dismiss the employee because he would not join the closed shop.

Secondly, the view that a repudiation of the contract of employment by one party automatically brings the contract to an end. The innocent party cannot ask the court to order the continuance of the contractual relationship because there is no longer any contract to maintain. This view has been described as the 'automatic theory' of termination and it is the change of judicial attitude in relation to this proposition which may in future broaden the scope for alternative challenges to disciplinary action beyond an unfair dismissal claim.

Automatic Termination or Elective Termination?

Since the early 70s the balance of judicial opinion has tipped in the opposite direction towards the elective theory, i.e., a repudiation requires acceptance by the innocent party before the contract comes to an end (see *Hill* v *C. A. Parsons & Co. Ltd* [1972] Ch 305; *Thomas Marshall (Exports) Ltd* v *Guinle* [1979] Ch 227; *Gunton* v *Richmond-upon-Thames London Borough Council* [1981] Ch 448; *London Transport Executive* v *Clarke* [1981] ICR 355; *R* v *British Broadcasting Corporation, ex parte Lavelle* [1983] ICR 99).

It is true to say, however, that even if the elective theory is now dominant it will not mean that employees will find it easy to obtain an injunction to keep the contract alive.

The factors which have militated against the granting of specific performance remain strong in the judicial mind and employee acceptance of the repudiation can be implied from making an application for unfair dismissal or electing to claim damages for wrongful dismissal (see *Dietman* v *Brent London Borough Council* [1987] ICR 737). In *Gunton* v *Richmond-upon-Thames London Borough Council* a dismissed employee was granted a declaration that his dismissal was void because of the employer's failure to comply with a contractually binding disciplinary procedure. However, the Court of

Appeal went on to hold that, on electing to claim damages for breach of contract, Gunton was only entitled to damages for the period up to the time when the employer could have terminated the contract lawfully by going through the proper procedure. Gunton did not get his job back but received only a few weeks extra pay as damages. It would seem that the adoption of the elective theory will only help smooth the way for the granting of specific performance in the exceptional case such as *Hill* v *C. A. Parsons & Co. Ltd*; *Irani* v *Southampton & South West Hampshire Health Authority* [1985] ICR 590 and *Powell* v *London Borough of Brent* [1987] IRLR 466 where trust and confidence can be said to be preserved.

It is thus too early to say that common law and public law developments represent a viable alternative to the statutory claim of unfair dismissal for the majority of employees. The courts have been most reluctant to open up the availability of public law remedies whilst, in the sphere of private law, it remains to be seen whether the courts, having adopted the elective theory of termination, will be prepared to go further and relax their traditional reluctance to exercise their discretion to order an injunction.

There are commentators who detect in the reasoning used in *Irani* and in the Australian case of *Turner* v *Australian Coal & Shale Employees' Federation* (1984) 55 ALR 635 evidence of a considerable relaxation of the 'rule' against specific performance (see Smith (1985) 14 ILJ at p. 248) and *Hughes* v *London Borough of Southwark* [1988] IRLR 55. On the other hand, there are still senior judges who have strong doubts about the validity of the elective theory (see the judgment of May LJ in *R* v *East Berkshire Health Authority, ex parte Walsh* [1985] QB 152).

In these circumstances, for most employees the best hope of redress against the employer's abuse of disciplinary powers remains the statutory claim for unfair dismissal, to be discussed in chapter 7.

READING

Ewing, K.D., 'Job security and the contract of employment' (1989) 18 ILJ 217.

Ewing, K.D., 'Remedies for breach of the contract of employment' [1993] CLJ 437.

McColgan, A., 'Remedies for breach of employment contracts' (1992) 21 ILJ 58.

Sedley, S., 'Public law and contractual employment' (1994) 23 ILJ 201.

7 UNFAIR DISMISSAL

INTRODUCTION

The right to claim unfair dismissal has been part of the legal scenery since 1971 when it was introduced as part of the now repealed Industrial Relations Act. It was introduced because the common law was perceived to be obsolete and unjust and also in an attempt to reduce the number of strikes over dismissals.

The unfair dismissal remedy is undoubtedly regarded as the most important of the 'statutory floor' of employment rights. Certainly in quantitative terms, unfair dismissal claims dominate the work of industrial tribunals accounting for more than 60% of their work-load. In addition, the introduction of the claim produced significant changes in industrial relations practices during the 70s encouraging the reform or formalisation of procedures adopted by employers in taking disciplinary action. The significance of this particular employment right is further enhanced because it is popularly portrayed as a powerful, perhaps too powerful, constraint on managerial prerogative. Your course of study should introduce you to judicial decisions, research and statistics which might cause you to question the extent to which the legislative code on unfair dismissal does effectively control management's power of discipline.

In the decade or so since the introduction of the right, the amount of case law has burgeoned and so has its complexity. As early as 1975 the first President of the EAT, Phillips J, was moved to remark: 'The expression unfair dismissal is in no sense a common-sense expression capable of being understood by the man in the street' (*W. Devis & Sons Ltd* v *Atkins* [1976] ICR 196).

So, while the industrial tribunals and the procedure under which they operate were designed to provide a speedy, cheap and informal mechanism for the resolution of disputes over dismissal, the law they have to apply is often of great complexity. It is therefore not surprising that just over one third of applicants and over a half of respondent employers are legally represented at tribunal hearings (see W. R. Hawes and G. Smith, *Patterns of Representation of the Parties in Unfair Dismissal Cases: A Review of the Evidence*).

This tendency towards excessive legalism is not just a problem for applicants and respondents: it poses potentially serious difficulties for students. Faced with the veritable torrent of case law, how do you go about making sense of it without risking your own sanity? The secret to success in this area is to focus your attention on the cases which lay down principles, provide an interpretation of the statute or offer guidance to industrial tribunals in deciding a particular issue. We would recommend the following advice offered by Smith and Wood in *Industrial Law*, p. 361:

> . . . precedents in this area are, to adopt Noël Coward's saying on wit, to be taken like caviar, not like marmalade.

OVERVIEW

At various points in this book we have suggested that a useful aid to understanding an area of employment law is to construct an overview of the topic under consideration. Alternatively, certain areas, such as equal pay and unfair dismissal, lend themselves to the construction of flowcharts. A flowchart on unfair dismissal might look something like the one set out in figure 7.1

You will see that for analytical purposes the law of unfair dismissal may be divided into four parts or stages.

Stage One: Has a Dismissal Taken Place?

We discussed the three forms of statutory dismissal in chapter 6. If there is a dispute on whether dismissal has taken place, the burden of proof is on the employee.

Stage Two: Is the Applicant Qualified to Make a Claim?

The tribunal must be satisfied on three issues, namely:

(a) that the applicant is an 'employee' (we have already discussed this question in chapter 3);

Figure 7.1

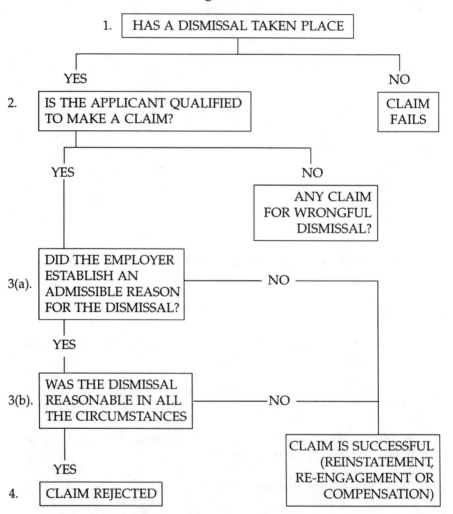

(b)   that the applicant's employment does not fall within an excluded category; *and*

(c)   that the applicant has presented the complaint in time.

Excluded categories

Excluded categories of employment include police and armed forces, workers on fixed-term contracts for at least one year who have waived their rights in writing (EPCA 1978, s. 142(1)), those who 'ordinarily' work outside Great Britain (EPCA 1978, s. 141) and persons excluded for reasons of national security (EPCA 1978, sch. 9, para. 2(1); see *Council of Civil Service Unions* v *Minister for the Civil Service* [1985] ICR 14).

Even employees who are not encompassed within the excluded categories will be unable to bring a claim if they do not possess the requisite continuity of employment. Only in exceptional cases is no period of qualification required, e.g., dismissals related to union membership or activities or to non-unionism and sex or racial discrimination. In the vast majority of claims, the employee must be continuously employed for a period of two calendar years ending with the 'effective date of termination' (we examine this phrase below, whilst the complexities surrounding continuity of employment will be tackled in the following chapter).

It is also worth mentioning one other area of exclusion which has caused the courts a degree of difficulty: that of retirement age. Indeed it has taken three House of Lords decisions to clarify matters. An employee will not be able to claim if, on or before the effective date of termination, the employee has reached the 'normal retiring age' or, if there is no normal retiring age, has reached the age of 65. It has been held that where the contract specifies a retiring age then it can be presumed to be the 'normal retiring age' (see *Nothman* v *Barnet London Borough Council* [1979] ICR 111). But this presumption can be rebutted by evidence that the contractual age has been abandoned in practice. The test of whether this has happened is to ascertain what would be the reasonable expectation or understanding of employees holding that position at the relevant time (*Waite* v *Government Communications Headquarters* [1983] ICR 653).

The third House of Lords case in this area, *Hughes* v *Department of Health & Social Security* [1985] AC 776, concerned the question whether employers can effectively alter a normal retirement age established by practice by a simple announcement to that effect. Their lordships held that this was possible, since such an announcement would vary the expectations of the employees affected.

Claim in time

In common with the enforcement of other employment protection rights, an applicant must present a claim within three months of the effective date of termination. This time-limit is fairly rigorously applied although EPCA 1978, s. 67(2), confers upon a tribunal a discretion to allow a claim to be presented within a reasonable time outside the three-month period where it considers that it was not reasonably practicable for the complaint to be presented in time. The leading authorities in this area tell us that the test to be applied in determining whether a late claim should be considered is not confined to whether the applicant knew of the right to claim but extends to considering whether the applicant should have known (*Dedman* v *British Building & Engineering Appliances Ltd* [1974] ICR 53; *Wall's Meat Co. Ltd* v *Khan* [1978] IRLR 499). In other words, ignorance of rights is not an excuse, unless it appears that the applicant could not reasonably be expected to be aware of them. Such is the stringency of the rule that it has been held that an applicant may not use the excuse that his or her failure to claim in time was due to a mistake of a 'skilled adviser' such as a lawyer, trade union official or CAB worker (*Riley* v *Tesco Stores Ltd* [1980] ICR 323). However, where the erroneous advice was given by an industrial tribunal clerk, this did provide an excuse for a late claim (*Jean Sorelle Ltd* v *Rybak* [1991] IRLR 153).

One recurring problem in this area is whether it is reasonable for the applicant to delay making a claim until the outcome of an internal appeal is known. The balance of authority would now suggest that this would not be a reason for admitting a late claim (see *Palmer* v *Southend-on-Sea Borough Council* [1984] ICR 372).

Examples of valid reasons for delay might be physical incapacity, absence abroad or a postal strike (given as examples in *Wall's Meat Co. Ltd* v *Khan*). If an employee does not discover a fundamental fact until more than three months after the date of dismissal an extension may also be granted. This was the approach taken by the EAT in *Churchill* v *A. Yeates & Sons Ltd* [1983] ICR 380 where the applicant did not discover evidence that his dismissal purportedly for redundancy may have been a sham until after the three-month deadline. This was subsequently approved by the House of Lords in *Machine Tool Industry Research Association* v *Simpson* [1988] IRLR 212.

It is difficult to offer much more guidance on this point because the Court of Appeal has made it clear that the application of the exemption is essentially a matter of fact for the tribunal to decide whether it was 'reasonably feasible' to claim in time (*Palmer* v *Southend-on-Sea Borough Council*).

Effective date of termination (EDT)

At various stages in our discussion, this phrase has cropped up. The identity of the date of termination will determine whether a claim is made in time, whether the applicant possessed the requisite continuity of employment at the date of dismissal, whether the retirement age exclusion is to operate in any particular case and, if the claim is successful, when to calculate compensation.

EPCA 1978 offers a statutory definition of the date of termination for both unfair dismissal and redundancy payment claims and, although for unfair dismissal purposes it is called the 'effective date of termination' and for redundancy payments the 'relevant date', the definition is largely the same in both cases:

(a)   Where the contract of employment is terminated by notice, whether by employer or employee, the date of termination is the date on which the notice expires (ss. 55(4)(a) and 90(1)(a)). Where notice is given orally on a day when work is carried out, the notice period does not begin to run until the following day (*West* v *Kneels Ltd* [1986] IRLR 430). If an employee is dismissed with notice but is given a payment in lieu of working out that notice, the EDT is the date when that notice expires (*Adams* v *GKN Sankey Ltd* [1990] IRLR 416). As will be seen below, a fine distinction is drawn between the latter situation and one where the employee is dismissed with no notice with the payment being in lieu of notice.

(b)   Where the contract of employment is terminated without notice, the date of termination is the date on which the termination takes effect (ss. 55(4)(b) and 90(1)(b)). Two useful cases to be aware of in this area are *Robert Cort & Sons Ltd* v *Charman* [1981] ICR 816 and *Stapp* v *The Shaftesbury Society* [1982] IRLR 326 which both uphold the view that the effective date of termination is the actual date of termination regardless of whether the employment was lawfully or unlawfully terminated. So where, as in *Robert Cort & Sons Ltd* v *Charman*, an employee is summarily dismissed with wages in lieu of notice, the 'effective date of termination' is the actual date on which the employee is told of dismissal and not the date on which notice would expire (see also *Batchelor* v *British Railways Board* [1987] IRLR 136).

(c)   Where the employee is employed under a contract for a fixed term, the date of termination is the date on which the term expires.

One easy way of cutting through the complexities of this section is to remember that in most cases the effective date of termination is the date on which the employee physically leaves work for the last time. The only exception to this rule is provided by s. 55(5) which artificially extends the effective date of termination, either where summary dismissal has occurred despite a period of statutory minimum notice being due under s. 49 or where the statutory notice required to be given is longer than the actual notice given. In either case, the date at the ending of the s. 49 notice period is treated as the effective date of termination.

Stage Three: Is the Dismissal Fair or Unfair?

Assuming that the employee has managed to navigate safely the shark-infested waters of qualification and exclusion, the tribunal will then proceed to determine whether the dismissal is fair or unfair.

This stage involves the tribunal producing answers to two broad questions:

(a)   Has the employer established that the reason or principal reason for the dismissal was an 'admissible' reason?

(b)   In the circumstances has the employer acted reasonably in treating it as a sufficient reason for dismissing the employee?

The reason for the dismissal
It is for the employer to establish that there was an 'admissible' reason for dismissal. These are as follows:

(a)   capability or qualifications;
(b)   conduct;
(c)   redundancy;
(d)   that the employee could not continue to work without contravention of a statute;
(e)   some other substantial reason.

This stage in the process of justifying the dismissal will generally not be difficult to satisfy since it does not involve any consideration of fairness. All that must be proved is the employer's subjective motivation for dismissal. As Cairns LJ put it in *Abernethy* v *Mott, Hay & Anderson* [1974] ICR 323: 'A reason for the dismissal of an employee is a set of facts known to the employer or beliefs held by him which cause him to dismiss the employee'.

In order to maintain credibility, the employer should maintain a consistent story throughout the proceedings. In this regard you should note that EPCA 1978, s. 53, provides that an employee who is under notice or who has been dismissed has a right to be provided by the employer with a written statement of reasons for the dismissal. The procedural significance of s. 53 is that a written statement provided under the section is expressly made admissible in subsequent proceedings. Any basic inconsistency between the terms of the statement and the reason actually put forward before the tribunal could seriously undermine the employer's case.

If an employer gives several reasons for dismissal and one of the reasons is not made out, the burden is on the employer to show that the reason formed 'no important part' of the reason or principal reason for the dismissal (see *Smith* v *Glasgow City District Council* [1987] ICR 796, a relatively rare House of Lords decision on whether a dismissal is fair or unfair).

An employer will only be allowed to rely upon facts known at the time of dismissal to establish what the reason for the dismissal was. Facts which come to light after the dismissal cannot be relied upon to justify the dismissal. This was the conclusion of the House of Lords in the important case of *W. Devis & Sons Ltd* v *Atkins* [1977] AC 931.

Certain reasons for dismissal are regarded as automatically unfair. They are as follows:

(a) Dismissal for trade union membership and activity, or because of refusal to join a trade union or particular trade union (TULR(C)A 1992, s. 152).

(b) Dismissal of a woman because she is pregnant or a reason connected with her pregnancy (EPCA 1978, s. 60 as amended).

(c) Dismissal because of a conviction which is spent under the terms of the Rehabilitation of Offenders Act 1974 (see s. 4(3)(b)).

(d) Dismissal connected with the transfer of an undertaking unless there are economic, technical or organisational reasons entailing changes in the workforce (see the Transfer of Undertakings (Protection of Employment) Regulations 1981 (SI 1981 No. 1795), reg. 8, discussed in chapter 8).

(e) Dismissal on the ground of redundancy if the circumstances constituting the redundancy also applied equally to one or more employees in the same undertaking who held posts similar to that held by the dismissed employee and they have not been dismissed and:

(i) the reason (or, if more than one, the principal reason) for selecting the employee for dismissal was union-related (TULR(C)A, s. 153); or

(ii) the reason for selection was because of pregnancy or childbirth or because the employee had been involved in raising or taking action on health and safety issues (see (f) below) or asserted certain statutory rights (see (g) below) (EPCA 1978, s. 59(1)(a)); or

(iii) the employee was selected for dismissal in contravention of a customary arrangement or agreed procedure relating to redundancy and there were no special reasons justifying a departure from that arrangement or procedure in the circumstances of the case (EPCA 1978, s. 59(1)(b), though this will be repealed when the Deregulation and Contracting Out Act 1994, s. 36(1), is brought into force, which is likely to be in early 1995).

(f) Dismissal on the grounds that the employee:

(i) carried out, or proposed to carry out, duties as a safety representative or as a member of a safety committee;

(ii) where there was no representative or committee, or it was not reasonable to raise the matter with them, brought to the employer's attention, by reasonable means, harmful or potentially harmful circumstances;

(iii) left the place of work, or refused to return to it, in circumstances of danger which the employee reasonably believed to be serious or imminent and which he or she could not reasonably have been expected to avert; or

(iv) in such circumstances, took or proposed to take appropriate steps to protect him or herself or others from danger (EPCA 1978, s. 57A).

(g)   Dismissal where the employee had brought proceedings against the employer to enforce a 'relevant statutory right' or had alleged an infringement of such a right. 'Relevant statutory rights' are those conferred by EPCA 1978 or the Wages Act 1986 for which the remedy is by way of complaint to an industrial tribunal; notice rights under EPCA 1978, s. 49; and rights relating to deductions from pay, union activities and time off under TULR(C)A 1992.

There is one situation where a dismissal will not be subjected to the scrutiny of the tribunal. This is a dismissal for taking part in a strike or other industrial action where all the strikers have been dismissed and there has been no selective re-engagement of those dismissed within a three-month period (TULR(C)A, s. 238). Moreover, by virtue of an amendment introduced by the EA 1990, no employee can complain of unfair dismissal if at the time of dismissal he or she was taking part in *unofficial* industrial action. In such a situation the employer may selectively dismiss or re-engage any participating employee without risking unfair dismissal liability.

An employee's action will be unofficial unless:

(a)   he or she is a member of a trade union and the action is authorised or endorsed by that union; or

(b)   he or she is not a trade union member, but members of a union which has authorised or endorsed the action also take part; or

c)   no trade union members are taking part in the industrial action (TULR(C)A 1992, s. 237).

The reasonableness of the dismissal
Prior to 1980, the burden of proof in unfair dismissal claims at this stage was on the employer. Section 6 of the Employment Act 1980 amended EPCA 1978, s. 57(3), primarily by removing the requirement that the employer *shall* satisfy the industrial tribunal as to the reasonableness of his action, and so rendered the burden of proof 'neutral'. Section 6 also required tribunals to have regard to the size and administrative resources of the employer's undertaking in assessing the reasonableness of the dismissal.

In assessing the test of reasonableness, the question is what a reasonable employer would have done in the circumstances and not what a particular tribunal would have thought right. As such, the reasonableness test is viewed by a number of commentators as not unduly challenging managerial prerogatives in the matter of discipline. In its current formulation, the test is whether the dismissal fell within 'the band of reasonable responses to the employee's conduct within which one employer might take one view, another quite reasonably another' (per Browne-Wilkinson P in *Iceland Frozen Foods Ltd* v *Jones* [1982] IRLR 439 at p. 432, a judgment worth reading because of its clear exposition of the contemporary position).

Provided the industrial tribunal follows the 'band of reasonable responses' test and does not substitute its own view, it will have considerable discretion in reaching its decision and it will only be in rare cases that its decision will be overturned on appeal. This is because the fairness of the dismissal is essentially a question of fact and, provided the tribunal has properly directed itself as to the law then its decision will only be overturned if it was perverse, i.e., no reasonable tribunal could possibly have come to that decision on the particular facts.

The scope of the industrial tribunal's discretion has been further enhanced by the Court of Appeal's rejection of the EAT's attempts to provide guidelines for tribunals to follow when confronted with major issues of unfair dismissal law, e.g., redundancy procedure, suspected theft, long-term sickness absence. The nature of the Court of Appeal's attack on what was seen as the EAT's unduly interventionist role is clearly illustrated by the following statement of Lawton LJ in *Bailey* v *BP Oil (Kent Refinery) Ltd* [1980] IRLR 287:

> Each case must depend on its own facts. In our judgment it is unwise for this court or the Employment Appeal Tribunal to set out guidelines, and wrong to make rules and establish presumptions for industrial tribunals to follow or take into account.

This attack on legalism and the proliferation of appeals, however, may be at the cost of certainty and consistency.

In reaching a conclusion on the reasonableness of the dismissal, the tribunal may have regard to two broad questions: the substantive merits and procedural fairness.

The substantive merits may involve the tribunal taking into account mitigating factors such as the employee's length of service, previous disciplinary record and any explanation or excuse. These factors may have to be balanced against the business needs of the employer which, as we shall see, are regarded as a particularly relevant factor in cases of dismissal for long-term sickness or those resulting from business reorganisations. Remember that s. 57(3) requires a dismissal to be fair in all the circumstances — fair to the employee and fair to the employing organisation.

The second element of the test of fairness relates to the question of the fairness of the procedures adopted by the employer in the events leading up to the dismissal. The concept of procedural fairness is not expressly articulated in the legislation but its development was influenced by the codes of practice which were introduced to accompany the legislation. The provisions relevant to discipline and dismissal are presently contained in the ACAS Code of Practice No. 1, *Disciplinary Practices and Procedures in Employment*. The Code's guidelines do not carry the force of law but any of its provisions which appear to a court or tribunal to be relevant to a question arising in the proceedings must be taken into account in reaching a decision (see TULR(C)A 1992, s. 207).

It is important that you are fully familiar with the guidance contained in the code (fortunately it is a relatively short document). You should also try to get hold of the ACAS advisory handbook, 'Discipline at Work'. Though the handbook has no statutory force, it concisely summarises the views of the leading cases on what constitutes a fair dismissal and it is well worthy of careful study. It also reproduces the Code of Practice as an appendix and is free from ACAS. When you obtain your copy of the Code, you will see that its main requirements are as follows:

(a)   Warnings (para. 12). The code recommends that in the case of minor offences there should be a formal oral warning followed by a written warning, and then a final written warning which should make it clear that any recurrence will result in dismissal.

(b)   Careful investigation by the employer (paras 10(i) and 11).

(c)   An opportunity to state a case and a right to be accompanied (paras 10(f), (g) and 11).

(d)   The right to appeal against any disciplinary decision (paras 10(k) and 16).

In the early 70s the courts and tribunals laid much emphasis on the importance of employers adhering strictly to the basic procedural requirements of fairness, taking the code as their guide. In one of the earliest cases, Sir John Donaldson thought that the only exception to the need for the employee to be allowed to state his case was 'where there can be no explanation which could cause the employer to refrain from dismissing the employee' (see *Earl* v *Slater & Wheeler (Airlyne) Ltd* [1972] ICR 508). So it had to be almost inconceivable that the hearing could have made any difference. This test was, however, replaced by more lenient standards.

Whilst the earlier approach could result in a dismissal being found to be unfair on procedural failings alone, the contemporary position is to view procedural matters as just one of a number of factors to be taken into account (see *Bailey* v *BP Oil (Kent Refinery) Ltd* [1980] IRLR 287).

The highpoint of this dilution of procedural requirements is to be found in the test laid down by the EAT in *British Labour Pump Co. Ltd* v *Byrne* [1979] ICR 347. This test allowed the employer to argue that an element of procedural unfairness (such as a failure to give a proper hearing) may be 'forgiven' if the employer can show that, on the balance of probabilities, even if a proper procedure had been complied with the employee would still have been dismissed and the dismissal would then have been fair.

This decision received considerable academic and judicial criticism but was specifically approved of by the Court of Appeal in *W. & J. Wass Ltd v Binns* [1982] ICR 486. The major criticism of the *British Labour Pump Co. Ltd v Byrne* principle was that it was irreconcilable with the ruling of the House of Lords in *W. Devis & Sons Ltd v Atkins* [1977] AC 391 that the employer was not entitled to rely on evidence acquired after dismissal and that fairness must be judged in the light of facts known to the employer at the time of dismissal.

This forceful criticism of the logic of *British Labour Pump Co. Ltd v Byrne* was accepted by the House of Lords in *Polkey v A. E. Dayton Services Ltd* [1988] AC 344 and the principle has been overruled. This decision is perhaps the most important unfair dismissal decision of the past decade and must be included in the portfolio of employment law cases with which you are closely familiar. In the judgments we find a re-emphasis of the importance of following a fair procedure. In the view of Lord Bridge of Harwich:

> . . . an employer having prima facie grounds to dismiss . . . will in the great majority of cases not act reasonably in treating the reason as a sufficient reason for dismissal unless and until he has taken the steps, conveniently classified in most of the authorities as 'procedural', which are necessary in the circumstances of the case to justify that course of action.

Lord Mackay of Clashfern was of the view that what must be considered is what a reasonable employer would have had in mind at the time he decided to dismiss:

> If the employer could reasonably have concluded in the light of the circumstances known to him at the time of dismissal that consultation or warning would be utterly useless he might well act reasonably even if he did not observe the provisions of the code.

It has been argued that there is a significant practical difference between asking whether at the time of the dismissal the employer had reasonable grounds for believing that a fair procedure would have been 'utterly useless' (the new test) and asking whether, in retrospect, it would have made any difference to the outcome (the old test). As a result it is predicted that failure to follow a fair procedure may well lead to a finding of unfair dismissal in a much increased proportion of cases (but see *Duffy v Yeomans and Partners Ltd* [1994] IRLR 642, CA, discussed at page 171).

For those who recognise the value of natural justice in discipline the decision will be welcome along with an earlier ruling of the House of Lords in *West Midlands Co-operative Society Ltd* v *Tipton* [1986] AC 536. As with *Polkey* v *A. E. Dayton Services Ltd* the point at issue was the precise scope of the *W. Devis & Sons Ltd* v *Atkins* principle. Ever since *W. Devis & Sons Ltd* v *Atkins* it was not clear whether, and to what extent, that decision prevented matters arising out of internal appeals from being considered by tribunals as part of their 'reasonableness' assessment under EPCA 1978, s. 57(3). In *West Midlands Co-operative Society Ltd* v *Tipton* the House of Lords confirmed that both the denial of a contractual right to appeal and matters arising out of an appeal, if one is held, can be taken into account by tribunals when they assess the reasonableness of the employer's conduct. Lord Bridge of Harwich felt that the rule in *W. Devis & Sons Ltd* v *Atkins* simply prevented conduct unrelated to the real reason for dismissal from affecting the question whether an employer acted unreasonably in dismissing the employee for the reason he did. But there was:

> nothing in the language of the statute to exclude from consideration . . . evidence relevant to show the strength or weakness of the real reason for dismissal which the employer has the opportunity to consider in the course of an [internal] appeal.

As a result of the Lords' ruling in *West Midlands Co-operative Society Ltd* v *Tipton*, in the context of internal appeals, a dismissal will be unfair if:

(a) the employer unreasonably treated his real reason as a sufficient reason to dismiss the employee — either at the time the original decision to dismiss was made or at the conclusion of an internal appeal; *or*

(b) the employer refused to entertain an appeal to which the employee was contractually entitled and thereby denied him the opportunity to show that, in all the circumstances, the real reason for dismissal could not reasonably be treated as sufficient.

Remedies

Once the tribunal is satisfied that an employee has been unfairly dismissed, it has to consider one of three forms of remedy:

(a) an order for reinstatement,
(b) an order of re-engagement,
(c) an award of compensation (see EPCA 1978, ss. 67 to 69).

Although reinstatement and re-engagement are regarded as primary remedies by the statute, in practice compensation is the normal remedy for unfair dismissal, such orders only being made by tribunals in roughly 3% of successful cases. As a result, the re-employment of dismissed workers has been described as the 'lost remedy'.

We can summarise the rules relating to the calculation. of unfair dismissal compensation as follows:

(a) Basic award (EPCA 1978, s. 73). An award of $\frac{1}{2}$, 1 or $1\frac{1}{2}$ weeks' pay for each year of continuous service (depending on age), subject to a maximum of 20 years. The maximum allowable for a week's pay is currently £205 (1994/95): this figure is reviewed each year.

If aged	But less than	No. of weeks' pay for each year
	22	$\frac{1}{2}$
22	41	1
41	65	$1\frac{1}{2}$

If the applicant is aged 64, entitlement goes down one twelfth for each month after 64th birthday.

Therefore the maximum payment under this head of calculation in the year 1994/95 will be:

$$£205 \times 20 \times 1\frac{1}{2} = £6,150$$

(b) The tribunal may also make a compensatory award (EPCA 1978, s. 74). This is an amount which the tribunal considers just and equitable. The maximum here in 1994/95 is a sum of £11,000.

Both heads of compensation may be reduced if the applicant contributed to his dismissal or as a result of any conduct before dismissal.

(c) Additional award. This award is made where an order for reinstatement or re-engagement is not complied with. If the original dismissal was for a reason other than sex, race or trade union discrimination, the award may be between 13 and 26 weeks' pay. If the reason was for discrimination, then there is a discretion to award between 26 and 52 weeks' pay. (Current maximum 52 × £205 = £10,660.)

You should also be aware that, by virtue of the Employment Act 1982, the amount of compensation to be awarded for unfair dismissal on grounds of trade union membership and activities or non-membership is much higher than for other types of dismissal because a 'special award' is made in addition to the basic and compensatory elements (see now TULR(C)A 1992, ss. 155 to 167, as to how this award is arrived at).

Before you start to think that a career as an 'employment protection rip-off artist' might be lucrative, we should warn you that the median average compensation awards are relatively low: £2,773 in 1993/94 (see *Employment Gazette*, October 1994).

THE EXAMINATION

In revising this area, remember what we said at the beginning about the dangers of being submerged in the torrent of decisions flowing from the courts and tribunals. Try to concentrate your attention on cases which establish principles, authoritative interpretation of the statute or, more rarely these days, offer guidance to industrial tribunals in deciding a particular issue.

Remember also that an unfair dismissal problem will have a number of issues not all of which will be necessarily drawn from the lecture series concerned with the law of unfair dismissal. A slick examiner can weave in issues from other parts of the course such as employee status, construction of the contract, discrimination, redundancy, etc. This is how it should be because, after all, employment problems which occur in real life do not come neatly compartmentalised.

One thing that you can safely rely on is that there will be at least one and maybe more question(s) featuring unfair dismissal on your examination paper. In the next section, we shall discuss several problem questions which will allow us to examine the case law surrounding some frequently recurring factual situations: dismissals for suspected theft, long-term illness and persistent absenteeism. We shall then discuss an essay question which will allow us to grapple with some of the policy debates in this area.

Question One

Fanfare Ltd is a manufacturer of hi-fi equipment. Fred and Bert work as storemen in the CD warehouse in which Fanfare's compact disc players are stored. Fred has been employed with Fanfare since the company started trading some 10 years ago. Bert started employment with the firm on 1 December 1992.

Recently, the company discovered stock deficiencies in its compact disc players. As a result, the firm's security officer was asked to carry out an investigation into the cause of these deficiencies. Having maintained close surveillance of the CD warehouse over a period of a month, the security officer reports that it is his view that either Fred or Bert or both of them were pilfering the machines. His reasons for forming this view are based on an anonymous tip-off, that Fred and Bert have recently purchased new cars and that the two workers were left alone in the warehouse for long periods.

Mr Snyd, the CD warehouse manager, received this report on 24 November 1994. On the same day, he called Bert and Fred to his office and told them: 'This company can't go on subsidising your ambitious life-styles. One or both of you are dishonest and you're both sacked.'

Two days later, Fred and Bert, through their union representative, sought to appeal under Fanfare's disciplinary procedure. This request was rejected by Mr Snyd on the grounds that he had called in the police and 'It was a matter for them now'.

Fred and Bert were charged with theft and released on bail pending their trial. Some four months later they were acquitted of the charges in the Crown Court. At the trial, evidence was adduced by the defence that the apparent stock shortage was due to an accounting error in the finance department of the company.

Fred lodged an application to an industrial tribunal two days after his dismissal. Bert, on the other hand, was advised by his full-time union official to await the outcome of the criminal proceedings.

Advise Fred and Bert.

Analysis

In approaching this problem you might find it useful to adopt the four-stage structure for analysis which we have set out earlier in the chapter. In adopting this framework, however, you should always pay close attention to the main thrust of the problem. For example, it is clear that in this question employment status is not the issue so there is no point in embarking on a long discourse on the tests used to determine whether Fred and Bert are 'employees'. This will just waste time and gather absolutely no marks.

Stage one. It is clear that both Fred and Bert have been dismissed without notice and this, of course, falls within EPCA 1978, s. 55(2)(a).

Stage two. Are Fred and Bert qualified to claim? It would appear that Fred will have no difficulty overcoming this particular obstacle.

There are, however, two serious problems in relation to Bert's claim: the sufficiency of his continuous employment and the time at which his claim was lodged.

Bert's period of continuous employment. The issue here is whether at the 'effective date of termination' Bert can establish that he has been employed for the necessary qualifying period of two years. As we have seen, normally under s. 55(4), the effective date of termination will be the date on which a period of notice expires, the date on which a dismissal without notice takes effect, or the date on which a fixed-term contract expires without being renewed under the same contract. For certain purposes, however, s. 55(5) extends the effective date of termination, either where summary dismissal has occurred despite statutory minimum notice being due under EPCA 1978, s. 49, or where the statutory notice required is longer than the notice actually given. In both situations, the date of the s. 49 notice is treated as the effective date of termination. In Bert's case, the statutory minimum notice extension of one week would just give him the requisite qualifying period. (You can guarantee that if dates are included in a problem, they are there for a reason!)

However, an unresolved problem is whether the s. 55(5) extension of the effective date of termination will apply in the event of a dismissal for 'gross misconduct'. This doubt arises because s. 49(5) declares that the minimum notice entitlement under the section 'does not affect any right of either party to treat the contract as terminable without notice by reason of such conduct by the other party as would have enabled him so to treat it before the passing of this Act'.

The only authority on this point is *Lanton Leisure Ltd* v *White and Gibson* [1987] IRLR 119. In this case, the EAT ruled that an employer cannot avoid the effect of s. 55(5) merely by dismissing summarily and labelling his reason for dismissal as gross misconduct. The EAT decided that, in such a case, it is first necessary to find out by means of an enquiry on the merits whether there was in fact such conduct which would enable an employer to terminate without notice. Since the tribunal's decision on whether there has been conduct meriting summary dismissal will be virtually the same as whether the dismissal was fair or unfair, it would appear that in practice s. 49(5) does not prevent the operation of s. 55(5). It would thus appear that Bert might be able to overcome this initial obstacle.

Bert's late claim. The question here is whether the industrial tribunal will be prepared to exercise its discretion under s. 67(2) to allow Bert's claim to be presented outside the three-month period. Bert has been advised by the full-time official to await the outcome of the criminal matter before lodging his complaint. This advice may well be regarded as faulty because the weight of authority would suggest that delay in making a complaint of unfair dismissal because of a pending criminal proceeding will not be accepted as an excuse (see the views of Lord Denning MR in *Wall's Meat Co. Ltd* v *Khan* [1978] IRLR 499 at p. 501 and *Porter* v *Bandridge Ltd* [1978] ICR 943).

The full-time official may well be regarded as a 'skilled adviser' and his negligence will be imputed to Bert (see *Times Newspapers Ltd* v *O'Regan* [1977] IRLR 101).

Stage three: fair or unfair? The important authority you need to employ at this stage of the problem is *British Home Stores Ltd* v *Burchell* [1978] IRLR 379. The test formulated by the EAT in that case is whether the employer:

(a)   entertained a genuine belief in the guilt of the employee;
(b)   had reasonable grounds for that belief; and
(c)   had carried out as much investigation into the matter as was reasonable.

This test was approved by the Court of Appeal in *W. Weddell & Co. Ltd* v *Tepper* [1980] ICR 286.

You might have a degree of reservation about the reasonableness of the grounds on which Mr Snyd acted: the evidence would appear to be highly circumstantial.

One potential obstacle standing in the way of a successful claim is the decision of the Court of Appeal in *Monie* v *Coral Racing Ltd* [1981] ICR 109 that if an employer can only narrow down his suspicions to one of two employees, it may be reasonable to dismiss both. Similarly, in our problem Mr Snyd cannot identify which of his two employees is the alleged thief. Nevertheless, we should emphasise that the tribunal would still have to be satisfied that a reasonable investigation had been carried out. (For a recent application of the *Monie* principle to a case of capability or conduct not involving dishonesty see the EAT's decision in *Whitbread & Co. plc* v *Thomas* [1988] IRLR 43.)

The fact that Fred and Bert are subsequently acquitted of the criminal charges is, however, one factor which will not help them. This is because the employer is judged by the state of evidence known to him at the time of the dismissal — not on the basis of what happens afterwards (see *Ferodo Ltd* v *Barnes* [1976] ICR 439; *Harris (Ipswich) Ltd* v *Harrison* [1978] ICR 1256).

Once the process of investigation has ascertained the facts, the employees have the right to have the accusations put to them. This is not done in our problem and Fred and Bert are not given a clear indication of why they are being dismissed. This lapse, together with the failure to allow an appeal against the dismissal, should be an additional reason for holding the dismissal to be unfair because the employees are being denied an opportunity to show that the employer's suspicions are ill-founded (*Polkey* v *A. E. Dayton Services Ltd* [1988] AC 344; *West Midlands Co-operative Society* v *Tipton* [1986] AC 536).

The reason given for not allowing the right of appeal — police involvement — may be found to be somewhat unconvincing by the tribunal. It is true that there is one case in which it was suggested that where the employee's actions are being actively investigated by the police, it may be improper for the employer to run through the usual disciplinary procedures and expect the employee to explain his conduct (*Carr* v *Alexander Russell Ltd* [1976] IRLR 220). The weight of authority, however, would appear to favour the view that the employer should at least give the employee an opportunity to make representations (*Harris (Ipswich) Ltd* v *Harrison*; *Harris* v *Courage (Eastern) Ltd* [1982] ICR 530).

Stage four: remedies. It is clear that the problem is not focused on remedies and therefore an extremely brief reference to the remedies available to Fred and Bert, should they succeed, is quite sufficient.

Question Two

(a) Widgets Ltd has a work-force of one thousand. Alf has been employed as a machine operator for the past 15 years. He has been absent for the past three months as a result of a skin complaint. Last week, the company requested that Alf be examined by the company's occupational health officer. The report shows that Alf has developed an allergy to the coolant which is used on the machine on which he works. The company dismisses him with wages in lieu of notice. At the time of his dismissal Alf had not exhausted his company sick-pay entitlement.

(b) Tricia is also employed as a machine operator by the company and has seven years' service. Over the past 18 months her attendance record was in the region of 65%. Most of these absences were self-certificated by Tricia. The reasons given by Tricia included influenza, cystitis, virus infection, food poisoning and flatulence. During this period she was warned by the works manager that her absence level was unacceptable. Two months ago a final written warning informed her that if her attendance did not improve then her cards would follow. Last week the company dismissed her.

Advise Widgets Ltd.

Analysis

Alf v Widgets Ltd

The first issue to discuss here is whether the contract is frustrated. We have fully discussed the operation of the doctrine of frustration in our chapter on termination. Remember that the Court of Appeal has recently held that the doctrine is applicable in appropriate cases of long-term sickness (*Notcutt v Universal Equipment Co. (London) Ltd* [1986] ICR 414).

In *Marshall v Harland & Wolff Ltd* [1972] ICR 101 Sir John Donaldson suggested that in order to determine whether sickness frustrated the contract regard should be had to a number of factors:

(a) The terms of the contract, including any provision for sick pay.

(b) How long the employment was likely to last in the absence of sickness, a temporary or specific hiring being more likely to come within the doctrine.

(c) The nature of the employment, the contract being more likely to survive the period of absence if the employee does not occupy a key post.

(d) The nature of the illness, how long it has already continued and the prospects of recovery.

(e) The period of past employment. 'A relationship which is of long duration is not so easily destroyed as one which has but a short history.'

The 'frustration checklist' was recognised by Sir John as not necessarily exhaustive and was added to by the EAT in *Egg Stores (Stamford Hill) Ltd* v *Leibovici* [1977] ICR 260. The additions were:

(f) The risk to the employer of acquiring obligations in respect of redundancy payments or compensation for unfair dismissal to the replacement employee.

(g) Whether wages had continued to be paid.

(h) The acts and statements of the employer in relation to the employment, including the dismissal of, or failure to dismiss, the employee.

(i) Whether in all the circumstances a reasonable employer could be expected to wait any longer.

These factors should help you answer the fundamental question: Was Alf's incapacity, looked at before the purported dismissal, of such a nature, or did it appear likely to continue for such a period, that further performance of his obligations in the future would either be impossible or would be a thing radically different from that undertaken by him under the contract? If frustration is found, then there will be no dismissal and Widgets will not have its actions subjected to the scrutiny of the industrial tribunal under s. 57(3).

The alternative argument available to the employers is that the dismissal related to capability and that it has behaved reasonably in treating Alf's absence as sufficient reason for the dismissal.

In analysing the tribunals' approach to the fairness or otherwise of a dismissal for ill health it is possible to identify two broad tests: (a) the substantive and (b) the procedural.

The substantive aspect revolves around the question of whether it was reasonable of the employer to dismiss in the particular circumstances of the case and involves a consideration of the employer's and employee's circumstances. Such an approach is evidenced in the judgment of Phillips J in *Spencer* v *Paragon Wallpapers Ltd* [1977] ICR 301 when describing the relevant elements of the reasonableness test:

> . . . the employers' need for the work to be done and the employee's need for time in which to recover his health . . . The basic question which has to be determined in every case is whether, in all the circumstances, the employer can be expected to wait any longer and, if so, how much longer? Every case will be different, depending upon the circumstances.

The question of the time the employee must be away from work before it may be reasonable for an employer to dismiss depends, as was stated in *Spencer* v *Paragon Wallpapers Ltd*, on the circumstances of each case. A significant factor may be the size of the employer's undertaking. In a large firm, the disruption caused by sickness absence may be minimal but in a small business such absences may be extremely serious. Remember that s. 57(3) has been amended so as to draw the industrial tribunal's attention to thesize and administrative resources of the employer's undertaking' when considering the question of reasonableness.

Where an employee is covered by a contractual sick pay scheme, can the employer dismiss before the sick-pay entitlement period lapses? It may be assumed that if an employer has contracted to provide a certain period of sick pay it would not normally be reasonable to dismiss before this time has elapsed. However, this does not mean that it will always be unfair to dismiss during the currency of a sick-pay period, if urgent business needs demand it (see *Coulson* v *Felixstowe Dock Co.* [1975] IRLR 11).

The second aspect of the reasonableness test under s. 57(3) involves the consideration of the adequacy of the procedures the employer has adopted in coming to the conclusion that dismissal is necessary. An employer will be expected to make a reasonable effort to inform himself of the true medical position and this will normally entail consulting the employee and seeking, with the employee's consent, a medical opinion.

The need for consultation with the employee was stressed in *Spencer* v *Paragon Wallpapers Ltd* and strongly affirmed by the EAT's decision in *East Lindsey District Council* v *Daubney* [1977] IRLR 181:

Unless there are wholly exceptional circumstances, before an employee is dismissed on the ground of ill health it is necessary that he should be consulted and the matter discussed with him, and that in one way or another steps should be taken by the employer to discover the true medical position. . . Discussions and consultation will often bring to light facts and circumstances of which the employers were unaware, and which will throw new light on the problem. Or the employee may wish to seek medical advice on his own account, which, brought to the notice of the employers' medical advisers, will cause them to change their opinion.

On the other hand, consultation has not always been required by industrial tribunals. In *Taylorplan Catering (Scotland) Ltd* v *McInally* [1980] IRLR 53 it was suggested that where a tribunal finds that the circumstances were such that consultation would have made no difference to the result it will not be required. In this case, the EAT was of the view that the guidelines in *British Labour Pump Co. Ltd* v *Byrne* [1979] ICR 347 could be applied to cases of dismissal for ill health. With the rejection of those guidelines by the House of Lords in *Polkey* v *A. E. Dayton Services Ltd* [1988] AC 344 it is likely that consultation will be required in the vast majority of cases.

Assuming that the tribunal is satisfied that the employer could not reasonably wait any longer before replacing the sick employee and that he has made reasonable efforts to establish the true medical position, the employer may find that he has one further duty to comply with before he can successfully defend the claim for unfair dismissal: an obligation to look for alternative work for the sick employee within the organisation. Where there is a suitable job in existence which the employee is capable of performing, a failure to offer it to the employee may well cast doubt on the fairness of the dismissal.

In Alf's case the company probably did take reasonable steps to establish the true medical position. However, it would appear that it failed to consult Alf once the allergy problem had been identified. One response from the company may be that the nature of the allergy made it impossible for Alf to return to his old job and therefore consultation would have been pointless. On the other hand, consultation may have produced a solution to the problem. Could Widgets use a different coolant mixture on Alf's machine, was there alternative work available which Alf might find acceptable?

Tricia v Widgets Ltd
The principles discussed thus far relate to situations where an employee is absent from work for a substantial period of time through illness. Until relatively recently, it was not clear whether the same rules covered persistent absenteeism, i.e., frequent absences generally covered by medical certificates. However, the decisions of the EAT in *International Sports Co. Ltd v Thomson* [1980] IRLR 340 and *Rolls-Royce Ltd v Walpole* [1980] IRLR 343 clarified matters, making it clear that these principles are not applicable in dealing with frequent absenteeism through sickness. According to the EAT in *International Sports Co. Ltd v Thomson* this type of situation comes under the heading of dismissal for conduct (s. 57(2)(b)) or possibly some other substantial reason (s. 57(1)(b)) rather than capability and therefore the use of warnings was an appropriate means of dealing with the problem.

In such a case, it would be placing too heavy a burden on the employer to require him to carry out a formal medical investigation and, even if he did, such an investigation would rarely be fruitful because of the transient nature of the employee's symptoms and complaints. What is required, in our judgment, is, firstly, that there should be a fair review by the employer of the attendance record and the reasons for it; and, secondly, appropriate warnings, after the employee has been given an opportunity to make representations. If then there is no adequate improvement in the attendance record, it is likely that in most cases the employer will be justified in treating the persistent absences as a sufficient reason for dismissing the employee.

In our problem, Widgets seems to have complied with these guidelines should Tricia take her claim to the industrial tribunal.

An Essay Question on Unfair Dismissal

'. . . far from controlling managerial discretion and therefore protecting the interests of employees in job security, the law [of unfair dismissal] endorses and legitimates a strong conception of managerial authority' (Hugh Collins).

Discuss. What reforms if any would you advocate in the law of unfair dismissal?

This quotation is taken from Collins's radical critique of unfair dismissal law, 'Capitalist discipline and corporatist law' (1982) 11 ILJ 78, 170. In answering this question it will be an advantage if you are familiar with the article, allowing you to expand on the position taken by Collins and to contrast his views with those of other writers. What should you do if, on the other hand, you feel that you have enough information with which to answer the question but are not familiar with the particular article from which the quote is taken? In this particular instance, it is probably safe to embark on an answer. After all, the question does not specifically ask you to discuss Collins's views and the use of the quote may be seen as a way of flagging that a critical analysis of the law of unfair dismissal is called for. But one final word of warning before you embark on this question: do make sure you have sufficient ammunition with which to tackle it. You will need to refer to the works of writers and researchers in addition to discussing selected areas of case law in some detail. A mere catalogue of statutory provisions and decided cases is not going to impress the examiner. If you have any doubts then look for a problem question to answer instead.

Analysis

The first part of the question is asking you to discuss the proposition that the law has been unsuccessful as an effective control upon managerial prerogative in relation to dismissals. Collins puts forward the view that the explanation for this lies in the attitudes of the appellate court judges to the legislation. The judges, Collins argues, are not happy with the unfair dismissal provisions because they are perceived to be 'corporatist' in that they overstep the boundary between matters which are suitable for State intervention and those which are not. The judges feel unhappy about meddling in affairs they have always thought should be left to individuals to resolve. Consequently the courts and tribunals are unwilling to substitute their own standards of fairness for management opinions and instead have a tendency to endorse the ordinary practices of employers. Once this occurs it is inevitable that the concept of fairness will tend to favour managerial control. Collins is therefore unable to agree with another commentator, Elias, 'Fairness in unfair dismissal: trends and tensions' (1981) 10 ILJ 201, who suggests that overall the appellate courts have ensured that 'the pursuit of profits must be tempered by consideration of the employee's interests in the enterprise'.

Whilst the views of these writers represent two broad perspectives on the operation of the law of unfair dismissal, it is possible to identify a third school of thought which views the legislation as far too favourable to employees and, as a result, has the effect of discouraging employers from taking on new employees. This line of thinking is broadly representative of the current government and, as we shall see, has informed its policy towards amendments to the law of unfair dismissal since it came to office in 1979.

Whichever perspective you adopt, there are certain key areas which you will need to advert to in answering the first part of the question. We should declare at the outset that we share many of the criticisms which Collins makes of the law but we will seek to present the evidence as dispassionately as possible. Remember, we all have our own frames of reference.

The concept of the reasonable employer

Earlier in the chapter we stated that in assessing reasonableness, the question is what the reasonable employer would have done in the circumstances and not what the industrial tribunal would have thought fair (*Iceland Frozen Foods Ltd* v *Jones* [1982] IRLR 439). In this sense the courts do not set norms of behaviour but merely reflect existing managerial standards. A stark illustration of the results of this approach can be seen in *Saunders* v *Scottish National Camps Association Ltd* [1980] IRLR 174. The employee was a maintenance handyman at a children's camp. He was dismissed on the grounds of being a homosexual. The dismissal was held fair on the grounds that a considerable proportion of employers would take the view that the employment of a homosexual should be restricted, particularly when required to work in proximity and contact with children. So, instead of laying down its standards, the EAT relied on the commonly held and perhaps highly prejudicial views of some employers.

The adoption of the band of reasonable responses test has meant that tribunals have been reluctant to criticise the decision to dismiss on the ground that a lesser penalty would have been more appropriate. As long as the action of dismissal is found to fall within the spectrum of reasonable responses, the tribunal will not intervene (see *British Leyland UK Ltd* v *Swift* [1981] IRLR 91).

Overriding contractual rights
The test of fairness is not inevitably controlled by the content of the contract
of employment. As a result, the courts and tribunals have been prepared to
hold as fair dismissals where the employee has refused to agree to a change
in terms and conditions of employment in line with the employer's
perception of business efficacy. Dismissals for refusal to agree to unilateral
changes in job content, pay, location and hours of work have been held to
be for 'some other substantial reason' and fair (see, for example, *Ellis* v
Brighton Co-operative Society [1976] IRLR 419; *Hollister* v *National Farmers'
Union* [1979] IRLR 238).

Whilst the courts and tribunals will expect the employer to lead evidence
to show why it was felt to be necessary to impose the changes (*Banerjee* v
City & East London Area Health Authority [1979] IRLR 147), they have not
imposed particularly strict criteria when judging the 'substantiality' of those
decisions. In *Ellis* v *Brighton Co-operative Society* it was suggested that the test
was whether, if the changes were not implemented, the whole business
would be brought to a standstill. A much less stringent test was formulated
by Lord Denning MR in *Hollister* v *National Farmers' Union* where he felt that
the principle should extend to situations 'where there was some sound,
good business reason for the reorganisation'. In subsequent cases, the EAT
has been prepared to dilute the test even further; in one case requiring only
that the changes were considered as 'matters of importance' or to have
'discernible advantages' to the organisation (*Banerjee* v *City & East London
Area Health Authority*) and in another demanding that the reorganisation be
'beneficial' (*Bowater Containers Ltd* v *McCormack* [1980] IRLR 50).

Surveys of the case law on reorganisation or 'business efficacy' tend to
show the adoption of a strong conception of managerial prerogative by the
courts and tribunals (see Painter, 'Any other substantial reason: a managerial prerogative?' (1981) 131 NLJ; Bowers and Clark, 'Unfair dismissal
and managerial prerogative: a study of 'other substantial reason'' (1981) 101
LJ 34). Indeed, Collins points to the irony that, in this sphere, even the
discredited remedy of wrongful dismissal offers greater protection to a
worker faced with a unilateral change of terms.

Dilution of procedural fairness
Critics of the operation of the law of unfair dismissal lay much emphasis
on the tendency of the courts and tribunals to put less weight on the
employer's failure to follow a fair procedure (see, for example, Williams,
'Unfair dismissal: myths and statistics' (1983) 12 ILJ 157).

This particular criticism, however, has lost much of its potency with the
decision of the House of Lords in *Polkey* v *E. A. Dayton Services Ltd* [1988]
AC 344. As a result, failure to follow a fair procedure may well now lead
to a finding of unfair dismissal in a much increased proportion of cases.

Not all commentators are entirely convinced that the renewed emphasis on procedural rectitude will assist applicants. McLean (1986) 15 ILJ 205 suggests cynically that the renewed attachment to procedural justice is in inverse proportion to the likelihood of compensation being awarded to an 'undeserving' dismissed employee. In the early days of unfair dismissal, the industrial tribunals could reduce compensation to nil in this sort of situation. When this power was removed with the introduction of the minimum basic award in EPCA 1978 the *British Labour Pump Co. Ltd* v *Byrne* principle developed. Following the repeal of the minimum basic award by the Employment Act 1980 there has been a return to the earlier approach. Of course, as McLean recognises, holding that the dismissed employee contributed to his or her own dismissal will not mean zero compensation in every case, whereas a finding of fair dismissal will mean just that.

Recent developments may confirm some of McLean's doubts. First it is clear that the 'no difference' test still has a significant part to play in reducing compensation awards (see *Rao* v *Civil Aviation Authority* [1994] ICR 495, CA; *Red Bank Manufacturing Co. Ltd* v *Meadows* [1992] ICR 204, EAT). Furthermore, in *Duffy* v *Yeomans and Partners Ltd* [1994] IRLR 642, CA, it was held that *Polkey* does not require that the employer must have consciously taken a decision not to consult with the employee. According to Balcombe LJ, it is sufficient that, judged objectively, the employer does what a reasonable employer might do. The danger inherent in this objective test is that it resembles the 'did it make any difference?' test that *Polkey* rejected.

An alternative perspective to that of Collins — and in its own way equally as radical — argues that the law of unfair dismissal has unduly hampered management and the law should be amended to render it less restrictive. As we have stated above, the current government subscribes to this view. Since 1979, the government has introduced a number of changes to the law: it has 'neutralised' the burden of proof; introduced the pre-hearing assessment in an attempt to discourage the continuance of claims which are unlikely to succeed; and it has increased the qualification period necessary to claim from 26 weeks, where it stood in 1979, to the current requirement of two years. More recently, the Employment Act 1989 exempted employers of less than 20 employees from the requirement to include a note specifying any disciplinary rules and any appeals procedure which are applicable to the employee (see now EPCA 1978, s. 3(3) as amended). The same Act empowered the Secretary of State to make regulations authorising whoever conducts a 'pre-hearing review' to require either party to pay a deposit of up to £150 'if he wishes to continue to participate in the proceedings': a renewed attempt to discourage claims that have 'no reasonable prospect of success' (see the Industrial Tribunals (Constitution and Rules of Procedure) Regulations 1993).

These changes were introduced because it was felt that the employment protection legislation has had a 'negative employment effect', i.e., it has discouraged employers from recruiting. However, surveys of management attitudes and responses have shown the legislation to have had only a minor impact, inducing greater care in selection in order to ensure the right quality of recruits rather than reducing quantity (see W. W. Daniel and E. Stilgoe, *The Impact of the Employment Protection Laws*; A. Clifton and C. Tatton-Brown, *The Impact of Employment Protection on Small Firms*. The latest research found that only 8% of firms surveyed expressed reluctance to recruit additional labour on account of the law of unfair dismissal (Evans, Goodman & Hargreaves, 'Unfair dismissal law and employment practice in the 1980s', DES Research Paper 53).

Your view of reform in this area, as with so many issues in employment law, will be affected by your ideological perspective. You may disagree with the thrust of the quotation in the question and argue that high economic performance is best achieved by firms having complete flexibility of labour, untrammelled by legislation.

Alternatively you may take the view that in advanced industrial societies, some minimum legal protection should be present as a moral right. You may feel that the present legal regime, particularly as a result of recent case law developments, broadly succeeds in striking a balance between the employer's pursuit of profits and the employee's interest in job security. As opposed to this, you may agree with Collins that the protection provided against unfair dismissal is insufficiently strong and managerially orientated, pointing to the very low proportion of successful claims which result in re-employment and the relatively low levels of compensation awarded.

A number of reforms have been mooted by those who see the need to strengthen the present system, including amending the law so that a dismissal decision, if challenged, could not be implemented unless and until justified before an industrial tribunal (a similar approach already exists under the 'interim relief' procedures presently used for dismissals for union reasons, see TULR(C)A 1992, ss. 161 to 167).

A more radical approach would be to remove unfair dismissal from the jurisdiction of industrial tribunals and introduce a system of private arbitration which it is claimed would be cheaper, quicker and generally much less formal and legalistic. On this proposal and many other aspects of the working of the law of unfair dismissal see Dickens et al., *Dismissed: A Study of Unfair Dismissal and the Industrial Tribunal System*. See also R. Lewis, R and Clark, J. *The Case For Alternative Dispute Resolution* (London: Institute of Employment Rights, 1993).

READING

Collins, H., *Justice in Dismissal* (Oxford: Clarendon Press, 1992).
Collins, H., 'The meaning of job security' (1991) 20 ILJ 227.
Hepple, B.A., 'The fall and rise of unfair dismissal', in McCarthy, W. (ed.)
  Legal Intervention in Industrial Relations: Gains and Losses (Oxford: Black-
  well, 1992), ch. 2.
Pitt, G., 'Justice in dismissal: a reply to Hugh Collins' (1993) 22 ILJ 251.

8 REDUNDANCY PAYMENTS

INTRODUCTION

The Redundancy Payments Act 1965 is of historical significance for a number of reasons. It was the first statute to provide compensation to workers who lost their jobs through no fault of their own. In addition, it was this legislation which was the first to utilise the industrial tribunal as a forum for the resolution of disputes between employer and employee.

The policy aims behind the legislation remain obscure (see Davies and Freedland, *Labour Law: Text and Materials*, pp. 528–30). It is probable, however, that the government was concerned to promote labour flexibility in order to accommodate technological advances in industry during the 60s. As a result, the government of the day enacted a statute which provided for a lump-sum payment for workers who were classified as redundant whether or not they were able to find new work immediately after dismissal. But if the aim was to increase labour mobility, its achievement via the Redundancy Payments Act 1965 is open to doubt. The Act hardly provides strong incentives for workers to be more mobile in search of jobs because the statutory payment is so small. Furthermore, in the radically different economic context of the 80s and 90s with high unemployment levels, retraining for new skills is not a realistic option for many redundant workers.

It is, therefore, not surprising to find that, since the advent of the unfair dismissal remedy with its more generous compensation levels, employees, who had previously sought to argue that they were dismissed for redundancy, are now seeking to deny this and argue that they have been dismissed unfairly. Conversely, employers, who, between 1965 and 1971, might have strenuously opposed a contention that any dismissal was for redundancy, now seize upon it as a reason to justify a fair dismissal.

In this chapter we shall seek to achieve three objectives. First, we hope to clarify some of the major issues concerned with qualification to claim, especially those arising from the calculation of continuity of employment. Of course, statutory continuity of employment is not only of importance in redundancy cases, it is also a gateway to other employment protection rights such as unfair dismissal and maternity leave. Therefore, much of our discussion on continuity will have a relevance beyond the area of redundancy. Our second objective is to try to cut through the complexities of the case law surrounding the concept of redundancy. Finally we wish to examine the relationship between redundancy and unfair dismissal and focus on situations where a redundancy dismissal may be held to be unfair.

QUALIFICATION TO CLAIM

Continuity of Employment

In order to qualify for a redundancy payment the 'employee' must have been employed for at least two years on the 'relevant date' (defined by EPCA 1978, s. 90(1), and substantially similar to the 'effective date of termination' discussed in our chapter on unfair dismissal).

The complicated provisions relating to the calculation of a period of continuous employment are set out in sch. 13 to EPCA 1978. The schedule attempts to ensure that 'continuity' is preserved despite certain changes of employer, certain periods where the employee is away from work or where the employee's hours of work fluctuate.

Continuity: change of employer (sch. 13, paras 17 and 18)

Normally only employment with the present employer counts. But there are six circumstances set out in EPCA 1978, sch. 13 paras 17 and 18, in which a change of employer does not break continuity. These include a transfer which occurs on the death of an employer, a change in the constitution of a partnership which acts as an employer and where an Act of Parliament causes one corporate body to replace another as employer. The two most important situations provided for are:

(a) If a trade, business or undertaking is transferred, the period of employment at the time of transfer counts as a period of employment with the transferee. In other words, the transfer does not break continuity (para. 17(2)).

In order for this provision to operate, the business must be transferred as a going concern, a mere sale of the physical assets of the business is insufficient. An example of this distinction is provided by *Woodhouse* v *Peter Brotherhood Ltd* [1972] ICR 186. In this case the nature of the business changed after the transfer from the manufacture of diesel engines to the manufacture of compressors and steam turbines. The Court of Appeal held that in this situation there was only a transfer of physical assets and not a transfer of a business.

In the important case of *Melon* v *Hector Powe Ltd* [1981] ICR 43 Lord Fraser of Tullybelton thought that the essential distinction between the transfer of a business or part of business and the mere sale of assets was:

> that in the former case the business is transferred as a going concern so that the business remains the same business but in different hands . . . whereas in the latter case the assets are transferred to the new owner to be used in whatever business he chooses. Individual employees may continue to do the same work in the same environment and they may not appreciate that they are working in a different business, but that may be the true position on consideration of the whole circumstances. A change in the ownership of a part of a business will, I think, seldom occur, except when that part is to some extent separate and severable from the rest of the business, either geographically or by reference to the products, or in some other way.

What factors should you be looking for in any problem involving a change of employer? What counts as the essence of the business? In many cases a decisive factor will be the transfer of the 'goodwill', i.e., the acquisition of the right to trade with the transferor's former customers. It is also likely that if the product changes after transfer then the 'business' has not been transferred. In *Crompton* v *Truly Fair (International) Ltd* [1975] ICR 359, for example, it was held that there was only a change of ownership of the physical assets where a factory, together with its machinery, was sold and was used for the manufacture of men's trousers, whereas the premises had originally been used for the manufacture of children's clothes.

Do not be seduced into thinking that because the employees featured in any problems continue to work after transfer in the same factory, at the same bench and under the same supervision, that their continuity has necessarily been maintained (the extract from Lord Fraser's speech above tells you that this is an irrelevance). This was exactly the trap which workers in *Woodhouse* v *Peter Brotherhood Ltd* fell into: so that when they were made redundant by the 'new' employer, they could only claim for the six years they had worked for it rather than the 20 years they had been at the factory.

(b) If the employee is taken into the employment of an 'associated employer', the period of employment with the old employer counts as a period of employment with the 'associated employer' (EPCA 1978, sch. 13 para. 18). The concept of 'associated employers' is an important one which is not only relevant in assessing continuity but also crops up in other areas of your course. Thus, offers of 'suitable alternative employment' made to redundant workers or those who have taken maternity leave may be by the employer or an associated employer. We shall also see that it is lawful, in the course of a trade dispute, to black supplies to and from an associated employer of the primary employer in dispute to whom production has been switched as a result of that dispute.

The definition of this key concept is to be found in EPCA 1978, s. 153(4), which states that 'any two employers are to be treated as associated if one is a company of which the other (directly or indirectly) has control, or if both are companies of which a third person (directly or indirectly) has control'.

Two major issues arise from this definition. First, 'control' means voting control rather than *de facto* control. In *Secretary of State for Employment* v *Newbold* [1981] IRLR 305, Bristow J stated:

> In the law affecting companies, control is well recognised to mean control by the majority of votes attaching to shares, exercised in general meeting. It is not how or by whom the enterprise is actually run.

Secondly, the definition has been held to be exhaustive, so that only companies can be associated — local authorities or health authorities fall outside the definition (see *Merton London Borough Council* v *Gardiner* [1981] QB 269).

Transfer of Undertakings (Protection of Employment) Regulations 1981 (SI 1981 No. 1794)

These complex regulations overlay additional rules which apply where there is a change of employer. They provide for the automatic transfer of contracts of employment, collective agreements and trade union recognition in the case of certain transfers of commercial ventures, hold any dismissal in connection with such transfers automatically unfair unless it occurs for an 'economic, technical or organisational' reason, and impose a duty on employers to inform and consult recognised trade unions.

Relevant transfers

None of the provisions of the regulations operate unless there is a 'relevant transfer' under reg. 3(1), i.e., 'a transfer from one person to another of an undertaking situated immediately before the transfer in the United Kingdom or a part of one which is so situated'. An undertaking was originally defined by reg. 2(1) to include 'any trade or business but excluding any undertaking or part of an undertaking which is not in the nature of a commercial venture'. But, under TURERA 1993, the definition was extended to cover non-commercial undertakings. This is designed to bring UK legislation into line with EC law (see Directive on acquired rights (77/187); *Dr Sophie Redmond Stichting* v *Bartol* [1992] IRLR 366, ECJ, and *Rask* v *ISS Kantineservice A/S* [1993] IRLR 133, ECJ). It would appear that, as under EPCA 1978, sch. 13, para. 17(2), a mere transfer of assets which falls short of a transfer of the undertaking as a going concern will fall outside the regulations.

Effect of a transfer on the contract of employment
In *Nokes* v *Doncaster Amalgamated Collieries Ltd* [1940] AC 1014 the House of Lords held that at common law an employee could not be transferred without his or her consent from one employer to another. This rule was explicable on the basis of freedom of contract. This 'freedom', however, could work against the employee because, equally, a person to whom a business was transferred was under no obligation to employ existing employees working in the transferred business.

As we have seen above, if an employee who was employed at the time of the transfer is re-engaged by the transferee employer, statutory continuity is preserved by EPCA 1978, sch. 13, para. 17(2). But the logic of the *Nokes* v *Doncaster Amalgamated Collieries Ltd* principle meant that the employer was under no obligation to offer either to renew the contracts or to re-engage in suitable alternative employment. If no such offer was made by the transferee, the employee was left with no alternative but to claim redundancy payment from the transferor employer.

The important change brought about by the regulations is to override the position at common law as set out in *Nokes* v *Doncaster Amalgamated Collieries Ltd* and provide that a transfer does not terminate the contracts of the employees of the business. Instead, the contracts continue with the substitution of the transferee as employer and the transferee taking all the transferor's 'rights, powers, duties and liabilities under or in connection with any such contract' (reg. 5(1) and (2)).

By virtue of reg. 5(3), however, this transfer of liability will only occur where the employee was employed in the undertaking 'immediately before the transfer'.

Differing divisions of the EAT reached different conclusions on the precise interpretation of the crucial phrase 'immediately before the transfer'. This conflict of authority was apparently resolved by the decision of the Court of Appeal in *Secretary of State for Employment* v *Spence* [1987] QB 179 that only when employees are employed at the very moment of a business transfer does the purchaser take over the vendor's liabilities under or in connection with their employment contracts. In other words, a business purchaser cannot be made liable for dismissals carried out by the vendor before transfer.

The scope of this decision is now heavily constrained by the judgment of the House of Lords in *Litster* v *Forth Dry Dock & Engineering Co. Ltd* [1990] 1 AC 546. The House of Lords held that liability for a dismissal by the vendor prior to the transfer passes to the purchaser if the employee has been unfairly dismissed for a reason connected with the transfer.

Although reg. 5(3) provides that liability is to be transferred only where the employee is 'employed immediately before the transfer', in order for the regulations to give effect to the EEC Employee Rights on Transfer of Business Directive 77/187, as interpreted by the ECJ, reg. 5(3) must read as if there were inserted the words 'or would have been so employed if he had not been unfairly dismissed in the circumstances described in reg. 8(1)'.

Without such a purposive interpretation, the regulations would, according to Lord Keith,

> be capable of ready evasion through the transferee arranging with the transferor for the latter to dismiss its employees a short time before the transfer becomes operative

thereby leaving the employees, as in this case, with 'worthless claims for unfair dismissal' against an insolvent vendor (see also *P Bork International A/S* v *Forgeningen af Arbejdsledere i Danmark* [1989] IRLR 41).

The approach advocated by the House of Lords is in two stages. First, it must be determined whether the dismissal by the vendor was unfair within the meaning of reg. 8. If yes, then unfair dismissal liability under reg. 5 passes to the purchaser, even if the dismissal was not, in temporal terms, immediately before the transfer. Secondly, it is only where the dismissal does not breach reg. 8 that the construction of 'employed immediately before the transfer' laid down in *Spence* continues to apply. So, if the reason for the dismissal is unconnected with the transfer, liability passes to the transferee only if the employee had not been dismissed before the moment of transfer.

Dismissal of an employee in connection with the transfer
Regulation 8(1) deems a dismissal caused by a transfer or a reason connected with it to be automatically unfair. This position is modified by r. 8(2) which allows the employer to argue that the dismissal was for an 'economic, technical or organisational reason entailing changes in the work-force of either the transferor or the transferee before or after a relevant transfer'. The latter is deemed to be a substantial reason of a kind to justify dismissal under EPCA 1978, s. 57(1)(b), and the fairness of that

dismissal is then determined in the normal way. However, it is now clear that an employee can claim a redundancy payment if redundancy was the reason for the transfer dismissal (*Gorictree Ltd* v *Jenkinson* [1984] IRLR 391).

It is implicit from the decision of the House of Lords in this case that the mere insistence of the transferee that the transferor dismiss as a condition of sale will not be regarded as an 'economic, technical or organisational reason entailing changes in the workforce'. (This supports the approach adopted in *Wheeler* v *Patel* [1987] IRLR 211 and *Gateway Hotels Ltd* v *Stewart* [1988] IRLR 287.)

Continuity: Periods Away from Work

An employee's service may be continuous in a statutory sense even where the employee has been away from work for certain periods.

First, EPCA 1978, sch. 13, para. 4, makes it clear that each week during which there is in existence a contract of employment that would normally involve employment for 16 hours or more per week counts as a week of continuous employment. This is so whether the employee is actually at work or not. It follows that periods of absence from work by reason of sickness or pregnancy will count as periods of continuous employment without reliance on any other provision so long as the contract of employment has not been terminated. Note that following *R* v *Secretary of State for Employment, ex parte EOC* [1994] 2 WLR 409, employment for eight hours per week will suffice for continuity (see below at p. 183).

Secondly, even where an employee is away from work and no longer has a contract, service may still be deemed to be continuous in certain situations should the employee eventually return to work. These situations are set out in paras 9 and 10:

(a)   Absence through sickness or injury, provided the absence does not exceed 26 weeks.

(b)   Up to 26 weeks' absence wholly or partly because of pregnancy or confinement (e.g., where a woman with less than two years' service with her employer has been dismissed while absent because of pregnancy and is later re-employed by that employer).

(c)   The whole of statutory permitted absence for leave on the grounds of pregnancy or confinement.

(d)   Absence through a 'temporary cessation of work'. This phrase has caused some difficulty and you should have a good grasp of two decisions by the House of Lords and one of the Court of Appeal which have provided guidance on its interpretation. The first authority is *Fitzgerald* v *Hall, Russell & Co. Ltd* [1970] AC 984 where it was held that the phrase refers to the cessation of the individual employee's work for some reason: there is no need to show that 'at the same time the whole works would close down or a department was closed down or a large number of other employees were laid off at the same time' (per Lord Upjohn).

This decision also tells us that in order to determine whether the absence is temporary we should view it in the context of the employment relationship as a whole. With the benefit of hindsight, we should be able to determine whether the absence was of a transient nature.

The second important House of Lords authority is *Ford* v *Warwickshire County Council* [1983] 2 AC 71. The applicant in that case was a teacher who had been employed by the county council under a series of consecutive short-term contracts, each for an academic year, for a total of eight years. There was, therefore, a break between the end of one contract and the beginning of the next. The House of Lords held that para. 9(1)(b) could apply in order to preserve the continuity of her employment. In the course of his judgment, Lord Diplock offered the following guidance:

> . . . the continuity of employment for the purpose of the Act . . . is not broken unless and until, looking backwards from the date of the expiry of the fixed-term contract on which the employee's claim is based, there is to be found between one fixed-term contract and its immediate predecessor an interval that cannot be characterised as short relatively to the combined duration of the two fixed-term contracts.

This approach is undoubtedly of benefit to many workers, such as part-time or temporary teachers, and makes it much more difficult for employers to avoid the employment protection laws by offering a succession of fixed-term contracts. However, it may not be appropriate where patterns of employment are not regular, as they were in *Ford's* case, but are subject to fluctuation. To look only at a particular period of unemployment and to compare that period with the combination of the periods either side could lead to some unjust results.

This issue arose before the Court of Appeal in *Flack* v *Kodak Ltd* [1986] ICR 775. This is the third important case on para. 9(1)(b) which you should have in your armoury. In this case, Mrs Flack had been employed by Kodak in its photo-finishing department over a number of years for periods which fluctuated markedly. Following her final dismissal, she and the other 'seasonal employees' claimed redundancy payments.

An industrial tribunal, purporting to follow what Lord Diplock had said in *Ford* with regard to temporary cessation, rejected their claims. In coming to this conclusion, the tribunal confined itself to a purely mathematical comparison of gaps in employment falling within the two years preceding the final dismissal with the period of employment immediately before and after that gap. Both the EAT and Court of Appeal thought that this was the wrong approach in the context of this particular case. They were of the view that the correct approach was to take into account all the relevant circumstances and, in particular, consider the length of the period of employment as a whole. Whilst it was true that the only absences from work on account of temporary cessations of work which were relevant for the purposes of redundancy payments and unfair dismissal claim qualifications were those which occurred during the two years prior to the dismissal, the characterisations of those cessations as temporary may be crucially affected by the whole history of the employment. As Sir John Donaldson MR put it:

A much longer gap in the course of a long period of work extending over many years might well be considered temporary, whereas if the same gap occurred in the course of a shorter period, it would not.

(e)   Absence from work 'in circumstances such that by arrangement or custom', the employee is regarded as continuing in the employment of the employer for all or any purposes.

It would appear that in order to fall within this provision, the arrangement or understanding must be established at the time the absence commences (see, for example, *Murphy* v *A. Birrell & Sons Ltd* [1978] IRLR 458). The absences that might be encompassed could be leave of absence arrangements, employees placed upon a 'reserved list' to be called upon as necessary and employees on secondment. A number of commentators, including Smith and Wood and Bowers, argue that the EAT's broad application of the subparagraph in *Lloyds Bank Ltd* v *Secretary of State for Employment* [1979] ICR 258 is no longer good law following the judgments of the Lords in *Ford* v *Warwickshire County Council*. In *Lloyds Bank Ltd* v *Secretary of State for Employment* the EAT held that where an employee works on a one week on and one week off basis, the weeks which she does not work count towards continuity by virtue of para. 9(1)(c). This was despite the fact that the heading to para. 9 reads: 'Periods in which there is no contract of employment'. In *Lloyds Bank Ltd* v *Secretary of State for Employment* a contract did exist throughout the period of employment. In *Ford* v *Warwickshire County Council* the House of Lords placed considerable emphasis on the requirement that there be no subsisting contract before para. 9 could operate. On that basis, the authority of *Lloyds Bank Ltd* v *Secretary of State for Employment* looks decidedly shaky.

Strikes and Lock-outs

If an employee takes part in a strike or a lock-out, the beginning of the period of employment is treated as postponed by the number of days between the start of the strike or lock-out and the resumption of work (para. 15). In other words, the period of the industrial dispute does not count towards continuity, but it does not break it.

Continuity: Changes in Hours of Work

For a week of employment to count for the purposes of calculating continuous service, the employee must either actually work (para. 3), or be employed under a contract of employment normally involving (para. 4) 16 hours per week. Employees who cannot meet this criterion will only cross this particular threshold of employment law rights after five years' continuous employment at eight hours or more per week (para. 6).

Workers whose weekly hours fluctuate above and below the hours threshold are not allowed to 'average' (see *Opie* v *John Gubbins (Insurance Brokers) Ltd* [1978] IRLR 540) and, in general, if weekly hours fall below the relevant eight or 16 hours per week, continuity will be broken and the worker will be back at square one in attempting to qualify for employment protection (see paras 5 and 7 for the two exceptions to this rule).

An important recent decision in this area is *Lewis* v *Surrey County Council* [1988] AC 323 where the House of Lords held that where an employee is employed under separate but concurrent part-time contracts, she is not entitled to aggregate the number of weekly hours worked under each contract for continuity purposes. You might recall that we focused on the case in our lecture extract in chapter 1 and there expressed the view that the decision weakens the protection offered to part-time and casual workers.

More recently, the House of Lords has determined that the hours thresholds for claims for unfair dismissal and redundancy payments constitute indirect discrimination against women employees, contrary to European law (*R* v *Secretary of State for Employment, ex parte EOC* [1994] 2 WLR 409). In the light of this decision, the government will have to amend the employment protection laws so as to give redundancy payment and unfair dismissal rights to any employee with two years' service. The one point of uncertainty is whether the amendments will apply to those working less than eight hours a week or only those working eight to 16 hours a week.

THE CONCEPT OF REDUNDANCY

Assuming that the employee establishes the requisite continuity of employment, the next question is whether the dismissal was by reason of redundancy. A dismissal is taken to be by reason of redundancy under s. 81(2) only if it is attributable wholly or mainly to:

(a)   the fact that his employer has ceased, or intends to cease, to carry on the business for the purposes of which the employee was employed by him, or has ceased, or intends to cease, to carry on that business in the place where the employee was so employed, or

(b)   the fact that the requirements of that business for employees to carry out work of a particular kind, or for employees to carry out work of a particular kind in the place where he was so employed, have ceased or diminished or are expected to cease or diminish.

One way of simplifying this definition is to remember that paragraph (a) covers the total closure of the employer's business and also the closure of the part of the business which, under the contract of employment, was the employee's place of work. Paragraph (b), on the other hand, requires us to consider whether the business requires so many employees to carry out certain work.

You will find that there is relatively little in paragraph (a) redundancy of legal difficulty. This is more than can be said about (b) and it is around this part of the definition that any examination question on redundancy is likely to revolve. Later in the chapter we will examine two problem questions concerned with redundancy, but it is equally possible that an examiner could set an essay question on the area. A quote, taken from Anderman's chapter on unfair dismissal and redundancy in R. Lewis (ed.), *Labour Law in Britain*, provides the basis for the following essay question:

'. . . the case law suggests that the decisions on whether or not an employee qualifies for a [redundancy] payment are strongly influenced by a concern that employee rights under their contracts should be construed to provide a measure of flexibility and adaptability to the needs of the business.
Discuss

Analysis

This question might largely be answered by examining the way the courts have interpreted the phrase 'work of a particular kind'.

Is 'work of a particular kind', the work which the employee actually performs or is it the work which the employee could be obliged to perform under the contract of employment'?
It would appear that the phrase should be defined by reference to the contract of employment rather than merely to the job the employee was habitually performing prior to dismissal. This test, of course, gives management a wide power to write into the contract a requirement of occupational

and geographical mobility. A case which clearly illustrates the working of this contractual approach is *Nelson v British Broadcasting Corporation* [1977] ICR 649 where the contract of employment of a radio producer who worked on the Caribbean service contained a clause which required him to work when, how and where the BBC demanded. The Court of Appeal held that Nelson was not redundant when the Caribbean Service was closed down because the 'particular kind of work' Nelson was employed to do was general radio production work (see also *Cowen v Haden Ltd* [1983] ICR 1 and *Pink v White* [1985] IRLR 1489).

The contractual approach has also been employed to determine the scope of another element of the definition — that is, the 'place where [the employee] was so employed'. This phrase has been interpreted to mean the place where the employee could be obliged to work under the terms of the contract of employment, not merely where the employee had been working prior to the instruction to move (see *Sutcliffe v Hawker Siddeley Aviation Ltd* [1973] ICR 560 and *United Kingdom Atomic Energy Authority v Claydon* [1974] ICR 128). More recently, this conventional approach was challenged by the EAT in *Bass Leisure Ltd v Thomas* [1994] IRLR 104, in which the EAT ruled that 'the place' where an employee was employed for redundancy payment purposes does not necessarily extend to any place where he or she could be contractually required to work, but is to be established by a factual inquiry, taking into account the employee's fixed or changing places of work and any contractual terms which go to evidence or define the place of employment and its extent, but not terms which provide for the employee to be transferred.

An employment contract cannot be silent on the place of work. If there is no express term, there must be an implied term. The geographical scope of the place of work to be implied depends on the circumstances of the case. In this respect relevant factors include: the nature of the employer's business, whether the employee has been moved during the employment, what the employee was told when employment started and whether there is any provision to cover expenses when working away from home. Three useful cases on the implication of terms in respect of workplace are *O'Brien v Associated Fire Alarms Ltd* [1968] 1 WLR 1916; *Stevenson v Teesside Bridge & Engineering Ltd* [1971] 1 All ER 296 and *Jones v Associated Tunnelling Co. Ltd* [1981] IRLR 477.

If in the process of a reorganisation, an employer substantially changes the contractual terms and conditions relating to the existing job, has there been a cessation of that 'particular kind of work'?
One might argue that the answer must be in the affirmative as a result of the logical application of the contractual approach. If we view the job as a package of terms and conditions wrapped up in the contract of

employment then surely significantly changing the contents of the package changes the very nature of the job itself?. This has not, however, been the approach usually adopted by the courts who have generally taken the view that, so long as job function remains, there is no redundancy where the employee is dismissed for refusing to agree to changes of terms and conditions of employment designed to save labour costs. The adoption of this approach means that a withdrawal of free transport which enables an employee to get to work or a change in shift pattern have been held not to amount to redundancy where the employer could show that there was still a requirement for the work of the employees in question (see *Chapman* v *Goonvean & Rostowrack China Clay Co. Ltd* [1973] ICR 310; *Johnson* v *Nottinghamshire Combined Police Authority* [1974] ICR 170 and *Lesney Products & Co. Ltd* v *Nolan* [1977] ICR 235).

The courts have also taken a wide view of the scope of the job function, resulting in findings that technological or social changes in the way it is performed do not render it a different 'particular kind of work'. Three cases are worthy of your attention in this area. In *North Riding Garages Ltd* v *Butterwick* [1967] 2 QB 56, a long-serving workshop manager was dismissed because of his inability to adapt to added responsibilities and new working methods introduced by the new owner of the business. His redundancy claim, based on the contention that the requirement of the business for a workshop manager of the 'old type' had ceased, was ultimately unsuccessful. The following extract from the judgment of Widgery J finds an echo in the *Cresswell* decision which we discussed in chapter 3:

> For the purpose of this Act an employee who remains in the same kind of work is expected to adapt himself to new methods and techniques and cannot complain if his employer insists on higher standards of efficiency than those previously required.

The court in this case largely ignored the question of when demands for greater efficiency reach the stage when the nature of the job changes. Critics of this decision have argued that there is not one single class of workshop manager and that the applicant, who had done nothing but manage a small workshop, had strong grounds to claim that the extra responsibilities meant that he was engaged in an entirely different job rather than being inefficient in the old one.

The second example is provided by the amazing case of *Vaux & Associated Breweries Ltd* v *Ward* (1969) 7 KIR 308. (Along with the **** off! cases in unfair dismissal, this is a case you will be unlikely to forget.) The owner of a public house decided to modernise it and install a discothéque. In line with the pub's new 'trendy' image, the brewers wanted to employ young blonde 'bunny girl' barmaids and dismissed the existing middle-aged barmaid, Mrs Ward, who could not compete in terms of physical attraction. When the case came before an industrial tribunal, Mrs Ward was awarded a redundancy payment. However, the Divisional Court held that the tribunal's approach of contrasting 'a barmaid of a very quiet bar' with attendants of more glamour and younger, who might attract the young, or perhaps the old, to the premises, was wrong. The correct test was: Was the work that the barmaid in the altered premises was going to do work of a different kind to what the barmaid in the unaltered premises had been doing? The Divisional Court thought that there was no change in the kind of work and therefore no redundancy. (This case was, of course, decided before the introduction of the right to claim unfair dismissal. Had it been available, Mrs Ward might have met with greater success.)

The final case of the trilogy is *Hindle v Percival Boats Ltd* [1969] 1 WLR 174 where it was held that a skilled woodworker on boats was not dismissed for redundancy after his employers started to build fibreglass as opposed to wooden boats. This case, however, is more notorious for the confusion it has generated in relation to the burden of proof in redundancy claims.

Is the employer's honest belief that the dismissal is for reasons other than redundancy sufficient to defeat the claim?
For the purposes of a redundancy payments claim, there is a statutory presumption that the dismissal was for the purposes of redundancy (s. 91(2)). The burden of proof placed on the employer is discharged if it can be shown either that there was no redundancy situation within the meaning of the Act (an objective test) or, if there was, that the dismissal was not wholly or mainly attributable to it. Following the majority judgments in *Hindle v Percival Boats Ltd* it would appear that this second alternative may be proved by showing that there was some other genuine reason for the dismissal even if it was based on a mistaken belief (a subjective test). The matter was expressed by Sachs LJ in this way:

> . . . once the tribunal is satisfied that the ground put forward by the employer is genuine and is the one to which the dismissal is mainly attributable the onus is discharged — and it ceases to be in point that the ground was unwise or based on a mistaken view of facts, though such matters may well be relevant for consideration by the tribunal when assessing the truth of the employer's evidence.

Prior to the enactment of the unfair dismissal remedy, this approach would mean that a worker who was objectively redundant would receive no compensation where his employer could establish that he honestly believed he dismissed on another ground. This issue is of less practical importance these days because the industrial tribunal will now be able to determine whether the reason which the employer puts forward is sufficient to render the dismissal fair.

Hindle v *Percival Boats Ltd,* however, is important in the sense that it, together with the judicial approaches to the phrase 'particular kind of work', illustrates the narrowness in scope of the statutory concept of redundancy and the support given to managerial prerogative. (For a detailed discussion of these issues see Davies and Freedland, *Labour Law:, Text and Materials,* 2nd ed., pp. 530–52.)

Unreasonable Refusals of Suitable Employment and other Disqualifications from Payment

Employees who fall within the statutory concept of redundancy will be disqualified from payment if they unreasonably refuse a contractual renewal or suitable alternative employment to take effect immediately or within four weeks, which is offered to them by their employer (s. 82(3) to (5)), or an associated employer (s. 82(7)), or a new employer to whom the business has been transferred (s. 94). If the new job offer differs in terms of capacity or place of employment, the employee is entitled to a statutory trial period of four weeks (s. 84(3) to (7)). At the end of the trial period the employee must then make a decision whether to accept the new job in the knowledge that to decline it may constitute an unreasonable refusal, resulting in disqualification from payment (s. 82(6)). (Further discussion of the working of, these provisions will take place in one of our problems later in the chapter.)

Employees may lose entitlement to all or part of redundancy payments in the following circumstances:

(a) If the claim is made out of time, i.e., after a period of six months from the 'relevant date'. However, as with unfair dismissal, an industrial tribunal may allow an extension in the time-limit if it is 'just and equitable' to do so (s. 101).

(b) If they leave their employment prematurely. If an employee leaves employment, having been warned of the possibility of redundancy in the future, there is no dismissal (see *Morton Sundour Fabrics Ltd* v *Shaw* (1967) 2 ITR 84; *International Computers Ltd* v *Kennedy* [1981] IRLR 28).

An employee under notice of dismissal who leaves before the notice expires may also lose the right to a payment. If the employee gives written notice to terminate employment on a date earlier than that given by the employer, the employee will not lose the right to a payment if the employer has no objections to the premature departure. If, however, the employer does object and serves on the employee a written request to withdraw the notice, warning that if this is not done any claim for redundancy payment will be contested, the employee may lose entitlement. It will then be up to the industrial tribunal to decide whether it is just and equitable for the employee to receive a full, part or nil payment (s. 85).

(c)   In cases where the employee is guilty of misconduct. Entitlement will be lost if the employer was entitled to terminate the contract by reason of the employee's misconduct (s. 82(2)). For this provision to apply, the employer must dismiss either (i) without notice, (ii) with shorter notice than that to which the employee is entitled, or (iii) with full notice accompanied by a written statement that the employer actually had the right to dismiss at once. You may be somewhat puzzled by this provision. After all, if an employee is dismissed for misconduct then that would be the principal reason and not the redundancy situation: the provision seems to be superfluous. There is no clear decision on what the provision is intended to achieve. In *Sanders* v *Ernest A. Neal Ltd* [1974] ICR 565, however, it was suggested that s. 82(2) will exclude a claim where the employee is dismissed for redundancy but in circumstances where the employer could have dismissed for cause.

The disentitlement imposed by s. 82(2) is subject to two significant exceptions:

(i)   If the dismissal for gross misconduct takes place when the employee is already under the 'obligatory period' of notice for redundancy, the employee may apply to the industrial tribunal which can award all or part of the redundancy payment. (The obligatory period is defined by s. 85(5) and is the period of notice which, by statute or the contract, the employer is obliged to give in order to lawfully terminate the contract.)

(ii)   If the misconduct takes the form of participation in a strike during the 'obligatory period' of notice for redundancy, then any dismissal for that form of 'misconduct' will not operate to disqualify the payment claim (s. 92). You should note that any participation in a strike which takes place before notice of dismissal for redundancy has been given will be classed as misconduct and s. 82(2) may be operated to disqualify any redundancy claim (see *Simmons* v *Hoover Ltd* [1977] ICR 61).

UNFAIR REDUNDANCY DISMISSALS

As we saw in chapter 7, redundancy is a prima facie fair ground for dismissal. It is important to note, however, that the statutory presumption that a dismissal is for redundancy under s. 91(2) does not apply in relation to an unfair dismissal claim. Therefore, it is up to the employer to prove that redundancy was the reason for dismissal.

Even where the employer has succeeded in this task, the dismissal for redundancy may still be attacked as unfair on one of three grounds:

(a) Selection for redundancy for trade union membership or activity or non-membership (TULR(C)A 1992, s. 153). We discussed trade union membership discrimination in chapter 7.

(b) Selection for redundancy in contravention of a customary arrangement or agreed procedure relating to redundancy where there were no 'special reasons' justifying departure from that arrangement or procedure in the circumstances of the particular case (EPCA 1978, s. 59(1)(b)). This provision, as with TULR(C)A 1992, s. 153, is subject to the proviso that another employee holding a similar position as the one selected for redundancy has been retained, although the circumstances constituting redundancy applied equally to that employee. The most common basis for selection under a redundancy agreement is last in, first out (LIFO). Such agreements may also allow other criteria to be taken into account such as skill, competence, attendance and disciplinary records. (This provision is likely to be repealed early in 1995 as a result of the Deregulation and Contracting Out Act 1994.)

(c) The reason for the redundancy selection was because of pregnancy or childbirth or because the employee had made health and safety complaints or asserted certain statutory rights (EPCA 1978, s. 59(1)(a)).

(d) Unreasonable redundancy under s. 57(3). Whilst it is an automatically unfair dismissal not to comply with a redundancy agreement or arrangement, it does not follow that it is necessarily fair to follow it. Under s. 57(3), the industrial tribunal still has to decide whether an employer's selection of a particular employee for redundancy was reasonable (see *N. C. Walling & Co. Ltd* v *Richardson* [1978] ICR 1049). Also, as we point out in chapter 5, certain types of selection agreements, such as 'part-timers first' may amount to indirect sex discrimination (see *Clarke* v *Eley (IMI) Kynoch Ltd* [1983] ICR 165 and compare with *Kidd* v *DRG (UK) Ltd* [1985] ICR 405).

Whether or not there is a redundancy agreement, the employee may challenge the fairness of the redundancy dismissal under s. 57(3). (This was decided by the Court of Appeal in *Bessenden Properties Ltd* v *Corness* [1977] ICR 821.)

The leading case in this area is *Williams* v *Compair Maxam Ltd* [1982] ICR 156 where the EAT laid down five principles of good industrial relations practice which should generally be followed in redundancies where the employees are represented by an independent and recognised trade union. These guidelines were as follows:

(a) To give as much warning as possible.

(b) To consult with the union, particularly relating to the criteria to be applied in selection for redundancy. (Principles (a) and (b) find an echo in TULR(C)A 1992, ss. 188 to 192, which oblige employers to consult recognised unions 'at the earliest opportunity'. If the employer is proposing to dismiss 100 or more employees at one establishment over a 90-day period, consultations must commence not less than 90 days before the first dismissal. If it is proposed to dismiss 10 or more over a 30-day period, consultations should take place not less than 30 days before the first dismissal takes effect. There is no minimum period where the employer proposes to dismiss fewer than 10 employees. An employee who suffers loss by the lack of consultation may receive a compensation in the form of a 'protective award'.)

(c) To adopt objective rather than subjective criteria for selection, e.g., experience, length of service, attendance, etc.

(d) To select in accordance with the criteria, considering any representations made by the union regarding selection.

(e) To consider the possibility of redeployment rather than dismissal.

These guidelines have since been approved and applied by the Northern Ireland Court of Appeal in *Robinson* v *Carrickfergus Borough Council* [1983] IRLR 122, whilst in *Grundy (Teddington) Ltd* v *Plummer* [1983] IRLR 98, the EAT emphasised that the guidelines should be applied flexibly as one or more of the five points may not be appropriate in the particular circumstances of the case.

Whilst the EAT in England has been in favour of a flexible but general application of the *Williams* v *Compair Maxam Ltd* guidelines, this approach has not found favour north of the Border. In *A. Simpson & Son (Motors) Ltd* v *Reid and Findlater* [1983] IRLR 401, the Scottish EAT felt that the principles had been misapplied by the tribunals and that they only had application in situations where there was an independent recognised trade union. The Scottish EAT was of the view that the principles had no application in a situation, such as that before it, of a small business faced with a selection of two out of three people where no trade union was involved. In *Meikle* v *McPhail (Charleston Arms)* [1983] IRLR 351, Lord McDonald, referring somewhat disparagingly to the 'so-called principles' set out in *Williams* v *Compair Maxam Ltd*, stated:

These principles must primarily refer to large organisations in which a significant number of redundancies are contemplated. In our view they should be applied with caution in circumstances such as the present where the size and administrative resources of the employer are minimal.

(See also *Buchanan* v *Tilcon Ltd* [1983] IRLR 417.)

We have been awaiting a decision from the Court of Appeal as to whether it approves of the *Williams* v *Compair Maxam Ltd* principles or adopts the restrictive Scottish approach. If the latter view was adopted then the law would return to rarely challenging management's approach to redundancy. These cases, as John Bowers has argued, 'tended to treat the employer as though he were an administrative agency whose decisions in this respect should be challenged only *in extremis*' (*A Practical Approach to Employment Law*, 2nd ed., p. 193).

Strong implicit support for the need for the *Williams v Compair Maxam Ltd* principles, however, may now be derived from the recent and important House of Lords decision in *Polkey v A. E. Dayton Services Ltd* [1988] AC 344, which we have discussed in chapter 7. This decision rejected the so-called no difference rule, i.e., the rule that an unfair procedure leading to a dismissal does not render the dismissal unfair if it made no difference to the outcome. In the course of his judgment, Lord Bridge of Harwich, whilst not referring to *Williams v Compair Maxam Ltd* by name, stated:

> . . . in the case of redundancy, the employer will normally not act reasonably unless he warns and consults any employees affected or their representative, adopts a fair basis on which to select for redundancy and takes such steps as may be reasonable to avoid or minimise redundancy by redeployment within his own organisation.

Lord Bridge felt that if an industrial tribunal felt it likely the employee would have been dismissed even if consultation had taken place, the compensation could be reduced by 'a percentage representing the chance that the employee would still have lost his employment'. This was a better approach than the 'all or nothing' decision which resulted from the application of the 'no difference rule'. Moreover, Lord Bridge was of the view that:

> In a case where an industrial tribunal held that dismissal on the ground of redundancy would have been inevitable at the time when it took place, even if the appropriate procedural steps had been taken, I do not, as at present advised, think this would necessarily preclude a discretionary order for re-engagement on suitable terms, if the altered circumstances considered by the tribunal at the date of the hearing were thought to justify it.

THE EXAMINATION

As with unfair dismissal, you can virtually guarantee that a question involving redundancy payments will make an appearance on the examination paper. Unfortunately, you cannot be certain of the form the question or questions will take. As we have seen, redundancy may appear in an essay question. Alternatively it can appear in a number of guises as part of a problem question. Examiners will often link a redundancy issue with an aspect of the rules relating to continuity of employment: the effect of a transfer of business may be a particularly attractive bedfellow for a point on redundancy. Equally, as the last section of the chapter has demonstrated, there is also much to discuss in a problem involving the interface between unfair dismissal and redundancy. For this reason it would be foolhardy to leave redundancy payments out of your revision scheme if you want to answer confidently any question on unfair dismissal that might be on the paper. With these thoughts in mind let us turn our attention to two sample problem questions on redundancy.

Question One

Mrs Brown, a widget polisher, has been employed by Widgets Ltd for 10 years. Her written particulars of employment describe her job as 'widget polisher (nights)' and she has always worked on the night shift from 10.00 p.m. to 6.00 a.m. The other two shifts were 6.00 a.m. to 2.00 p.m. and 2.00 p.m. to 10.00 p.m. In December 1994, because of a decline in the demand for widgets, her employer, in consultation with the trade union, replaced the three shifts with just two days shifts, i.e., 6.00 a.m. to 2.00 p.m. and 2.00 p.m. to 10.00 p.m. No one from the shop-floor was made redundant but some managers were. The new shifts required alterations to the working hours of the night-shift workers. Mrs Brown, a non-union member, refused to work either of the new shifts on the grounds that it was only by working nights that she was able to take proper care of her family. She was therefore dismissed.

Advise Mrs Brown.

Analysis

There may be two possibilities open to Mrs Brown: (a) a redundancy payments claim and (b) a complaint of unfair dismissal.

Redundancy claim
Two decisions of the Court of Appeal in *Johnson* v *Nottinghamshire Combined Police Authority* [1974] ICR 170 and *Lesney Products & Co. Ltd* v *Nolan* [1977] ICR 235 are well worthy of discussion here. Both stand for the proposition that an employer can reorganise a business to improve efficiency and in doing so unilaterally change the terms and conditions of employment without necessarily incurring liability for a redundancy payment.

In *Lesney Products & Co. Ltd* v *Nolan* a decline in sales had forced the company to reduce overtime by reorganising a day and a night shift into a double day shift. The Court of Appeal held that the employees dismissed for refusing to move from the old day shift to the new double day shift were not entitled to redundancy payments. The requirements of the business for employees to carry out work of a particular kind had not ceased or diminished. The amount and type of work had not changed and the number of employees required to do it had remained constant.

This is similar to the situation which Mrs Brown finds herself in. There is still the same requirement for those performing her job function, the only reduction in the work-force occurred at supervisory level.

On the other hand, Mrs Brown could call to her aid the decision of the EAT in *Macfisheries Ltd* v *Findlay* [1985] ICR 160, where it was held that a change from night shift to day shift may be construed as a reduction in demand for that particular kind of work. According to the EAT, whether such a change should be so construed depended on the nature of the work to be done, whether it differed in ind from that done on the day shift and whether the employee had a contractual right not to be required to transfer to the day shift. The EAT was of the view that there is neither a rule of law that a change from night shift working to day shift constitutes a change in the particular kind of work, nor does *Johnson* v *Nottinghamshire Combined Police Authority* lay down a contrary rule that a change of hours cannot amount to a change in the kind of work to be performed. It is a question of fact for the industrial tribunal.

The reasoning in *Macfisheries Ltd* v *Findlay* accords with the approach of the Court of Appeal in *Cowen* v *Haden Ltd* [1983] ICR 1 in treating the phrase 'work of a particular kind' as meaning the work the employee is contractually obliged to do. (It also evidences the confusion caused when the courts are prepared to juggle with two competing tests for redundancy.)

If the industrial tribunal finds that there was a cessation or diminution of work of a particular kind, the question remains whether the offer of work on one of the day shifts was an offer of suitable alternative work which was unreasonably refused by Mrs Brown. In considering the suitability of the offer, it has been held that the tribunal should ask itself the question whether the new post is substantially equivalent to the old (*Taylor* v *Kent County Council* [1969] 2 QB 560). Ultimately, however, the question of suitability is one of fact for the industrial tribunal, weighing up objective criteria such as pay, conditions, status, the nature of the work, etc. If the offer is suitable, the tribunal must then proceed to determine whether it was unreasonably refused. On this question it is permissible to take into account personal or subjective considerations, e.g., domestic circumstances.

Unfair dismissal
If there was no redundancy, an alternative claim may be that by dismissing her when she refused to work the new shift pattern the employers had behaved unreasonably.

We saw in the previous chapter that dismissal for refusal to agree to changes in terms and conditions of employment resulting from a reorganisation of the business may result in a dismissal being held to be fair under some other substantial reason' (s. 57(1)(b)).

To what extent should Mrs B's domestic commitments have been taken into account by the employer? In *Evans v Elemeta Holdings Ltd* [1982] ICR 323, a case involving the imposition of an obligation to work overtime, the EAT did express the view that, if it was unreasonable to expect an employee to accept the changes proposed by the employer, it was unfair for the employer to dismiss. This view, however, was not accepted by a differently constituted EAT in *Chubb Fire Security Ltd v Harper* [1983] IRLR 311. In its view the correct approach, in accordance with the decision of the Court of Appeal in *Hollister v National Farmers' Union* [1979] ICR 542, is for the industrial tribunal to concentrate on whether it was reasonable for the employer to implement the reorganisation by terminating existing contracts and offering new ones. It may be perfectly reasonable for an employee to decline to work extra overtime, having regard to his family commitments. Yet from the employer's point of view, having regard to his business commitments, it may be perfectly reasonable to require an employee to work overtime.

Some form of consultation over the reorganisation has been expected in the past in order to maintain the fairness of the dismissal. The dilution of the importance of consultation in *Hollister v National Farmers' Union* should be reassessed following the decision of the House of Lords in *Polkey v A. E. Dayton Services Ltd* [1988] AC 344. Having said that, there is no clear guidance on the form the consultation should take. In *Ellis v Brighton Co-operative Society* [1976] IRLR 419, the EAT was satisfied that the requirement of consultation had been fulfilled by union agreement to the scheme even though Ellis, as a non-union member, had little chance in participating in the scheme. In *Martin v Automobile Proprietary Ltd* [1979] IRLR 64, on the other hand, there are suggestions that non-union members should expect to be individually consulted.

Question Two

Alan and Brian had been employed for four years by Toys Ltd. The company had been trading at a loss for some time and in January 1994 agreed to a sale of the factory premises and machinery to Funtime Ltd. Funtime Ltd also purchased the right to manufacture and sell a number of Toys Ltd's best-selling toy products. As part of the agreement, Toys Ltd was to dismiss all its work-force prior to the transfer. Consequently, Toys Ltd issued dismissal notices to all its work-force which took effect one day before the completion of the sale to Funtime Ltd. Two months later, Funtime re-engaged the whole of Toys Ltd's work-force, with the exception of Alan and Brian.

Advise Alan and Brian as to their rights.

Analysis

This problem is concerned with Alan and Brian's rights where their work place is transferred to a new owner.

Do the Transfer of Undertakings (Protection of Employment) Regulations 1981 apply? It would appear that for a transfer of undertaking to be classed as a 'relevant transfer', there has to be a transfer of the business as a going concern (see *Woodhouse* v *Peter Brotherhood Ltd* [1972] ICR 186; *Melon* v *Hector Powe Ltd* [1981] ICR 43). For this to occur we are looking for something more than the mere transfer of assets. In our problem, not only are the factory premises and machinery transferred but also the manufacturing and sales rights to a number of Toys Ltd's best-known lines. If there is no transfer of business then the regulations do not apply and Alan and Brian must seek a redundancy payment and/or claim unfair dismissal from Toys Ltd (see below).

If the regulations operate then the transferee will inherit all the transferor's 'rights, powers, duties and liabilities' in connection with Alan and Brian's contract. This would include liability for any unfair dismissal compensation or redundancy payments which might arise out of their dismissal. In order, however, for this liability to arise Alan and Brian must be employed 'immediately before the transfer' (reg. 5(3)). The decision of the House of Lords in *Litster* v *Forth Dry Dock & Engineering Co. Ltd* [1990] 1 AC 546, discussed earlier, is now the leading authority on the meaning of this phrase. You will remember that the House of Lords held that, if the dismissal was for a reason connected with the transfer, it will be caught by the regulations even though it took place some time before the transfer was effected. On that basis, it would appear that Alan and Brian will be treated as employed at the time of the transfer notwithstanding their dismissals and that Funtime Ltd will become liable for the potential unfair dismissal liabilities.

Are the dismissals automatically unfair?
We have seen that reg. 8 of the Transfer of Undertakings (Protection of Employment) Regulations 1981 provides that a dismissal which is connected with the transfer of a business is automatically unfair unless it is for an 'economic, technical or organisational reason entailing changes in the work-force'. By virtue of reg. 8(2) such dismissals are deemed to be for a substantial reason for the purpose of EPCA 1978, s. 57(1), and are fair provided they pass the statutory test of reasonableness.

This part of our problem raises an issue which has been the subject of much debate: namely, whether a dismissal by the transferor on the insistence of the transferee is justifiable as an 'economic, technical or organisational reason'.

In *Anderson* v *Dalkeith Engineering Ltd* [1985] ICR 66 the Scottish EAT held that a dismissal by the transferor at the behest of the transferee was an 'economic' reason and therefore fell within reg. 8(2). The EAT was of the view that to get the best deal for the sale of the business, the vendor had to accede to the purchaser's demand that the work-force be dismissed and that was clearly an 'economic' reason.

The *Anderson* v *Dalkeith Engineering Ltd* approach was not adopted by the EAT south of the Border in *Wheeler* v *Patel* [1987] ICR 631, where the EAT thought that the word 'economic' should be given a more restricted interpretation. It was felt that:

> The references to 'technical' and 'organisational' reasons seem to us to be references to reasons which relate to the conduct of the business. In our view, the adjective, 'economic', must be construed *eiusdem generis* with the adjectives 'technical' and 'organisational'. The 'economic' reasons apt to bring the case within paragraph (2) must, in our view, be reasons which relate to the conduct of the business.

As we have seen, the *Anderson* approach has been effectively overruled by the House of Lords in *Litster* which held that to find a dismissal at the behest of the transferee fair would frustrate the purposes of the regulations.

CONCLUSION

In this chapter we have attempted to help you understand three important facets of the law relating to redundancy: continuity of employment (which, of course, also has a general relevance in employment protection), the concept of redundancy and its relationship to unfair dismissal. You will now readily appreciate that these prove to be complex areas of law, made all the more so by a barrage of often contradictory case law. As a result, you may be tempted to give these areas a miss when it comes to your revision. We would advise you not to take that course of action because these three areas often put in an appearance on examination papers. Resolving to grapple with these issues should pay dividends. We hope this chapter will help you to capitalise on your studies.

READING

Anderman, S.D., *Labour Law: Management Decisions and Workers' Rights*, 2nd ed. (London: Butterworths, 1993), chs. 9, 10 and 11.

Collins, C., *Justice in Dismissal: the Law of Termination of Employment* (Oxford: Clarendon Press, 1992), ch. 5.

9   HEALTH AND SAFETY AT WORK

INTRODUCTION

In this chapter we shall be considering the extent to which the law promotes health and safety within the working environment. Although this is not a topic always found in an employment law course all students will have come across it in other areas of legal study; most probably as an example of a strict liability offence in criminal law and also as the main example of the law relating to breach of statutory duty in tort. The law has chosen to promote safety in the workplace by imposing upon employers duties, a breach of which may give rise to both criminal and civil liability. As civil liability aspects are commonly dealt with in tort you may well find that your particular lecturer will assume an existing knowledge and accordingly will, at most, only sketch over the major safety sections of the Factories Act 1961. In this chapter we have also assumed a previous study of breach of statutory duty as imposed under the Factories Act 1961 and other legislation, and our observations in this regard are intended to act as a refreshing of the memory. However, civil liability must never be overlooked when answering any question on health and safety in the examination. We trust that the example given below to illustrate the ambit of the subject will also serve to impress upon you the interaction of both the criminal and civil law in this area. The width of the liability imposed by the Health and Safety at Work etc. Act (HASAWA) 1974 must also be appreciated at the outset. Since the 1974 Act health and safety have become a matter for everyone, not just occupiers, employers and employees. The Act has the ability to affect everyone's daily life, something which cannot be said of many other areas of law. It specifically relates to an accident arising out of a work activity, rather than an accident at work, so it could involve a member of the public not just an employee. For example, a spillage at a chemical plant may well affect local residents and could result in criminal liability under HASAWA 1974. The impact of EU law in this area should be appreciated and you should therefore familiarise yourself with the main regulations arising from the Directives, namely, the Management of Health and Safety at Work Regulations 1992; Health and Safety (Display Screen Equipment) Regulations 1992; Workplace (Health, Safety and Welfare) Regulations 1992; Provision and Use of Work Equipment Regulations 1992; Personal Protective Equipment at Work Regulations 1992; Manual Handling Operations Regulations 1992.

OVERVIEW

X is employed as a machine operator by a company manufacturing preformed moulded plastic panels for use in the fitting out of the interior of motor cars. The machine operated by X is a plastic moulding machine which requires X to feed into the machine a length of plastic which is moulded by the two parts of the machine pressing together. Clearly there is a danger of injury to X if part of his body were to come into contact with the machine during this moulding operation. If X was to have his arm crushed by the machine and it was shown that the accident would not have happened if the machine had been properly guarded then X would probably have an action for negligence (the tort of employer's liability) and/or breach of statutory duty under the Factories Act 1961, s. 14, or against his employer. However, in addition, the Health and Safety Executive, which has the task of enforcing the criminal responsibilities imposed by HASAWA 1974, may decide to bring criminal proceedings against the employer as well.

The above example can be put into the following diagrammatical form:

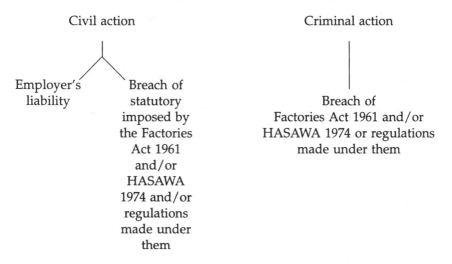

Civil action | Criminal action

Employer's liability | Breach of statutory imposed by the Factories Act 1961 and/or HASAWA 1974 and/or regulations made under them | Breach of Factories Act 1961 and/or HASAWA 1974 or regulations made under them

Let us now turn to look at both civil and criminal liability in more depth.

CIVIL LAW

EMPLOYER'S LIABILITY

Where an employee is acting within the course of his employment and is injured at work he may pursue a claim against his employer in tort on the basis of employer's liability. There are two important things for you to remember:

(a)   Once an employer/employee relationship is established, the employer is under a general duty to take reasonable care for the safety of his employees. The scope of this duty can be found in *Wilsons & Clyde Coal Co. Ltd v English* [1938] AC 57. This duty is of a personal nature and cannot be delegated by the employer. In *Morris v Breaveglen Ltd* [1993] IRLR 350 it was held that the duty applies even where the employer has subcontracted the employee's labour to another contractor. However, you should note that it does not include a duty to protect the employee from economic loss caused through the wrongdoing of a person for whom the employer is not responsible; nor does the employer have to inform his employee of such risks (*Reid v Rush & Tomkins Group plc* [1989] IRLR 265).

(b)   A breach of this duty and subsequent liability can only be established by reference to the law of negligence so you must have an understanding of this area of law. As you may recall many of the leading authorities in negligence are in fact employer's liability cases, e.g., *Doughty v Turner Manufacturing Co. Ltd* [1964] 1 QB 518.

We shall now consider, albeit briefly, the nature of the duties with particular reference to any substantive difficulties. The duties are sometimes referred to as being 'threefold', however, there are in effect four distinct duties imposed on the employer. Note that not all aspects of the employer's duty will fall easily within the four categories. For example, the consideration of whether a requirement on hospital doctors to be available for 48 hours overtime each week, in addition to the requirement that they should work a 40-hour week, was held to fall within the scope of the employer's duty to take reasonable care not to injure his employee's health (*Johnstone v Bloomsbury Health Authority* [1991] IRLR 119).

Duty to employ competent employees
This issue with which you are faced is whether the employer knew or should have known about the 'incompetence' of the employee causing the injury. This is a question of fact in each case. You should refer to the

'practical joker' cases: *O'Reilly* v *National Rail & Tramway Appliances Ltd* [1966] 1 All ER 499; *Hudson* v *Ridge Manufacturing Co. Ltd* [1957] 2 QB 348; *Coddington* v *International Harvester Co. of Great Britain Ltd* (1969) 6 KIR 146.

Duty to provide safe plant and equipment

You must decide whether the equipment provided as part of the job is safe, the test being that of the reasonable employer. The duty is not confined to provision but includes maintenance as well. In a number of cases liability has hinged upon reasonable foresight (see *Bradford* v *Robinson Rentals Ltd* [1967] 1 WLR 337; *Taylor* v *Rover Co. Ltd* [1966] 1 WLR 1491). You must refer to the Employer's Liability (Defective Equipment) Act 1969 which imposes additional liability on the employer. Flagstones have been held to be equipment within the meaning of the 1969 Act (*Knowles* v *Liverpool City Council* [1993] 1 WLR 1429).

Duty to provide a safe place of work

This includes not only the actual place where the employee is expected to work but also access and egress from that place as long as it is under the control of the employer (see *Smith* v *Vange Scaffolding & Engineering Co. Ltd* [1970] 1 WLR 733).

Duty to provide a safe system of work

Whether a safe system has been provided is a question of fact in each case by reference to what the reasonable employer would have done. Your main problem is what exactly fits under the heading of safe system of work. In a way this duty can be used as a 'catch-all' in that anything which does not fit into the other duties will probably come under this heading. However, it really involves consideration of the following factors: the physical layout of the job, warning notices, training and supervision, special precautions and instructions, protective clothing etc. As is pointed out in *Winfield and Jolowicz on Tort*, the employer has to have regard for the fact that his work people may be careless and he must do all he can to minimise the dangers as far as they are reasonably foreseeable. The scope of the duty can be seen from the following cases: *Charlton* v *Forrest Printing Co. Ltd* [1978] IRLR 559; *Woods* v *Durable Suites Ltd* [1953] 1 WLR 857; *Bux* v *Slough Metals Ltd* [1973] 1 WLR 1358; *McWilliams* v *Sir William Arrol & Co. Ltd* [1962] 1 WRL 295; and *Crouch* v *British Rail Engineering Ltd* [1988] IRLR 404. This duty may extend to the prevention of work-related upper limb disorders, but in *Mughal* v *Reuters Ltd* [1993] IRLR 571 it was concluded that repetitive strain injury (RSI) was not a recoverable form of injury because it had no pathology; see also *Bettany* v *Royal Doulton (UK) Ltd* (1993) 219 HSIB 20 in which a contrary decision was reached. A further extension of the remit of safe system of work to work-related stress can be seen in *Walker* v

Northumberland County Council [1995] IRLR 36 in which it was held that the employer had failed to provide a safe system of work resulting in a social worker suffering two nervous breakdowns from overwork. The council had failed to act as a reasonable employer in not providing effective help.

Finally can we remind you that the employee is within the course of his employment whilst he is doing something reasonably incidental to his main employment (see *Davidson* v *Handley Page Ltd* [1945] 1 All ER 235 and the case of *Smith* v *Stages & Darlington Insulation Co. Ltd* [1989] IRLR 177, which discusses the position of peripatetic employees, those who use the employer's transport and those who are in receipt of wages whilst travelling to and from work). Also that the rule that you must take your victim as you find him appears to be extended to illiterate employees and therefore the standard of care may be increased where such are employed (see *James* v *Hepworth & Grandage Ltd* [1968] 1 QB 94; *Hawkins* v *Ian Ross (Castings) Ltd* [1970] 1 All ER 180).

Breach of Statutory Duty

In respect of health and safety at work, this has become a particularly important tort as many actions are brought alleging a breach, for example, of ss. 12 to 14 of the Factories Act 1961. Whether this remains so once the Factories Act 1961 has been repealed is open to debate, though the regulations made under the HASAWA 1974 may give rise to such an action.

When you studied breach of statutory duty as part of the law of tort one of the more contentious areas involved establishing whether the statute in question gave rise to a civil action. As a general rule, at least in respect of many of the sections of the Factories Act 1961, this does not pose a problem for the student as it is firmly established that a civil action lies (see *Lonrho Ltd* v *Shell Petroleum Co. Ltd* [1981] 2 All ER 456, per Lord Diplock). A word of warning: where a breach of a section which has not been considered by the courts before is alleged, you may have to argue that a civil remedy should be available, i.e., it may well be that parts of the Act do not confer a civil remedy, e.g., the welfare sections. Clearly the safety sections do provide a civil remedy (see *Groves* v *Lord Wimborne* [1898] 2 QB 402; *Lochgelly Iron & Coal Co. Ltd* v *M'Mullan* [1934] AC 1).

You must establish three things in order to prove liability:

(a) That the statute imposes a duty on the defendant and that duty is owed to the plaintiff. The Factories Act 1961 places a duty on occupiers (of a factory) and the duty is owed to all persons working on the premises, including contractors (see *Wigley* v *British Vinegars Ltd* [1964] AC 307).

(b) That the defendant is in breach of that duty. This involves looking at the nature and extent of the duty (see *Close* v *Steel Co. of Wales Ltd* [1962] AC 367). See also *Whitfield* v *H. & R. Johnson (Tiles) Ltd* [1990] IRLR 525.

(c) That the harm suffered is of the kind contemplated by the statute and that the plaintiff has been injured as a result of the breach (see *Gorris v Scott* (1874) LR 9 Ex 125; *Wearing v Pirelli Ltd* [1977] ICR 90; *Millard v Serck Tubes Ltd* [1969] 1 WLR 211; *Larner v British Steel plc* [1993] ICR 551).

It should be clear to you that merely to establish breach is insufficient and this is where many students make their mistake; they forget causation! All of the above points depend on the construction and interpretation of the section in question.

Finally the conduct of the plaintiff is relevant to an action for breach of statutory duty as the defendant may be able to show that the injured person's conduct was the sole cause of the accident — this will only be upheld as a defence if the occupier has done all that he should; or that the injured person was contributorily negligent — a claim of 100% contributory negligence has been upheld (see *Jayes v IMI (Kynoch) Ltd* [1985] ICR 155).

Vicarious Liability

Whilst it is not within the remit of this book to discuss the law relating to vicarious liability (you can refer to any standard text on tort for a full discussion), you need to be familiar with the principles. There may be circumstances where the employer does not have primary liability, or for whatever reason, this cannot be proved, but may be vicariously liable for the torts of his employees as they affect their fellow employees (see *Smith v Stages & Darlington Insulation Co. Ltd* (1989) and *Sime v Sutcliffe Catering Scotland Ltd* [1990] IRLR 229).

CRIMINAL LAW

Introduction

The criminal law in this area is very detailed and wide-ranging; see *Redgrave Fife & Machin Health and Safety* — the 'Bible' on health and safety — or the *Encyclopedia of Health and Safety at Work Law and Practice*. It is extremely unlikely that in your employment law course you would have been able to do more than consider the main statutes. In the past these would have been the Factories Act 1961 and the HASAWA 1974. However, as the former is gradually being repealed, you may have focused on the latter, the Directives and the regulations which implement the Directives. Remember that for the time being regulations made under the Factories Act 1961 are still in force, although there are plans to repeal many of them and replace them where necessary with new regulations made under the HASAWA 1974.

Historically protection for people at work in the form of legislation has only been around for a relatively short time, i.e., just over 100 years. It is perhaps a comment on Victorian values that the first cruelty to animals legislation preceded their workers' safety legislation by over 50 years. The need for legislation arose out of the effects of the industrial revolution which took its toll in the high rate of deaths and accidents in the work place. At the same time the working environment was generally appalling as were the wages; also men were not the only bread-winners — women and children were expected to do the same work as the men.

The remit of the Robens Committee was to look at what was wrong with the existing legislation, It was felt by the committee that there was too much law, much of it obsolete, unsatisfactory and out of date. The result was HASAWA 1974, the watershed of the current approach to health and safety at work. It attempts to bring about a completely different approach to health and safety; whether the amount of 'law' has been reduced is questionable in the light of the new regulations either in force or proposed.

Factories Act 1961

It is still pertinent at this stage to consider the Factories Act 1961 as much of the Act continues to apply to existing workplaces and work equipment until the new regulations are gradually phased in; also, in many areas, the standards required by new regulations are the same or similar in practical terms to the requirements of the 1961 Act. Obviously we cannot consider the whole of the Factories Act 1961. We shall consider one area which highlights the substantive difficulties and at the same time is probably the most important section of the Act, s. 14, which deals with machinery guarding. Before we consider this section it is important for you to understand the approach and application of the Factories Act 1961 so that you can compare it with HASAWA 1974.

Approach and application

Most of the Factories Act 1961 imposes an absolute duty on the occupier of a factory. By now you should know the effect of this, i.e., no proof of negligence on the part of the occupier is necessary to establish liability; nor can the employer plead that it was not practicable to meet the requirements of the Act (unless this is specifically allowed by the section, e.g., s. 4). The effect of this is that enforcement is easy once the facts are established, e.g., if the walls have not been painted within the last seven years there is a clear breach of s. 1 and enforcement action can be taken. Furthermore if you glance at any of the sections on health, safety and welfare you will see that they spell out what the occupier must or must not do. These duties are therefore very specific and the only thing left to the discretion of the occupier is how he should comply with the Act; the method used must be acceptable to the Inspectorate in the light of current standards and codes of practice. It is important for you to appreciate that this approach has, over the years, resulted in the 'policing' of the Factories Act 1961. This has meant that some occupiers have taken a negative attitude towards health and safety because they have come to realise that they need do very little until the inspector calls, and, because of the shortage of inspectors, there could be on average six years between visits. This has been aggravated by the weakening of the influence of the trade union movement.

You should have noted by now that the duties are imposed on the occupier of the factory; at no time is the word 'employer' used. In real terms it is usual for the employer to be the occupier of the premises, but should this not be the case, it will be the person in occupation who is responsible for what goes on in the premises. You should also have noted that the application of the Act is confined to 'factory premises'. This is given a fairly wide definition in s. 175 to include slaughterhouses, laundries etc., but is basically confined to manual labour in manufacturing industry or anything incidental to it. This highlights the real issue which is that there are many employees not afforded protection under the Factories Act 1961, e.g., those employed in the health service, local government, Post Office etc. (The Robens Report calculated that there were 8 million employees without any health and safety protection.) Finally, although the application of the Act is confined to factories, anyone working on the premises so defined is protected, not just employees but also contractors (see *Wigley* v *British Vinegars Ltd* [1964] AC 307).

Fencing

We shall now consider our illustrative section (s. 14). We appreciate that many law students are put off this area by what appears to be a requirement that they should understand items of a technical nature. First this is an extremely blinkered view, especially as many engineering courses involve the study of law, and secondly there is no need for you to rush out and purchase books on engineering as it is the principle of law which you should grasp, not what the machine looks like, although we will admit it does help you to relate to the topic if you can visualise these things.

Section 14(1) is expressed in the following terms (note we shall not be considering the whole of the section):

Every dangerous part of any machinery shall be securely fenced.

In considering this section you are faced with a number of issues. The first being, what is included in the word 'machinery'? It is well established that s. 14 only applies to machinery which is installed as part of the factory equipment.

We can therefore safely assume that machinery which is being manufactured is outside the provisions of the Act (see *Parvin* v *Morton Machine Co. Ltd* [1952] AC 515). Although, of course, it would have to be guarded to the correct standard by the time it reached the purchaser (HASAWA 1974, s. 6). The machinery in question does not have to be power driven, although in practical terms most machinery with dangerous parts is power driven. 'Machinery' can be static or mobile, such as an overhead crane (see *British Railways Board* v *Liptrot* [1969] 1 AC 136).

Once you have decided that the machine in question is 'machinery' within the meaning of the section, you can proceed to consider whether there is a 'dangerous part'. Remember it is not the whole machine which has to be fenced, only the 'dangerous part'. This is probably the most contentious part of s. 14. You must know the test for establishing what amounts to a dangerous part. This is the test laid down in *John Summers & Sons Ltd* v *Frost* [1955] AC 740 as affirmed in *Close* v *Steel Co. of Wales Ltd* [1962] AC 367. The part must be:

> . . . a reasonably foreseeable cause of injury to anybody acting in a way in which a human being may be reasonably expected to act in circumstances which may be reasonably expected to occur.

Although this may sound complicated, in effect it is a similar test to that of reasonable foresight in negligence — something with which you should be familiar — to the extent that in *Eaves* v *Morris Motors Ltd* [1961] 2 QB 385 the judgment of Lord Porter in *Bolton* v *Stone* [1951] AC 85 was applied, i.e., 'there must be sufficient probability to lead a reasonable man to anticipate the cause of injury'.

However, this issue does not rest here. The behaviour of the work people has to be taken into account when considering foresight; to the extent that even stupid behaviour has to be catered for if it is reasonably foreseeable. This was illustrated in *Uddin* v *Associated Portland Cement Manufacturers Ltd* [1965] 2 QB 582 where Uddin climbed a ladder in order to attempt to catch a pigeon which had flown up into the roof of the factory. Whilst Uddin was up there his clothing became entangled in an unfenced part of the machinery (the line shafting) and he was injured. As far as the court was concerned there was a clear breach of s. 14; the behaviour of Uddin in climbing the ladder was being the case it was foreseeable that unfenced line shafting could cause injury. Obviously the occupier need not guard against 'sheer perversity' (see *Carr* v *Mercantile Produce Co. Ltd* [1949] 2 KB 601).

This criterion is probably better expressed by Lord Cooper in *Mitchell* v *North British Rubber Co. Ltd* 1945 JC 69 where he said that a machine is dangerous if.

. . . in the ordinary course of human affairs danger may reasonably be anticipated from its use unfenced, not only to the prudent, alert and skilled operative intent upon his task but also to the careless and inattentive worker whose inadvertent or indolent conduct may expose him to risk of injury or death from the unguarded part.

It is important for you to appreciate that as a matter of policy it would be wrong for the employer to be able to plead, in order to avoid fencing the dangerous part, that he has given proper instructions etc. and that the employee should be aware that if he puts his fingers in the machine he will be injured. Employers are primarily (at least in the private sector) motivated by profit. Having to take safety into account eats into those profits. Therefore in times of recession safety is one of the first things to be affected. It is morally wrong to place the onus in respect of safety on, for example, someone employed on piece-work who is having to work extremely fast in order to collect a basic wage.

When you are considering whether there is a 'dangerous part', as a general rule you do not have to take into account the item being machined. The obligation is only to fence the dangerous part of the machinery (see *Eaves* v *Morris Motors Ltd* [1961] 2 QB 385). However, you should be aware that if the juxtaposition of the item being machined and the moving part creates, for example, an in-running nip, then there would be a duty to fence the moving part (see *Midland & Low Moor Iron & Steel Co. Ltd* v *Cross* [1965] AC 343).

The standard of secure fencing
Finally in respect of s. 14 you need to establish what amounts to secure fencing. Obviously to some extent this is a question of fact in each case depending on the nature and operation of the machine in question. However, there are certain criteria which you should apply. Secure fencing:

(a)   Should prevent the operator from coming into contact with the dangerous part (see *John Summers & Sons Ltd* v *Frost* [1955] AC 740).
(b)   Need not prevent pieces of the dangerous part, e.g. a broken drill bit or the workpiece, from flying out of the machine (see *Close* v *Steel Co. of Wales Ltd* [1962] AC 367).
(c)   Must comply with s. 16, i.e., it must be of substantial construction, constantly maintained and kept in position while the dangerous part is in motion and use.

We should briefly consider these points. First, remember that protection is not confined to the operator of the machine. The occupier must take into account the other work people. It is therefore not adequate to fence the front or sides of a machine in order to protect the operator if one of his or her colleagues has access to the dangerous part from the rear of the machine. Furthermore you have to consider the behaviour of the persons employed in deciding whether your fencing is secure; this brings us back to the test of reasonable foresight discussed earlier (see *Burns* v *Joseph Terry & Sons Ltd* [1951] 1 KB 454 and *Carr* v *Mercantile Produce Co. Ltd* [1949] 2 KB 601).

Secondly, the interpretation of 'secure fencing' culminating in the decision in *Close* v *Steel Co. of Wales Ltd* [1962] AC 367 has created a loophole in s. 14 which is in no way justifiable. In theory this loophole can be blocked by regulations made under the Factories Act 1961. However, the regulations which have been made to supplement the requirements of the Factories Act relate to particular machinery, e.g., Woodworking Machines Regulations 1974 (SI 1974 No. 903), and do not cater for such things as drill bits flying out of machines, a not unusual occurrence.

A wide interpretation has been given to the word 'use' (see *Irwin* v *White, Tomkins & Courage Ltd* [1964] 1 WLR 387). As stated in *Redgrave's*:

> . . . the fencing provisions apply notwithstanding that the machine is not at the material time being used in the manufacturing process, provided that it is intended to be so used and capable of being so used.

Finally, in practice there are accepted standards of guarding for certain types of machinery. These standards are published in booklets and guidance notes by the Health and Safety Executive. There is also a British Standard on machinery guarding (BS 5304: 1988, 'Code of Practice for Safety of Machinery').

Health and Safety at Work etc Act 1974

In considering this Act, it is important for you to be aware of its effect and the implications for the future, although you should make sure you are familiar with the general requirements. You should also be able to make a comparison with the effect and requirements of the Factories Act 1961.

As stated earlier the 1974 Act was passed as a direct result of the report of the Robens Committee which was particularly critical of the existing legislation on health and safety. It was felt that although the Factories Act had resulted in a substantial decline in the number of fatalities and injuries at work, this reduction had 'bottomed out' and therefore the likelihood of future improvements under the existing system looked bleak. As a result the whole system was given an overhaul. As we shall see some things are an improvement on the old system whereas others are not. We have referred to it as the 'old system' although you must remember that it will be with us until the Factories Act 1961 is finally repealed.

Approach

One of the most important things for you to understand is the approach taken by HASAWA 1974. The main aim of the Robens Report was to use the legislation to bring about a change in attitude of management to health and safety in the work place. Obviously if management could be persuaded to take a positive approach to health and safety this would be reflected, albeit gradually, in an improvement in standards. Robens also recognised the need and importance of employee and trade union participation with management in striving for better conditions at work. This was certainly not recognised under the old system where health and safety were used as a means of bringing the trade unions and management into conflict rather than as the centre of discussion. You should therefore refer to the Safety Representatives and Safety Committees Regulations 1977 (SI 1977 No. 500) which attempted to achieve this result. See also TURERA 1993, s. 28 which gives employees the right not to be dismissed for taking action on grounds of health and safety, either where there is a serious or imminent danger or for performing their health and safety responsibilities (see *Harris* v *Select Timber Frame Ltd* (1994) IT case No. 59214/93).

In order to bring about this positive approach by employers, there is a requirement for all employers with five or more employees to have a written safety policy (s. 2(3)). This safety policy is supposed to be a statement of the employer's commitment to the enhancement of the health and safety of his employees. It should state the arrangements made in respect of health and safety and the organisation for implementing these arrangements. However, for many employers the statement is merely a token gesture and little constructive thought has gone into the writing of the policy. Only the larger companies can now afford to employ safety officers who are likely to have the greater understanding of what is required. Whilst the HSE has produced guidance on what amounts to an effective safety policy, it has maintained quite rightly that it is not prepared to produce model policies as this is akin to writing the document for the employer. One thing is certain: every policy should be different if it is to be effective.

Effect

The Act itself is to some extent a codification of the common law although it is wider in scope. One of the most wide-sweeping effects was that for the first time 8 million employees had some protection whilst at work, e.g., Health Service staff, telephone engineers, teachers etc. Indeed it is horrendous to think that prior to 1974 there was no protection for these people.

The Act streamlined the enforcement agencies by setting up the Health and Safety Commission and the Health and Safety Executive (HSE). Although you are unlikely to be asked about the structure of the HSE it would be wise to look at it so that you can understand who is responsible for the enforcement of the statutory provisions and in which premises. You should also be aware of the Health and Safety (Enforcing Authorities) Regulations 1977 (SI 1977 No. 746) and Health and Safety (Enforcing Authority) (Amendment) Regulations 1985 (SI 1985 No. 1107) and 1986 which pass the enforcement of the law in some premises to the local authority. Originally this was confined to 'low-risk premises', however, the current political approach is to transfer more and more premises to the local authorities and to adopt a more advisory role for the HSE. This is further evidence of the undermining of the principal enforcement agency.

One of the changes which has had a beneficial effect was the award of greater powers to inspectors under the 1974 Act, ss. 20 to 22. The introduction of the improvement notice and the prohibition notice gave greater flexibility and discretion to inspectors. The use of notices has increased at the expense of prosecutions. You should appreciate that this is not necessarily a bad thing as prosecution does not necessarily have the desired effect, especially as the maximum fine was a mere £2,000, and fines rarely reached these giddy heights — even when a man's head is crushed in a machine which is not satisfactorily guarded — the average fine being £877. The impact of prosecutions is under greater scrutiny in the light of the increase in fines in the magistrates' courts from £2,000 to £5,000 for breaches of the legislation and fines of up to £20,000 for a serious breach. For a critical review of the enforcement of the legislation, see 'Accounting for Workplace Deaths', D. Bergman, Legal Action, June 1991; D. Bergman, The Perfect Crime (1994), Health and Safety Advisory Centre, Birmingham.

When considering enforcement you should refer to the latest Report of the Chief Inspector of Factories as this gives the statistics in respect of the number of notices issued and prosecutions brought as well as the accident statistics. For example, the current statistics show that there has been a steady increase in the number of notices issued and prosecutions brought by HSE. Remember that not every accident is reportable so the statistics do not reflect the true figure; nor can you assume any correlation between the number of notices issued and prosecutions brought and the decline in fatalities — always remember that statistics can be used to prove or disprove whatever you want!

Scope
The 1974 Act is much wider in scope than the existing statutory provisions. It applies to all premises where persons are employed with the exception of private households. The main duties are placed on the employer although there are corresponding duties on the self-employed, persons in control of premises, designers, manufacturers, suppliers etc. of articles and substances, and employees. The duties are owed to employees and people who might be affected by any acts or omissions, e.g., the public.

The duties are laid down in ss. 2 to 7. It is not within the scope of this book to consider each individual duty so, as we stressed earlier, it is in your interests to make sure you are familiar with the Wording of them. You should also be aware of decisions such as *R v Swan Hunter Shipbuilders Ltd* [1981] ICR 831 where the duty under s. 2(2)(c) to provide instruction and training was extended to cover the situation where in order to protect one's own employees' safety, the instruction and training should also be given to contractors. See also *HM Inspector of Factories v Austin Rover* [1989] IRLR 405. In *Bolton Metropolitan Borough Council v Malrod Insulations Ltd* [1993] ICR 358 it was held that s. 2 is breached when an employer makes available plant which is not safe, even though it has not been used; it is the provision which is the breach. Another recent case has decided that in order to establish a breach of s. 3(1) there is no need to establish actual harm to the public: exposure to the risk is sufficient; risk being defined as the possibility of danger (*R v Board of Trustees of the Science Museum* [1993] 1 WLR 1171). A further contentious issue relating to s. 3 has arisen from the need to establish that the defendant's actions fell within the conduct of the defendant's undertaking. A restrictive approach was taken by the Divisional court in *RMC Roadstone Products Ltd v Jester* [1994] ICR 456, in which it was held that the mere capacity or opportunity to exercise control over an activity is not enough to bring that activity within the ambit of the employer's undertaking — the employer needs to involve himself in some way. However, in the later case of *R v Associated Octel Co. Ltd* [1994] IRLR 540, the Court of Appeal held that, contrary to the decision in *RMC Roadstone Products Ltd v Jester*, it is not necessary to show that the employer has some actual control over how the work is done. 'The ingredients of an offence under s. 3(1) are that the accused is i) an employer, ii) who so conducts his undertaking iii) as to expose to risk to health and safety iv) a person not employed by him v) who may be affected by such conduct of the accused's undertaking . . .'

The most contentious issue in respect of the duties is that most of them (ss. 2 to 6) are subject to the term 'so far as is reasonably practicable'. The problem with which you are faced is: What does this mean and what is the effect?

If we consider the meaning first, the most influential decision in this field is *Edwards v National Coal Board* [1949] 1 KB 704. Although the case was decided under the Coal Mines Act 1911 it is accepted as the correct interpretation of this term. You should therefore make sure you know the gist of it. Asquith LJ at p. 216, stated that:

'Reasonably practicable' is a narrower term than 'physically possible', and seems to me to imply that a computation must be made by the owner in which the quantum of risk is placed on one scale and the sacrifice involved in the measures necessary for averting the risk (whether in money, time or trouble) is placed in the other, and that, if it be shown that there is a gross disproportion between them — the risk being insignificant in relation to the sacrifice — the defendants discharge the onus on them. Moreover this computation falls to be made by the owner at a point of time anterior to the accident. The questions he has to answer are: (a) what measures are necessary and sufficient to prevent a breach? (b) are these measures reasonably practicable?

In practical terms this interpretation means that the employer is allowed to balance the risk to his employees or the public against the time, money etc. involved in minimising or eliminating the risk. If, for example, the cost outweighs the risk then he need not do anything about the risk. He does not have to take into account all three factors, i.e., time, trouble and money, one will suffice. You may wish to refer to other cases in which this judgment has been approved (*McCarthy* v *Coldair Ltd* [1951] 2 TLR 1226 and *Marshall* v *Gotham Co. Ltd* [1954] AC 360).

We shall now consider the effect of the term 'so far as is reasonably practicable' in the light of the interpretation in *Edwards* v *National Coal Board*. It introduces a lower standard than the general standard of absolute duty under the Factories Act 1961 and its subordinate legislation. We would suggest that the use of the word 'sacrifice' in Asquith LJ's judgment indicates a certain attitude to health and safety at work and clearly favours the employer's viewpoint at the expense of the employee's safety. This interpretation raises the issue whether as a matter of policy such things as money or economic factors should be taken into account.

We would contend, whilst recognising that the financial resources for safety are not necessarily a bottomless pit, that within reason money, and indeed time or trouble, should not be the prime considerations when people's safety is at stake. The counter-arguments are generally of an economic nature, e.g., the cost of safety makes it difficult for UK industry to compete at home and abroad because safety is paid for in higher prices. The HSC's 'Plan for Work 1994/5 and Beyond' places the emphasis on effective safety management as the key to improving health and safety in the workplace.

The future
It is essential that you give some thought to the future of health and safety at work. Changes have resulted from Directives and the regulations made to implement them. These regulations will reinforce the change of emphasis from a prescriptive approach to a risk-based approach leading to the inculcation of a self-regulatory ethos amongst industrial management so that risk assessment forms an integral part of the management process.

Further regulations arising from European Directives are proposed and some are in the process of being implemented, e.g., the health and safety provisions of the pregnant workers Directive 92/85.

Whether the new regulatory regime will maintain the standards achieved under the old system remains to be seen.

You should also consider the more positive aspects of HASAWA 1974 and how it might influence the future. Certainly there is plenty of scope for using it to protect employees from violence which they may encounter as part of their jobs, e.g., teachers, social workers and Health Service employees. This has been considered by Kate Painter in 'It's part of the job: violence at work', *Employee Relations*, vol. 9, No. 5 (1987); see *Violence to Staff: A Basis for Assessment and Prevention* (1986) HSE. Also it can be used to counter the effects of passive smoking. You can see, therefore, that there is more flexibility within the 1974 Act.

Public awareness of the effects of industry on health, safety and welfare is growing; unfortunately usually as a result of a major incident affecting them directly, e.g., gas leaks resulting in explosions, Chernobyl, release of toxic substances. The regulations made under the 1974 Act cater mainly for employees but can also take into account the importance of public safety, an area which has been neglected in the past, e.g., the Control of Industrial Major Accident Hazards Regulations (SI 1984 No. 1902), which require the preparation of on-site emergency plans for notifiable hazardous installations such as LPG storage depots; these plans have to take into account members of the public who may be affected by an incident at the site.

However, the future role of the Factories Inspectorate gives some cause for concern. Its fortunes are dependent upon current economic and political policy. The economic recession is seen as a burden which slows down industry's recovery; industry perceives safety as an additional economic burden which it can do without and pressure is brought to bear on the government to recognise this position. As we have stated, the average interval between basic inspections at premises where persons are employed is approximately six years and the self-employed are an even lower priority although they may be the employers of tomorrow. If Japan is accepted as the competitive and economic role model then safety is bound to decline further as Japan and indeed most of our competitors have deplorable safety standards compared with the UK.

Whilst HSE should be encouraged to adopt an advisory rather than a policing role, as inspectors must be seen to be approachable if management are to adopt a more positive approach to health and safety, a purely advisory role may not bring about the required decline in accidents at work. This is illustrated by the Site Safe '83 campaign to improve conditions in the construction industry which has the worst fatality statistics. Inspectors spent a lot of time advising the construction industry yet fatalities increased in 1987 and have continued to rise.

Risk assessment and appraisal by management are important but we would suggest that few firms can afford to employ safety officers with the necessary expertise. As a result safety is given to the personnel department who may have less understanding than the men on the shop-floor. Advice alone to industry will never be sufficient to improve the current accident statistics and safety standards because safety alone is not the prime concern of management.

THE EXAMINATION

You may find that this topic either appears on the examination paper as a topic in its own right, which is most likely; or possibly with a problem on unfair dismissal or implied terms of a contract of employment. If it appears as a single topic you may be faced with either an essay question or a problem. An essay is likely to involve a discussion of the wider issues and so should not be attempted unless you are confident that you can write about the effects of policy. A problem will probably cover both the Factories Act 1961 and HASAWA 1974 and may even draw on your knowledge of the civil law. If you attempt to answer the problem you must be familiar with the contentious issues arising out of the particular sections which you are required to apply.

A Typical Essay Question

'The importance of economic and commercial considerations in a manufacturing country like the UK is bound to inhibit the development of "ideal" health and safety legislation.'
Discuss.

Analysis

The first thing you must do when faced with an essay question like this is think carefully about what is required. If you misinterpret the question you could easily go off at a tangent and lose valuable marks; on the other hand if the question implies two possible requirements then as long as you give a complete answer you will not necessarily be marked down for placing a different emphasis than that placed by the examiner. We can only stress once more the importance of making a plan.

Clearly in answering this question you must consider the wider issues as well as the law. You must be able to discuss the arguments against the existence of a comprehensive system for controlling and maintaining health and safety at work.

Let us first consider the economic factors. Obviously you need to refer to the cost of health and safety to industry in general, especially manufacturing industry. It is argued that the cost of implementing health and safety measures is too high. This cost is passed on to the consumer at home and abroad which in turn makes the goods uncompetitive in comparison with countries where the health and safety laws are not so strict or are non-existent. It is also argued that the cost to industry is further increased by the time lost because of compliance with health and safety requirements, e.g., guarding machinery, wearing protective clothing etc. This may reduce productivity which again affects industry in its competitive markets. You should be prepared to use counter-arguments if they are available, e.g., if you have looked at the position in the USA or preferably West Germany you will have noted that both countries have fairly strict laws in this field yet are able to be competitive, although the USA does not have to rely as heavily on exports as the UK and it also has strict import controls.

You need also to look at the political influence on health and safety legislation as to some extent this is tied in with the economic factors. Whilst the promotion of manufacturing industry is important to all of the political parties, the Conservative party is keener to remove anything which is seen as a hindrance; for example, small businesses no longer have to concern themselves with writing safety policies — the safety policy being the key to self-regulation under HASAWA 1974; also the enforcement agency has had until recently few recruitment drives to replace inspectors who have left. This has undermined the role of the inspectorate and has increased the time between 'basic inspections'. Furthermore the future role of the inspectorate is seen as advisory rather than 'policing'. There will therefore be less to restrict industry from its main aim of increasing profits.

If you then consider the counter-argument to this, you will need to look at the approach of the Labour party which is that any promotion of industry should not be at the expense of health and safety of the employees. Certainly in a healthier economic climate health and safety are potentially contentious issues between the trade unions and management. In firms where the health and safety of the work-force are actively promoted rather than seen as a hindrance, health and safety cannot be used as a wedge between management and the unions. Furthermore it can be argued that any reduction in the standards imposed by the legislation or its applicability will result in greater cost to the State and industry in the form of sick pay, industrial injuries benefits and working days lost through illness, all as a result of the increase in accidents which is bound to happen and which can be seen from the position in the construction industry, where cutting corners has increased the number of deaths and injuries on construction sites.

The aim of the essay is to get you to discuss whether the factors referred to above have prevented the UK from having 'ideal' health and safety legislation. You then need to consider what is 'ideal'. You may argue, for instance, that what the UK has at present is 'ideal'. Let us consider the relevant factors. You can argue that there are two distinct approaches to health and safety. The first is the absolute duty approach as for the most part adopted by the Factories Act 1961 and its subordinate legislation. This approach, while placing the onus solely on the occupier, depends on policing by the enforcement agencies if it is to be successful. Secondly there is the 'reasonably practicable' approach which is laid down in HASAWA 1974. This approach places the onus on the employer using self-regulation as the basis for promoting health and safety in the work place. It also recognises the importance of the role of the employee, safety committees and safety representatives through its subordinate legislation. You need to refer to the advantages and disadvantages of the two approaches bearing in mind that at least for the moment both are in force in the UK. However, you must refer to what is potentially the biggest drawback of the second approach which is the judicial interpretation of 'reasonably practicable' — i.e., the balancing of cost against risk — this certainly goes some way to supporting the question. You may like to argue that there is a third approach which is a compromise in that an absolute duty is placed on the employer in respect of hazardous activities or processes and a self-regulatory approach is maintained for such things as welfare; this would allow some consideration of cost and not be seen to be safety at all costs. In real terms whichever approach is seen as the 'ideal' there must be some cost to the employer in insurance premiums which he cannot avoid.

CONCLUSION

We readily admit that health and safety can seem a frightening topic for the student. However, if you have studied it in any detail it is almost bound to appear on your examination paper. If you are prepared to read widely, an essay question could be a 'banker'. If you are faced with a problem, it should be fairly straightforward as it is bound to be on a section or sections of the statutes which you have covered, probably s. 14 of the Factories Act 1961 and ss. 2 to 7 of HASAWA 1974. You are unlikely to have studied many of them as time is of the essence in an employment law course.

READING

Barrett, B., and James, P., 'Safe systems: past, present — and future?' (1988) 17 ILJ 26.

Bergman, D., *Deaths at Work: Accidental Death or Corporate Crime* (London Hazards Centre, 1991).

Committee on Safety and Health at Work. *Safety and Health at Work: Report of the Committee 1970–72* (Cmnd 5034) (London: HMSO, 1972).

Drake, C.D., and Wright, F.B., *Law of Health and Safety at Work: the New Approach* (London: Sweet & Maxwell, 1983).

Health Services Advisory Committee, *Violence to Staff in the Health Services* (London: HMSO, 1987).

Hendy, J., and Ford, M., *Redgrave, Fife and Machin Health and Safety*, 2nd ed. (London: Butterworths, 1993).

HSC, *Plan of Work for 1993/94 and Beyond* (London: HMSO, 1993).

HSE, Annual Reports of HM Chief Inspector of Factories.

HSE, *Drug Abuse at Work*.

HSE, *Successful Health and Safety Management* (London: HMSO, 1991).

HSE, *Workplace Health and Safety in Europe* (London: HMSO, 1991).

James, P., 'Reforming British health and safety law: a framework for discussion' (1992) 21 ILJ 83.

Moore, R., *The Price of Safety: the Market, Workers' Rights and the Law* (London: Institute of Employment Rights).

Munkman, J., *Employer's Liability at Common Law*, 10th ed. (London: Butterworths, 1990).

Painter, R.W., 'Smoking policies: the legal implications' (1990) 12(4) Employee Relations 17.

Poyner, B., and Warre, C., *Violence to Staff: a Basis for Assessment and Prevention* (London: HMSO, 1986).

10 THE LAW OF INDUSTRIAL CONFLICT 1: THE ECONOMIC TORTS AND TRADE DISPUTE IMMUNITIES

INTRODUCTION

We shall now turn our attention to certain aspects of the law relating to collective relationships between employers and trade unions. Collective labour law includes the following matters: the legal status of trade unions; trade union membership and government; provisions relating to collective bargaining such as disclosure of bargaining information, consultation over redundancies and transfers of undertaking and the legal effects of collective agreements.

However, the most important, complex and controversial part of collective labour law is the law relating to industrial conflict. As a result, it is this area which is given particular emphasis on most, if not all, employment law course programmes and it provides the focus for the last two chapters of this book.

THE IMPORTANCE OF A HISTORICAL PERSPECTIVE

A study of the law relating to industrial conflict should begin by examining the historical background to labour law in Britain. This is necessary in order to understand its unique character: most importantly, the fact that the law does not provide a positive right to strike but instead operates a system of negative 'immunities' from civil or criminal liability. In addition, a historical analysis of the interplay between the legislation on industrial action and the judges' decisions helps to explain the British trade union movement's traditional suspicion of legal intervention in industrial relations. It is not unusual to find an essay question making an appearance in examinations relating to this area. The following might be a typical example:

> Any account of the law cannot ignore the fact that its present shape has been a result of cat and mouse, played between the courts and legislature for more than a century, in which Parliament has consistently tried to maximise and the courts almost as consistently to minimise the extent to which the taking of industrial action attracts legal sanctions (Elias, Napier and Wallington, *Labour Law*, p. 210).
> Discuss.

Analysis

The writings of Lord Wedderburn of Charlton will provide you with a penetrating analysis of these issues (see *The Worker and the Law*, ch. 1 and 'Industrial relations and the courts' (1980) 9 ILJ 65). On the issue of 'why immunities?', Wedderburn finds the major reason in the nature of the labour movement in the formative period of our labour law. That period lies between 1867 (the year of the first royal commission on trade unions) and 1906 (when the Trade Disputes Act was passed):

> The central feature of that period was a labour movement which was relatively strong but which was a wholly industrial movement. Unlike its European counterparts it had as yet no ideological political wing. The Labour party was not born until 1906. It was, therefore, a movement which made pragmatic not ideological demands. And those demands registered upon bourgeois parties in Parliament as they encountered a gradual extension of the franchise in 1867 and 1884 — although the universal franchise did not come until the end of this formative period. (9 ILJ at p. 71.)

Wedderburn observes that, from its inception, the modern labour movement in countries such as France and Italy was accustomed, in both its industrial and political wings, to talk in terms of political ideology and rights. The industrial and political wings grew up together — this was not the case in Britain.

The system of immunities from civil or criminal liability reflected the tradition of legal abstention in British industrial relations: the courts were to be excluded from matters that were deemed to be the private concerns of workers, unions and employers.

The unique British approach to the freedom to strike, however, can be vulnerable to judicial intervention where judges develop the common law in ways unforeseen by those who drafted the statutory immunities. Indeed a number of writers have characterised British labour law as a pendulum that has swung between judge-made law and Parliament's enactments. The major developments in the law of industrial conflict are listed in the following paragraphs.

Trade Union Act 1871
Removed the doctrine of 'restraint of trade' which rendered trade unions unlawful associations at common law (see *Hornby* v *Close* (1867) LR 2 QB 153).

Conspiracy and Protection of Property Act 1875
This Act offered an immunity against the crime of 'simple conspiracy' which had been used against strikers in *R* v *Bunn* (1872) 12 Cox CC 316. The legislation provided that an agreement by one or more persons to do an act in contemplation or furtherance of a trade dispute should not be a criminal conspiracy unless the act itself was punishable as a crime. You will see that the statute did not abolish the crime of conspiracy to injure, it offered an immunity provided that the action was taken 'in contemplation or furtherance of a trade dispute'. This phrase, often described as the 'golden formula', became the foundation stone of subsequent immunities.

Trade Disputes Act 1906
This important statute overturned four judicial decisions which posed serious threats to the freedom to strike.

Section 1 provided that an act done in pursuance of an agreement by two or more persons in contemplation or furtherance of a trade dispute should not be actionable unless the act would amount to a civil wrong if done without combination. In other words, the provision was intended to overrule the decision in *Quinn* v *Leathem* [1901] AC 495 which had developed the tort of conspiracy to injure.

Section 2 provided an enlarged definition of what constituted lawful picketing and was designed to overcome the highly restrictive effects of the decision in *J. Lyons & Sons* v *Wilkins* [1896] 1 Ch 811; [1899] 1 Ch 255.

Section 3 provided immunity for a person who, in contemplation or furtherance of a trade dispute, induced another to break a contract of employment. This provided a limited immunity from the tort established in *Lumley* v *Gye* (1853) 2 E & B 216.

Section 4 stated that no action in tort could be brought against a trade union and its funds for acts by its members or officials even though carried out on its behalf. In other words, the House of Lords decision in *Taff Vale*

Railway Co. v *Amalgamated Society of Railway Servants* [1901] AC 426 was overturned and trade unions as such were provided with a complete immunity in tort and could not be sued for damages.

Trade Union Act 1913

This statute was enacted in order to restore the right of unions to spend money on political objects following the decision of the House of Lords in *Amalgamated Society of Railway Servants* v *Osborne* [1910] AC 87. This decision held that it was unlawful for a union to impose on its members a compulsory levy for the purposes of creating a parliamentary fund to promote Labour MPs. Whilst the Act allowed trade unions the right to maintain a political fund, it imposed a series of restrictive conditions on their ability to incur expenditure in respect of certain specified political objects. The union was required to ballot its members in order to approve the adoption of political objects: payment in furtherance of such objects had to be made out of a separate political fund, individual members were allowed to 'contract out' and were safeguarded against discrimination arising from their failure to contribute to the fund. You should note that the two major changes made to this system by the Trade Union Act 1984 relate to the introduction of ballots held at 10-yearly intervals in order to test continued support for the political objects of the union and an enlarged definition of those items of expenditure which must be met out of the political, as opposed to general, funds.

Trade Disputes Act 1965

This measure extended immunity to the tort of intimidation. This was necessary because in *Rookes* v *Barnard* [1964] AC 1129 the House of Lords had expanded this tort to include threats to break a contract as well as threats of violence.

Trade Union and Labour Relations Act 1974

At the same time as repealing the interventionist Industrial Relations Act 1971, this legislation sought to deal with some of the new tortious liabilities developed by the judiciary during the 1960s — most notably extending trade dispute immunity to liability for inducing breaches of commercial contracts (*J. T. Stratford & Son Ltd* v *Lindley* [1965] AC 269) and for interference with contractual relations short of breach (*Torquay Hotel Co. Ltd* v *Cousins* [1969] 2 Ch 106).

Commentators who thought that TULRA 1974's extension of the scope of the immunities had severely restricted any further interventions by the judiciary had badly underestimated the judicial creativity of Lord Denning. In *Meade* v *Haringey London Borough Council* [1979] ICR 494, the then Master of the Rolls and Eveleigh LJ both stated *obiter* that it was tortious to induce a breach of statutory duty, e.g., to cause a local education authority to break its statutory duty to provide education. This potential head of liability has particular relevance for public sector industrial relations and is not encompassed by the framework of immunities set out in TULRA 1974 (cf. *Barretts & Baird (Wholesale) Ltd* v *Institution of Professional Civil Servants* [1987] IRLR 3 and the case note by Bob Simpson 50 MLR 506).

In addition, the late 70s saw Lord Denning and the Court of Appeal seeking to undermine the scope of the immunities by putting a narrow construction on the phrase 'in contemplation or furtherance of a trade dispute'. In a series of cases the Court of Appeal held that a union official could not claim immunity for certain types of sympathetic action because it found, using an objective test, that it was not capable of furthering the primary dispute, being too remote from it (see, for example, *Star Sea Transport Corporation of Monrovia* v *Slater* [1978] IRLR 507; *Express Newspapers Ltd* v *McShane* [1979] ICR 210; *Associated Newspapers Group Ltd* v *Wade* [1979] ICR 664; *Beaverbrook Newspapers Ltd* v *Keys* [1978] ICR 582). This particular attempt to control 'sympathetic' industrial action was rather regretfully rejected by the House of Lords, with Lord Diplock observing that the wide scope of the statutory immunities provided to trade unions 'not surprisingly, have tended to stick in judicial gorges' (*Express Newspapers Ltd* v *McShane* [1980] ICR 42 at p. 57). As we shall see, the Employment Act 1980 subsequently returned us to much the same position as that reached by the Court of Appeal.

This catalogue of developments helps to explain the British trade union movement's deep distrust of the courts and its firm commitment to a policy of legal abstention in relation to industrial conflict.

The reasons for the degree of tension between the trade union movement and the judiciary are complex. In part it may derive from the common law's emphasis on the importance of individual property and contractual rights, and the inability of judges trained in the common law tradition to give sufficient recognition to the rights of collectivities. A number of writers would also point to the narrow social base from which judges are recruited and the inevitable effect that this background has on the frame of reference they adopt (see J. A. G. Griffith, *The Politics of the Judiciary*, 4th ed., 1991, especially chs. 1, 3, 8 and 9). Wedderburn observes:

> . . . it is of significance that the eras of judicial 'creativity' of new doctrines hostile to trade union interests have been largely, though not entirely, coterminous with the periods of British social history in which trade unions have been perceived by middle-class opinion as a threat to the established social order (9 ILJ at p. 78).

The perceived problems with the immunities approach as a means of protecting the freedom to strike have produced calls from a number of quarters for the enactment of a positive right to strike perhaps adjudicated by a specialised labour court (for some thought-provoking contributions to this debate see K. D. Ewing, 'The Right to Strike' (1986) 15 ILJ pp. 143–160); K. D. Ewing, 'A Bill of Rights for Britain', Institute of Employment Rights, 1990; Lord Wedderburn, *The Worker and the Law*, 3rd ed., 1986, ch. 10; R. Welch, 'The Right to Strike: A Trade Union View', The Institute of Employment Rights, 1991).

BREAKING THE MOULD: THE NEW POLICIES OF RESTRICTION

With the exception of war-time and the brief interlude of the Industrial Relations Act 1971, the non-interventionist model established by the 1906 Act was maintained until the Conservative government came to power in 1979. At this point the pattern described above changed and we see Parliament adopting the traditional judicial role of restricting the scope of the immunities.

The Employment Act 1980 marked the first step towards the fulfilment of the Conservative party manifesto pledge of 'striking a balance between the rights and duties of the trade union movement'. This piece of legislation was designed to restrict two forms of industrial action which had come to the forefront of public debate during the so-called 'winter of discontent' in 1978–9, namely, secondary picketing and certain types of 'sympathetic' industrial action. The Act also sought to limit the effectiveness of the closed shop by enlarging those situations in which dismissal for failure to join a particular union was unfair and allowed the employer to reclaim any compensation from the union itself if its action had contributed to the dismissal. Individuals were given a right to complain of unreasonable exclusion or expulsion from a union in a closed shop.

Unlike the last Conservative government's attempts, via the Industrial Relations Act 1971, to accomplish fundamental industrial relations law reform 'at a stroke', the Thatcher/Major administrations have adopted a much more subtle and incremental approach. Following the legislation of 1980, the Employment Act of 1982 narrowed further the parameters of lawful industrial action and, for the first time since 1906, exposed trade union funds to damages claims. The 1982 Act added further to the restrictions on the closed shop, rendering it unfair to dismiss a worker for non-membership unless the closed shop arrangement had received a specified level of support by the workers affected in a ballot conducted Within five years of the dismissal.

Two years later, the Trade Union Act 1984 contained provisions which sought to limit the autonomy of trade unions in three areas. First, it required that unions ballot their members every ten years as to whether they wished to maintain a political fund. Secondly, all voting members of a trade union's principal executive committee, henceforth, had to be elected by ballot at least every five years. Finally, the Act removed immunity in tort where a trade union authorised or endorsed industrial action without first calling a ballot which meets the criteria laid down by the Act. This legislation did not mark the completion of the government's industrial relations law reform strategy.

The Employment Act 1988 extended the rights of individual trade union members where the existing framework was thought by the government to be deficient and also strengthened aspects of the law in the light of experience during the miners' strike of 1984–85. The Act's major provisions are summarised below:

(a) Union members gained the right to apply for a court order to end industrial action which has not been authorised or endorsed by a union without the support of a ballot. Under the Trade Union Act 1984, the cause of action was restricted to employers.

(b) Where those likely to take part in industrial action have different places of work, the union must either hold separate ballots at each workplace or ballot only complete bargaining units.

(c) Members were given a right not to be unjustifiably disciplined. Discipline is treated as unjustifiable, inter alia, if the reason for it is that the member has refused to take part in industrial action.

(d) Further curbs on the closed shop. Without making the closed shop illegal, the Act made the post-entry closed shop virtually impossible to enforce.

(e) Workplace ballots for the purposes of union elections and political funds were replaced by postal ballots.

(f) The requirement for members of a union's principal executive committee to hold their position by virtue of an election was extended to non-voting members of that committee and the president and general secretary.

(g) A post of Commissioner for the Rights of Trade Union Members (CROTUM) was created. The Commissioner's function is to assist union members who wish to bring proceedings to enforce certain of their statutory rights against the union.

More recent, and the fifth piece of legislation since 1979, is the Employment Act 1990. Its contents reflect the proposals set out in two 1989 Green Papers: 'Removing Barriers To Employment' and 'Unofficial Action and the Law'.

Commenting on the Bill, the (then) Secretary of State for Employment, Norman Fowler stated:

This Bill will strengthen the rights of people at work and help to protect the community as a whole against irresponsible industrial action. It tackles three long-standing problems: the closed shop, secondary action and unofficial strikes . . .

A Summary of the 1990 Act's Main Provisions

The closed shop

(a)   It is now unlawful to refuse to employ someone because he or she is, or is not, a trade union member, or because he or she refuses to become or cease to be a member. This provision seeks to outlaw so-called pre-entry closed shops.

(b)   It is also unlawful for an employment agency to refuse any of its services to someone on those grounds.

(c)   Complaints that the above rights have been infringed may be taken to an industrial tribunal.

Industrial action

(a)   The statutory immunity for industrial action taken in 'contemplation or furtherance of a trade dispute' will not apply in cases where there has been secondary action' except in the case of peaceful and lawful picketing.

(b)   Trade unions are made liable in tort for the acts of all their officials (including shop stewards) and committees, unless the union effectively repudiates the action in accordance with the Act's requirements.

(c)   Section 62 of the EPCA 1978, which removes the unfair dismissal jurisdiction of an industrial tribunal where the applicant was taking part in industrial action at the time of the dismissal, and all other 'relevant' employees were treated the same, is amended. There is now no right to claim unfair dismissal if an employee was dismissed while taking 'unofficial industrial action', regardless of how other employees were dealt with.

(d)   There is now no statutory 'immunity' for any industrial action taken in support of a worker dismissed in the above circumstances.

In a clear and perceptive analysis of the 1990 Act, Hazel Carty concludes:

Overall, the Act lacks justification. At the heart of the provision is the attempt to prevent effective trade union pressure. Even those who seek to keep within the rules for taking lawful industrial action will find it difficult to apply those rules. It is hard not to agree with Tony Blair, the Opposition spokesman, that it is a leftover from the old agenda of the industrial cold war. No doubt the severe reduction in the ability to take industrial action will fuel the need for guaranteed rights to take industrial action. The Employment Act 1990 leaves industrial action immunities in tatters. ((1991) 20 ILJ 1 at p. 20.)

In 1991 the government published plans for yet further changes to trade union law. Under the proposals contained in a Green Paper, *Industrial Relations in the Nineties*:

(a)   unions would have to give seven days' notice of industrial action following a ballot;

(b)   workers would be given the right to join a union of their choice, thus undermining the TUC's so-called 'Bridlington Principles' which prevent affiliated unions from poaching each other's members;

(c)   union dues could not be deducted without the written consent of the individual worker;

(d)   members of the public would be given new rights to seek an injunction to halt unlawful industrial action that disrupts public services;

(e)   unions would be obliged to conduct independently scrutinised postal ballots before strikes;

(f)   collective agreements were to be legally binding unless they include a provision making them unenforceable.

All of the proposals, with the exception of the one conerned with making collective agreements legally enforceable, are given statutory force by the Trade Union Reform and Employment Rights Act (TURERA) 1993.

At first sight there would appear to be a contradiction between the neo liberal philosophy of the Conservative administration, which essentially believes in keeping the business of the State and the business of government to a minimum, and the highly interventionist policy adopted in relation to trade union reform. There is no contradiction. For the free marketeer, the market is the mechanism by which individual wants and desires can be controlled. The only valid function of government is to protect this mechanism from interference. According to this philosophy, trade unions not only distort the market, but also infringe the political liberty that the free market offers. The basis of trade union power is seen to be coercion resting on legal privileges:

No salvation for Britain until the special privileges granted to trade unions three-quarters of a century ago are revoked. (F. von Hayek, *Unemployment and the Unions* (1980).)

FINDING YOUR WAY THROUGH THE LEGAL MAZE

The incremental approach adopted by the government has obviously proved a successful political strategy, but it has meant that an already complex area of law has become even more difficult to unravel. The consolidation of these changes by the Trade Union and Labour Relations

(Consolidation) Act (TULR(C)A) 1992 has gone some way to reduce the confusion, but we now have to deal with further amendments introduced by the Trade Union Reform and Employment Rights Act (TURERA) 1993. In trying to make sense of this area it is important that you adopt a structured approach. We suggest that you adopt the three-stage framework of analysis developed by Brightman LJ in *Marina Shipping Ltd* v *Laughton* [1982] QB 1127 and which was subsequently employed by Lord Diplock in *Merkur Island Shipping Corporation* v *Laughton* [1983] 2 AC 570:

(a)   Stage one. Does the industrial action give rise to civil liability at common law?
(b)   Stage two. If so, is there an immunity from liability provided by what was TULRA 1974, s. 13 (now TULR(C)A 1992, s. 219)?
(c)   Stage three. If so, has that immunity now been removed by virtue of the changes introduced by the Employment Acts 1980, 1982, 1988 and 1990 and the Trade Union Act 1984?

Let us try to add a little detail to our analytical framework.

STAGE ONE: CIVIL LIABILITIES FOR INDUSTRIAL ACTION

Breach of Contract

The traditionally accepted view is that a strike is a breach of contract: it being a breach of the obligation on the part of the employee to be ready and willing to work. This is so even if strike notice has been given: it merely being construed as notice of impending breach. You should be aware of Lord Denning's attempt to challenge the traditional analysis in *Morgan* v *Fry* [1968] 2 QB 710 at p. 730, where he suggested that the giving of strike notice corresponding in length to that required to terminate the contract resulted in suspension rather than breach. This alternative analysis, however, has not found favour (see *Simmons* v *Hoover Ltd* [1977] QB 284).

Most other forms of industrial action short of a strike also amount to contractual breaches. If workers 'black' (refuse to carry out) certain work then they are in breach for refusing to comply with a reasonable order. A 'go-slow' or 'work to rule' probably breaches an implied term not to frustrate the commercial objectives of the business (see *Secretary of State for Employment* v *ASLEF (No. 2)* [1972] 2 QB 455 and *Drew* v *St Edmundsbury Borough Council* [1980] ICR 513). An overtime ban would also amount to breach if the employer is entitled under the contract to demand overtime, but not if overtime is voluntary on the part of the employee. However, you should note that a ban on voluntary overtime was classed as 'Industrial action' for the purposes of EPCA 1978, s. 62, in *Power Packing Casemakers Ltd* v *Faust* [1983] QB 471, with the somewhat surprising result that the industrial tribunal had no jurisdiction to hear the workers' unfair dismissal claims.

Where the industrial action does constitute breach, the employer may summarily dismiss or also sue for damages. But in practice the true significance of a finding of breach is that it constitutes the 'unlawful means' element necessary for certain of the economic torts to which we now will turn our attention.

The Economic Torts

It is possible to place the torts relevant to industrial action under four broad headings:

(a) Inducement of breach of contract.
(b) Interference with contract, trade.
(c) Intimidation.
(d) Conspiracy.

If matters were not confusing enough, the classification of these torts differs across the academic texts and even in the cases. For our part, we have adopted what we hope is the simplest format for the purposes of explanation and one which broadly accords with that found in the texts on employment law by Smith and Wood and Bowers and Honeyball.

Inducement of breach of contract

This is the main economic tort and derives from *Lumley* v *Gye* (1853) 2 E & B 216 in which it was established that it was a tort to induce a person to break a contract to which he or she is a party. Since, as we have seen, virtually all industrial action involves a breach of contract, you can readily appreciate that anyone who calls on workers to take industrial action commits the tort. The inducement may take one of two forms: direct and indirect. Direct inducement occurs where the defendant induces a third party to break an existing contract which that third party has with the plaintiff who thereby suffers loss. It may help you conceptualise this and other torts if you express the position in diagram form:

Inducement   Breach of contract of employment

    Albert   Brenda   Capital plc
(union official) ----▶   (employee) ----------------------------▶   (employer)

In the above example, Brenda is employed by Capital plc. Albert, a trade union officer, instructs her to strike. Albert is directly inducing Brenda to break her contract with Capital and is therefore committing a tort.

The necessary elements of this form of tort are:

(a) Knowledge of the contract.
(b) Intention to cause its breach.
(c) Evidence of an inducement.
(d) Actual breach.

We offer further guidance on the content of these elements below. Note that this form of the tort can also be committed where a union directly puts pressure on one of the employer's suppliers to cease delivery of vital supplies, thereby inducing a breach of a commercial contract. However, 'blacking' the employer in dispute usually arises in the second form of the tort, i.e., indirect inducement.

Indirect inducement occurs where unlawful means are used to render performance of the contract by one of the parties impossible.

	Breach of		Breach of	
Albert ----------------▶	Bert ----------------▶	Capital ----------------▶	Delta
	employment contract	commercial contract		

In this example, Delta plc's workers are in dispute with their employer. Capital plc is a supplier of Delta. Bert is employed by Capital as a lorry driver. Albert, a union official, persuades Bert not to make deliveries to Delta. Not only has Albert directly induced Bert to break his contract of employment with Capital, he has also used unlawful means through which he has indirectly induced a breach of commercial contract between Capital and Delta.

In *D. C. Thomson & Co. Ltd* v *Deakin* [1952] Ch 646 at p. 659, Jenkins LJ helpfully breaks down the requirements of this form of the tort into four:

(a) Knowledge and intention. Whether the tort is in its direct or indirect form, the defendant must know of the contract and intend to procure its breach. You will find that these requirements have been interpreted broadly by the courts. As a result, it is not necessary for the precise terms of the contract to be known, a knowledge of the contract's existence will suffice (*J. T. Stratford & Son Ltd* v *Lindley* [1965] AC 269). Similarly, the requirement for intention to induce the breach has been extended to encompass a reckless indifference as to whether the contract could be terminated lawfully or not (*Emerald Construction Co. Ltd* v *Lowthian* [1966] 1 WLR 691).

(b)   An inducement. In *D. C. Thomson & Co. Ltd* v *Deakin* inducement was held to involve an element of 'pressure, persuasion or procuration'. There is an extremely confused boundary between the giving of advice or information on the one hand and inducement on the other. Once again, the courts have on occasion taken a broad view, as can be seen in the homely analogy provided by Winn LJ in *Torquay Hotel Co. Ltd* v *Cousins* [1969] 2 Ch 106:

> A man who writes to his mother-in-law telling her that the central heating in his house has broken down may thereby induce her to cancel an intending visit.

(For a stricter interpretation see *D. C. Thomson & Co. Ltd* v *Deakin* and *Camellia Tanker Ltd SA* v *International Transport Workers' Federation* [1976] ICR 274.)

(c)   An actual breach of contract of employment on the part of those induced.

(d)   A breach of commercial contract ensuing as a necessary consequence of the breaches of the contracts of employment.

This four-element approach has been approved by the House of Lords in *Merkur Island Shipping Corporation* v *Laughton* [1983] 2 AC 570.

Interference with contract, trade or business
In contrast with well-established inducement to breach of contract, this tort is of more recent vintage. In several cases, Lord Denning MR expressed his view that 'if one party interferes with the trade or business of another, and does so by unlawful means, then he is acting unlawfully, even though he does not procure or induce any actual breach of contract' (*Daily Mirror Newspapers Ltd* v *Gardner* [1968] 2 QB 762; see also *Torquay Hotel Co. Ltd* v *Cousins* [1969] 2 Ch 106). Therefore, it will be tortious to interfere with a contract short of breach, for example, by preventing performance in cases where the contract contains *a force majeure* clause, exempting a party in breach from liability to pay damages. (For an interesting application of this tort, see the county court judgment in *Falconer* v *ASLEF and NUR* [1986] IRLR 331, where a commuter succeeded in claiming damages for the expenditure and inconvenience caused to him by a rail strike.)

More recently, it would appear that this head of liability is even broader in scope, encompassing any intentional use of unlawful means aimed at interfering with the plaintiff's trade or business. The existence of this 'super tort', as Smith and Wood aptly describe it, was recognised by Lord Diplock in *Merkur Island Shipping Corporation* v *Laughton* [1983] 2 AC 570.

Intimidation

The tort of intimidation may take the form of compelling a person, by threats of unlawful action, to do some act which causes him loss; or of intimidating other persons, by threats of unlawful action, with the intention and effect of causing loss to a third party. Prior to 1964, it was assumed that the tort was confined to threats of physical violence but in that year the House of Lords held that threats to break a contract were encompassed by the tort *Rookes* v *Barnard* [1964] AC 1129).

Conspiracy

This tort may take two forms:

(a)   Conspiracy to commit an unlawful act. A conspiracy to commit a crime or tort is clearly included in this category. Before the decision in *Lonrho Ltd* v *Shell Petroleum Co. Ltd (No. 2)* [1982] AC 173 it had been assumed that if there were unlawful means the purpose or motives of the conspirators was irrelevant. However, one interpretation of the decision of the House of Lords in the *Lonrho* case was that even in cases where the act complained of was a criminal offence, the civil tort of conspiracy should not be extended beyond acts done in the execution of the agreement by two or more persons for the purpose not of protecting their own interests but of injuring the plaintiff. However, in *Lonrho plc* v *Fayed* [1992] 1 AC 448, the House of Lords denied that its earlier decision involved any major change in the previous law. As a result, a conspiracy by unlawful means does *not* require proof of predominant intent to injure.

(b)   Conspiracy to injure by lawful means. It is, however, the second form of conspiracy which is most dangerous, because it makes it unlawful when two or more do something which would have been quite lawful if performed by an individual. A conspiracy to injure is simply an agreement to cause deliberate loss to another without justification. As with the other form of the tort, the motive or purpose of the defendants is important. If the predominant purpose is to injure the plaintiff, the conspiracy is actionable. If, on the other hand, the principal aim is to achieve a legitimate goal, the action is not unlawful, even if in so doing the plaintiff suffers injury. Whilst it took the courts some time to accept trade union objectives as legitimate (see *Quinn* v *Leathem* [1901] AC 495), later decisions adopted a more liberal stance (see *Crofter Hand-Woven Harris Tweed Co.* v *Veitch* [1942] AC 435). As a result, this form of the tort does not pose the threat it once did to trade union activities.

STAGE TWO: THE IMMUNITIES

The next stage of our analysis is to examine the scope of the statutory immunities from liability for the four categories of economic torts which we have just described. These are now contained in TULR(C)A 1992, s. 219.

Inducement of Breach of Contract

Under the Trade Disputes Act 1906, the immunity for inducements to breach in contemplation or furtherance of a trade dispute only extended to contracts of employment. This had allowed the courts in the 60s to find ways of holding trade unionists liable for inducing breaches of commercial contracts (see *J. T. Stratford & Son Ltd* v *Lindley* [1965] AC 269).

TULRA 1974 (as amended) extended the immunity to cover the breach of any contract. The relevant provision states that an act done by a person in contemplation or furtherance of a trade dispute shall not be actionable in tort on the ground only 'that it induces another person to break a contract or interferes or induces any other person to interfere with its performance' (TULR(C)A 1992, s. 219(1)(a).

As we shall see, however, it is important to view this immunity in the context of subsequent legislative developments. Section 219(1)(a) provides a prima facie immunity, but this immunity may be lost in certain instances, i.e., by taking unlawful secondary action; engaging in secondary picketing; enforcing trade union membership; or taking 'official' industrial action without first having called a secret ballot.

Interference with Contract, Trade or Business

Section 219(1)(a) provides an immunity against the tort of interference with contract. It does not, however, offer any explicit protection against the wider 'genus' tort of interference with trade or business by unlawful means. As a result it is of crucial importance to discover whether an act which is immune by virtue of s. 219 (inducement to breach of contract, for example) may nonetheless constitute the 'unlawful means' for the tort of interference with trade or business. Before the passage of the Employment Act 1980, TULRA 1974, s. 13(3), had stated, 'for the avoidance of doubt', that acts already given immunity could not found the unlawful-means element of other torts. When the 1980 statute repealed s. 13(3), the legal position became confused. However, it would appear that the correct view is that the repeal of s. 13(3) has not changed the position. According to the House of Lords in *Hadmor Productions Ltd* v *Hamilton* [1983] 1 AC 191, s. 13(3) merely confirmed what was obvious anyway from s. 13(1), i.e., inducement is 'not actionable'. So if the unlawful means are immune, then no liability in tort can arise.

Intimidation

This immunity is contained in TULR(C)A 1992, s. 219(1)(b), which states that an act done by a person in contemplation or furtherance of a trade dispute shall not be actionable in tort on the ground only 'that it consists in his threatening that a contract (whether one to which he is a party or not) will be broken or its performance interfered with, or that he will induce another person to break a contract or to interfere with its performance'.

Conspiracy

Section 219(2) now provides the immunity against simple conspiracy originally contained in the Trade Dispute Act 1906.

The Trade Dispute Immunity

In order to gain the protection of the immunities the individual must be acting in contemplation or furtherance of a trade dispute.

For analytical purposes you should ask yourself four questions in order to determine whether the industrial action qualifies:

(a)   Is it between the correct parties? (see below)

(b)   Is there a dispute? (Note that there may still be a dispute even if the employer is willing to concede to the demands of the union (s. 244(4)). Thus if an employer ceases to supply another company on receiving a threat of strike action by its work-force if it continues supplies, there is still a dispute.)

(c)   Is the subject-matter of the dispute wholly or mainly related to one or more of the matters listed in s. 244(1)? (See below.)

(d)   Is the action in contemplation or furtherance of a trade dispute (ICFTD)? (We will say more about this troublesome phrase when we discuss secondary action.)

The scope of the 'golden formula' was amended by the Employment Act 1982 and significantly narrowed in the following ways:

(a)   A trade dispute must now be 'between workers and their employer' not between 'employers and workers' as laid down by the unamended s. 29 of TULRA 1974. Furthermore, because what was s. 29(4) of TULRA 1974 has been repealed the Act no longer allowed trade unions and employers' associations to be regarded as parties to a trade dispute in their own right.

Under the law as it stood before the Employment Act 1982, it was possible for there to be a 'trade dispute' between a trade union and an employer, even though none of the employer's work-force was involved in the dispute. In NWL Ltd v Woods [1979] ICR 867, for example, the House of Lords held that there was a trade dispute between the owners of a 'flag of convenience' ship and the International Transport Workers' Federation, although there was evidence that the crew did not support the union's action. As a result of the 1982 amendment, the ITF's action would not now be protected within the ICFTD formula (see now TULR(C)A 1992, s. 244(1) and (5)).

(b)   Disputes between 'workers and workers' are now omitted from the 'trade dispute' definition. Whilst this means that disputes not involving an employer are unlawful, in practice it is rare for an employer not to be a party to an inter-union dispute. A demarcation dispute between unions will usually involve a dispute with an employer regarding terms and conditions of employment.

(c)   A trade dispute must now relate 'wholly or mainly' to terms and conditions of employment and the other matters listed as legitimate in TULR(C)A 1992, s. 244. Under the law existing prior to the Employment Act 1982, the dispute merely had to be 'connected' with such matters.

The amended phrase marks a return to the form of words used under the Industrial Relations Act 1971 and was inserted to overrule the decision of the House of Lords in *NWL Ltd* v *Nelson* [1979] ICR 867. In this case it was argued that the predominant purpose behind the 'blacking' of the *Nawala* was the ITF's campaign against flag of convenience shipping and little to do with the trade dispute. The House of Lords did not agree, stating that as long as there was a genuine connection between the dispute and the subjects listed in TULRA 1974, it did not matter that other issues were predominant.

The amendment wrought by the Employment Act 1982 means that a mere connection with the matters specified in s. 244 will no longer suffice. So a dispute which is held to be predominantly a trade dispute will fall outside the trade dispute formula.

In many instances it will be extremely difficult to decide which is the predominant element in the dispute and this can be illustrated by the first case which dealt with the issue: *Mercury Communications Ltd* v *Scott-Garner* [1984] Ch 37. Mercury had been granted a government licence to run a private telecommunications system. The Post Office Engineers Union (POEU) objected to the government's policy of 'liberalisation' and ultimate 'privatisation' of the industry. The union instructed its members employed by British Telecom (BT) to refuse to connect Mercury's telecommunications system to the BT network. The Court of Appeal, in granting an injunction to prevent the union continuing its instruction, held that this action related wholly or mainly to opposition to the government's policy rather than fear of future redundancies in the industry should those policies be implemented.

(d)   Since 1982, disputes relating to matters occurring outside the UK are excluded from the immunity, unless the UK workers taking action in furtherance of the dispute are likely to be affected by its outcome in terms of the matters listed in s. 244 (see s. 244(3)). This means that sympathetic action taken by British workers in order to advertise the plight of workers in other countries will be unlawful. In any event, this sort of solidarity action would probably be regarded as political rather than a trade dispute (*British Broadcasting Corporation* v *Hearn* [1977] ICR 685).

In Contemplation or Furtherance

As we have seen, in several cases in the mid 70s the Court of Appeal held that an individual could not properly claim to be within the trade dispute immunity if, objectively, the action he or she had taken was not furthering the trade dispute because it was too remote from it. This meant that certain types of 'secondary action', i.e., action taken against a customer or supplier of the employer in the dispute, lost their immunity.

A classic example of this approach is the case of *Express Newspapers Ltd* v *McShane* [1980] AC 672. In the course of a dispute with provincial newspapers, the National Union of Journalists (NUJ) called on journalists employed by the Press Association (who were still supplying vital copy to the newspapers) to strike. When this call was not fully supported, the NUJ called on its members on the national newspapers to refuse to handle any copy from the Press Association. This action was restrained by the Court of Appeal on the ground that it was not reasonably capable of achieving the objective of the trade dispute.

The Court of Appeal's attempt to restrict secondary action, however, was subsequently rejected by the House of Lords. The main thrust of the decision of the Lords in *Express Newspapers Ltd* v *McShane* was that if a person taking action honestly believes it will further the trade dispute, then this is all that matters: there is no room for an objective test (see also *Duport Steels Ltd* v *Sirs* [1980] ICR 161).

It was, however, the approach of the Court of Appeal, and Lord Denning MR in particular, which most closely accorded with the newly elected Conservative government's perspective on industrial relations. As a result, the Employment Act 1980 included provisions which aimed to control, *inter alia*, secondary action and, to use the words of one government spokesman, to 'return the law to Denning'. This legislation commenced the new legislative policy of stripping away the immunities.

STAGE THREE: REMOVAL OF THE IMMUNITIES

The scope of the immunities has been restricted by the legislation of the 80s and early 90s: the Employment Acts of 1980, 1982, 1988 and 1990 and the Trade Union Act 1984. In this section we examine: the restriction of secondary action; the provisions removing immunity in respect of actions aimed at enforcing the closed shop or trade union recognition on an employer; the loss of immunity for unlawful picketing; the requirements for secret ballots before industrial action; and industrial action taken in support of dismissed 'unofficial strikers'.

Statutory Control of Secondary Action

The Employment Act 1980, s. 17, removed the protection provided by TULRA 1974, s. 13(1), against liability for interfering with commercial contracts by secondary action unless it satisfied conditions which enabled it to pass through one of three 'gateways to legality', the most important of which being the so-called 'first customer/first supplier' gateway. This gateway permitted secondary action to be organised if it involved employees of persons who were in direct contractual relations with the employer involved in the primary dispute.

The second gateway extended the 'first customer/first supplier' rule to cover cases where the supply, which was disrupted, was between the secondary employer and an employer 'associated' with the primary employer. This gateway only applied where the supplies, which were disrupted, were in substitution for the goods which, but for the dispute, would have been supplied by or to the primary employer. The third gateway maintained immunity where the secondary action was a consequence of lawful picketing.

Whilst the policy behind s. 17 was straightforward, its drafting was massively complex. Indeed, Lord Denning described it as 'the most tortuous section I have ever come across' (*Hadmor Productions Ltd* v *Hamilton* [1981] IRLR 210). Indeed, the complexity of the section was one of the reasons put forward for its repeal by the Employment Act 1990, s. 4. News of the demise of s. 17 will be music to the ears of those students of labour law who have been forced to grapple with its intricacies over the last decade: the news will be less welcome to trade unionists who are now confronted with even greater restriction. The aim of s. 4 of the 1990 Act is that only direct disputes between an employer and its workers should attract immunity under TULRA 1974, s. 13. The only exception is secondary action arising out of lawful picketing: the only 'gateway to legality' to be retained from the repealed s. 17 of the 1980 Act. The relevant law is now consolidated in TULR(C)A 1992, s. 244.

As we have said, your task in determining whether secondary action attracts immunity is much simpler than it used to be but we should still adopt a structured approach in determining the legality of the action featured in any problem. Ask yourself the following questions:

(a) Is there a trade dispute within TULR(C)A 1992, s. 244?
If so,
(b) Does the basic immunity contained in s. 219 apply?
If so,
(c) Is there secondary action as defined by s. 244? This occurs if a person:

(i)   induces another to break a contract of employment or interferes or induces another to interfere with its performance, or
(ii)   threatens that a contract of employment under which he or another is employed will be broken or its performance interfered with, or that he will induce another to break a contract of employment or interfere with its performance,
and the employer under the contract of employment is not a party to the trade dispute.

At this point, we have to establish which employer is in dispute with its workers (the primary dispute). If a person acting in support of this primary dispute induces a breach of the employment contracts of the employees of a different employer, then there is secondary action.

Example
Company A's employees are on strike for higher wages. Company B supplies Company A. Company B's employees are instructed to strike in furtherance of the trade dispute with A.
The instruction to Company B's employees constitutes secondary action.
Section 224(4) seeks to limit any attempt to extend the notion of the primary employer. The section states that an employer is not to be regarded as a party to a dispute between another employer and that employer's workers. This section would appear to confirm the thinking of the House of Lords in *Dimbleby & Sons Ltd* v *National Union of Journalists* [1984] ICR 386, that an employer, even though associated with the employer involved in the primary dispute, was not to be regarded as party to that dispute.
If there is secondary action, then move to the final question.

(d) Does the case pass through the lawful picketing 'gateway' in s. 224(1) and (3)? If not, immunity is lost and the action is unlawful.

The basic immunity of s. 219, only applies if the picket is acting lawfully within s. 220, of which the main requirement is that workers may only picket their own place of work.
Even if the workers do picket their own place of work, their actions may still amount to secondary action because they may induce a breach of the contracts of employment of employees of other employers.

Unlawful Picketing

Unlawful picketing, such as picketing a place other than your own place of work, will cease to attract immunity under TULR(C)A 1992, s. 219 (see chapter 11).

Enforcing Union Membership

We have already adverted to the fact that the EA 1988 put further curbs on the closed shop. Section 10 removed the immunities contained in s. 13 of TULRA 1974 from primary industrial action where the reason, or one of the reasons, for the action is that the employer is employing, has employed or might employ a person who is not a member of a trade union or that the employer is failing, has failed or might fail to discriminate against such a person. As we saw in chapter 7 on unfair dismissal, s. 11 made it unfair for an employer to dismiss or to take action short of dismissal against an employee on the ground of the employee's non-membership of a union or a particular union. In both the situations covered by ss. 10 and 11, the fact that the closed shop has been approved in a ballot is an irrelevancy (see now TULR(C)A 1992, s. 222).

The EA 1982, s. 14, withdrew the immunity where the reason for the industrial action is to compel another employer to 'recognise, negotiate or consult' one or more trade unions or to force the employer to discriminate in contract or tendering on the ground of union membership or non-membership in the contracting or tendering concern (see now TULR(C)A 1992, s. 225).

Secret Ballots before Industrial Action (TULR(C)A 1992, ss. 226 to 235)

Official industrial action will only attract the immunity offered by TULRA(C)A, s. 219, unless the majority of union members likely to be called upon to take industrial action have supported that action in a properly conducted ballot. While labour law students have now been spared the brain twisting niceties of EA 1980, s. 17, the complexities posed by the ballot rules now pose an equally formidable challenge! As we saw earlier, the requirements for a lawful ballot and the ways in which a union can be held to be vicariously responsible for industrial acts have seen considerable additions and modifications as a result of the Employment Acts of 1988 and 1990. To supplement these requirements, the Department of Employment has issued a Code of Practice on Trade Union Ballots on Industrial Action. Breach of the Code does not of itself give rise to civil or criminal liability, but any court or tribunal must, where it is relevant, take it into account as evidence of good industrial relations practice (TULR(C)A

1992, s. 207). In what follows, we will try and offer some guidance through the minefield.

When is a ballot required

A ballot is only required in respect of an 'act done by a trade union'. By TULR(C)A 1992, s. 20(2), an act is taken to have been authorised (beforehand) or endorsed (afterwards) by a trade union if it was done, or was authorised or endorsed by:

(a)   any person who is empowered by the rules so to do;

(b)   the principal executive committee, the president; or

(c)   any other committee of the union or any official of the union (whether employed by it or not).

The latter provision, introduced by the EA 1990, will mean that a shop steward could render a union liable where he or she authorises or endorses action without a ballot. Moreover, by virtue of a further amendment, it is sufficient that such an official is a member of a group, the purpose of which includes organising or coordinating industrial action, and that *any member of that group* has authorised or endorsed the action (see TULR(C)A, s. 20(3)(b)).

A union may repudiate the purported authorisation or endorsement by the third group, viz other committees and officials, but can *never* repudiate the actions of the principal executive committee, president, general secretary or those acting under the rules. The requirements for an effective repudiation are far more stringent and complicated as a result of changes introduced by the 1990 Act. To escape liability, the action must be repudiated by the principal executive committee or the president or the general secretary as soon as reasonably practicable. Furthermore:

(a)   written notice of the repudiation must be given to the committee or official in question without delay; and

(b)   the union 'must do its best' to give individual written notice of the fact and date of repudiation, without delay:

(i)   to every member of the union who the union has reason to believe is taking part, or might otherwise take part, in industrial action as a result of the act, and

(ii)   to the employer of every such member (TULR(C)A 1992, s. 21(2)).

The notice given to members must also contain the following 'health warning':

Your union has repudiated the call (or calls) for industrial action to which this notice relates and will give no support to unofficial action taken in response to it (or them). If you are dismissed while taking industrial action, you will have no right to complain of unfair dismissal.

Should these requirements not be complied with, the repudiation will be treated as ineffective. In addition, there is no repudiation if the principal executive committee, president or general secretary subsequently 'behaves in a manner which is inconsistent with the purported repudiation'.

At this stage, we think it important to emphasise the fundamental point that whilst a properly conducted ballot is vital to maintain the protection of the immunities for any action authorised or endorsed by the union, a lawful ballot, per se, will not accord immunity to the action if it is unlawful for other reasons, e.g., secondary action or action to enforce the closed shop.

Ballot requirements
Official industrial action will only attract immunity if the following conditions are met

Separate ballots for each workplace
As originally enacted, the Trade Union Act 1984 required a single ballot of all those who were expected to take part in the industrial action. This position was, however, changed by the EA 1988 and a union intending to organise industrial action, generally, must organise separate ballots for each place of work. Industrial action may not be lawfully taken at a particular workplace unless a majority of members have voted in favour of the action at that workplace (TULR(C)A 1992, s. 228).

The requirement of separate ballots is subject to the following major exceptions:

(a)   Where the union reasonably believed that all the members had the same workplace.

(b)   Where there is some factor:

(i)   which relates to the terms, conditions or occupational description of each member entitled to vote;

(ii)   which that member has in common with some or all members of the union entitled to vote.

This allows a trade union to hold a single aggregated ballot covering members from different places of work if all belong to a complete bargaining unit, e.g., all electricians or all members employed by that employer. If you can make sense of this highly convoluted provision, you will also note that there does not have to be a factor which is common to all voters. There can be several factors, each of which is common to some, e.g., all skilled and semi-skilled grades, all part-time workers and electricians. The union must ballot *all* its members who possess the same relevant factor. So, for example, if it wishes to conduct a ballot of part-time employees employed by a particular employer, it cannot ballot those at workplace A but not those at workplace B.

Ballot papers (TULR(C)A 1992, s. 229)
The ballot paper must ask either whether the voter is prepared to take part or continue to take part in a strike; or whether the voter is prepared to take part or continue to take part in action short of a strike; or it may ask both questions separately. The voter must be required to answer 'Yes' or 'No' to each question and the questions must not be rolled up into one (see *Post Office* v *Union of Communication Workers* [1990] IRLR 143). Every voting paper must contain the following statement: 'If you take part in a strike or other industrial action, you may be in breach of your contract of employment'.

The ballot paper must also specify the identity of the person(s) authorised to call upon members to take industrial action in the event of a vote in favour. This person need not be authorised under the rules of the union, but must be someone who comes within TULR(C)A, s. 20(2)(4) (see above and the decision by the Court of Appeal in *Tanks and Drums Ltd* v *Transport and General Workers' Union* [1992] ICR 1).

Conduct of the ballot
The ballot must have complied with ss. 227 and 230 as to equal entitlement to vote, secrecy etc. The Trade Union Act 1974 offered a union a choice of voting methods: fully postal, semi-postal (voting papers are returned but not distributed by post) or workplace balloting. However, the Code of Practice on Trade Union Ballots on Industrial Action, strongly advocates the fully postal method as the most desirable (para. 20) and TURERA 1993 has now made it a legal requirement (see s. 17). The Code also recommends the appointment of independent scrutineers to oversee the ballot, and, once again, TURERA 1993 has now imposed a legal obligation to do this (see TULR(C)A, s. 226B).

Section 227(1) provides that all those who the union might reasonably believe will be induced to take part, or to continue to take part, in the strike or industrial action should be entitled to vote. Section 227(2) provides that that requirement is not satisfied where a trade union member who is called out on strike 'was denied entitlement to vote in a ballot'. Section 230(3) relates to the opportunity to vote and provides that: 'So far as is reasonably practicable, every person who is entitled to vote in the ballot must' be given an opportunity to vote.

In *British Railways Board* v *NUR* [1989] IRLR 349, the Court of Appeal rejected the employer's argument that what is now s. 227(2) invalidates a ballot if anyone who is entitled to vote, but did not have an opportunity of voting, is invited to strike. The court held that there was a profound difference between denying someone's entitlement to vote and inadvertently failing to given an individual an opportunity to vote. Wrongly denying a member's entitlement to vote is an absolute obligation with draconian consequences. However, s. 230(3) expressly makes the opportunity to vote subject to a test of practicability. Therefore, a 'trifling error' (200 members out of 60,000 not having an opportunity to vote) did not invalidate the ballot.

Timing of the industrial action
The normal rule is that the action must be called within four weeks, beginning with the date of the ballot (s. 234(1)). However, the 1989 Docks Dispute and the litigation surrounding it showed the harsh effect of this time limit where the union was prevented from calling industrial action during the four-week period because of an injunction. The TGWU succeeded in getting the injunction lifted but then had to re-ballot because it was outside the four-week limit.

Under s. 234(2) a union may now apply for an extension of time to allow for the period during which they were prohibited from calling the action. An application has to be made 'forthwith upon the prohibition ceasing to have effect' and no application may be made after the end of the period of eight weeks, beginning with the date of the ballot.

We saw earlier that the ballot paper must identify the person(s) authorised to call for industrial action and, indeed, industrial action will only be regarded as having the support of the ballot if called by this 'specified person' (s. 233(1)). Finally, there must be no authorisation or endorsement of the action before the date of the ballot.

TURERA 1993 has introduced yet more requirements for a lawful ballot. A union is required to give the employees seven days' written notice of any industrial action to which the ballot relates. The notice has to identify which workers are to be called upon to take industrial action, and on which specific date the industrial action will begin. Where a union proposes to call for intermittent action, such as a series of one-day strikes, it is required to give at least seven days' notice of each day or other separate period of industrial action. Moreover if the union suspends or withdraws its support of the action, further notice would be required before there is any subsequent call to resume the action (see now TULR(C)A 1992, s. 234A). Under the TURERA 1993 amendments, employers also have the right to the following information:

(a)   at least seven days' notice of intent to hold the ballot, with details of which workers will be entitled to vote (see *Blackpool and the Fylde College* v *National Association of Teachers in Further and Higher Education* [1994] ICR 648, CA);

(b) a sample copy of the ballot paper, to enable the employer to know which questions are to be asked and what other information is to appear on the ballot paper; and

(c) the same details of the result as the law requires to be given to the union's members, and a copy of the report of the independent scrutineer for the ballot (TULR(C)A 1992, ss. 226A, 231A and 231B).

The member's statutory right to prevent unballoted action

Whilst the failure to hold a ballot will result in the loss of immunities, the Employment Act 1988 created an additional legal consequence. Where a trade union authorises or endorses an 'industrial action' without first holding a ballot, one of its members who has been, or is likely to be induced to take action, may apply to the High Court for an order requiring the union to withdraw the authorisation or reverse the effect of its authorisation or endorsement (see now TULR(C)A 1992, s. 62). In bringing this action, the member may be assisted by the Commissioner for the Rights of Trade Union Members.

The precise scope of the phrase 'industrial action' is unclear. But interpretation of that phrase under what is now TULR(C)A 1992, s. 238 (dealing with the dismissal of those taking part in a strike or other industrial action), would suggest it encompasses action which does not necessarily involve a breach of contract (see *Power Packing Casemakers* v *Faust* [1983] QB 471). The practical significance of this is not lost on the editors of *Harvey on Industrial Relations and Employment Law:*

> In the first place, there is no statutory immunity from suit in tort for a union which takes industrial action without the support of a ballot (TULR(C)A 1992, s. 226) . . . .. In the second place, a member of the union who is being asked to participate in industrial action may demand that the union hold a ballot (TULR(C)A 1992, s. 62) . . . .. In the third place, any member of the public may seek an injunction to restrain any unballoted action if it is likely that he will be materially affected by it (TULR(C)A 1992, s. 235A — the so-called 'citizen's charter' . . .). In other words, the law does not *compel* the union to hold a strike ballot in every case, but the union takes a risk by not holding a ballot. (N [3003.01].)

Industrial Action in Support of Dismissed 'Unofficial Strikers'

In chapter 7, dealing with unfair dismissal, we have described how the 1990 Act removed the limited unfair dismissal protection to 'unofficial' strikers (see now TULR(C)A 1992, s. 237). In order to strengthen the employer's

position in such a situation, the 1990 Act removed the statutory immunity
from any industrial action if 'the reason, or one of the reasons, for doing it
is the fact or belief' that an employer has selectively dismissed one or more
employees who were taking unofficial action (see now TULR(C)A 1992,
s. 223).

CIVIL REMEDIES AND ENFORCEMENT

Injunctions

An injunction is an order either requiring the defendant to cease a
particular course of action (a negative injunction) or, in its mandatory form,
an order requiring the defendant to do something. The most frequent form
of order in industrial disputes is the interlocutory injunction requiring the
organisers to call off the industrial action pending full trial of the action.
Employers who succeed at this stage rarely proceed to full trial: they have
achieved their aim of halting the action. They know that the suspension of
the industrial action, although theoretically on a temporary basis, will
defeat the strike in practical terms because the impetus will be lost. Given
the crucial effect the obtaining of injunctive relief will have on the outcome
of a dispute, the principles on which the court's discretion is based are of
great importance:

It used to be the case that in order to be granted interim relief the plaintiff
had to establish a prima facie case. However, in *American Cyanamid Co.* v
Ethicon Ltd [1975] AC 396 (a case involving patents law) the House of Lords
substituted a less arduous test, namely, whether there is 'a serious issue to
be tried'.

Secondly, the plaintiff must show that the defendant's conduct is causing
him irreparable harm: harm that cannot be remedied by a subsequent
award of damages (the status quo concept).

Finally, the plaintiff must convince the court that the harm being suffered
by him is greater than will be incurred by the defendants if they are
ordered to cease their activities pending full trial (the 'balance of convenience' test).

The application of these tests generally produced a favourable result for
a plaintiff employer. In determining the status quo and balance of convenience tests, it is easy to quantify the economic loss to an employer as a result
of a strike but far more difficult to assess the enormous damage that can be
done to the union's bargaining position if the injunction is granted. This,
together with the fact that interlocutory relief can be obtained on affidavit
evidence, at very short notice and without the defendants even having an
opportunity to answer the complaint, meant that the process was very
much tilted in favour of management.

TULR(C)A 1992, s. 221, contains two provisions which seek to do something to redress the imbalance:

(a) Section 221(1) requires reasonable steps to be taken to give notice of the application and an opportunity to be heard to a party likely to put forward a trade dispute defence.

(b) Section 221(2) provides that where a party against whom an interlocutory injunction is sought claims that he acted in contemplation or furtherance of a trade dispute, the court shall have regard to the likelihood of that party succeeding in establishing a trade dispute defence at full trial of the action. This was an attempt to mitigate the effects of the *American Cyanamid Co.* v *Ethicon Ltd* test in labour injunction cases.

In *NWL Ltd* v *Woods* [1979] ICR 867 Lord Diplock was of the view that the provision was intended as a reminder to judges that, in weighing the balance of convenience, they should consider a number of 'practical realities', particularly the fact that the interlocutory injunction stage generally disposes of the whole action. However, in *Dimbleby & Sons Ltd* v *National Union of Journalists* [1984] ICR 386, his lordship revised his view of the practical realities, given that in the interim period the Employment Act 1982 had made it possible to pursue actions for damages against trade unions themselves and therefore it was wrong to assume that the matter will be disposed of at the interlocutory stage. Lord Diplock appears to suggest that this should make a judge more willing to grant an interim injunction. But surely this factor should weight the balance of convenience against the grant of an injunction, given that the employer is now able to recover damages and costs at full trial from a solvent defendant.

You will find suggestions in several cases (*NWL Ltd* v *Woods*; *Express Newspapers Ltd* v *McShane* [1980] AC 672 and *Duport Steels Ltd* v *Sirs* [1980] ICR 161) that the courts have a residual discretion to grant an injunction. Consequently, in cases where a strike posed serious consequences to the employer, a third party or the general public, what is now s. 221(2) might be overridden. This possibility is of much less practical importance in the 80s, given the considerable narrowing of the scope of the immunities which has taken place (for a detailed discussion of this highly complex area see Wedderburn, *The Worker and the Law*, 3rd ed. pp. 681–717).

Damages

Probably the most significant change in the structure of labour law during the 80s was contained in the Employment Act 1982 which enabled a trade union itself to be sued for unlawful industrial action. In doing so, the Act 'broke the mould' of British labour law which had been used, but for the brief interlude of the Industrial Relations Act 1971, since 1906.

Under what is now TULR(C)A 1992, s. 20, a union will be held vicariously liable for the unlawful industrial action of its membership where such action 'was authorised or endorsed by a responsible person' (see page 239 for a definition).

Limits on damages awarded against trade unions in actions in tort
The TULR(C)A 1992, s. 22, places limits on the amounts which can be awarded against trade unions in actions brought against them where they have authorised or endorsed unlawful industrial action. The limits, which depend on the size of the trade union, are as follows:

(a) £10,000 for unions with less than 5,000 members.
(b) £50,000 for unions between 5,000 and less than 25,000 in membership.
(c) £125,000 for unions with more than 25,000 but less than 100,000 members.
(d) £250,000 if the union has 100,000 or more members.

These limits apply in 'any proceedings in tort brought against a trade union'. The effect of this phrase is that where a union is sued by various plaintiffs (e.g., the employer in dispute, customers, suppliers etc.) for the damages caused to them by the unlawful action, then the maximum will be applied to them separately. In this way, a large union, such as the T & GWU, could find it will be liable to pay well over the £250,000 in damages arising from any one dispute. You should also note that these maxima do not apply in respect of the size of any fine imposed for contempt of court where there is a failure to comply with the terms of an injunction. Nor do the limits on damages include the legal costs the defendant union may have to pay. Hepple and Fredman cite the example of the *Stockport Messenger* action in 1983 against the National Graphical Association as a result of which the union lost one tenth of its assets.

The damages against the union were assessed at £131,000 plus interest (which included aggravated and exemplary damages in relation to proved losses). When this was added to the £675,000 fines for contempt of court for non-compliance with an injunction, and legal costs of sequestration, it was estimated in December 1985 that the union had lost over £1 million. (*Labour Law and Industrial Relations in Great Britain*, p. 212; see also *Messenger Newspapers Group Ltd* v *National Graphical Association (1982)* [1984] ICR 345.)

THE EXAMINATION

It is highly likely that your examination paper will contain at least one question concerned with the issues discussed in this chapter. Earlier we looked at the possible content of an answer to an essay question involving the historical development of the law on strikes. In the last part of the chapter we shall analyse a sample problem question on the scope of the immunities.

Question

Dirty Den Enterprises plc is a newspaper publisher. On 1 January 1994 Dirty Den management announced that its printing works in London would close in six months' time and that it was proposed to transfer all printing operations to its plant in Manchester.

On hearing of the management's plans, Caxton '85, the union which represented the printing workers, organised a strike ballot of its London members employed by Dirty Den. The ballot took place on 6 January 1994. The ballot paper required members to vote yes or no to the following question: 'Are you prepared to strike in order to prevent redundancies?' Nothing other than this single question appeared on the ballot paper. In a 35% turnout, 60% were in favour of strike action.

Following the announcement of the ballot result, there were renewed negotiations between Dirty Den management and Caxton '85 officials. On 15 February 1994, however, the talks broke down and Caxton '85's national executive called an immediate strike at the London printing works.

Dirty Den immediately transferred the printing of all its titles to Manchester.

The printing in Manchester was carried out by a subsidiary of Dirty Den Enterprises, namely, Inky Den Ltd. In an attempt to prevent an undermining of the London print workers' action, Ned, the Caxton '85 Manchester area full-time official, instructed his members at the Manchester printing works to institute a work to rule. As a result, the number of newspapers produced for distribution to wholesalers was reduced by 50%.

One week after the institution of the work to rule, Vera, the general secretary of Caxton '85 wrote to Ned in the following terms:

Dear Ned,

Whilst the National Executive fully appreciate the reasons for the position you have taken with regard to Inky Den in Manchester, you will realise that we must formally distance ourselves from your action.

Yours fraternally

Vera

Having received the letter, Ned took no steps to withdraw the work-to-rule instructions and called on members employed by Manchester newspaper wholesalers to black distribution of all Dirty Den titles to retail outlets. As a result, Trevor, an avid reader of one of the Dirty Den newspapers failed to receive his daily delivery.

Advise Caxton '85 on the legality of the various forms of industrial action which have been taken.

Analysis

This might look a rather daunting prospect but don't despair. The secret of success when confronted by a complex factual situation such as this is to adopt a logical and structured approach. Let's adopt the step-by-step framework of analysis described earlier in the chapter.

Stage one. Does the industrial action give rise to civil liability at common law?
Yes, there is a prima facie tortious liability arising in the following ways:

(a)   When the union called the London printers out on strike this amounted to the tort of inducement to breach of contract (of employment).

(b)   The same can be said of Ned when he persuaded the Manchester workers to work to rule. Following *Secretary of State for Employment* v *ASLEF (No. 2)* [1972] 2 QB 455, it would appear that this particular withdrawal of cooperation can amount to a breach of contract.

(c)   Assuming that there is a supply contract between Inky Den and the newspaper wholesalers, Ned also indirectly induced a breach of those commercial contracts by unlawful means. The unlawful means are the probable breaches of contract he induced by organising the work to rule.

(d)   Even if there is no continuous umbrella contract for the supply of the newspaper to the wholesalers, it is probable that Ned has committed the tort of interference with trade by unlawful means (see *Hadmor Productions Ltd* v *Hamilton* [1983] 1 AC 191).

(e)   The torts described in (b), (c) and (d) were also committed by Ned when he instigated the blacking of distribution of all Dirty Den titles by his members employed by the Manchester wholesalers. (We shall consider the union's liability for Ned's action in a moment.)

Stage two. If there is prima facie civil liability, is there an immunity from liability provided by TULR(C)A 1992, s. 219?
Remember that the issue here is whether any or all of these actions fall within the trade dispute immunity offered by s. 219. The actions must be taken in contemplation or furtherance of a trade dispute. It has been held that a dispute which relates wholly or mainly to fears for jobs is a trade

dispute falling within TULR(C)A, s. 218(1)(b) (i.e., engagement or non-engagement, or termination or suspension of employment or the duties of employment, of one or more workers: see *Hadmor Productions Ltd* v *Hamilton*). Therefore the primary dispute between the London printers and Dirty Den would appear to fall within the formula. Section 219(1)(a) would then offer the immunity against the tort of inducement to breach the contracts of employment.

Ned's actions, however, are not taken against the primary employer in dispute (Dirty Den). Ned is organising action by employees of Inky Den and the wholesalers — employers not party to the primary dispute. Does this mean his actions are not taken in contemplation or furtherance of a trade dispute? No, that is not the case. The House of Lords in *Express Newspapers Ltd* v *McShane* [1979] ICR 210 held that the question whether the acts complained of were done in contemplation or furtherance of a trade dispute is a subjective test, i.e., whether the individual honestly believed that his actions would further the dispute.

So it would also appear that Ned's prima facie tortious actions are covered by s. 219.

Stage three. If the actions are covered by s. 219, has that immunity now been removed by virtue of the changes introduced by the Employment Acts 1980, 1982, 1988 and 1990 and the Trade Union Act 1984?

It is at this stage of the problem that you may begin to appreciate the significance of the legal restrictions on industrial action introduced during the 80s and early 90s. In our scenario, immunity from actions in tort is likely to be lost for two reasons: the conduct of the ballot and the form of secondary action organised by Ned.

The ballot As we have seen the Trade Union Act 1984 (as amended), removed immunity against certain actions in tort where a trade union 'authorises or endorses' industrial action without first calling a ballot which meets the criteria laid down by the Act.

Therefore, Caxton '85 will be exposed to tortious action unless the action it has authorised or endorsed meets the requirements now set out in TULR(C)A, ss. 226 to 234. The union's conduct of the ballot may be legally deficient in several respects:

(a) In order to be valid, the authorisation or endorsement of industrial action must be within four weeks of the date of the ballot (s. 234). Unfortunately for Caxton '85, the strike call was made outside this period. Once the four-week period elapsed, the union should have organised a fresh ballot.

(b) Section 229(4) requires that the following statement must (without being qualified or commented on by anything else on the voting paper) appear on every voting paper, namely, 'If you take part in a strike or other industrial action, you may be in. breach of your contract of employment'. Caxton '85's failure to include this statement on the ballot paper will also invalidate the ballot.

(c) The ballot paper also fails to specify who, in the event of a vote in favour of industrial action, is authorised for the purposes of s. 233 to call upon members to take part or continue to take part in industrial action (s. 229(3)).

(d) Entitlement to vote must be accorded equally to all those members of the union who it is reasonably believed, at the time of the ballot; will be called upon to take strike or other industrial action (TULR(C)A, s. 227(1)). In our problem, the industrial action escalates to the Manchester membership and this raises the question whether this particular constituency should also have been entitled to vote. Much will depend on whether the union has actually authorised or endorsed the action taken by the Manchester workers (see below). If it was reasonable to believe that the Manchester workers would be called upon to take industrial action, then they should have been balloted separately as they obviously have a different place of work from the London printers (s. 228).

(e) The relatively low turnout in the ballot, however, is a 'red-herring'. Provided those entitled to vote are accorded the opportunity, a simple majority of those voting is all that is required (s. 226(2)(iii)). However, it should be noted that the Code of Practice on Trade Union Ballots *advises* unions that in deciding whether to call industrial action a relevant consideration should be the size of that majority and the number of those voting in the ballot. It is also possible, that a low turnout may provide evidential support for a claim by the employer or a member that the ballot is invalid because certain members have been denied their entitlement to vote or that the union has not taken reasonably practicable steps to ensure that those entitled to vote have an opportunity to do so (ss. 227(1) and 230(1) and (2) and see *British Railways Board* v *NUR* [1989] IRLR 349).

(f) TURERA 1993 has introduced yet more traps for the unwary in the balloting process. In particular, the facts of our problem make no reference to whether or not Caxton '85 supplied the employer with the requisite notice of the intention to hold a ballot and to take strike action (TULR(C)A, ss. 226 and 234(A)).

Secondary action Ned is involved in the organisation of secondary action in Manchester. Remember that secondary action can be broadly defined as industrial action by employees of an employer who is not party to the trade dispute (s. 224(2)). Although there is a close association between Dirty Den Enterprises plc and Inky Den Ltd, we have seen that the courts have evidenced a reluctance to lift the corporate veil where business is carried on by companies with the same owners (*Dimbleby & Sons Ltd* v *National Union of Journalists* [1984] ICR 386). This judicial ruling is now confirmed by the terms of s. 224(4). Therefore, the work to rule by the employees of Inky Den Ltd is not taken against an employer who is party to the primary dispute. More obviously, the blacking action taken by employees of the Manchester newspaper wholesalers also amounts to secondary action.

Responsibility and remedies A ballot complying with the terms of the TULR(C)A 1992 is required in respect of 'an act done by a trade union'. We have examined the meaning of this phrase earlier in the chapter and know that it includes the principal executive committee. Therefore, the union will be exposed to tortious liability flowing from the invalid ballot it organised for its London membership.

Determining whether the union has authorised or endorsed Ned's action will also, of course, tell us whether the union is vicariously responsible for the unlawful secondary action in Manchester and vulnerable to an injunction and/or damages action.

We have seen that the TULR(C)A 1992, s. 20(2), includes a full-time official within the class of persons who may act on behalf of the union in order to authorise or endorse industrial action. However, we also noted that the union may escape liability for its official's actions if the executive committee, president or general secretary repudiate the official's actions (s. 21(1)). The requirements for an effective repudiation have become very much more stringent following amendments introduced by the EA 1990. Consequently, Vera's letter, written one week after the institution of the work to rule and expressed in implicitly supportive terms, is not sufficient to constitute such a repudiation. Moreover, Vera has not communicated in writing the fact of her repudiation to Inky Den Ltd or to the Manchester members engaged in the work to rule as required by what is now TULR(C)A 1992, s. 21(2)(b), nor, of course, has she issued the 'health warning' to the members regarding loss of unfair dismissal rights as required by s. 21(3).

The union will also be held responsible for the 'blacking' of Dirty Den titles by members employed by the newspaper wholesalers unless a legally effective repudiation of Ned's actions is issued.

Finally, by virtue of a new right created by TURERA 1993, Trevor, a consumer, may apply to the High Court for an order preventing the continuance of the unlawful industrial action which is preventing or delaying the supply of his newspaper (see now TULR(C)A 1992, s. 235A). In mounting his legal challenge, Trevor may apply to the new Commissioner for Protection against Unlawful Industrial Action for assistance in relation to the proceedings (TULR(C)A 1992, s. 235B).

READING

Auerbach, S., Legislating for Conflict (Oxford: Clarendon Press, 1990).

Morris, G. S., and Archer, T. J., *Trade Unions, Employers and the Law*, 2nd ed. (London: Butterworths, 1993), ch. 6.

Smith, I. T., and Wood, Sir John, *Industrial Law*, 5th ed. (London: Butterworths, 1993), ch. 11.

Wedderburn, Lord, *Employment Rights in Britain and Europe: Selected Papers in Labour Law* (London: Laurence & Wishart: 1991) ch. 1–4, 8–9 and 10.

11 THE LAW OF INDUSTRIAL CONFLICT 2: PICKETING

INTRODUCTION

The practice of peacefully picketing a place of work in order to persuade other workers not to enter the work place has been traditionally perceived by trade unions as an essential weapon in their strike armoury. The vast majority of picket lines are conducted in an entirely peaceful and orderly manner, often without the need for a police presence (see S. Evans 'Picketing under the Employment Acts', in P. Fosh and C. Littler (eds), *Industrial Relations and the Law in the 1980s: Issues and Trends*). During the 70s and 80s, however, we have witnessed the practice of 'mass picketing' and instances of violent confrontation between strikers and the police, e.g., the miners' strikes of 1972, 1974 and 1984/5, Grunwick in 1977 and Wapping in 1986. Such atypical *causes célèbres* prompted statutory intervention aimed at more closely controlling the conduct of picketing through the use of both the civil and criminal law. Indeed, you should note that picketing is the one area of industrial conflict where the criminal law plays a significant part in regulation.

The law's approach to picketing raises the question whether there is an adequate recognition of an individual right of assembly. Indeed, essay questions on this area commonly address this issue and require an analysis of the fragile legality of picketing. A typical essay question might be as follows:

'There is no legal right to picket as such, but peaceful picketing has long been recognised as lawful' (Department of Employment Code of Practice on Picketing, para. 2).
Discuss.

Analysis

As with strike action, English law provides no right to picket. Instead it offers an extremely limited immunity from civil and criminal liability. This is now contained in TULR(C)A 1992, s. 220. Section 220(1) states that:

It is lawful for a person in contemplation or furtherance of a trade dispute to attend—

(a)   at or near his own place of work, or
(b)   if he is an official of a trade union, at or near the place of work of a member of that union whom he is accompanying and whom he represents,

for the purpose only of peacefully obtaining or communicating information, or peacefully persuading any person to work or abstain from working.

Notice that picketing will only receive the protection of the immunities if the pickets are attending at or near their own work place. So-called 'secondary picketing' was rendered unlawful by the Employment Act 1980. It is important that you do not confuse secondary picketing with secondary action under the TULR(C)A 1992, s. 224 (see chapter 10). The latter comprises any form of industrial action taken by employees of an employer not party to the primary dispute. Secondary picketing, on the other hand, will be unlawful even if the workers are employees of the employer in dispute: it is the place of work of the pickets which is the all-important question. There is no statutory definition of 'place of work'. However, the Code of Practice on Picketing, published in 1980 and revised in 1992, offers the following guidance:

The law does not enable a picket to attend lawfully at an entrance to, or exit from any place of work other than his own. This applies even, for example, if those working at the other place of work are employed by the same employer, or are covered by the same collective bargaining arrangements as the picket. (Paragraph 18.)

In *Rayware Ltd* v *TGWU* [1989] IRLR 134, pickets assembled on the public highway at an entrance to an industrial estate which included the factory unit where they worked. They were actually ¾ mile from their factory unit. The majority view of the Court of Appeal was that the pickets were 'near' their workplace and, therefore, acting lawfully.

The statute provides three exceptions to the 'own place of work' requirement:

(a) If workers normally work at more than one place (mobile workers) or if it is impractical to picket their place of work (e.g., an oil rig) then the section allows them to picket the place where their work is administered by the employer (s. 220(2)).

(b) Workers who are dismissed during the dispute in question are permitted to picket their former place of work (s. 220(3)).

(c) As you will see from s. 220(1)(b), a trade union official may attend at any place of work provided that:

(i) the official is accompanying members of his or her trade union who are picketing at their own place of work; and

(ii) the official personally represents those members within the trade union.

(An official — whether lay or full time — is regarded, for this purpose, as representing only those members he or she has been specifically appointed or elected to represent. So it is lawful for a regional official to attend a picket at any place within that region, whereas a shop steward can only picket the work place of the work group he or she represents (see s. 220(4)).

CIVIL LIABILITIES

The Economic Torts

Without the protection of the immunities, picketing will generally result in an economic tort being committed. If workers assemble at the entrance to a work place and attempt to persuade other employees not to work, the pickets could be liable for inducing a breach of contracts of employment. However, provided the picketing is lawful within s. 220, the general immunity provided by s. 219, in respect of tortious liability applies (see s. 219(3)).

Private Nuisance

Private nuisance is an unlawful interference with an individual's enjoyment or use of his land. Unreasonable interference with that right by, for example, blocking an access route to the employer's property, may give rise to a cause of action. So, even though the pickets stand outside the employer's premises they may be liable for the tort of private nuisance.

Picketing which exceeds the bounds of peacefully obtaining or communicating information may involve liability for private nuisance. However, there is still doubt whether peaceful picketing itself amounts to a nuisance when not protected by the 'golden formula'. In your studies you will come across the case of *J. Lyons & Sons* v *Wilkins* [1896] 1 Ch 811; [1899] 1 Ch 255, where the Court of Appeal held that peaceful picketing which involved persuasion went beyond mere attendance for the purpose of informing and was a common law nuisance. In *Ward Lock & Co. Ltd* v *Operative Printers' Assistants' Society* (1906) 22 TLR 327, a differently constituted Court of Appeal thought otherwise. In this case it was said that picketing a person's premises is not unlawful unless it is associated with conduct which constitutes nuisance at common law: some independent wrongful act such as obstruction, violence, intimidation, molestation or threats.

In *Hubbard* v *Pitt* [1976] QB 142 (a rare non-industrial picketing case) Lord Denning MR sided with the view of the Court of Appeal in *Ward Lock & Co. Ltd* v *Operative Printers'Assistants' Society*, stating:

> Picketing is not a nuisance in itself. Nor is it a nuisance for a group of people to attend at or near the plaintiffs' premises in order to obtain or communicate information or in order peacefully to persuade. It does not become a nuisance unless it is associated with obstruction, violence, intimidation, molestation or threats.

The majority of the Court of Appeal, on the other hand, merely affirmed the High Court judge's exercise of his discretion to grant an interlocutory injunction to the plaintiffs whose premises were being picketed and had little to say on the substantive issue.

However, Orr LJ did feel that the defendants' intentions and states of mind formed what he called 'a crucial question' in this matter and he was satisfied that in this case the pickets intended to interfere with the plaintiff's business.

This sort of reasoning was applied subsequently in *Mersey Dock & Harbour Co.* v *Verrinder* [1982] IRLR 152 where the High Court held that the picketing of the entrances to container terminals at Mersey Docks amounted to private nuisance despite the fact that the picketing was carried out in an entirely peaceful manner by a small group of pickets.

On the basis of this approach, it would appear that if the intention of the pickets is to achieve more than the mere communication of information and is actually to interfere with the picketed employer's business, then the picket will be tortious.

As you can see, the conflict between the *Lyons* and *Ward Lock* approaches is unresolved, though you will find the weight of academic opinion favouring the *Ward Lock* approach (see, for example, R. Lewis (ed.), *Labour Law in Britain*, p. 199; P. L. Davies and M. Freedland, *Labour Law: Text and Materials*, 2nd ed., p. 852).

You will also find that the tort of nuisance was interpreted to be considerably broader in scope in *Thomas v National Union of Mineworkers (South Wales Area)* [1986] Ch 20, a case arising out of the protracted miners' strike of 1984/5. In this case, a group of working miners obtained injunctions restraining the area union from organising mass picketing at the collieries where they worked.

Whilst Scott J expressed his agreement with the *Ward Lock* approach that picketing *per se* does not amount to a common law nuisance, he held that it could be tortious if it amounted to an unreasonable interference with the victims' rights to use the highway. This was the situation in the case before the court:

> . . . the picketing at the colliery gates is of such a nature and is carried out in a manner that represents an unreasonable harassment of the working miners. A daily congregation on average of 50 to 70 men hurling abuse and in circumstances that require a police presence and require the working miners to be conveyed in vehicles do not in my view leave any real room for argument.

Two important points arise from this decision:

(a) Private nuisance is concerned with interference with the use of or enjoyment of land in which the plaintiff has an interest. In this case, a species of the tort was held to extend to interference with the right to use the highway (cf. *News Group Newspapers Ltd v Society of Graphical & Allied Trades 1982* [1986] IRLR 337).

(b) The terms of the injunction granted by the court restricted picketing at the collieries to peacefully communicating and obtaining information and in numbers not exceeding six. This number is not a purely arbitrary figure, it comes from the Code of Practice on Picketing which, at para. 51, advises that 'pickets and their organisers should ensure that in general the number of pickets does not exceed six at any entrance to or exit from, a work place; frequently a smaller number will be appropriate'. This would suggest that the judge was using the guidance in the code to fix the parameters of lawful picketing. If this view is correct, then any picketing numbering more than six will lose the immunity offered by s. 220 and will be tortious.

Trespass

Section 220 tells us that picketing is lawful where pickets attend 'at or near' their own place of work. To mount a picket on the employer's land without consent will mean that the immunity will be forfeited and that the tort of trespass has been committed (see *British Airports Authority* v *Ashton* [1983] ICR 696).

CRIMINAL LIABILITY

Whilst it is important to grasp the range of possible civil liabilities which may attach to certain types of picketing, it is the criminal law which is of the greatest practical significance in terms of the control of the activity. This can be clearly seen from the employment of the criminal law during the miners' strike, where over 11,000 charges were brought in connection with incidents arising out of the dispute. These ranged in gravity from the serious offences of riot and unlawful assembly to the less serious charge of obstruction of the highway. Additional criminal offences which may be relevant to the conduct of picketing have been created by the Public Order Act 1986. We shall offer you a brief survey of the potential criminal liability of pickets (more detailed accounts of developments in this area are provided by Gillian Morris, 'Industrial action and the criminal law', IRLIB, 5 May 1987, pp. 2–9, and J. Bowers and M. Duggan, *The Modern Law of Strikes*, ch. 4).

Obstructing a Police Officer in the Execution of Duty

If a police officer reasonably apprehends that a breach of the peace is likely to occur, the officer has the right and duty at common law to take reasonable steps to prevent it. If the officer is obstructed in the exercise of this duty then an offence is committed (Police Act 1964, s. 51(3)). In practice, this gives the police a wide discretion to control picketing. While there must be an objective apprehension that a breach of the peace is a real as opposed to a remote possibility, the courts tend to accept the officer's assessment of the situation. The leading case on this question is *Piddington* v *Bates* [1961] 1 WLR 162, where the officer's decision to restrict the number of pickets at an entrance to a work place to two was held to be legally justified. (You should note that the Code of Practice on Picketing, para. 47, makes it clear that its recommended number of six pickets does not affect in any way the discretion of the police to limit the number of people on any one picket line.)

The common law duty to preserve the peace also allows the police to set up road-blocks to prevent pickets joining picket lines some distance away, provided that there is a reasonable apprehension that the risk to the peace is in close proximity both in time and place (see *Moss* v *McLachlan* [1985] IRLR 76 and the commentary on the case by Morris (1985) 14 ILJ 109). Under the Police and Criminal Evidence Act 1984, s. 4, police officers may also operate road checks' for purposes which include ascertaining whether a vehicle is carrying a person intending to commit an offence which a senior officer has reasonable grounds to believe is likely to lead to serious public disorder.

Obstruction of the Highway (Highways Act 1980, s. 137)

Under this provision, it is an offence wilfully to obstruct free passage along a highway without lawful authority or excuse. Before the offence is established, there must be proof of an unreasonable user of the highway. This is a question of fact and depends upon all the circumstances including the length of time the obstruction continues, the place where it occurs, its purpose and whether it causes an actual as opposed to potential obstruction (*Nagy* v *Weston* [1965] 1 WLR 280). It would appear that peaceful picketing carried out in the manner envisaged by TULR(C)A 1992, s. 220, and within the numbers advised by the code will be held to be a reasonable user. If, however, these boundaries are crossed the offence will be committed as where the pickets, for example, stood in front of a vehicle in order to stop it entering the employer's premises (*Broome* v *Director of Public Prosecutions* [1974] AC 587) or walked in a continuous circle in a factory entrance (*Tynan* v *Balmer* [1967] 1 QB 91).

Public Nuisance

This offence derives from common law and is committed where members of the public are obstructed in the exercise of rights which are common to all Her Majesty's subjects, including the right of free passage along the public highway. As with the more frequently charged offence under the Highways Act 1980, it is necessary for the prosecution to prove unreasonable user.

Where an individual suffers special damage, over and above that suffered by the rest of the public, an action in tort for public nuisance may also be brought.

Intimidation or Annoyance by Violence or Otherwise

The Conspiracy and Protection of Property Act 1875 made the following five acts criminal if they are done 'wrongfully and without legal authority' with a view to compelling any person to do or abstain from doing any act which that person has a legal right to do (s. 7):

(a)   Using violence or intimidating that person or his wife or children or injuring his property.

(b)   Persistently following that person about from place to place.

(c)   Hiding any tools, clothes or other property owned or used by such other person, or depriving him or hindering him in the use thereof.

(d)   Watching or besetting his house, residence or place of work, or the approach to such house, residence or place, or wherever the person happens to be.

(e)   Following such a person with two or more other persons in a disorderly manner in or through any street or road.

Until relatively recently, it was assumed that this quaintly worded provision was only of historical interest and virtually obsolete in practical terms. During the miners' strike of 1984/5, however, at least 643 charges were brought under s. 7, mainly to deal with 'watching and besetting' working miners' homes. In the view of the government, the section had demonstrated its continued efficacy in the circumstances of the strike and should not only be retained but strengthened (see *Review of Public Order Law*, Cmnd 9510). Consequently, the Public Order Act 1986 increased the maximum penalty of three months' imprisonment and a £100 fine to six months' imprisonment and/or a fine (currently £5,000). The 1986 Act also made breach of s. 7 an arrestable offence. The five offences are now contained in TULR(C)A 1992, s. 241.

Of the five offences listed in what is now s. 241, watching and besetting is the one which is most likely to arise out of the course of picketing. As we have seen earlier in this chapter, the weight of authority would suggest that the watching and besetting must be of such a nature as to amount in itself to tortious activity before it can give rise to liability under s. 241. If peaceful picketing is not tortious then it cannot amount to a criminal watching and besetting either.

One final point on this section concerns the question whether mass picketing amounts to intimidation for the purposes of s. 241. In *Thomas v National Union of Mineworkers (South Wales Area)* [1986] Ch 20 Scott J was of the view that not only was mass picketing a common law nuisance but it also amounted to intimidation under s. 241, even where there was no physical obstruction of those going to work.

Public Order Act 1986

In putting forward the proposals which were later largely translated into the provisions of the Public Order Act 1986, the White Paper of 1985, *Review of Public Order Law*, stated:

The rights of peaceful protest and assembly are amongst our fundamental freedoms: they are numbered among the touchstones which distinguish a free society from a totalitarian one. Throughout the review the government has been concerned to regulate these freedoms to, the minimum extent necessary to preserve order and protect the rights of others.

A number of commentators, however, have expressed a general concern that the provisions contained in the Act impose a dangerous restriction on the civil liberties of assembly and protest and, particularly in the light of events during the 1984/5 miners' strike, make it increasingly more difficult for the police to be seen to maintain a position of neutrality in the policing of industrial disputes (see R. Lewis (ed.) *Labour Law in Britain,* pp. 216–19; Wedderburn, *The Worker and the Law,* 3rd ed., pp. 550–3).

Part I of the Public Order Act 1986 contains five new statutory offences which may have a relevance in the context of picketing. Sections 1 to 3 of the Act contain the offences of riot, violent disorder and affray and replace the common law offences of riot, rout, unlawful assembly and affray whose ambit was confused and uncertain. Sections 4 and 5 contain the more minor offences of causing fear or provocation of violence and causing harassment, alarm or distress.

Riot (s. 1)
Where 12 or more people are present together and use or threaten violence for a common purpose and their conduct (taken together) is such that a person of reasonable firmness — if present — would fear for his safety, each person using the violence is guilty of riot and liable on conviction to a maximum possible penalty of 10 years' imprisonment.

Violent disorder (s. 2)
Where three or more people who are present together use or threaten violence and their conduct, taken together, would cause a person of reasonable firmness — if present — to fear for his safety, each person using or threatening violence is guilty of the offence and liable on conviction to a maximum of five years' imprisonment. Note the contrast with the more serious offence of riot: fewer people are required, the accused need only threaten violence as opposed to using it and there is no requirement for a common purpose.

Affray (s. 3)
The offence of affray is committed if a person uses or threatens unlawful violence towards another and his conduct is such as would cause a person of reasonable firmness — if present — to fear for his personal safety. The maximum sentence on conviction is three years' imprisonment.

You should note that 'violence' is given a wide definition by s. 8 of the Act and, except in the context of affray, includes violent conduct to property as well as towards persons. In addition, the term is not restricted to conduct intended to cause injury or damage: it covers any 'violent conduct'. Rather unusually, the section provides us with an example of what it means, i.e., throwing at or towards a person a missile of a kind capable of causing injury which does not hit or falls short.

Note also that it is not necessary for the prosecution to prove that anyone actually feared for their safety: the fear of a hypothetical bystander is sufficient.

Causing fear of or provoking violence (s. 4)

The most frequently charged public order offence prior to the passage of the 1986 Act was that contained in the Public Order Act 1936, s. 5. This section made it an offence to use threatening, abusive or insulting words or behaviour with intent to cause a breach of the peace or whereby a breach of the peace was likely to be occasioned. During the miners' strike in 1984/5, some 4,107 prosecutions were brought under this section.

Section 4 of the 1986 Act replaces s. 5 of the 1936 Act with a modified and extended version of the offence. A person is guilty of the offence if he:

(a) uses towards another person threatening, abusive or insulting words or behaviour, or

(b) distributes or displays to another person any writing, sign or other visible representation which is threatening, abusive or insulting,

with intent to cause that person to believe that immediate unlawful violence will be used against him or another by any person, or to provoke the immediate use of unlawful violence by that person or another, or whereby that person is likely to believe that such violence will be used or it is likely that such violence will be provoked.

The new provision is broader in scope than its predecessor in two respects. First, the new offence can be committed in a public or private place. The limitation of s. 5 of the 1936 Act to conduct in public places meant that during the miners' strike a number of summonses were dismissed where men charged with threatening words or behaviour were able to show they were on National Coal Board or other private property at the time of the alleged offence. (Indeed, the extension of coverage to both public and private places applies in respect of all five of the statutory public order offences contained in the Public Order Act 1986.) Secondly, case law suggested that the Public Order Act 1936, s. 5, did not cover a situation where the victim (for example, a policeman or an elderly lady) was someone who was not likely to be provoked to breach the peace. Under the new provision, a belief that immediate violence will be used against himself or another is sufficient.

The maximum penalty on conviction is six months' imprisonment and a £5,000 fine.

Causing harassment, alarm and distress (s. 5)
This 'catch-all' and controversial offence is committed where a person:

(a)   uses threatening, abusive or insulting words or behaviour, or disorderly behaviour, or
(b)   displays any writing, sign or other visible representation w' .h is threatening, abusive or insulting,

within the hearing or sight of a person likely to be caused h; ssment, alarm or distress thereby.

The maximum penalty is a £1,000 fine.
It is easy to foresee that this offence will be readily emplc ed to control the conduct of picketing. Shouts of abuse to workers as they ross the picket line, offensive gestures and insulting placards or banners may all fall foul of this section.

One of three defences provided by s. 5(3) is if the acc sed can prove that his conduct is reasonable. The scope of this defence for the picket is untried and uncertain though J. Bowers and M. Duggan, *The Modern Law of Strikes*, p. 44, are not optimistic:

A picket might claim that his conduct was reasonable when he called the strike-breaker names such as 'scab', because it is in the collective interest that the strike is successful and his conduct sought to achieve that result. One cannot, however, imagine the courts being very sympathetic to such a plea.

Marches and assemblies
Part II of the Public Order Act 1986 imposes new controls over the conduct of marches or processions and static assemblies.

Marches and processions   Section 11 imposes a new national requirement for organisers of 'public processions' to give at least six clear days' notice of their intention to the police. The notice must specify the date of the procession, its proposed starting time and route, and the name and address of one of the organisers.

Picketing, by definition, is a static assembly outside the entrance of a work place. However, protest marches are now a relatively frequent feature of larger industrial disputes, e.g., the protest marches held in support of the striking miners in 1984/5 and the marches, culminating in a mass picket outside the Wapping plant of News International, during 1986 in protest at the dismissal of some 5,500 print workers (see *News Group Newspapers Ltd* v *Society of Graphical & Allied Trades 1982* [1986] IRLR 337). In future such marches will have to comply with the terms of s. 11, though you should note that the notice requirement does not apply to processions 'commonly and customarily held', e.g., by trade unionists on May Day.

A notice may be delivered by post but only if it is by recorded delivery; otherwise it must be delivered by hand to a police station in the police area in which it is proposed the procession will start. The Act allows an exception to the six-day notice requirement in the case of a delivery by hand where it is not reasonably practicable to give that amount of advance notice. An example where this exception may be relevant in an industrial dispute would be the need for a rapid protest response to the summary dismissal of a shop steward or management's announcement of immediate plant closure and redundancies.

Failure to give the appropriate notice renders the organisers liable to a fine of up to £1,000. It is also made an offence to organise a march which differs in terms of start and route from the information given in the notice. Defences are available if it is proved that the accused did not know of and neither suspected, nor had reason to suspect, the failure to satisfy the requirements or the different date, time or route. In relation to a march being held on a different date or at a different time or following a different route, it is also a defence to prove that the difference arose from circumstances beyond the control of the accused or from something done with the agreement of a police officer.

Power to impose conditions on processions (s. 12) This section enables the most senior police officer present to impose conditions, including conditions relating to route and timing, on a procession when the officer reasonably believes that it may result in serious public disorder, serious damage to property or serious disruption to the life of the community or that the purpose of the organisers is to intimidate others. Where a march or procession is intended to be held, the 'senior police officer' with the power to impose conditions is the chief officer of police.

An organiser of a march who knowingly fails to comply with a condition imposed under the section commits an offence, whose maximum punishment is three months' imprisonment and/or a £2,500 fine. In addition, those who participate in a march who knowingly fail to comply with any imposed condition commit a summary offence punishable with a fine not exceeding £1,000. Finally, those who incite marchers to break a condition are also guilty of a summary offence and are liable on conviction to a maximum of three months' imprisonment or a fine not exceeding £2,500.

Ban on marches The power to ban marches for up to three months under the Public Order Act 1936 on the grounds of reasonable belief that they will result in 'serious public disorder' is retained. The major change is that the 1986 Act makes it an offence, punishable with a fine, to particpate in a banned march. It is also an offence to organise or incite others to participate in a banned march.

Static assemblies The Public Order Act 1986, for the first time ever, provides the police with a clear statutory power to impose conditions which prescribe the location, size and maximum duration of 'public assemblies' (defined as assemblies of 20 or more people in a 'public place' which is wholly or party open to the air). As with processions, the most senior officer present will be able to impose such conditions where he or she reasonably believes that the assembly may result in serious disorder, serious damage to property, serious disruption of the life of the community or the 'intimidation of others with a view to compelling them not to do an act they have a right to do, or to do an act they have a right not to do'.

This provision has the clearest relevance for pickets and provides a potent additional weapon of control for the police. As the White Paper (Cmnd 9510) observed: '. . . at Grunwick's or Warrington, for example, the police could have imposed conditions limiting the numbers of demonstrators, or moving the demonstration in support of the pickets further away from the factory' (para. 5.7).

Where conditions are imposed in advance of the assembly they may only be imposed by the chief officer of police or his deputy or assistant. The organisers of a static assembly which fails to abide by the conditions or those who incite disobedience face a maximum penalty of three months' imprisonment and/or a £2,500 fine. The participants in such an assembly risk a £1,000 fine.

THE EXAMINATION

As we have stated, the law of picketing is a traditional favourite for an essay question. We hope that the material we have presented in this chapter will help you to approach such a question with confidence. It is also often the case that the legality of the conduct of pickets provides the focal point for a problem question.

The following question is a good example of its genre.

LB Cars Ltd is a motor vehicle manufacturer with plants at Alton and Bursley. On 1 March 1994 the company announced plans to close the Alton plant on the grounds of over-capacity within the next 12 months. This would involve considerable redundancies amongst the work-force though some skilled workers will be transferred to the Bursley plant.

The closure plans are opposed by the Union of Bumpers and Grinders (the UBG), the union which represents the workers employed by LB Cars. Following negotiations, it became clear that no agreement could be reached and the union balloted its members about taking strike action and the result was overwhelmingly in favour.

On 25 March the strike began, whereupon the employer dismissed all the strikers and immediately transferred all production to the Bursley plant. In the following weeks the Bursley plant was picketed. The picketing took two forms.

First, the union organised an 'official picket'. This consisted of five pickets stationed at the main entrance to the plant, four of whom were dismissed workers from the Alton plant and the fifth being the regional full-time official of the UBG. The official picket was entirely peaceful. This picket has persuaded a number of delivery drivers employed by Tyres Ltd to refuse to enter the Bursley plant in solidarity with the Alton workers.

Secondly, there were daily assemblies of between 100 and 200 dismissed workers lining the road which led to the plant entrance. These congregations formed in the mornings and evenings when the Bursley workers arrived at or left work. The Bursley workers were frequently subjected to abuse and threats as they passed the assembly. This persuaded LB cars to provide buses, at some considerable cost, to transport its employees to and from work.

A number of Bursley workers have resigned as a result of the threats they have received from the mass pickets.

Advise the UBG as to its potential civil liability arising from the picketing of the Bursley plant of LB Cars Ltd.

Analysis

Problem questions on the law relating to industrial conflict often tend to be on the lengthy side because of the need on the part of the examiner to set up a sufficiently challenging factual scenario. This particular question is no exception to the rule. In building up to the picketing issue, the problem refers to other matters such as redundancy and consultation, strike ballots and the dismissal of strikers. Do not render an already challenging task more difficult by pursuing the legal issues surrounding these questions. You will receive absolutely no credit for a discourse on these matters. Note also that the question on this occasion does not require an analysis of criminal matters: it is solely concerned with civil liabilities arising out of the conduct of the picketing.

In answering this question let's adopt the structured question and answer approach we adopted in the previous chapter when dealing with the immunities.

Civil Liability

Which torts are committed?

Public nuisance We have seen that actionable nuisance comes in two distinct forms: private and public nuisance. Public nuisance occurs where members of the public are obstructed in the exercise or enjoyment of rights which are common to all Her Majesty's subjects. Obstruction of the public's right to use the highway might constitute a public nuisance if — and only if — the obstruction is regarded as an unreasonable user of the highway. Whilst an orderly and peaceful demonstration is therefore likely to be lawful, disorderly gatherings on the highway will fall foul of this crime/tort. In *News Group Newspapers Ltd* v *Society of Graphical & Allied Trades 1982* [1986] IRLR 337 the facts of which provide a partial basis for this problem, the conduct of the pickets and the daily demonstrations outside the Wapping plant of News International was held to be an unreasonable user of the highway.

Public nuisance is usually a crime, but is actionable as a tort if the plaintiff can prove that he has suffered particular damage over and beyond that suffered by the general public. In *Thomas* v *National Union of Mineworkers (South Wales Area)* [1986] Ch 20 Scott J held that because the working miners' access to the collieries was not being physically impeded by the pickets, they could not establish the requisite special damage which would allow them to sue in public nuisance. This may be contrasted with the *News Group Newspapers Ltd* case in which it was held that the employers could establish special damage given that they had to provide buses to bring their labour force past the mass picket and into the Wapping plant. The buses were specially adapted to protect them from missiles thrown from the crowd. In addition, it was accepted that the conduct of the pickets which had caused some journalists to leave and discouraged others from joining the organisation, amounted to special damage suffered by the employers. Following the News Group case, it would also be possible for any employee whose freedom of movement was constrained by the presence of disorderly picketing to mount an action for public nuisance. In that case, an employee plaintiff, who felt no longer able to leave the plant during the middle of the day for lunch breaks, 'who had to travel to and from the premises by taxi rather than on foot and complained of feeling drained by the pressure created by the mass picketing was also held to have suffered special damage.

Private nuisance It should be relatively straightforward for LB Cars to establish this tort. The disorderly picketing may amount to an unreasonable user of the highway which affects LB Cars' rights of access and enjoyment of the land which it owns.

Harassment   As stated above, in *Thomas* v *National Union of Mineworkers (South Wales Area)* the working miners were not able to rely on public nuisance because it was held that they could point to no special damage — their employer had provided transport so they could safely gain access to the colliery. Nor could their remedy lie in the traditionally formulated tort of private nuisance because they had no proprietary interest in the land being picketed. You will remember, however, that Scott J felt that there was a species of private nuisance, namely 'unreasonable interference with the victim's right to use the highway'. Such an action might have a relevance to the Bursley workers in our problem. In the *News Group Newspapers Ltd* case Stuart-Smith J, whilst not finding it necessary to express, a final view on the matter, thought that there was force in the defendant unions's argument that such a species of tort did not exist.

Intimidation   We have already referred to this tort in the previous chapter. In the *News Group Newspapers Ltd* case Stuart-Smith J described the tort in the following manner:

> The tort of intimidation is committed when A delivers a threat to B that he will commit an act or use means unlawful against B, as a result of which B does or refrains from doing some act which he is entitled to do, thereby causing damage either to himself or C. The tort is one of intention and the plaintiff, whether it be B or C, must be a person whom A intended to injure.

The threat may be one of violence or a threat to break a contract. The tort is not complete, however, unless the victim of the threat gives way to the threat and damage is suffered as a result. However, injunctive relief may be available to restrain both the unlawful act and serious threats to commit-the unlawful act (this was the case in the *News Group Newspapers Ltd* case).

This tort may have a relevance to the facts of our problem if threats of violence have been made to the Bursley workers unless they abstain from working for LB Cars. We are told that certain of the workers succumbed to threats of violence and in both cases this resulted in damage to LB Cars Ltd.

The economic torts   Don't forget the group of torts we discussed in the previous chapter. If the pickets are successful in persuading any of the Bursley workers not to work for LB Cars, then they may have induced breaches of employment contracts. In addition, dissuading the lorry drivers from delivering the tyres will amount to the tort of indirect inducement to breach of commercial contract.

Are the actions of the pickets covered by the immunities?
TULR(C)A 1992, ss. 219 and 220, provide immunity from actions done 'in contemplation or furtherance of a trade dispute'. It would seem clear that the dispute between the Alton workers and LB Cars Ltd over the future redundancies falls within this formula (see s. 244(1)(b)). Furthermore, whilst the trade dispute is required to be between workers and their own employer, this does include a dispute between an employer and a worker who has ceased to be employed by him where either the worker's employment was terminated in connection with the dispute or the termination was one of the circumstances giving rise to the dispute (s. 244(5)). Therefore the fact that the Alton workers have been dismissed in connection with the dispute does not exclude them from the scope of the formula.

Workers or union officials whose picketing falls outside the scope of s. 220 will lose the immunities for the economic torts. Remember the reason for this is because s. 219(3), provides that nothing in TULR(C)A 1992, s. 219(1) and (2) which contain the immunities, 'shall prevent an act done in the course of picketing from being actionable in tort unless it is done in the course of attendance declared lawful by' s. 220.

With these factors in mind let us analyse the two forms of picketing being conducted outside the Bursley plant.

The 'Official Picket'

We are told that this was an entirely peaceful picket: it would appear that the five pickets are attending — to use the statutory phrase — 'for the purpose only of peacefully obtaining or communicating information, or peacefully persuading any person to work or abstain from working'. So it would appear that their purpose, is lawful.

The next question we should ask ourselves concerns the number of pickets. We have seen that the Code of Practice on Picketing states that six pickets will usually be a sufficient number. Although the code's provisions are not of binding effect, the decisions in *Thomas v National Union of Mineworkers (South Wales Area)* and *News Group Newspapers Ltd v Society of Graphical & Allied Trades 1982* can both be read as regarding six as the maximum number for lawful picketing. Once again, the pickets in the problem fall within the advised number.

The official picket loses the immunity when location is considered. Remember that pickets may generally only attend at or near their own place of work. Workers whose employment was terminated in connection with the trade dispute can picket their own place of work. The four sacked Alton workers are, of course, outside the scope of this exception. This fact also renders the trade union official's presence on the picket line unlawful. He may only attend 'at or near the place of work of a member of that union whom he is accompanying and whom he represents' (s. 220(1)(b)).

Thus this group of entirely peaceful pickets commit the tort of inducement to breach of contract (of employment) when they persuade the lorry drivers to refuse to deliver the tyres and, by these unlawful means, indirectly induce a breach of the commercial contract between LB Cars Ltd and Tyres Ltd.

The Mass Picket

Section 220 only encompasses peaceful picketing and it is clear that the courts will readily infer that pickets who assemble in unreasonably large numbers are there other than for a purpose declared lawful by the section (see the views of Lord Reid in *Broome* v *Director of Public Prosecutions* [1974] AC 587). In our case, the secondary pickets and the threats used by some of them should leave us in no doubt that s. 220 immunity is lost.

Responsibility for the Torts

Given that a number of torts appear to have been committed, the next question is the extent of the union's liability. We can divide this complex issue into two parts for the purpose of analysis: (a) liability for the economic torts under statute, (b) vicarious liability at common law.

Liability under statute

As we saw in chapter 10, the TULR(C)A 1992, s. 20, imposes a statutory vicarious liability on a trade union for certain unlawful acts of its officials and members where those acts have been 'authorised or endorsed' by a 'responsible person'. But it is important to note that this statutory vicarious liability only applies in respect of the economic torts of inducing breach of contract, intimidation and conspiracy. (Now TULR(C)A, s. 20(1).)

In our problem it may be possible that the union will be held responsible for the economic torts committed by the 'official picket', but will the union's responsibility extend to the torts of nuisance and intimidation which appear to have been committed as a result of the mass picket? This involves a consideration of the common law.

Vicarious liability at common law

Given that trade unions were granted a complete statutory immunity in tort by the Trade Disputes Act 1906, there had been relatively little discussion of a union's liability for the acts of its members until the major statutory change wrought by the Employment Act 1982. However, during the currency of the Industrial Relations Act 1971 a leading case did emerge on the question of common law vicarious responsibility: *Heatons Transport (St Helens) Ltd* v *Transport & General Workers' Union* [1973] AC 15. In this case the union was held liable for the unofficial acts of its shop stewards, on the basis that shop stewards had an implied authority to act on the trade union's behalf. The trade union could only escape responsibility if it had expressly forbidden its members to take particular unlawful actions, perhaps going as far as disciplining members or withdrawing shop stewards' credentials.

This precedent was applied by the court in *Thomas v National Union of Mineworkers (South Wales Area)* to hold the South Wales Area of the NUM responsible for the part played by its constituent lodges in organising the mass picketing. We have little evidence to rely on as to the level of involvement of UBG officials in the mass picket, though in the *Thomas* case, one important factor leading to the South Wales Area's responsibility for the mass picket was the lack of evidence that on any occasion any lodge officer had discouraged the attendance at the colliery gates of large numbers.

This leads us again to the *News Group Newspapers Ltd* case where the union resisted the plaintiff's claim that it was responsible for the torts committed during the course of the mass picketing and demonstrations outside the Wapping plant.

Stuart-Smith J held that the union was not vicariously liable simply because it organised a march or picketing during the course of which tortious acts were committed by third parties, even though such acts could have been foreseen. However, a defendant may be taken to have authorised the commission of a nuisance or other torts, where the defendant continues to organise events which, in the light of experience, amount to a nuisance or other tort and in the knowledge or presumed knowledge that such nuisance or tort is being committed by those whom it organises, notwithstanding that the defendant condemns rather than encourages the tortious conduct.

Following the reasoning in the above cases, the union in our problem will only avoid liability for the tortious acts arising from the mass picket if the union and its officials are completely dissociated from the organisation of the gathering.

Remedies?

In a problem such as this, a brief reference to remedies is probably all that is necessary. From LB Cars' point of view, it would probably be most interested in obtaining an interlocutory injunction in order to restrict the picketing, rather than suing the union in damages. We discussed the factors which influence the courts in exercise of their discretion whether to grant an injunction in chapter 10.

READING

The suggested further reading for this chapter is the same as that recommended for chapter 10.

BIBLIOGRAPHY

Anderman, S. D., *Labour Law: Management Decisions and Workers' Rights*, 2nd ed. (London: Butterworths, 1993).

Bain, G. S. (ed.), *Industrial Relations in Britain* (Oxford: Blackwell, 1983).

Bourn, C., & Whitmore, J., *Race and Sex Discrimination*, 2nd ed. (London: Sweet & Maxwell, 1993).

Bowers, J., *Bowers on Employment Law*, 4th ed. (London: Blackstone, 1993).

Bowers, J., & Duggan, M., *The Modern Law of Strikes* (London: Financial Training Publications, 1987).

Bowers, J., & Honeyball, S., *Textbook on Labour Law*, 3rd ed. (London: Blackstone Press, 1990).

Clifton, R., & Tatton-Brown, C., *The Impact of Employment Protection on Small Firms* (DE Research Paper 6) (London: Department of Employment, 1979).

Committee on Safety and Health at Work (Chairman: Lord Robens), *Safety and Health at Work* (Cmnd 5034) (London: HMSO, 1972).

Daniel, W. W., *The Impact of Employment Protection Laws* (London: Policy Studies Institute, 1978).

Davies, P. L., & Freedland, M., *Labour Legislation and Public Policy* (Oxford: OUP, 1993).

Davies, P. L., & Freedland, M., *Labour Law: Text and Materials*, 2nd ed. (London: Weidenfeld & Nicolson, 1984).

Department of Employment, *Building Businesses — Not Barriers* (Cmnd 9794) (London: HMSO, 1986).

Dickens, L., et al., *Dismissed: A Study of Unfair Dismissal and the Industrial Tribunal System* (Oxford: Blackwell, 1985).

Employment Department, *Industrial Relations in the 1990s* (Cm 1602), (London: HMSO, 1991).

Equal Opportunities Commission, *Men's Jobs? Women's Jobs?* (London: HMSO, 1986).

Ewing, K. D., *A Bill of Rights in Britain* (London: The Institute of Employment Rights, 1990).

Fosh, P., & Littler, C. (eds), *Industrial Relations and the Law in the 1980s: Issues and Future Trends* (Aldershot: Gower, 1985).

Goodman, M. J. (general ed.), *Encyclopedia of Health and Safety at Work Law and Practice* (London: Sweet & Maxwell, looseleaf).

Griffith, J. A. G., *The Politics of the Judiciary*, 4th ed. (London: Fontana Press, 1991).

Grunfeld, C., *The Law of Redundancy*, 3rd ed. (London: Sweet & Maxwell, 1985).

Harvey, R. J. (ed. in chief), *Industrial Relations and Employment Law* (London: Butterworths, looseleaf).

Hawes, W. R., & Smith, G., *Patterns of Representation of the Parties in Unfair Dismissal Cases: A Review of the Evidence* (DE Research Paper 22) (London: Department of Employment, 1981).

Hayek, F. A., *1980s Unemployment and the Unions* (London: Institute of Economic Affairs, 1980).

Hendy, J., & Ford, M., *Redgrave Fife & Machin Health and Safety*, 2nd ed. (London: Butterworths, 1993).

Hepple, B. A., & O'Higgins, P. (general eds), *Encyclopedia of Labour Relations Law* (London: Sweet & Maxwell, looseleaf).

Home Office & Scottish Office, *Review of Public Order Law* (Cmnd 9510) (London: HMSO, 1985).

Kahn-Freund, Sir Otto, *Kahn-Freund's Labour and the Law*, 3rd ed. by P. Davies & M. Freedland (London: Stevens, 1983).

Lewis, R. (ed.), *Labour Law in Britain* (Oxford: Blackwell, 1986).

McMullen, J., *Business Transfers and Employment Rights*, 2nd ed. (London: Butterworths, 1992).

Morris, G. S., & Archer, T. J., *Trade Unions, Employers and the Law*, 2nd ed. (London: Butterworths, 1993).

Painter, R. W., & Puttick, K., *Employment Rights* (London: Pluto, 1993).

Painter, R. W., Holmes, A. E. M., & Migdal, S., *Cases and Materials in Employment Law* (London: Blackstone, 1994).

Pitt, G., *Cases and Materials in Employment Law* (London: Pitman, 1994).

Rogers, W. V H., *Winfield and Jolowicz on Tort*, 12th ed. (London: Sweet & Maxwell, 1984).

Smith, I. T., & Wood, Sir John, *Industrial Law*, 5th ed. (London: Butterworths, 1993).

Wedderburn of Charlton, Lord, *The Worker and the Law*, 3rd ed. (Harmondsworth: Penguin/London: Sweet & Maxwell, 1986).

Wedderburn of Charlton, Lord, & Murphy, W. T. (eds), *Labour Law and the Community: Perspectives for the 1980s* (London: Institute of Advanced Legal Studies, 1982).

Welch, R., *The Right to Strike: a Trade Union View* (London: Institute of Employment Rights, 1991).

INDEX

Agency incorporation   44, 45
Assemblies   265
Assessment
    assignment work   20–2
    oral assessment   23–4
    portfolio assessment   23
    tutorial performance   24
    see also Examinations
Assignments   12–13, 20–2
Associated employers   176–7, 236

Ballots   238–43, 249–50
    ballot papers   241
    conduct of   241–3
    political funds and   223–4
    prevention of unballoted action   243
    requirements of   240
    separate workplaces   224, 240–1
    timing of industrial action after   242–3,
        249
    union executives, for   224
    when required   239–40
    written notice   242–3
Breach of contract, inducements   228–31,
    232, 237, 270
Bridlington Principles   226

Closed shop   224, 225
    enforcing union membership   238
Collective bargaining, employment contract
    and   41–2, 44, 62
Commissioner for Protection against
    Unlawful Industrial Action   251

Commissioner for the Rights of Trade
    Union Members   224
Comparators, equal pay   80–2, 88–9
Compensation
    for sex and race discrimination   113–14
    unfair dismissal   158–60
Competition see Fidelity, duty of
Conduct incorporation   47
Confidential information   57–8
Conspiracy and Protection of Property Act
    1875   220, 259–60
Continuity of employment
    for redundancy payment   175–83
    for unfair dismissal   149, 161–2
Contract of employment
    collective agreements in   41–2, 44, 62
    construction of contract   40–61
    custom and practice   60
    employment status   35–40
    examination questions   61–5
    express terms   41–4
    holiday entitlement   63–4
    implied terms   47–60
        common law   48–9
        duties of employees   49, 55–9
        duties of employers   48, 49–55
    new skills development   65
    relocation   64–5
    statement of particulars   41–4, 62
    statutory interventions   61
    termination see Termination of
        employment
    work rules   60

Contracts
  interference with 230
  strikes and breach of 232
Control test 36
Custom and practice 60

Damages, in industrial conflict 245–6
Dismissal *see* Termination of employment:
  Unfair dismissal

Employees *see* Employees' duties:
  Employment status
Employees' duties 49, 55–9
  duty to cooperate 55
  fidelity *see* Fidelity, duty of
  obedience to reasonable orders 49, 55–6
Employers' duties 48, 49–55
  duty to co-operate 55
  obligation to pay wages 49–55
  obligation to provide work 54–5
Employment Act 1980 223
Employment Act 1982 223
Employment Act 1988 224
Employment Act 1990 225–7
  ballots 238–43
  closed shop 225, 238
  industrial action 225–6
Employment contract *see* Contract of
  employment
Employment status 35–40
  atypical workers 36–8
  in business on own account 38
  control test 36, 39
  essay question 35–8
  integration test 36
  mutuality of obligation 36–7
  payment method 37
  problem question 38–40
  taxation differences 35
  temps
Equal pay 66–90
  comparator 80–2, 88–9
  Equal Pay Act (1970) 68, 69, 71, 74–85,
    114
  European Community law 68, 70–3
    UK law and 72–3
  examination questions 85–9
  genuine material difference defence 71,
    78, 83–5
  indirect discrimination 71–2
  job evaluation 76–8
  like work 68, 75–6, 77
  market forces 83, 84
  part time workers 70, 71–2, 84–5
  pay 74–5
  pension schemes 70
  qualifying limits 71

Equal pay – *continued*
  red-circled agreements 85
  redundancy schemes 70
  sick pay 70
  simultaneous employment 83
  time at which person works 76
  work of equal value 72, 76, 78–80
  work rated as equivalent 76–8
  see also Sex and race discrimination
European Community
  equal pay 68, 70–3
  UK law and 72–3
  sex and race discrimination 93–4
  social policy 5–7
Examinations
  before the examination 27
  essay questions 31–2
  in the examination room 27–9
  problem questions 30–1, 32
  purpose 18
  reasons for failure 19
  revision 19, 24–7
  style and content 29–30
  see also individual topics
Express incorporation 45–7
Express terms 41–4

Factories Act 1961
  approach and application 204–5
  fencing
    dangerous part 205–7
    machinery definitions 205–6
    reasonable foresight 206
    secure, standards of 207–8
    stupid and perverse behaviour 206–7
Factories Inspectorate 213
Fencing *see* Factories Act 1961, fencing
Fidelity, duty of
  competition by ex-employee 57–9
  competition whilst in employment 57
  confidential information 57–8
  impeding employer's business 59
  trade secrets 57–8
Frustration 124–5
  illness and 124, 125, 164–8
  imprisonment and 124, 125, 134, 136–8

Gipsies 97

Harassment
  picketing 263, 268
  sexual or racial 99–101, 111
Health and safety at work 198–217
  absolute duty approach 216
  breach of statutory duty 202–3
  civil law 200–3
  competent employees duty 200–1

Health and safety at work – *continued*
    criminal law   203–4
    duty of reasonable care   49
    economic considerations   212, 214–15
    employer's liability   200–3
    examination questions   214–16
    Factories Inspectorate   213
    passive smoking   213
    physically possible   211–12
    political factors   215
    reasonably practicable   211–12, 216
    Robens Report   205, 208
    safe place of work duty   201
    safe plant and equipment duty   200
    safe system of work duty   201
    vicarious liability   203
    violence   213
    see also Factories Act 1961: Health and
        Safety at Work etc Act 1974
Health and Safety at Work etc Act 1974
        208–14
    approach   209
    effect   209–10
    future of   212–14
    scope   210–12
Holidays, entitlement to   63–4

Immunities
    conspiracy   220, 233
    inducement to break contract   220, 232,
        237
    interference with contract, trade or
        business   232
    intimidation   221, 232–3
    removal of   235–44
    restriction to   223, 224
    secondary action   248–9
    trade dispute immunity   233–5
        in contemplation or furtherance of
            233, 235
        for picketing   269
Implied terms *see* Contract of employment
Incorporation
    by agency   44, 45
    by conduct   47
    express   45–7
Industrial conflict
    ballots and *see* Ballots
    civil liabilities   227–31, 248
        breach of contract   227
    civil remedies
        damages   245–6
        injunctions   244–5
    conspiracy   231, 233
    deduction from wages for   50–3
    examination questions   246–52
    historical perspective   218–23

Industrial conflict – *continued*
    immunities *see* Trade Unions, immunities
    inducement to breach contract   228–31,
        237, 270
    immunity   220, 232, 237
    interference with contract, trade or
        business   230, 232
    intimidation   221, 231, 232–3
    notice of   227
    secondary action *see* Secondary action
    trade dispute immunities *see* Immunities
    see also Picketing: Trade Unions
Industrial Relations Act 1971   223
Insults   100
Intimidation   221, 231
    or annoyance by violence or otherwise
        259–60
    immunity   232–3
    picketing and   268

Language requirements   94
Law reports   14
Lay-off without pay   49–50
Lectures   7–11
Lewis, Roy   3
Lockouts, redundancy and   182–3

Maastricht summit, social policy   5–7
Machinery *see* Factories Act 1961, fencing
Marches   263–5
Marxist frame   4
Mass picket   257, 270, 271

New skills development   65
Note-taking   7, 8–11
Nuisance during picketing
    private nuisance   255–7, 267
    public nuisance   259, 267

Overpayment of wages   53

Part-time work
    equal pay   70, 71–2, 84–5
    sex discrimination   108–9
Pension schemes discrimination   70,
        111–12
Picketing   253–71
    civil liability
        defendant's intentions and state of
            mind   256–7
        economic torts   255, 268, 270–1
        harassment   263, 268
        intimidation   268
        private nuisance   255–7, 267
        trespass   258
    Conspiracy and Protection of Property
        Act   259–60

Picketing – *continued*
  criminal liabilities 258–65
    intimidation or annoyance by violence
      or otherwise 259–60
    obstructing highway 259
    obstructing police officer 258–9
    public nuisance 259
  examination questions 265–71
  harassment 263, 268
  immunities *see* Immunities
  liability
    under statute 270
    vicarious, at common law 246, 270–1
    see also civil liability: criminal liabilities
  mass picketing 257, 270, 271
  official picket 269–70
  'own place of work' 254–5, 267, 269
  private nuisance 255–7, 267
  public nuisance 259, 267
  Public Order Act *see* Public Order Act
    1986
  road checks to prevent 258–9
  secondary 254
    lawful 236, 237
    unlawful 238
Pregnancy 107–8, 120
Private nuisance, picketing 255–7, 267
Processions 263–5
Protected office 142
Public nuisance, picketing 259, 267
Public Order Act 1986 260–5
  affray 261–2
  assemblies 265
  causing fear of or provoking violence
    262
  causing harassment, alarm or distress
    263
  marches 263–5
  reasonable conduct defence 263
  riots 261
  violent disorder 261

Race discrimination *see* Sex and race
  discrimination
Radical pluralists 4
Rastafarian hair styles 97, 116, 118–19
Reasonable employer concept 169
Red-circled agreements 85
Redundancy payments 174–97
  continuity of employment
    associated employers 176–7
    change of employer 175–7
    changes in hours 183
    periods away from work 180–2
    strikes and lockouts 182–3
  duty to obey reasonable orders 49

Redundancy payments – *continued*
  employer's belief dismissal not
    redundancy 187–8
  equal pay 70
  examination questions 192–7
  leaving before notice 188–9
  misconduct and 189
  place of employment 185
  qualifications to claim 175–83
  redundancy concept 183–9
  relevant date 150
  transfer of undertakings 177–80, 195–7
    dismissal in connection with transfer
      179
    effect on contract of employment
      178–9
    'immediately before' 179
    relevant 177–8
  unfair redundancy dismissals 189–92,
    194–5
  unreasonable refusal of alternative
    employment 188–9, 194
  see also Work of particular kind
Re-engagement 158
Reference frames 3–4
Reinstatement 158
Relevant date 150
Relocation 64–5
Retirement age 111–12
Revision 19, 24–7
Robens Report 205, 208

Secondary action
  associated employers 236
  first customers/suppliers 236
  inducement to breach contract 228–31,
    232, 237, 270
  personal liability for 225
  picketing *see* Picketing
  repudiation by Trade Union 225, 247–8,
    251
  statutory control 236–8
  in support of dismissed 'unofficial
    strikers' 243–4
Segregation 101
Self-employment *see* Employment status
Sex and race discrimination 91–121
  advertisements 114
  against applicants and employees 95
  burden of proof 97–8
  compensation 113–14
  detriment 105–6, 111, 117, 119
  direct discrimination 95, 98–9
  employment linked 110–11
  EOC and CRE roles 114
  European Community Law and 93–4
  examination questions 115–20

Sex and race discrimination – *continued*
  genuine occupational qualification   113
  hair styles   116, 118–19
  harassment   99–101, 111
  indirect discrimination   95, 101–13
    requirement or condition   102–3, 105
  instructions to discriminate   114
  insults   100
  justification   106–7
  language requirements   94
  married persons   109, 112
  need for statutes   93
  part-time workers   108–9
  pension schemes   111–12
  personal service   113
  pregnancy   107–8, 120
  proportion of compliance   103–5
  racial grounds and groups   96–7
    'ethnic'   97
    gipsies   97
    hair styles   97
    nationality and national origins   97
    Rastafarians   97, 116, 118–19
    travellers   97
  restrictions on types of work   112–13
  retirement exception   111–12
  SDA and EPA   114
  segregation   101
  victimisation   95, 109–10, 119
  see also Equal pay
Sickness leave, obligation to pay wages
    and   48, 49
Social Charter   6
Strikes
  redundancy and   182–3
  see also Industrial conflict: Picketing:
    Trade Unions
Study methods
  assignments   12–13, 20–2
  lectures   7–11
  literature, use of   13–16
  note-taking   7, 8–11
  tutorials   11–12, 24
  see also Examinations

Temporary workers status   37
Termination date   150–1
Termination of employment   122–45
  automatic   127, 130, 139, 144–5
  by agreed notice   141
  constructive dismissal   128, 129–33
    fairness and   133
  constructive resignation   139–40
  direct dismissal   128
  dismissal at common law   141–5
  dismissal by statute   123, 128
  elective termination   144–5

Termination of employment – *continued*
  employer's breach *see* constructive
    dismissal
  examination questions   134–44
  fixed-term or 'task' contracts   125–6,
    138–9
  frustration   124–5, 134, 136–8, 164–8
  mutual agreement   126–7, 138
  not involving dismissal at common law
    123, 124–33
  private law remedies   143–4
  protected office   142
  public law remedies   142–3
  reduction in pay   129, 140
  resignation under threat   128
  unaccepted repudiation   139–40, 144
  unfair dismissal   141, 142
  words used   128–9
  wrongful dismissal   141
  see also Unfair dismissal
Trade Disputes Act 1906   220–1
Trade Disputes Act 1965   221
Trade secrets   57–8
Trade Union Act 1871   220
Trade Union Act 1913   221
Trade Union Act 1984   223
Trade Union and Labour Relations Act
    1974   221–3
Trade Unions
  ballots   224, 238–43, 249–50
    at each workplace   224, 240–1
    ballot papers   241
    conduct of   241–3
    for executives   224
    political funds and   223–4
    requirements of   240
    secret, before industrial action   239–43
    timing of industrial action after
      242–3, 249
    when required   239–40
    written notice   242–3
  Bridlington Principles   226
  closed shop   224, 225, 238
  Commissioner for the Rights of Trade
      Union Members   224
  enforced membership   238
  fund open to damages   223, 246
    limits on   246
  immunities *see* Immunities
  political funds   221
    ballots regarding   223–4
  repudiation of actions   247–8, 251
  sympathetic action   222, 223
  unjustified disciplining   224
  vicarious liability   246, 270–1
  see also Industrial conflict: Picketing:
      Secondary action

Traditional pluralists 3–4
Transfers of undertakings *see* Redundancy
   payments
Travellers 97
Trespass 258
Tutorials 11–12, 24
   assessment of performance 24

Unfair dismissal 141, 142, 146–73
   business efficacy 170
   compensation 158–60
   consultation 166
   date of termination 150–1
   duty to obey reasonable orders 49, 55–6
   examination questions 160–72
   fairness and unfairness 151–8
      automatically unfair 152–3, 179,
         196–7
      dilution of procedural fairness 170–2
      reasons for dismissal 152–4
   hearing and appeals 156–7
   ill health 164–8
      failure to offer alternative
         employment 167
   legal representation 147
   management authority and 168–72
   overriding contractual rights 170
   persistent absenteeism 167
   proof of dismissal 148
   qualifications to claim 147–51
      continuity of employment 149, 161–2
      excluded employments 148–9
   reasonable employer concept 169
   reasonableness test 154–8, 165–6, 169

Unfair dismissal – *continued*
   procedural fairness 155–8, 170–2
   substantive merits 155
   redundancies 189–92, 194–5
   re-engagement 158
   reinstatement 158
   remedies 158–60, 163
   time limit for claim 149–50, 162
      skilled adviser mistake 150, 162
   warnings 156, 157
   see also Termination of employment
Unitary reference frame 3

Vicarious liability
   health and safety 203
   secondary action 246, 270–1
Victimisation 95, 109–10, 119

Wages
   deduction from 50–3
      industrial action 50–3
   lay-off without pay 49–50
   obligation to pay 49–55
   overpayment 53
   sickness leave and 48, 49
Warnings 156, 157
Wedderburn of Charlton, Lord 219
Work of particular kind 184–7, 194
   employer changes terms and conditions
      184–7
   greater efficiency requirement 186
Work rules 60
   working to 60, 227

TITLES IN THE SERIES

SWOT Constitutional and Administrative Law
SWOT Law of Evidence
SWOT Company Law
SWOT Law of Contract
SWOT Revenue Law
SWOT Family Law
SWOT Land Law
SWOT Criminal Law
SWOT Equity and Trusts
SWOT Commercial and Consumer Law
SWOT A Level Law
SWOT Law of Torts
SWOT Jurisprudence
SWOT Employment Law
SWOT English Legal System
SWOT EC Law
SWOT Conveyancing
SWOT Law of Succession